They Were the Rough R

They Were the Rough Riders

Inside Theodore Roosevelt's Famed Cavalry Regiment

RICHARD E. KILLBLANE

McFarland & Company, Inc., Publishers

Jefferson, North Carolina

Library of Congress Cataloguing-in-Publication Data

Names: Killblane, Richard, author.
Title: They were the Rough Riders : inside Theodore Roosevelt's
famed cavalry regiment / Richard E. Killblane.
Other titles: Inside Theodore Roosevelt's famed cavalry regiment
Description: Jefferson, North Carolina : McFarland & Company, Inc., Publishers, 2022
| Includes bibliographical references and index.
Identifiers: LCCN 2022013853 | ISBN 9781476687148 (print) | ISBN 9781476645483 (ebook) ∞
Subjects: LCSH: United States. Army. Volunteer Cavalry, 1st—History.
| Spanish-American War, 1898—Regimental histories. | Spanish-American War,
1898—Campaigns. | Roosevelt, Theodore, 1858-1919—Military leadership. |
San Juan Hill, Battle of, Cuba, 1898. | BISAC: HISTORY / Military / United States
Classification: LCC E725.45 1st .K55 2022 | DDC 973.8/94—dc23/eng/20220505
LC record available at https://lccn.loc.gov/2022013853

British Library cataloguing data are available

ISBN (print) 978-1-4766-8714-8
ISBN (ebook) 978-1-4766-4548-3

On the cover: "Teddy's Rough Riders" by W.G. Read (Library of Congress);
officers of the Rough Riders at military camp, Montauk Point, New York,
Benjamin Johnston 1864–1952, photographer (Library of Congress)

Printed in the United States of America

*McFarland & Company, Inc., Publishers
Box 611, Jefferson, North Carolina 28640
www.mcfarlandpub.com*

Table of Contents

Preface

One would think that with a subject as popular as Theodore Roosevelt and the Rough Riders, there would be very little new to write about it. Surprisingly, historians overlooked a wealth of personal accounts. The most common question to a historian is where or how did you find the information. Each project is different and has its own journey. The information can be found anywhere and often where one least expects it. Mine began with a photograph.

I began my research into the Rough Riders from Oklahoma when I moved back to my hometown of Ponca City, Oklahoma, after leaving the Army and earning a Master of Arts in history from the University of San Diego in 1992. I knew that some of the Rough Riders had been recruited from my home state and thought there might be some readily accessible information. Who knows, there might even be a few of the relatives still living in the area. I did a quick survey of the local newspapers and historical societies yet found very little. A few years later, Ray Falconer gave me a photograph of a company of soldiers in downtown Ponca City around the time of the Spanish–American War. Excited by this new find, I searched the records to determine the date of the photograph based upon the buildings in the background. We knew the exact street corner, and, with the help of Lloyd Bishop at the Ponca City Library, we narrowed the photo to 1897, one year before the Spanish–American War.

As time permitted, I then began to search through the Ponca City newspapers of that year looking for information on who those soldiers were. I discovered that they were most likely the local militia company. As I read through the newspaper articles about the early Oklahoma National Guard, they led me to the Spanish–American War. I stumbled onto what I had previously overlooked. As usual, when looking for one thing, I found something else. The papers had printed letters from the Rough Riders. Here were unknown firsthand accounts of the Rough Riders.

The Spanish–American War had become very personal when the sons of Oklahoma joined the fight. People did not care as much for the politics of the war or analysis of the action. They wanted to know what their friends or relatives experienced. So family members took their letters to the newspapers. The editor most likely edited out the personal parts and printed the rest. Just from the towns of Ponca City and Newkirk I found a treasure trove of letters.

I also noticed that the local paper printed interesting letters from other newspapers. Many of them came from the same source, the *Guthrie Leader*. When I went through that roll of microfilm, I found that nearly every issue had printed a letter. One Rough Rider, Paul Hunter, wrote regularly to the paper to keep folks back home informed of their progress. This was the motherlode of firsthand accounts.

1

This provided a good start for a book. I had a wealth of letters written by members of the same cavalry troop. The next obvious place to look for more information would be the state archives. As luck would have it, the Oklahoma Archives had the letters of the commander of the Oklahoma troop and the diary of an Oklahoman who had served in another troop. Letters and diaries are great because they are not subject to selective memory. Soldiers begin to forget things as soon as they return home, and their memory becomes subject to interpretation.

I also began to search local historical societies to see what they might have hidden away in their file drawers and managed to strike up some friendships with the local historians. The coup came when Karen Dye, of the Newkirk Community Historical Society, handed me a letter from Dale Coil seeking information about those Rough Riders from her town. Evidently he wrote every hometown listed in the muster-out roll. Since everything she knew about the Rough Riders from Newkirk I had told her, she figured that I ought to answer him. That began a tremendous exchange of information between the two of us. It was a privilege to talk with someone who shared the same passion of the subject. Dale Coil had begun his exhaustive research of the Rough Riders after watching the TNT movie *Rough Riders*. Inspired by a desire to learn more about the individuals and what happened to them after the war, he began his research.

Dale was so enamored with the subject that he traveled the country in search of material. Through him I received the materials housed in the New Mexico and Arizona archives. It was through one of his trips that I had the privilege to meet him face to face, not knowing I would never get to see him again. He died shortly afterwards. His family donated his collection of research to the archives in New Mexico. Dale's greatest fascination was with those Rough Riders of the social elite. Had he lived to write about them, it would have proven another very interesting story. I enjoyed his telling of it.

I found that journalists during the Spanish–American War saw themselves as the eyes and ears of the public. They did not pass judgment or analyze, interpret or predict the consequences of the events. They just wrote what they saw and heard. Their descriptions were extremely detailed, a writer's dream. They painted pictures with words that later readers could add to their own canvas.

This was the most popular regiment during the war, and, fortunately, Americans wanted to know all they could about it. For that reason, many veterans published their stories. A number of Rough Riders' stories besides Theodore Roosevelt's were published: Tom Hall, Thomas Rynning, Theodore Miller, Allen and Kirk McCurdy. Two journalists, Richard Harding Davis and Edward Marshall, both published their accounts. Before the smoke had cleared the battlefield, journalists who had accompanied them rushed to the publishers to get their collections of interviews out in print. This was raw material. For the big picture of the campaign, Major General Joseph Wheeler and Lieutenant John D. Miley published their accounts. Sadly, most of the later works on the Santiago Campaign simply rehashed the same old material. It had gotten to where I could read a statement and know where the author had found it. Once in a while, one of the authors found a published account that I had not seen.

Almost all the pieces of the puzzle were there just waiting to be assembled. They would reveal a picture that had not been clearly seen before. With the exception of Charles Johnson Post's work, *The Little War of Private Post*, I had found no work that painted a clear picture of what life was like in the Army of 1898. These letters, diaries, memoirs and books individually provided glimpses that when assembled reveal the entire picture. And the picture was not what many historians had thought. The view of the war from the vantage point of those who fought it was different from those of the armchair tacticians and critics.

I subtitled this book *Inside Theodore Roosevelt's Famed Cavalry Regiment*. While in my opinion it is the most detailed account of the history of the regiment, it is still just a story. There are still more stories to be told. Any one of the participants could be explored in more depth.

It is interesting to reread the views of Roosevelt, Hall and Miley after having seen the full picture. In the light of other accounts their own biases and personalities come through merely by what they describe or fail to describe.

Through collective research with the help of many others, I amassed enough information to write. The question was how to tell the story. I began by giving lectures on the Rough Riders. By judging my audiences' interest, I found that they wanted to know more about who these men were, what they did before the war and after. Since I had enough information, I decided to tell their story. Virtually the only question I received about Roosevelt was what did the men really think of him. This story was not intended to be about Roosevelt but the men who served under him.

My outlines for writing are usually very vague. I am more of a storyteller than a writer, having studied the art for many years under great practitioners in the Army. I learned that a story has a way of taking on a life of its own. The outbreak of war in 1898 generated a fever of patriotism like nothing we have seen in the latter half of the twentieth century. I felt it important to take a step back in time and let the reader know what life was like then, especially out West. I picked a few main characters I liked or had plenty of information on, then let the story tell itself.

To my surprise, Roosevelt, who started off almost comical, became more prominent as the story progressed. In fact, by the time of the charge up Kettle Hill, he had become the focus of the story. "What did the men think of Roosevelt?" In time they thought the world of him. He dominated their stories. It was hard to tell their story without telling his.

While a story is told to entertain, it usually has a moral or lesson for the reader. This story became a study of leadership, both good and bad. It is a study of leadership as seen from the bottom, which is probably the toughest evaluation to pass. Like life, chance plays an important role in who succeeds and who fails. There are plenty of examples of that in this story. Not everyone had their chance at glory or to test their courage under fire. As in real life, someone had to stay behind. Soldiers became sick prior to deployment. Like Admiral Sampson, who was absent when his fleet destroyed the Spanish fleet, some people were at the wrong place at the wrong time.

Writing this story was a journey. It could not have been taken without the help of a number of people. Not all historians have the financial resources to travel the country in search of records as Dale Coil did. Even then, success in finding that elusive document comes from archivists, librarians and historians who have a dedication to their profession or at least this subject. To them go my thanks.

There were the descendants of several of the Rough Riders: Viana Pribble and the granddaughters of Robert Huston; Beckey Hughey, the daughter of Ira Hill; and Mack Wetmore, son of Starr Wetmore. As with the children of most veterans, they did not know much about their fathers' service since the veterans did not talk much about it with their families. The children did provide an insight to the character of the veterans.

Jacqueline Davis, of the Army Medical Museum at Fort Sam Houston, Texas, had a similar interest in the Rough Riders during their stay in San Antonio. She provided me with a wealth of articles from the local newspapers during their stay in Texas.

Many little towns across America have historical societies or museums. The people who work there are often volunteers, but they are some of the most dedicated people in the preservation of local history. They have treasures tucked away in their files and shelves. Karen Dye discovered a photograph with the names of the Rough Riders on the back. Up until that time she had no idea of who and what they were. That started an interesting journey for both of us. The Pawnee City Historical Society and public library were also a big help. Lloyd Bishop of the genealogy research section of the Ponca City Library was a tremendous help in locating material. Through him, I acquired the microfiche roll on the *Guthrie Leader*, which had volumes of letters from the Rough Riders. It was probably the best source of personal accounts.

Joe Todd, of the Oklahoma Historical Society, was a tremendous asset. Old archival practices left much to be desired, and most archives do not have the resources to catalog the tremendous volumes of information that have been donated over the centuries. Consequently, much of what one finds comes by the memory of those who work there, accident, or personal interest. I had the fortune that Joe Todd shared my interest in Oklahoma military history. Together, we unearthed volumes of material on the early years of the Oklahoma National Guard. The Oklahoma Historical Society also had the fortune to save the letters of Robert Huston. They also had Ben Colbert's diary, and, fortunately, they had typed out both.

The library staff at the U.S. Army Transportation School, Timothy Renick, Diane Forbes and Nancy Gordon, were extremely helpful. If I identified a book, they acquired it for me on an interlibrary loan, even the rarest, Theodore Miller's.

Just when an author thinks he is finished, he finds another lead. I stumbled across a short biography of William Frank Knox. The author, George H. Lobdell, pointed me in the direction of the letters of William Frank Knox. My gratitude goes to Wallace Dailey of the Houghton Library at Harvard University and the staff at the Grand Rapids Public Library for finding the letters for me. The last biography I needed to complete was that of Schuyler McGinnis. There was no paper trail that told me where he left to. Again, Karen Dye came to my aid. Jim Fulbright contacted her about researching the biographies of Oklahoma Rough Riders to augment the McGinty memoirs that the family had finally agreed to publish. Jim had found the date and place of death of Schuyler. I contacted the Greenwood County Historical Society, and Loretta A. Smethers Stuber found and emailed the obituaries to me that same day. Without their help, this story would have remained incomplete.

No work is complete without imposing upon friends to read the draft product. Michael Pacella III, then the U.S. Army Transportation School Chaplain, inspired me to pay more attention to the role of Chaplain Henry Brown. My favorite mentor and friend, Gary Null, completed the first editing of the manuscript. My friend and former co-worker, Charles Bissett, has produced a number of maps for me in the past and was extremely helpful with this project. A perfectionist, he studied the current terrain along with the maps drawn by the participants (not to scale) and my interpretations to come up with what we believe is a more accurate depiction of the movements of the Rough Riders and Regular cavalry during the Battle of Las Guasimas.

The internet was in its infancy when I began this project but has come a long way since then. Photographers documented this war in detail, and their labor brings this story to life. A great thanks goes out to all the libraries and archives that have digitized their photos and put them online. They are cited in the captions under the photos. Similarly, the U.S. Military Academy at West Point has posted its collection of campaign and battle maps online to share with the world. The combination of maps and photos helps give the reader an understanding of the geography of the campaign and a feel for being there.

Although I began this project around 1995, I put it on hold when I started writing *The Filthy Thirteen*. Once it was published by Casemate in 2003, I could then pick up where I left off with writing about the Oklahoma Rough Riders. Finding a publisher takes time, and I became distracted in writing about convoy operations during the recent wars. With my retirement as a Department of Army historian in 2019, I finally had time to concentrate on finding a publisher for this project. My gratitude to my friend and fellow author Alexander Barnes for putting me in contact with McFarland. So now others will be able to enjoy this labor of love.

Chapter 1

Oklahoma National Guard

On September 12, 1918, the Eighty-Second Division lined up on the right flank of the U.S. I Corps for the St. Mihiel Offensive. It would be the first battle of the American army under its own command. Each of the two brigades in the divisions had a machine-gun battalion to provide fire support. Lieutenant Colonel Orlando G. Palmer commanded the 320th Machine Gun Battalion, which supported the 163rd Infantry Brigade.

By then Colonel Palmer was 54 years of age, which made him older than many of his peers. Eighteen of those years he had seen fighting in three other countries, and the St. Mihiel Offensive of the Great War would add France to the list. Yet, this war was far different from the others, with trenches, gas, tanks, airplanes, barbed wire, machine guns, and lots and lots of artillery. The latter three he had seen before but not in this quantity or combination. Palmer had hunted guerrillas in the Philippines and chased Pancho Villa into Mexico, but his baptism of fire in Cuba had left a lasting impression on him, causing his life to take a new course.

He began his career as a lawyer but fell in love with teaching instead. Cuba changed that. It was not just that the combat had whetted his appetite for more excitement; there was something special about the company of men whom he fought with. Palmer had begun his military career as one of Teddy Roosevelt's Rough Riders, a unit unlike any other, and he was not alone in his sentiment, as other Rough Riders still served on active duty. Frank Knox, who had served as a private in his company, was a major in the artillery over in the Seventy-Eighth Division. Gordon Johnston, also a lieutenant colonel, had started in the Eighty-Third Division but moved up to Corps staff. Lieutenant Colonel Ode Nichols, of Durham, Oklahoma, who had served in one of the Indian Territory troops, was freezing with the Thirty-First Infantry Regiment in Siberia. The list went on. Something special clearly had happened 20 years before.

Palmer had joined the Rough Riders from Oklahoma, which, during the Spanish–American War, was then known as the "Twin Territories," comprising both Oklahoma and the Indian Territories. Each territory contributed its own unique character to the Rough Riders. Oklahoma recruited its one troop solely from its existing National Guard. They were not the cowboys, hunters and mining prospectors that Roosevelt described in his book; instead, they were farmers, businessmen and lawyers. The neighboring Indian Territory provided two troops of men with Indian blood flowing through their veins. Sprinkled among these three troops were sons of millionaires and Ivy League college athletes. Men from the Twin Territories were also scattered throughout the other troops of the regiment. In total these men formed part of a regiment unlike any other. Their words speak from the pages of their letters, diaries and memoirs to describe life in this regiment as they saw it.

A martial tradition runs deep through American history, and every generation produces a certain percentage of citizens motivated by patriotism, family tradition of military service or adventure ready to answer the call of the bugle or drum to fight for causes not necessarily clear to them. The Spanish–American War was fought on such a small scale that it did not require a draft to spoil the adventure. This nation had enough Regular Army regiments to wage this popular little war in the Caribbean, but each state and territory demanded the opportunity for its militia or National Guard to participate in the fight. The militia system of the nineteenth century was a living testament to the martial spirit in America. As such, the birth of the Oklahoma National Guard provides an insight to this martial spirit as it flourished at the end of the nineteenth century and the caliber of the men who would fight in Cuba.

The circumstances which attracted settlers to a new territory and the subsequent creation of its militia identified the kind of men who would readily fight for the rights of others in foreign countries. To understand the caliber of men who served as Rough Riders one must understand the environment from which they came. The creation of the Oklahoma National Guard is integral to this story as it typified the growing pains in other territories. This was a crucial time in American history.

Having fought on both sides of the Civil War, the Five Civilized Tribes had to cede some of the western part of the Indian Territory back to the United States for allying with the Confederacy. This land was designated for the future relocation of Indian Nations from other territories. After two decades of removal, all the nations of the Great Plains had found their homes on reservations, and a fair amount of the Indian Territory remained unassigned. These uninhabited lands attracted a new generation of American adventurers looking to settle the last of the frontier. Throughout the 1880s, groups of farmers led forays into these lands in the hope to pressure the government to open them for white settlement. Finally, the "Boomers" won out, and the Creek and Seminole Nations sold their claims to the unassigned lands in the center of the territory. With that sale, two territories would grow out of one: Oklahoma and the Indian Territories.

President Benjamin Harrison issued a proclamation on March 23, 1889, to open the first unassigned lands in the Oklahoma district to white settlement. At noon on April 22, an empty prairie would spring forth with bustling "boomtowns" and farms. It required a sense of adventure to stake out a claim in the wilderness, and from this character of men would one of the greatest regiments of the Spanish–American War be recruited.

Endless opportunities abounded. Fortunes could be made by those who established their businesses early and survived. Consequently, boomtowns attracted men of different motivations, and not all were law abiding. In the early days of settlement, companies of soldiers camped throughout the territory enforced law and order.

On April 19, 1889, the newly promoted, 47-year-old Captain Daniel F. Stiles stepped off the train at the Santa Fe rail depot with his G Company of the Tenth Infantry. Overnight the small depot with its one government storehouse would grow into a town site known as Oklahoma City. Stiles's little army would represent the law in that part of the territory.

Born in Pictou, Nova Scotia, on June 5, 1841, his family immigrated to Boston, Massachusetts, while he was just two years old. The outbreak of the Civil War revealed the martial spirit of the 20-year-old Daniel, and he enlisted as a sergeant in the District of Columbia Volunteers, then received a commission as a lieutenant the next year. After his regiment's term of service expired, he raised and commanded the First U.S. Colored Volunteers. He later resigned from that post to enlist in the Second District of Columbia Volunteers where he again became a lieutenant. In total, Stiles fought in all the engagements in the Shenandoah Valley and discovered that army life appealed to him.

Two years after the war, he received a Regular Army commission as a lieutenant in the Twenty-Sixth Infantry. Occupation duty in the South, however, was not duty he relished. Instead, he wanted to rekindle the warrior spirit, so he later transferred out West to the Tenth Infantry where he campaigned for 12 years against hostile Comanche warriors in Texas. While in Texas, he married Margaret "Maggie" Bell in 1875, who provided him two

Capt. Daniel F. Stiles (courtesy Oklahoma Historical Society).

sons. He was later sent on detached service for five years as the lieutenant colonel of the New York National Guard. This National Guard experience would prove extremely useful in later years. After that assignment, he returned west to Fort Crawford, Colorado, but by that time hostilities with the native inhabitants had ended. In another five years his company was transferred to Fort Lyon, Indian Territory, for a new kind of duty—to prepare it for settlement. Stiles was a professional soldier with considerable experience fighting both Rebels and Indians and enforcing order in the South. The last phase of his life would play an integral part in the growth of the new territory.

When he arrived in Oklahoma City, crowds of eager '89ers from across the nation flooded the booming town awaiting the opening of the unassigned lands. They were men and women of the pioneering spirit. Each generation produced a new stock ready to push back the frontier, stake out their claim in the wilderness and till the land with their plows. Homesteading had become the American way of expansion, but available lands gradually disappeared. Because the national government anticipated more settlers wanted land than was available, it decided upon a land race. Everyone would gather at railheads and upon a given signal raced for the choicest lands. At the end of the day, that part of the territory had transformed into a settlement. The race attracted those with an adventurous spirit as well as those with other motivations.

Stiles's duties made him the town provost marshal with responsibility to preserve the peace and keep out intoxicating liquors, since the Indian Territory was a dry state. Times were wild, and so were the people. Whiskey peddlers and gamblers stirred up their own kind of trouble, but no group of people were more despised than land speculators.

Several land development companies had descended onto Oklahoma City with the intent to gain control of the land, survey the town site, then sell it off at a considerable profit. Sooners, Boomers, Colony and the Seminole Township companies each contested for control of the town site. In this environment land agents became the scourge of the land. Colony and Seminole settled on a compromise where they would maintain control, and each would survey and develop their half of the town. Yet, the laws of the nation had been founded to protect the rights of the individual. To get around this inconvenience, the speculators merely needed to gain control of the law.

On May 1, the citizens of Oklahoma City held their first election, through which the Seminole Company dominated the election and elevated two of their own to positions of authority. Mayor William L. Couch, one of the original Boomers, and Judge O.H. Violet would, therefore, rule over land disputes in favor of Seminole. Any citizen protesting would incur either a fine or incarceration.

It did not take long to stir up an opposition movement with the goal of limiting this abuse of power. Called "Kickapoos" by the Seminoles, they drafted up their own city charter, which they put up for public vote on July 16, 1889. The governing authorities predictably forbade the election and even confiscated the poll boxes. The Seminoles, in turn, drafted up their own charter, which merely gave sanction to their abuse of authority. The citizens voted it down. Coinciding with a congressional visit on September 17, the Kickapoos decided to hold another election on the 21st. Once again, the authorities forbade it, and Captain Stiles had the unfortunate duty to enforce this edict.

On September 21, a riotous mob of over 500 massed outside the polling station. Stiles appeared on the scene with only 25 soldiers and ordered the crowd to disperse. The angry crowd refused. Stiles demonstrated his courage by walking up to a man who pointed a Winchester rifle at his chest, then snatched it from his hands. In a test of wills, the professional soldier had won. The crowd lost heart and began to walk away but not fast enough for the army captain. An angered Stiles then ordered his soldiers to clear out the demonstrators. The infantrymen fixed bayonets and marched against the multitude of unarmed citizens, skewering several along the way. This bold act secured Stiles's reputation in Oklahoma.

Stiles was a professional soldier in an army which thrived on discipline. He believed in the unquestioned authority of the civil government. He had even appealed to the U.S. Marshals' office in Muskogee to have Marshal George Thornton removed for not supporting the unpopular laws. However, Stiles knew there was considerable controversy over that incident. Yet, he genuinely believed that he had done right by upholding the provisional government and refusing to permit the election. His actions evidently endeared him with the more law-abiding citizens who presented him with a $300 gold cane in appreciation of his services.

The journalist Richard Harding Davis had investigated accounts from both sides and praised Stiles for his conduct. "I heard these stories on every side, and I was rejoiced to think how well off our army must have been in majors, that the people in Washington could allow one who had served through the war and on the border, and in this unsettled territory, and whose hair grew white in the service to still wear two bars on his shoulder strap." Captain Stiles cared little about public opinion, but he carried out his orders with a zeal that would invariably make enemies.[1]

Stiles remained in charge of the garrison in Oklahoma City until 1892. He then returned to Fort Reno where he applied for a well-deserved leave of absence, and, finally in 1893, after 30 years, he retired from active duty service.

Oklahoma had become his newly adopted home, so he returned to Oklahoma City with James Geary to lay out the 160-acre Maywood addition. Even this caused commotion, as others contested his rights to the land for the next four years. In his first year of retirement, he had become quite an entrepreneur. He had also organized the Oklahoma National Bank and served as its president. On September 16, 1893, the Cherokee Outlet which had been purchased from the Cherokee Nation was also opened for settlement. Stiles headed north to stake his own claim in Ponca City.

The Cherokee Nation had used the Outlet for hunting. Yet, extensive hunting expeditions had killed off the buffalo by the late 1870s, so the Cherokee did not have much use for it other than ranging cattle. Enterprising as they were, they leased much of the land to Kansas cattle ranchers. Some Kansas citizens protested that the Cherokee did not deserve to own the land since they did not live on it. The economic depression of 1893 finally inspired the federal government to purchase the land from the Cherokee Nation and open it up for white settlement. This massive settlement of free land would give the economy its needed shot in the arm for recovery. The Cherokee Strip Land Run would become the last great race for land in America.

Lured by adventure, Orlando G. Palmer left his home in Jewell, Kansas, to line up at the railroad town of Arkansas City for the race across the Kansas border. Palmer had descended from good stock. Some of his ancestors had arrived on the *Mayflower*. His father, D.L. Palmer, was a distinguished attorney-at-law and prominent in Kansas politics. He had seen to it that his son received a fine education. After graduating from Kansas State Agricultural College with a Bachelor of Science in 1887, his father sent him off for the next three years to the Columbia University of Law in Washington, D.C. Palmer's heart, however, lay in education. He had taught school while attending college and only made a token effort at the practice of law. He was admitted to the bar at Mankato, Kansas, in 1891 but worked for three years in the census office in Washington, D.C. He had evidently studied for his law degree in honor of his father but did not practice. He returned home in time to make the run.

When the cannon bellowed, he joined one of the great races in history. At the end awaited 80 acres of prairie farmland. Palmer, however, had to contest his claim against a "Sooner," and justice in court prevailed in his favor over justice at the end of a gun. Most homesteaders would not make a living over the next few years and would have to give up their claim. Palmer fortunately had another occupation to bring in an income. He became Perry's first school superintendent, then moved over to Pawnee to hold the same post for the next two years. Born in Iowa and raised in Missouri and Kansas, Palmer became an Oklahoman.

Few people outside the Indian Nations could claim the territory as their birthplace. The identity of an Oklahoman belonged to a new generation of men and women who craved adventure or were willing to take a risk to stake their claim to the American dream of land ownership. The territory was not a place for the faint at heart. This last land run had brought the settlement process in the Oklahoma Territory to rapid fruition. Meanwhile, the Oklahoma militia with which Stiles would play a critical role had gotten off to a difficult start.

The Organic Act of 1890 which created the first government for the Territory of Oklahoma also allowed for the organization of a militia. The militia created the unique opportunity for men to explore their military interests as a hobby. If a man with substantial local support recruited enough men, he could form his own company and be elected its captain. It was also a requirement for statehood.

On April 28, 1891, 54 men gathered in the territorial capital at Guthrie to organize the first militia company of the territory. The men elected S.M. Decker as the captain with P.J. Cavanaugh as the first lieutenant and H.C. Olds, the second. They celebrated their success by passing out cigars. The company held further meetings like a social club, then drilled for a while. This routine only lasted for about three months before men lost interest and the company dissolved.

A militia had become an integral part of any state or territory. America's military tradition was built on the concept of the citizen soldier. State volunteer regiments had won honors in all the major wars of American history. Symbolically, the organization of a militia was as important a step toward statehood as the forming of a governing body. It was only a matter of time before a more permanent militia organization would take root in Oklahoma.

The militia by law answered directly to the governor. As their commander-in-chief, he could use it to put down rebellions, uprisings or other acts of armed violence. Yet, there was no apparent need of a militia for local security in Oklahoma. The Regular Army still had plenty of camps and forts scattered across the territory, and they provided the early law in the wild boomtowns. In the absence of any internal threat, the early militia would just serve more as social clubs for patriotic citizens.

The Civil War had tremendously changed American society. Nearly every man of that generation was a veteran. Every prominent politician in Oklahoma had fought in the Civil War, though it did not matter which side. There were plenty of veterans from both. Veteran officers retained the titles of their former ranks with honor. In the absence of war, the militia provided a reasonable substitute for veteran service. This martial tradition inspired many ambitious young individuals to don the army blue even though there were neither opportunities for glory nor pay. In fact, the captains would later have to post a substantial security bond for their company property. It was little surprise that attorneys comprised the majority of the early officers. They had the political ambition and economic resources to accept the job.

The territory during this early period obviously offered little in the way of organization and equipment for a militia. It was a "come as you are" militia. The men wore whatever uniforms they purchased themselves. Otherwise, they would drill in civilian clothes. The same went for firearms. Whatever the vintage or make, any rifle would do. Such a motley group of men represented Oklahoma's first attempt at a militia. Fortunately, the inspiration of patriotic men like Robert B. Huston and the desire to drill formed and held the later companies together.

In 1893, Harold Huston wrote his brother, Robert, asking if he knew of any boomtowns where they could open up a law practice. Born on a farm in Hamilton, Ohio, on January 25, 1864, Rob had aspired to be a lawyer from an early age. He studied for this end and graduated from the National Normal University in Lebanon, Ohio. In 1884, he moved to Salina, Kansas, where he taught school until he was admitted to the bar in 1892.

Ohio had a strong martial tradition, which produced its share of famous general officers during the Civil War. Growing up in this environment, young Rob also developed an early interest in military history. He read all he could about battles and wars of the world and the great men who fought them. His close friend F.H. Greer remembered conversations about the heroic men Rob would like to emulate.

Rob said, "In my mind Napoleon is the greatest man, whose influence has spread over the world, but I have no moral purpose behind him; therefore I would rather be like George Washington, whose ideas and moral influence have benefitted nations and gave liberty to his country; still rather would I be like Abraham Lincoln, who not only advocated national liberty, but who was instrumental in giving individual liberty to thousands of human beings."[2] This inspired in Rob a strong desire for military service. So, in 1892, he enlisted in the Kansas National Guard where he quickly rose to first lieutenant.

On the urging of his brother, Rob moved to Guthrie, the territorial capital, in 1893. There he renewed his martial interests when on July 12, 1894, Governor William C. Renfrow appointed him captain to organize a militia company. The Guthrie company held elections for its first and second lieutenants that July but did not confirm Rob as the captain with an election until March 25 of the next year. Rob's previous militia experience would make this militia experiment work. By then his law practice had prospered, and he married Vianna "Vite" J. Roads on June 12, 1895.

Rob was a modest and cultured gentleman who earned the admiration of others. Gifted with an artistic talent, he loved to paint. Yet his zeal and fidelity in the performance of his military duties would carry him far in his career in the Oklahoma National Guard and link his career path with that of Stiles's.

Company letters were designated generally in the order that the companies were formed. Guthrie became designated "A." In March 1894, Alva organized Company B, and Oklahoma City recruited Company C in July. The letter designations of other towns changed as companies appeared and disappeared. The first three remained the same until the Spanish–American War.

In addition, every regiment had a marching band, and Oklahoma had plenty to choose from. Before the invention of radios, local concerts provided the main form of musical entertainment at that time, so most towns had their own bands. The only question was which one would receive the honor of becoming the regimental band. Philip C. Rosenbaum did not delay recruiting the Guthrie band on June 12, 1894, and became its captain. This 21-piece military band fortunately became one of the best in the West. It repeatedly took honors in competition at the Kansas City Carnival over the next few years.

Phil was born in Staunton, Virginia, on October 3, 1867. The Reconstruction South provided too great a hardship for his family, so they moved to Washington, D.C. where they lived for five or six years. When conditions improved, the family returned to Staunton. There, Phil attended Hoover Military Academy, which sparked his keen interest in the military. Afterwards, he attended the Dunsmore Business College, then transferred to Otterbein College at Westerville, Ohio, where he also acquired an interest in music.

When Phil learned first about the opening of the Indian Territory, he read all he could about the territory and made plans to migrate there. He arrived in the booming town of Guthrie in 1890. There he established a real estate office and general insurance agency. In September 1893, he joined the great race for land in the Cherokee Strip like many others. Quite possibly he just participated in the run for the adventure of it. When he saw a destitute family which had failed to stake a claim, he gave them his. Phil then returned to Guthrie where he impressed Governor Renfrow enough to receive a promotion on July 7, 1894, to the office of quartermaster general with the rank of major. This position close to the territorial capital ensured Phil's further military success. His ambition set him on a collision course for the leadership of the National Guard.

While inspired individuals had broken ground for the Oklahoma militia, the appropriate infrastructure did not exist to complete their work. Governor Renfrow, a veteran of the Confederacy, wanted to transform his militia into a professional military organization. His wartime experience had "borne witness to the fact that upon the efficiency and thoroughness of the 'citizen soldier' depends the safety of the state." He needed a man of vast military experience to lay that foundation.

On December 23, 1894, he appointed James C. Jamison, then the Register of Deeds for Kay County in Newkirk, to replace Harry Clark as the second Adjutant General of Oklahoma. Renfrow had chosen well. Jamison would become the most instrumental man in the organization of the Oklahoma National Guard. He brought with him a wealth of military experience for the job.

Born on September 30, 1830, Jamison was 14 when his father died. His destitute mother sold the farm and sent the children to live with neighbors. Dreams of adventure inspired James to escape from farm life. At the age of 16, he had even tried to enlist to fight in the war with Mexico. Yet it was not until April 1849 that he finally left the farm to join the flood of immigrants flowing into the California goldfields. Five years of backbreaking labor in the mines provided neither the fortune nor adventure that he had sought. He instead found it in another country. In October 1855, he read about William Walker's victory in Nicaragua and learned that Walker was recruiting his "American Phalanx" in California.

In December 1855, James boarded the *Sierra Nevada* with 45 other soldiers of fortune bound for Nicaragua. In a short time, the six-foot-tall young man had made a favorable impression on the others. While en route, they elected him first lieutenant of their company. He inherited the difficult task to instill discipline in men whose motivations were not always admirable or patriotic. Over the next year and a half, he would find more than enough adventure to fill a lifetime.

He learned his military trade from Mexican War veterans and honed it quelling insurrections in the jungles of Nicaragua. The Second Battle of Rivas on April 11, 1856, provided his introduction to a large-scale battle. He narrowly escaped capture and execution at the hands of the Costa Ricans when abandoned with the wounded. Because of his courage and demonstrated leadership, General Walker promoted Jamison to captain of D Company, First Infantry. When the armies of neighboring countries tried to drive out Walker's army, Jamison courageously fought battle after battle against superior numbers until their final surrender on May 1, 1857. Afterwards, the young filibuster finally returned home to Missouri.

As his luck would have it, his interval of peace was short lived. Fate provided one more adventure with the outbreak of the Civil War. On June 13, 1861, the governor raised the Missouri State Guard to side with the Confederacy. Colonel John S. Marmaduke recruited the Guard at Booneville. Men with inadequate arms and no uniforms assembled on that field. Jamison's combat experience earned him the captaincy of Company D in Hull's Battalion. A well-trained and -equipped Union force soundly defeated Marmaduke on June 17, just a few days after their arrival. Disillusioned, Marmaduke left to join the Confederate Army in Richmond.

Jamison participated in other fights in Missouri to conclude with the nine-day siege and capture of Lexington on September 20. Unfortunately, he became ill and was left behind with the small garrison. On October 16, a squadron of Union cavalry recaptured the town and Jamison along with it. The captors paroled the prisoners with their pledge of allegiance never to fight against the Union again. Jamison's career as a Confederate officer came to a quick end, and the long war would never discover his full potential. During his parole, however, he courted and married Sarah Ann White.

After the war, he entered the newspaper business, and, in 1885, Governor Marmaduke, his old commander and former Confederate general, appointed Jamison the Adjutant General of Missouri. As the adjutant general, he quelled disturbances with railroad men in Hannibal, coal miners in Bevier and "Bald Knobbers" in southern Missouri. He performed well enough that Governor Albert Morehouse also retained him in that capacity during his term of office. In 1889, at the age of 49, he left for the opening of the Oklahoma Territory for one last adventure. There he served in various civil offices until Governor Renfrow sought his talents. This new challenge revived the martial spirit of the aging veteran.

On January 6, 1895, Governor Renfrow sent a message to the Third Legislative Assembly outlining a number of goals. Among them, he identified that a Congressional Act of February 1887 authorized the annual appropriation of funds for furnishing ordnance stores and equipment to the states and territories free of charge. The Session Laws of the First Legislative Assembly were wholly inadequate to encourage the organization of a militia. It made no provisions for office supplies or even the rent of offices or armories. Renfrow's directive started the momentum.

By March, the new adjutant general had received the appropriate uniforms, equipment and other property. For some reason, however, the War Department also sent Oklahoma a Gatling gun and six cavalry saddles and bridles. At that time, Oklahoma was only recruiting infantry companies. Neither was needed and were returned that same summer. What the militia said they needed were copies of the 1890 drill regulations. The secretary of war later answered that the officers had to purchase those with their own funds.

Based upon his Missouri experience, General Jamison articulated the articles pertaining to the organization of the militia in the 1895 Session Laws. These articles became his most significant contribution to Oklahoma. In this sense, Jamison should be considered one of the most important architects of Oklahoma's National Guard. His articles laid down the architectural framework for the territorial militia. It issued instruction for how property could be issued to the companies, and issue began almost immediately. The volunteer militia became officially designated as the Oklahoma National Guard.

The law authorized the organization of a regiment of infantry not to exceed 500 men in time of peace with only one troop of cavalry or one battery of artillery. While they could not have less than 34 men, the companies rarely exceeded it. On August 7 that same year, Jamison issued General Order Number 3 limiting the maximum strength of an infantry company to 50. At full strength this would have restricted the regiment to just ten companies.

By the end of 1895, more companies had sprung up in Cleveland, El Reno, Stillwater, Ponca City and Norman. After two years, the militia grew to eight companies, enough to form two battalions of the First Regiment, ONG. This finally created vacancies for regimental officers, and for the most part, very few of these early militia officers had any military background outside the militia. A colonel with vast military experience was then needed to supervise the training and instill the necessary discipline in a regiment.

On December 21, 1895, a group of officers gathered in Guthrie to vote for the regimental officers. Of all the Civil War veterans living in Oklahoma at that time, they elected Daniel F. Stiles as their colonel. The senior captain of the Guard, Robert Huston, proved to be just as popular, and they voted him their lieutenant colonel. Stiles and Jamison would both mentor Huston. Walter R. Jennings, of Oklahoma City, was elected the commander of the first battalion and William. P. Baker, of Cleveland, the commander of the second, both with the rank of major.

The new articles also defined how the companies would draw their issue of property. Each company had to submit accurate muster rolls, thus accounting for the total number of men actively participating in the unit. Correcting the muster rolls seemed to take the longest time. Each commander would then have to deposit a $2,500 security bond with the adjutant general before the government property could be issued. The Session Laws stated up front that the bond had to double the cost of replacement. This exceeded a year's salary for most men.

Once procured, each enlisted man received the standard issue of one dark blue fatigue blouse, blue trousers, blue flannel shirt and either the old Model 1873 forage cap or the Model 1894 "Pill Box" style cap. Brass crossed rifles with the regimental number above and the company letter below adorned the cap. The two company musicians wore brass hunting horns instead. A black leather belt with brass rectangular buckle, McKeever cartridge box and white cotton Berlin gloves completed the soldier's dress. The enlisted men had to turn their issue back in when discharged. Officers, on the other hand, had to purchase their own uniforms. General Order Number 2 of July 26, 1897, made "OK. N. G." the official abbreviation to be worn or embroidered on the collar and forage cap.

The men carried the obsolete Model 1873 or 1884 "Trapdoor" Springfield rifles. These recent "hand-me-downs" from the army fired a .45-caliber black powder cartridge. The Regulars had traded these Springfields in for the Model 1894 bolt-action, .30-caliber Krag rifle. The obsolete rifles would distinguish the militia apart from the Regular Army.

The legislature also provided money for the rent of drill halls in each town with a militia company. Each company received arms chests and racks for storage of their rifles, shell extractors, wooden cleaning rods, spring vises and tumbler punches. In addition, each company received ball cartridges, target cloth, silhouettes, revolving targets and pasters for marksmanship training. Training traditionally consisted of drill. The company commanders had to inspect their property and send in an annual report on this, actual strength and efficiency in training every December.

While Jamison articulated how the National Guard would function, Stiles supervised its discipline and training. At first, there was no official requirement for how often the companies should train. On November 21, 1896, Stiles issued General Order Number 8, requiring drill once a week. Company A, for example, met every Monday night at their designated armory. The order also specified that the training would comprise instruction in the school of the soldier and company. Noncommissioned officers or sergeants and corporals were required to recite the drill regulations, military code and Articles of War. This rudimentary training provided the building blocks for tactical training.

Jamison and Stiles also raised the necessary legislative funds for the National Guard's first encampment, which began on September 26, 1896. Once the War Department had equipped the Guard, it assumed the responsibility to supervise its maintenance and use. An encampment had become an integral part of training any militia. It provided the best opportunity for the Regular Army to inspect the quality of discipline, training, as well as the maintenance of the equipment. The War Department sent First Lieutenant Robert C. Van Vleit, of the Tenth Infantry, to Oklahoma's first encampment.

As the regiment took shape, names emerged within the officer ranks which would provide the leadership for the impending war with Spain. The First Regiment., ONG, assembled at the Guthrie fairgrounds for encampment and training. Only five of the eight companies attended the training. Newkirk was hosting a Grand Army of the Republic encampment for old Union Civil War veterans, so its company did not attend. Captain J. Milt Welch could not free himself from business, so he sent Lieutenant J.F. Vandervort in command of the Ponca City company. Alva's Company B marched an impressive 95 miles across country to the encampment. The assembled companies spent Monday erecting their tents along designated company streets with the commander's tent at the head. By Tuesday, the camp was in full military order.

This was the first chance for many of the militiamen to experience military life. The encampment conformed strictly to the Regular Army routine. Each morning reveille sounded at 6:30 when the first sergeants assembled their men and then called roll 15 minutes later. At 7 a.m., buglers sounded mess call, and each company marched under the charge of their first sergeant to breakfast, which consisted of a simple diet of bread, butter, coffee, pork and beans. After breakfast, the companies marched to their respective headquarters, where they policed the camp. They removed all litter, straw, or dirt, made beds and prepared the camp for inspection. At 9 a.m., each company conducted the ceremony of guard mount. The men assigned guard duty paced their respective beats for two hours on and four hours off, thus guarding the camp from any surprise attack.

Battalion drill followed guard mount. Instead of a routine event, guard mount became a major ceremony to inspect the standard of discipline inherent in professional soldiers. All companies formed in single line and drilled in the manual of arms or any other exercises the battalion commander designated. Once finished, each company marched back to its quarters and rested until noon. They then reassembled and marched to a dinner of hardtack, pork, beans and coffee—the staple field ration of the army for most of the century. General Jamison often ate with his soldiers.

At 2 in the afternoon, came company drill, when each company executed the manual of arms, bayonet exercise or other such exercises the commanding officer selected. Thirty minutes sufficed for company drill. Then the companies were again assembled at their respective headquarters for another rest or such duty as seen necessary.

The companies spent as much time drilling as possible in preparation for the competition scheduled for 4 p.m. Wednesday. The competition tested the performance of the manual of arms, bayonet exercises and school of the company, a total of about 160 movements. Colonel Stiles, Lieutenant Colonel Huston and General Jamison judged. Oklahoma City's Company C, commanded by Captain Ed O. Overholser, made a sharp impression in white duck trousers (instead of blue) and dark blue coats. They won the first place prize of $70. Alva's Company B, commanded by Captain William Whitworth, won a second place prize of $25. Ponca City's Company G won the third place prize of $15. This was quite a feat since it had not yet been in existence a year. More important, the men had just received their uniforms and equipment just a few weeks before this encampment. Thursday morning, the entire regiment marched in review before Governor Renfrow and his staff. He complimented them on their performance. At 2 p.m. came the highlight of the encampment—a mock battle. The regiment of five companies had orders to attack a natural fortress defended by a rebel army of about 500 men. The parade ground was ideally suited for the war game. Directly in front of and across the racetrack from the grandstand was a bluff, covered with a scrubby growth of timber and rocks, which served as the enemy earthworks.

G Company, Oklahoma National Guard, Ponca City, sometime around 1896 (author's collection).

The ONG formed a battle line. Ponca City led the attack as skirmishers. The enemy succeeded in repulsing the attack, forcing a retreat, which drew them from their strong-hold. Flushed with success, the enemy gave chase. Simultaneously, Oklahoma City, as the reserve, was ordered to make a flank attack, which they did double-quick on the ene-my's right flank. By this time, the regiment had rallied for another charge. This time the companies attacked the flank, and the enemy became an easy victim. Their arms were taken from them, and they were escorted from the fort. Both Alva and Ponca City were the first to scale the ramparts, but Alva earned the honor of securing the rebel colors. During the charge, the fortress in some way caught fire, and it was only saved by the heroic effort on the part of the Ponca City boys. One man, Private Pratt of Ponca City, was injured, for which he would be compensated with a liberal pension. In four years, some of the participants would be similarly charging up San Juan Hill.

Guthrie's A Company and the regimental band culminated the event with a mil-itary ball. The men in military dress showed off their best chivalry in celebration of a successful week of training. The encampment had provided the first chance for the regi-ment to train as a cohesive unit and allowed the men to actually live under military rule. The Guard was shaping up, and so was Huston.

Later alphabetical designations changed as companies fell below status and were disbanded. By 1897, the next year, the Cleveland, Stillwater and Norman companies had been disbanded. Yet the regiment had increased to 12 companies with the formation of new companies in Pawnee, Shawnee, Kingfisher, Newkirk, Enid, Perry and Medford. By the end of 1897, however, El Reno was disbanded.

A third battalion was then organized out of the four additional companies, thus creating another vacancy for a major. Jamison still commanded the first battalion with companies from Guthrie, Oklahoma City, Enid and Perry. Jerry J. O'Rourke, of El Reno, assumed his vacancy the next year. Overholser commanded the second battalion with El Reno, Kingfisher, Enid and Medford. The commanders of the two best companies of the encampment advanced either because of their skill or because of seniority. Baker commanded the third battalion with Alva, Ponca City, Newkirk and Pawnee.

Jamison's term of office ended on July 10, 1897, and he handed over to his successor a fully functioning National Guard. As the founder of the Oklahoma National Guard, Jamison did not leave with a sense of pride. Instead he feared financial destitution. At the age of 66, he evidently had no plan for retirement and was too old to work the farm. He had only a meager veteran's pension to live on. For the next two weeks he drank heavily; then on July 27, he consumed a 100-gram bottle of chloral. Fortunately, the doctors saved his life. Unknown to him, the territory had further need of his services.

Governor Cassius M. Barnes promoted Major Rosenbaum to the office of adjutant general with the rank of brigadier general. At 29, Phil was probably the youngest adjutant general in any state or territory. He continued the task of uniforming and equipping the remaining companies in his National Guard.

The legislation, unfortunately, provided no funds for an encampment in 1897. Instead, the Commander of the Department of Missouri sent Captain Summer H. Lincoln of the Tenth Infantry from Fort Reno to inspect the band and the Guthrie, Oklahoma City and Pawnee companies. From September 27 to October 11, he checked the records, inspected property and evaluated the drill and discipline.

Stiles kept himself busy traveling the territory inspecting his companies. He had moved his headquarters back to Oklahoma City in early 1897. By that time, Huston had accumulated nearly four years' experience in the Oklahoma National Guard. He had also been blessed with a new son. Meanwhile, reports on the Cuban struggle in the local newspapers only drew mild public sympathy. The front pages of the local newspapers reported on things more important to the citizens, fluctuating livestock and crop prices. Little did the Oklahomans know that this tropical island would draw them into a war. Instead, internal problems in the Guard festered.

On a cold winter night on Wednesday, December 22, 1897, scandal, however, rocked the Oklahoma National Guard. Colonel Stiles and his adjutant, Captain McGregor Douglass, waited at the Santa Fe Depot in Guthrie to return to Oklahoma City. As Stiles walked across the platform to one of the cars, several men sprang forth from the shadows to hurl rotten eggs at him. He turned and made a rush for the waiting room but found the door locked. The men continued to pelt him in the face and coat. Unable to escape, the elderly Stiles chased down and grabbed one of his assailants. The man wiggled free and ran off. The night watchman, Al Hixon, came up and shot at the assailants but missed. Smelling of spoiled "hen fruit," Stiles returned to the hotel.[3]

After reporting the incident to Governor Barnes, Stiles initiated his own investigation, with the help of a few friends, to identify the culprits. Accumulating evidence eventually pointed to the men of Company A and its commander, Captain David B. Arrell. Captain Douglass even suspected that he had identified Arrell that night in December. Stiles, however, suspected that Rosenbaum was also behind the plot.

During the midst of this scandal, the USS *Maine* exploded in Havana Harbor on February 15, 1898. Americans reading their papers did not care to wait for the conclusion of the investigation. To them it could have only been the dastardly work of the

Spaniards. The angered citizens demanded justice for the blood of the sailors and Marines. With war lurking in the near future, the growing battle in the ranks of the Oklahoma National Guard would determine the future of its wartime leadership.

Suspecting his end was near, Rosenbaum wrote a glowing letter of thanks on March 3 to the officers and men of the National Guard. He eulogized their service and thanked them for their support. On March 10, 1898, Stiles brought his accusations against the adjutant general to the governor in a closed-door session. Rosenbaum denied the charges and asked for a court of inquiry. Governor Barnes took a special interest in the affair and held the court in his office at 2 in the afternoon on March 21.[4]

He appointed Major Baker as the president, Captains Schuyler A. McGinnis and Fred Boynton as members and Captain A.W. Dunham, the recorder. After two days of questioning, they were unable to ascertain any guilt. Evidently six of the A Company men, who had allegedly boasted of their participation, hid out so they would not have to testify. They had claimed that the assault had been planned for several weeks in the company armory and that A Company was upset with Stiles's strict handling of Governor Barnes's inauguration. One man at the hearing claimed that Rosenbaum had even bought the eggs and arranged plans for the assault. Stiles was angered by the verdict of not guilty and was not about to let the issue rest.

On March 24, Stiles then filed charges and placed Arrell under arrest for failure to salute when both had met in uniform. Arrell and Major O'Rourke submitted their resignations, and the colonel appointed First Lieutenant Charles Laux to command A Company. On March 28, Arrell's company in protest asked for honorable discharges and refused to drill. That same day, Governor Barnes asked for both Rosenbaum's and Stiles's resignations. Rosenbaum resigned without protest.

Stiles was clearly the victim in this scandal, so Barnes's demand for his resignation had to have political motives. Either the governor had tired of the infighting in his Guard, or he wanted someone else to command it in time of war. With war and mobilization imminent, Oklahoma expected the opportunity to field its National Guard in battle. The commander of the Oklahoma National Guard and his officers would reap the laurels of a grateful territory.

Hesitant to resign, Colonel Stiles left for home. He expected to command the regiment if it was called up. While Barnes considered his other options against Stiles, the colonel finally submitted his letter of resignation on March 31. Colonel Stiles died two years later at his home in Oklahoma City on September 11, 1900. He would miss one last opportunity to serve his nation in war. He, to his credit, had established his name in the annals of Oklahoma history as its National Guard's first colonel. The Guard would continue to prosper as his legacy. The old veteran, however, had to leave the next war to a new generation.

Huston advanced one grade to become the new colonel and senior ranking officer of the regiment with war waiting just around the corner. With Stiles's resignation, there were no charges left against Arrell, and he was reinstated to command. Major William Baker assumed Huston's place as lieutenant colonel, and Captain Whitworth of Company B became a battalion commander with the rank of major. The scandal had run its course on the eve of war with Spain.

This did not end the problems for Rosenbaum though. Evidently, while he was the quartermaster general, he lavishly furnished his office at the expense of the territorial government. The territorial auditor, S.N. Hopkins, sought an audience with the governor to discuss the unlimited expenditures and other lost property. Barnes agreed to order a board of survey on May 11, which did not find Rosenbaum negligent. For some unexplainable reason though, Rosenbaum still had to pay $250 for lost property, his last month's salary. He then moved to the Indian Territory to recruit a volunteer company.

Barnes chose not to select a new adjutant general for the time being and left Second Lieutenant Bert C. Orner as the acting adjutant. He could, instead, count on the help of an old patriot. Jamison stepped out of retirement to assist in any preparations for an anticipated call for volunteers.

In anticipation of war, patriotism and ambition soared. Attorney Robert Lowry, of Stillwater, equally anxious to get into the war, recruited the first cavalry company of the Oklahoma National Guard from across the territory. Perkins also wanted to organize a cavalry troop. Farmers living in the Tohee township of Lincoln County boasted of organizing the first militia company outside a town.

In the spring of 1898, Oklahoma had a functioning National Guard with companies ranging from one to four years of training experience. It had an established infrastructure that could survive even scandal. The Oklahoma National Guard therefore provided a small population of Oklahomans trained and ready to respond to war and face its first test of combat.

CHAPTER 2

Mustering the Troops

The Oklahoma Territory was still in its infancy, and the opening of the last 6,000,000 acres of unassigned lands in the Cherokee Strip to white settlement in 1893 signaled the end of the Old West and the beginning of the new. Yet, it had a few rambunctious years left as the territory grew into statehood. In a rapid acceleration of growth, boomtowns sprang up overnight, and new settlements offered unlimited opportunities for resourceful and adventurous men, many of whom descended from families that had followed the frontier steadily westward, never resting until they found more open space. Oklahoma provided one of the last exciting opportunities to start completely anew. For men of this breed, war provided the greatest adventure, but having no threat on the nation's borders and completing the subjugation of the native population, the only prospect of war was overseas.

Some Americans had been following the plight of the Cubans in their fight for independence from Spain, with many identifying the struggle with the American War of Independence from England. On February 15, 1898, the battleship USS *Maine* mysteriously exploded and sank in Havana Harbor. Americans hastily blamed the Spaniards simply as an excuse to join the Cuban struggle, resulting in a war that would significantly change the lives of many Oklahomans.

Roy V. Cashion's family had settled in the western half of the Cherokee Strip in 1894, within a year after it opened. They first staked a homestead outside of the town of Okeene but later moved to Hennessey where Roy led the typical childhood life on the prairie, riding, exploring and playing tricks on his friends. He liked a variety of sports but enjoyed baseball the most. He similarly possessed an adventurous spirit and would take on challenges that would frighten others.

On Thanksgiving Day 1896, an important dispatch arrived for one of the citizens of Hennessey, who was 60 miles away on the range watching his herd of cattle. Roy volunteered to deliver the message to him, a journey that would take several days. He started off on horseback at noon. By 5 p.m., a northerner blew in, causing the warm afternoon to suddenly turn into a blizzard with freezing wind that stung when the snow hit his skin. He wandered lost through the blinding snow into the night until by providence he came across a lone house out on the prairie. Roy was nearly frozen, and the inhabitants offered him shelter and warmth for the night. The next morning, the determined youth borrowed heavier clothing and set out to complete his task. For four days his parents worried about him until finally he returned as happy as ever having delivered the message and acquired a personal story of adventure to tell.

An exceptional student and active Methodist, Roy was an idealistic youth with a promising future. He graduated at the top in his high school class of seven in May 1897.

Having closely followed the Cuban plight, he selected *"Cuba Libre"* or "Cuban Liberty" as the topic for his graduation speech. To prepare for his oration, he read everything available on the cruel treatment of Cubans by Spain, and on graduation night he spoke in ardent tones:

> The Cubans will soon redress their grievances. Maceo was not martyred in vain, nor has Gomez led these patriots for naught. The cause they have struggled for, is the rights of humanity. The oppression in Cuba has been tolerated too long. It is time to call Spain to a halt, for it is evident she can neither govern nor control Cuba. Her insults, not only to the Cubans, but to Americans, also, are insufferable, and should be avenged. The rights of Cuba ought to be the great subject of our solicitude. And the United States should be the first to salute Cuban Liberty, and I for one, am ready and willing to help break off the shackles.[1]

After school, Roy took a job with the grocery firm of Griffin & Griffin and joined the recently organized fraternal organization for boys, the Coming Men of America. Reared on war stories, military service was in his blood. His father and four uncles had fought for the Union cause during the Civil War, and Roy's great-grandfather had fought in the War of 1812. So he likewise joined the local vigilante unit, "Pat Hennessey Rifles," which was raised to respond to outlaw raids. It provided him an early substitute for military service. At 17, the news of the sinking of the *Maine* in February 1898 had inspired this young man's martial dreams of glory, and this martial spirit was contagious.

In the spring of 1898, Professor O.G. Palmer was finishing his first school year as superintendent in Ponca City on the eastern edge of the Cherokee Strip. When the 33-year-old heard the news of the *Maine*, he reflected on his father's military service during the Civil War. Inspired by patriotism, he told his friends that if his country went to war, he would also go, but to do so Palmer would have to resign his post and leave behind his pregnant wife and daughter. When he returned, he would probably not be able to pick up where he had left off but would have to wait until the beginning of the next school year for another job. Nonetheless, this may be his only chance to measure up to his father's war record. He anxiously awaited the outcome of the investigation into the sinking of the *Maine*.

Meanwhile, the nationwide clamor for war steadily increased. In the midst of the Stiles-Rosenbaum scandal, former Adjutant General Jamison stepped out of retirement to help ready the National Guard for the prospect of war. This gave him a new purpose in his life. In early March, he asked each company for a list of volunteers to determine how much Oklahoma interest there was in enlistment for a possible mobilization. With the numbers in hand, Jamison estimated that his territory could muster an entire regiment of infantry in 30 days and one of cavalry in 60. On March 21, a naval court of inquiry determined that since some metal plates on the hull of the *Maine* were bent inward, the cause of the explosion resulted from an underwater mine. (This was, much later, determined to be incorrect.) There was no stopping the clamor for war after that.

On April 3, Governor Barnes sent a telegram to Secretary of War Russell A. Alger stating Jamison's estimation of what Oklahoma could muster. As it turned out, others with the similar intent in mind were feeling the waters within their own territories while the press continued to enflame the furor for war. With great popularity for this fight, congressional representatives pressured the War Department to employ their volunteers in the upcoming war.

Back in Oklahoma on April 21, Acting Adjutant General Orner sent out General Order Number 4 revoking the 50-man limit and ordered the companies to recruit up to 80 men. The ranks of the local militia companies rapidly swelled with men affirming their desire to go to war. This would expedite the recruitment of a full regiment.

Remembering the disaster of the opening battles of the Civil War, the War Department, however, was hesitant to rely on hastily recruited volunteer regiments. Although the Regular Army was still small and wholly understrength, it felt it had enough men to whip the Spanish Army in Cuba. Additionally, there was not enough time to recruit, equip and train volunteer regiments effectively. Weather was a key factor as the rains would begin in June, heralding the season for such tropical diseases as yellow fever and malaria. However, to increase their territories' chances for participation in the war, a couple of politicians originated a logical idea.

In March, Honorable Jay L. Torrey, of Wyoming, proposed to Secretary Alger that the Army should recruit regiments of cavalry from the frontier territories. Since cowboys already knew how to ride and shoot, they made ideal recruits for the mounted branch and only needed rudimentary training in military drill and discipline, the easiest of martial skills to learn. Coincidentally, Adjutant General Melvin Grisby, of South Dakota, pressed the same idea to Alger, watering the seed Torrey had planted. Finally, on Saturday, April 23, Congress authorized the call-up of 125,000 volunteers to serve two years unless sooner discharged. Two days later Congress declared war with Spain.

The War Department also bought into the novel idea of recruiting a couple of regiments of cavalry with "special qualifications," so Congress attached the Grisby Amendment to the Volunteer Bill. Alger then offered command of the Second and Third U.S. Volunteer Cavalry regiments to both Grisby and Torrey as reward for their proposals. Alger, however, reserved the command of the First for Assistant Secretary of the Navy Theodore Roosevelt.

Confident that he had the skill to lead a regiment, Roosevelt knew he did not have the necessary military experience to organize and train the regiment in time to join the invasion. Showing great wisdom, the ambitious politician declined the post of command in favor of his personal friend and professional soldier, Captain Leonard Wood. To subordinate his ego to one more experienced proved his wisest decision.

Wood, a Harvard graduate and army surgeon, had earned the Medal of Honor while commanding an infantry detachment during the last Geronimo Campaign in 1886. Although a surgeon, Wood had always aspired for military command. This war provided another opportunity. Not only had Wood commanded men in combat, but he had also spent enough time living out West to know the nature of Westerners. As colonel, Wood would provide the needed military expertise to train and equip the regiment in the short time available, while Roosevelt, as lieutenant colonel, would provide the charisma to attract even the sons of the leading citizens of the nation and the political clout to expedite matters. Roosevelt was a wealthy Ivy Leaguer who went West to become a cowboy after the death of his first wife. Both stocks would provide the caliber of men he attracted. Although Wood was in command, in character it would be Roosevelt's regiment. The call for the First U.S. Volunteer Cavalry went out initially to Southern Colorado, Arizona, New Mexico and Oklahoma Territories. The newspapers quickly dubbed them the "Rough Riders," another term for cowboys.

The race was on, and Wood knew that he had very little time to recruit, equip, organize and train his regiment. Otherwise, any volunteer regiment not ready would miss the war, and this newly promoted colonel was not about to let this happen. While the other volunteer regiments received the obsolete "Trapdoor" Springfield rifles which fired black powder, Wood armed his regiment with the state-of-the-art Model 1896 bolt-action Krag carbines also used by the Regular cavalry. His experience campaigning in the sweltering heat of Arizona and Mexico also inspired him to adopt the Model 1884 brown cotton canvas fatigues as the field uniform. His would be the only American regiment to fight in the tropics of Cuba wearing cotton.

In a week, Wood and Roosevelt had completed the necessary arrangements for the regiment. On May 2, Colonel Wood boarded a train bound for the rendezvous station at San Antonio, Texas, ahead of his troops. He left Roosevelt behind in Washington to tie up any loose ends. In a small ceremony in his office on May 6, surrounded by senators, representatives and leading army officers, Adjutant General Henry C. Corbin administered the oath of commission to Theodore Roosevelt, making him a lieutenant colonel of volunteers. The others shook his hand in congratulations on his entrance into the military. By noon, millionaires, college athletes, and ex-policemen, who had mustered into his regiment the day before, crowded his office to add their congratulations. They would leave for San Antonio the next day. From there events progressed rapidly. Wood believed that as soon as his regiment was organized and equipped, it would sail for Cuba. Meanwhile, recruiting in the territories was well underway.

Back in Oklahoma on Monday, April 25, Governor Barnes had not yet received word of the call for volunteers. Impatient, he fired off a telegram to Secretary of Interior Cornelius N. Bliss, stating, "If the president calls for volunteers, I ask your good offices to urge that Oklahoma be allowed to furnish at least one full regiment of infantry." He even improved on the time estimated to mobilize them since men were still pouring into the companies. "Can perfect organization of First Regiment in a few days. Have reliable offers of men for regiment of cavalry, battery of light artillery and additional regiment of infantry if desired."[2]

He also sent a second telegram to Alger: "The population of Oklahoma is at least three hundred and fifty thousand. If apportionment of call four volunteers be based strictly on population we should be entitled to over six hundred, but we want a distinct Oklahoma regiment and I can place full regiment in rendezvous in five days."[3]

Almost at the same time, Alger had sent out telegrams to the respective territories assigning their quotas for volunteers. His and Barnes's probably passed each other going in opposite directions. At 5 that evening, Barnes received Alger's message.

Oklahoma received a disappointing quota for only 143 men and to furnish a cavalry company of 85 men. Alger requested that the men should be "good shots" and "good riders." He also asked that the territories draw the men from their existing militia or National Guard. Such men were already armed, equipped and drilled and should be ready for service by May 1.

This small quota came as much of a severe disappointment to Barnes, as he knew it would be to the companies. He answered Alger that same night that he would draw from his National Guard as he had always intended, making Oklahoma the only territory to do so. Barnes, however, could have filled that meager requirement with almost any company but at the displeasure of the other companies. Each company belonged to a town that hoped to secure its place in history, and the men had hoped to go to war with their hometown friends. After consultation with his staff, Barnes decided to do the fair thing and divide the quota equally among the companies. Acting Adjutant General Orner subsequently sent out Circular Order Number 1 directing the companies of the Oklahoma National Guard to pick their best eight volunteers.

For some reason the order did not include all the companies of the regiment, only Guthrie, Oklahoma City, Ponca City, Pawnee, El Reno, Shawnee, Kingfisher, Newkirk and North Enid. Alva, the second-oldest company in the Guard, was left off the list along with the two newest companies, Perry and Medford. Attorney Robert Lowry's newly recruited company of cavalry in Stillwater incidentally received a quota, evidently verifying his political influence.

That next day, Tuesday, April 26, Captain Arrell notified the 82 men of his Guthrie Company to meet at the armory that night. That night he fell them in formation and read the message from Barnes. He announced that the hour for action had finally arrived and then warned of the dangers awaiting any man who volunteered. Since not all could go, he promised he would recommend an honorable discharge for anyone who wanted one. Finally, he asked for volunteers. Sixteen men brought their rifles to right shoulder arms to indicate their desire, a scene which played itself out in almost every company in the territory.

Thirty-one-year-old Attorney-at-Law Schuyler A. McGinnis commanded Newkirk's Company I. His father, J.A. McGinnis, had settled in Bleeding Kansas in 1854 and practiced medicine under the tutorship of his father and Dr. J.D. Hitchcock. When the Civil War broke out, he enlisted in the Ninth Kansas Volunteer Infantry and was later commissioned in the First Kansas Colored Regiment, the first African American regiment raised during the Civil War. After the war, Schuyler Arthur was born in Coffee County, Kansas, on November 10, 1867, but his mother died before he was one-year-old, so the family of William H. Baxter raised the infant while his father practiced medicine. After high school, Schuyler attended the Kansas Agricultural College and then the newly opened Garfield University in Wichita. Descending from a family of veterans, little wonder he demonstrated an early interest in the military and participated in the military instruction at Garfield. Besides his father's service during the Civil War, Schuyler's grandfather had fought in the Mexican War and his great-grandfather had fought in the War of 1812. After graduation, Schuyler then joined the Kansas National Guard and rapidly advanced through the ranks from private to colonel of the Second Kansas National Guard. On the professional side, he was admitted to the bar in Butler County, Kansas, in 1890 and was also elected as county attorney that same year, therefore becoming the youngest county attorney, and served for two years. Right after the Cherokee Strip opened, he moved to Newkirk (the county seat) to practice law and again joined the National Guard. That night in April 1898, 12 Newkirk men volunteered when Captain McGinnis asked. One of those volunteers was a fellow lawyer.

Twenty-three-year-old Ira Hill had similarly arrived from Kansas after the opening of the Strip where he tried his hand at different kinds of work until he finally landed a job in an attorney's office where he studied and passed the bar. Ira then formed a law partnership with William S. Cline. Ira also had political aspirations having just that April 1898 thrown his hat in the ring for the Republican nomination for town clerk. War service might provide a boost to this ambitious young lawyer's political career.

Aside from the politically ambitious, McGinnis's list also included a cross sampling of the community that comprised any National Guard company. It included the young and adventurous type, like 19-year-old baker and fellow Knight of Pythias Starr W. Wetmore and 19-year-old John Frank Weitzel, who lived in the comfort of his father's brand-new, plush Windsor Hotel. Twenty-year-old John T. Brown listed himself as a student. Twenty-seven-year-old Jacob Milt Haynes, Junior, wanted a break from working in his father's dry goods store. Twenty-seven-year-old William Dick Amrine had just opened a bakery and small restaurant in an old meat market. He was also the only married enlisted volunteer from Newkirk. Most of the others could pick right up where they left, but to go to war Dick would have to shut down his business. The 23-year-old farmer Scott Reay, and Charles F. Fouts rounded out Newkirk's quota of eight, and Mac also included four alternates: 23-year-old farmer Thomas M. Holmes and three others in the event any of the eight failed to pass the mustering physical. Newkirk's selection represented a sample of the occupations of the men who had volunteered from across Oklahoma.

Kay County National Guard (Newkirk and Ponca City) quota and alternates: (1) James Brown; (2) Will Tauer; (3) Scott Reay; (4) Starr Wetmore; (5) Milt Haynes; (6) Capt. S.A. McGinnis; (7) unknown; (8) Dick Amrine; (9) Lawrence S. Hands; (10) Ira Hill; (11) Eugene Weitzel. Missing are Elisha Freeman and Tom Holmes (courtesy Newkirk Community Historical Society).

That same Tuesday, the local papers announced the news of war and the call for volunteers. This new generation had grown up during a time when Civil War officers retained their former ranks as honorary titles. Military service was rewarded with political appointments and at the polls of public office. Nearly every political official had served in the Civil War on one side or the other, and no one of the Civil War generation could expect to attain a political office without these military credentials. Many ambitious young patriots expected this war to provide the same benefits and likewise flocked to their local militia companies. Consequently, some of the most prominent men of the territory volunteered to go to war.

As a small war, there were not as many opportunities to serve, so nearly every National Guard officer and man of influence traveled to Guthrie to seek an audience with the governor. They flooded Barnes with requests for one of the three commissions in this new troop. Professor Palmer discovered that even with his position of leadership and military experience, he could not find a quota with the Ponca City company. He similarly hopped on a train bound for Guthrie to personally plead his case with the governor. He just wanted in at any rank and successfully returned with a vacancy in the Pawnee quota. Among Pawnee's eight was also one full-blood Indian.

William Pollock had been born in 1872 on the Pawnee Reservation in Nebraska. His Pawnee name was Syracrisout-Kuwyh. While a young boy, his elders had gone off to fight in the Great Sioux War of 1876 for the U.S. Army with the famed Pawnee Scouts. Pawnee Scout Companies had distinguished themselves for nearly a decade, and Pollock had grown up listening to tales of valor around the council fires. Yet, by the time he came of age, the Pawnee had no more enemies to fight. After completing schooling on the Pawnee Reservation in Oklahoma, Pollock was the product of assimilation and attended the Haskell Indian School in Lawrence, Kansas, where he demonstrated a talent for art. Graduating in 1894, he returned to Pawnee and became a deputy sheriff for the county, all the while continuing his painting. Raised as a Great Plains Indian and educated into the Anglo-culture, Pollock balanced both cultures. When the United States declared war on Spain, Pollock saw his chance to fulfill his warrior heritage and serve his country as his ancestors had. He secured a vacancy in the Pawnee quota.

By the end of the week, each company had chosen its quota of eight plus alternates, and on Friday, the 29th, Orner wired a telegram for each company to report with their quota to Guthrie by rail no later than Sunday, May 1. The adjutant general's office would reimburse the Santa Fe Railway for the transportation. Orner also included instruction for Captain J. Milt Welch of Ponca City to bring Palmer down with his quota.

Captain Arrell again assembled his company in the armory that Friday night, where he passed out the latest information from the governor and named his quota and six alternates. He granted the new recruits leave of absence and wrote down addresses where they could be reached, then dismissed them until their services would be needed. He then instructed the old members of his company to meet for their regular Monday night drill.

On Saturday, April 30, the Newkirk company escorted their volunteers dressed in army blue to the Santa Fe Depot while the local band played and crowds cheered. Family members said their good-byes, and ladies gave their loved ones the gift they thought would keep them safe—Bibles. The Newkirk boys became the first volunteers to arrive at the mustering station in Guthrie.

Captain Welch selected his own eight and alternates to represent Ponca City's Company D. A total of 14 Ponca City volunteers departed with similar fanfare on the noon train to Guthrie that Sunday, May 1; an unfortunate incident, however, soured the occasion. Twenty-three-year-old Ed Haley turned up at the depot and decided to insult the militia and their flag. While a respected "colored" population lived in Ponca City, Haley represented a recent group of undesirables who had immigrated within the last month. After calling the American flag an "old rag," he was warned by Corporal Imel to shut up and leave. An insolent Haley refused and then foolishly drew a knife. The militia then proceeded to beat the young black man senseless until his mother and wife threw their bodies across him to protect him from further injury. It was later reported that Haley subsequently beat his wife and mother terribly. This tarnished celebration left the local white community in a sour mood.[4]

That afternoon the militia and several citizens met to decide what to do. They then appointed a committee to run Haley out of town, which was a common practice to rid communities of undesirables regardless of their race. The problem escalated when the committee, followed by a mob of several hundred citizens, decided to lynch Haley instead. Sheriff Pierce, who had refereed the entire affair, interceded when the mob contemplated this act of murder. This was a little too far even for frontier justice. Haley was instead taken to the south edge of town and told to "hit the grit."

The incident regrettably did not end there, and after supper the unruly mob decided to rid the town of the whole black population. They then began to direct the rest of the blacks to pack up and leave. The mob went so far as to break into houses and take valuables. One law-abiding citizen was even beaten. Upon learning of this injustice, fair-minded Marshal Gillen rounded up a posse which included the editor of the local Republican paper. With rifles in hand, they dispersed the mob and threw 16 of the instigators in jail. While many settlers in the Strip had arrived from Kansas and other northern states, this new territory had also attracted considerable Southern influence that would taint the others. This incident reflected the attitude of the territory and times, but those who would fight in Cuba would return with greater respect for African Americans.

Meanwhile, 27 Kay County boys had arrived in Guthrie as men from other towns similarly answered the call. When 27-year-old William McGinty learned of this, he approached Robert Lowry about enlisting through one of his quotas. Roosevelt later claimed that the majority of his men were cowboys, miners and hunters. Oklahoma, however, was different. Most of the members of the Guard were lawyers, businessmen and farmers. Bill was one of the few great cowboys produced by Oklahoma, a kind of employment that usually caused one to move about, which was not conducive to maintaining membership in a militia. As such, cowboys for whom the regiment was organized had difficulty finding quotas for enlistment through the Oklahoma National Guard.

Born in Missouri, Bill's parents brought him to Oklahoma during the first opening of land in 1889 and settled in Ingalls, the hideout of the notorious Dalton and Doolin Gangs. Growing up, Bill worked on the Bar-X-Bar Ranch on the Pawnee Reservation where he learned his trade and built his reputation as a superb broncobuster and roper, one of the legendary cowboys of Oklahoma. Having secured his quota vacancy, he rode his horse for two days to Guthrie, checked into one of the hotels at the government's expense and waited for the others to arrive.

Governor Barnes had also favored the Hennessey Rifles by calling for three of their best men. Young Roy V. Cashion coaxed, begged and pleaded with his parents for their written permission to enlist. At last, they gave in, and on April 29, he bade farewell to his friends, and with his parent's written consent in his pocket, he rode the long journey to Guthrie on horseback along with J.E. Redman and John Rhoades, who had been elected captain of the company during the last meeting.[5]

The rest of the volunteers arrived that weekend at the Santa Fe Depot to the fanfare of martial music of the regimental band and the cheers of soldiers from Company A and as many as 1,000 citizens. The territorial capital came alive with excitement as nearly 200 arrivals were put up in local hotels courtesy of the Quartermaster General H.A. Platt. The men with quotas had priority in the enlistment, but rumors spread that some men offered a considerable amount of money for volunteers to give up their quota vacancies.

To facilitate the recruiting, Governor Barnes activated Arrell's Company A on Monday to assume command of Camp George B. Steele, named in honor of the first territorial governor. The camp assembled all the National Guard volunteers to help with the mustering. The appearance of officers and soldiers walking about in blue uniforms gave the camp a military air. In the meantime, the applicants were delayed in Guthrie for most of the week while waiting for the recruiting officer. Heavy rains had washed out tracks, which caused the Regular Army officer from Fort Sill, Oklahoma Territory, difficulty in reaching Guthrie. During the wait, excitement increased as Old Glory waved from the red brick buildings of the business center of the town. Old veterans passed out words of encouragement, and citizens wished the volunteers luck. There was nothing like a war to make citizens feel patriotic.

On Monday night, the town honored the volunteers with a rousing farewell at the Knights of Pythias Hall. Local dignitaries and Guard officers took their turns to praise the volunteers. The military band played patriotic music, and Governor Barnes presented the closing remarks by charging the Oklahoma volunteers to bring honor to their territory. As restlessness grew in the crowded town, many men flooded the "honkey-tonk" bars. Fights naturally broke out, and the men nearly tore one of the drinking establishments apart.

Aside from the excitement of the war, the officers of the National Guard felt slighted that they were only called upon to provide one company. It turned out the quotas for each of the territories and states were based upon an outdated census report. Oklahoma had just opened its first seven counties for settlement when the official census was taken. With all the officers in town, they met Tuesday night to organize a permanent association of officers for the betterment of the Oklahoma National Guard and elected Captain James Neal, of Pawnee, as the president and G.L. Finley, of Enid, as the secretary and treasurer. They sought to rectify the problem and see that Oklahoma received its fair quota in the future. They also hoped to complete the organization of the First Regiment, ONG, as soon as possible.

On Wednesday morning, May 4, Lieutenant Allyn K. Capron, Jr., of the Seventh Cavalry, and his First Sergeant, Ernest Stecker, finally arrived from Fort Sill. The 26-year-old, tall, athletic, blond-haired, blue-eyed Capron presented a striking figure, every bit the image of the ideal soldier. Capron had the right credentials for a professional soldier since he had descended from a family of career military men. His father, Captain Allyn Capron, was a career soldier and commanded a battery in the First Artillery Regiment. Rank was slow in the Army and even slower in the field artillery. Although his father was an 1867 graduate of West Point, Allyn Capron had served for four years as a private and noncommissioned officer in the Fourth Cavalry until he passed the examination for a direct commission in 1894. He married Lillian Morris two years after his commission. He would pass final judgment on the volunteers from Oklahoma after the doctors deemed them healthy enough for military service. Governor Barnes had chosen Dr. O.E. Barker, the Oklahoma Regimental Surgeon, and Dr. Harry Walker, of Oklahoma City, to assist the mustering officer in examining the volunteers.

Beginning at 7 that morning, 111 naked recruits hurried through the physical examination before the two local doctors. They checked eyesight, thumped here and there, turned the candidates around, then pronounced their verdict. If they were physically fit, the applicants then passed in front of Lieutenant Capron, who determined whether they met the height and weight qualifications for cavalry. Evidently, the examiners just had enough time for the original quota that day, and only 60 of those passed.

Forty-two-year-old Charles Hunter walked through the line that day. An original '89er, he had settled in Okarche and started the *Okarche Times*. He had successfully run that paper until the opening of the Cherokee Strip, when he moved north to Enid and started another newspaper up there. His accomplishments earned him the post as the Director of the Oklahoma Press Association from January 1895 to June 1896, and he also became the town site manager. He had succeeded at everything he had set out to do, but, after he passed the doctors' examination, Capron pronounced him a quarter of an inch too short for the cavalry. This devastated him to the point that he burst into tears and returned to his hotel room, vowing to try again the next day. His peers in the press joked that he would return wearing a wig to make up the difference in his height. He was not alone in his disappointment, as even Captain G.L. Finley, of Enid, had hoped to enlist as a private but did not pass the physical examination. Men of status wanted to serve in this war at any rank.

An elated Roy Cashion passed, and so did his friend, 26-year-old farmer, John Rhoades. McGinnis, of Newkirk, had chosen well, as seven of his eight had passed. Hill, Haynes, Brown, Reay, Amrine, Wetmore and Weitzel would go. Ponca City and Shawnee, however, fared the worst, as both towns only had two volunteers pass. Twenty-one-year-old laborer, William Tauer, and 32-year-old cowboy, Elisha A. Freeman would represent Ponca. Both were sons of land run families. Captain Welch was disappointed by the product of his selection, and the man he had turned down surprisingly passed. Palmer along with Pollock completed a total of eight men from Pawnee who qualified. McGinty was the only man from Stillwater to pass, hinting that everything about Lowry's role was political. Right at five feet and five inches, McGinty had feared that he might be rejected for being a little too short, but he just barely reached the minimum height requirements. The results of this examination reflected on the judgment of the Guard officers who made the initial selection, and their list alternates would be examined the next day.

All through the week, the officers had anxiously waited to see whom the governor would appoint to lead the first Oklahomans into battle. A Union veteran of the Civil War, Barnes made his decision based on military merit and not politics, since each of his officers belonged to a different political party. Neither was he about to leave the military reputation of the territory up to an election by the men, which was standard procedure in volunteer companies. This would be the first unit in combat to bear the name Oklahoma, and it had to consist of the best he could send.

That Wednesday, he appointed 34-year-old Robert B. Huston, of Guthrie, the captain of the cavalry troop. As the senior officer of the regiment, Colonel Huston, a Republican, still had the youth and energy to lead a troop in combat. Barnes remembered years later, "I knew his strong characteristics, a modest man, reserved, but over a genial, courteous gentleman, tender hearted as a woman, but withal a man of sound judgment and strong determined will, able and capable to assume the command of men and the responsibility for their best welfare." Stiles and Jamison had groomed this quiet professional for this day.

Newkirk's Captain McGinnis, a Populist, was appointed first lieutenant. The Populist movement championed the cause of the common man that would later be embraced by the Democratic Party, and McGinnis similarly identified with the average citizen on the street. With no airs of superiority, he endeared himself to his soldiers, and this appointment surprised him since he had not applied for the commission. The friends of this former colonel of the Kansas National Guard had nominated him.

Thirty-eight-year-old Captain Jacob Schweizer, a Democrat and hotel manager from El Reno, became the second lieutenant. Born in Germany, he had immigrated to America by himself when he was just 16. He then went West, and, like many immigrants looking for work while they breached the language barrier, he enlisted in the Sixth Cavalry in 1878. After completing a five-year enlistment in Arizona, he then tried his hand at business. Evidently, that did not work out, because after a few years, he again enlisted, this time in the Fifth Cavalry at Fort Reno in the Oklahoma Territory. He finished another five years of military service as a sergeant, then settled in the territory. Although the junior officer, he was the only officer with any active military service, and, like the other two officers, he was also married.

The Oklahoma officers represented the most experienced military men the Guard had, and most of the enlisted men who passed the muster exam that day had served in the National Guard. Jamison's effort to improve the Oklahoma National Guard had paid off. Although it would not deploy as a regiment, it would provide the material for a first-rate cavalry troop.

Thursday began with a heavy rain as a batch of 48 alternates paraded through the same routine as the others had the day before, competing for the remaining 25 vacancies left in the troop. Capron, who had impressed everyone with his impartiality, was more scrutinizing than the day before. The newly appointed officers also endured the same critical eye of the examiners that day. Fortunately, the Army allowed greater latitude in height and weight for officers, and all three passed. At the end of the line, a happy fellow would shout, "I have passed!" or a more solemn figure would otherwise sulk home.

Charley Hunter mustered up his confidence and returned to the examination. Evidently, he had not grown the necessary quarter of an inch overnight, and he received the same answer as before. Undaunted, he then returned to the end of the line and tried again. At last, Capron selected 18 men, and to everyone's approval, Charley Hunter was one of them. His undaunted spirit had won out over army regulations. Tom Holmes added one more to the list from Newkirk.

Capron then had the 78 enlisted volunteers fall into company formation on the parade ground as he explained the significance of their next step. Unlike previous patriotic speeches, this Regular Army lieutenant warned them that army life was no child's play. When they signed up, they would commit themselves for two years of service, and there was no backing out. He then asked if anyone had any reservations about going to war to take two steps back. The line held firm. Afterwards, each man proceeded into the office to sign his name to the muster roll. With a stroke of the pen, each became a soldier in the U.S. Volunteers. The volunteers then swore their oath before their mustering officer on Thursday, May 5.

Capron had impressed everyone with his fairness. He had that look of a soldier and the kind of charisma that left a lasting impression on every citizen who had a chance to meet him. The recruits from Oklahoma looked forward to seeing him again since Colonel Wood had offered him the position of regimental adjutant. Meanwhile, the other territories of the Southwest had made similar progress in recruiting.

That same evening, Major Alexander O. Brodie had wired Roosevelt at 6 p.m. that he had enlisted 250 men from Arizona and would leave the next day for Texas. Major

Henry B. Hersey also telegraphed from New Mexico that he had recruited 358 men and would leave soon. The floods, however, had washed out tracks at Purcell on the South Canadian River, and Roosevelt telegraphed Capron from Washington, D.C.: "Why don't you move that company?" Capron explained the problem of washed-out railroads and bluntly added, "Come out and build railroads and we will move it." Meanwhile, Robert H. Bruce, of Mineola, Texas, who would help him recruit in the Indian Territory, telegraphed Capron that he was similarly stranded at Ardmore and could move neither north nor south. Capron sent back the message, "Swim!" Capron's outward appearance as the consummate professional hid his sense of humor.[6]

Leaving his wife and child behind was Huston's only reservation about going off to war. He worried about whether his wife could take care of herself while he was gone. Both Huston and McGinnis then made last-minute preparations for war and signed up for $1,000 life insurance policies. Having passed the rigorous army physical, McGinnis then took another physical examination at the opera house for his insurance policy Friday morning. When asked his concern about the war, Mac quipped the only bad thing he could imagine was if the navy would sink the entire Spanish fleet; then the United States would be morally bound to buy each Spaniard a pair of rubber boots so they could wade home. Mac was an outgoing, friendly character that spent his week hanging out and drinking with his men to the objection of Huston's wife, Vite, who felt that was not the proper conduct of an army officer. Could Mac balance his familiarity and still inspire confidence?

As the commander, Captain Huston only had one day to determine who would wear chevrons in his troop. Friday, he announced his initial selection for noncommissioned officers. Volunteer regiments had an advantage over the Regular Army in choice for noncoms. Generally, volunteer soldiers had higher education and a vast array of experience from which the commanding officer could predict future performance.

Professor O.G. Palmer was the obvious choice for first sergeant. With a law degree from Columbia, a former captain in the Guard and school superintendent, he would have responsibility for the company administration, formations and would command the third platoon in combat for $20 a month.

Seniority among sergeants was designated in the numerical order of appointment. Sergeants commanded sections and served as left and right guides of platoons. The senior sergeants acted as platoon sergeants. Twenty-seven-year-old painter George H. Sands became the second sergeant and Gerald A. Webb the third. Both were from Guthrie and had previous active military service. The tall, handsome George was popular with the ladies and had served a hitch in the Navy. Gerald had served five years in the cavalry and had seen action in Arizona against Apaches. Joseph A. Randolph, a 39-year-old married cattleman from Waukomis, made the fourth sergeant. McGinnis had some influence in promoting fellow attorney, Ira Hill, to fifth sergeant. Huston's choice for sixth sergeant was the man who had demonstrated the greatest determination of all, Charley Hunter. This responsibility increased their pay from $13.50 of a private to $18.70 a month.[7]

Most of these men were proven leaders in their communities. Huston picked his corporals based on their training and discipline in the militia. They were assigned in order: 38-year-old married rancher Calvin Hill, of Pawnee; 21-year-old teacher George Norris, of Kingfisher; 18-year-old ranchman David V. McClure, of Oklahoma City; and John Rhoades, of Hennessey. These corporals would risk their lives leading squads of eight men each for $15.50 a month.

The remaining positions had little to do with military experience but were on the recommendation of the officers. McGinnis evidently had more say about this since his quota had fared so well. Starr Wetmore became the bugler and Dick Amrine the saddler. Thirty-seven-year-old former soldier Thomas Moran, of Oklahoma City, became the farrier. If and when the troop would increase to its ~~auth~~ 104 men, Huston could promote mor

At 4 p.m. _____ on, then marched them across the str _____ ion in Guthrie was coming to an end _____ taries, wives and friends along with al _____ ceremony. Capron then formed the m _____ 7 present. The one man missing was si _____

Barnes g _____ t they had the honor to be the first tro _____ . He assured them that they would be _____ only had to call on him. He reiterated h _____ He also hoped that they would bring h _____ the fortifications of the Morro Castle o _____ re he could say. The rest was up to them _____ s small contribution to the war effort w _____ ory's limelight. Capron then turned the _____ a double line so photographer Swea _____ glass negative.

Judge Frank Dale then stepped forward to make a presentation on behalf of the City of Guthrie. Since officers had to provide their own horses and saddles, the citizens presented Huston with a fine thoroughbred. Dale then called McGinnis forward and brought up a beautiful black thoroughbred charger. This was a personal gift from Guthrie's Chief of Police and Mac's foster father, William Baxter. This fine specimen of horse flesh had won a number of races at the local track. Mac prized the horse very much and named it "Ben Baxter."

The ceremony was concluded with three hearty cheers for Barnes, Capron and then the troop. Afterwards, they were dismissed until mess call. Huston then made quick arrangements with his brother, Had, to send down the two horses. Ed Miller, of Company C, would escort them to San Antonio, Texas, days later. The rest of the troop had only a few hours to bid farewell to family and friends.

At 9:30 p.m., the bugle sounded assembly at Camp Steele one last time, and the men fell in before a final crowd of militia, close friends and family. Huston, Palmer, officers of militia and even Sergeant Stecker made patriotic speeches. The crowd cheered the volunteers, and they marched to the Santa Fe Depot where a special railcar waited to take them to Texas.

At the depot, hands clasped in tight farewell grips as the men boarded. Final words of encouragement were given, uncertain of when or if they would see each other again. At that moment, Captain Robert B. Huston was the most important man in the Oklahoma Territory, but Vite's heart sank at the thought of being left alone. Her husband, Robert, had become her life, and he would not be around to watch their baby son grow. She was not alone in her feelings. One woman had even written the governor not to allow her fiancé to volunteer, and Starr Wetmore's mother would worry herself sick. While caught up in the moment, the men may have cast a casual thought to the possible consequences of war, but this possibility became a greater torment for those who had to wait at home.

The newly organized Women's Relief Corps contributed their part by packing a box lunch for each man. With every trooper onboard, the train lurched forward, then slowly rolled out of the station. The crowd cheered and waved. In high spirits, the volunteers headed for San Antonio by way of Oklahoma City, then west to El Reno and finally south.

Those left behind could only wait for letters and read the news. *The Guthrie Daily Leader* had taken a keen interest in the activities of the sons of Oklahoma who rode that train into history. The editor asked them to write *The Leader* about everything that would happen. With their duties complete in that territory, Capron and Stecker left for the Indian Territory.

The Indian Territory had been overlooked in the earlier plan for recruiting. On April 26, the day after telegraphing the other governors, the secretary of war wired Judges John R. Thomas and William M. Springer in Muskogee to inquire if they could enlist 175 volunteers. Since the native residents of the Indian Nations were not United States citizens, they could not be compelled to serve. They could only receive a quota if they accepted. The Five Civilized Tribes had fielded regiments on both sides during the Civil War, and they would eagerly serve the Union again. Thomas answered that he could provide as many as 200 and wired Judge Hosea Townsend in Ardmore to provide 50 of them. Thomas also informed Alger that Muskogee would provide the best place for recruiting, and that became the destination of Capron.

In reward for his four terms in Congress from Illinois, John Thomas had received a federal judgeship in the Indian Territory just the year before. As the senior government official to the Indian Nations, Judge Thomas served as the de facto governor of the territory. Right after he had received the telegram from Alger, he fired off another to his son in Chicago.

Twenty-five-year-old John Robert Thomas, Jr., a recent graduate of Dickinson College in Carlisle, Pennsylvania, worked as a reporter in the office of the Chicago *Interocean* newspaper. He was a large, powerfully built young man. A friend of his stepped in one morning, dressed in a new blue uniform, to bid his farewell since his volunteer regiment was about to leave.

Rob reflected on his own family tradition of service. His father, the judge, had served as a captain during the Civil War. His grandfather had fought as a captain in the Mexican War, and his great-grandfather had earned a captaincy during the War of 1812. The parting words of his dying mother came to him: "My son, I leave you my flag. If ever it needs defense, be willing to give your life for it."[8] Caught up in a moment of patriotism, Rob jumped up and exclaimed, "By thunder, I'll go with you!" He enlisted that very morning in Company I, First Illinois Volunteer Infantry.[9]

The judge's telegram found Rob out on the drilling field in Springfield. It informed him that the Indian Territory would muster two troops of cavalry for Roosevelt's regiment, and, if he could come down and help in the recruiting, he was sure he could secure his son a commission. Rob received a release from his enlistment from the Governor of Illinois and departed with his two Chicago friends: 21-year-old architect Dillwyn "Dill" Bell and Walter Sharpe. Bell's father was the supervisor architect of the Treasury at Chicago. Since the volunteers were supposed to be residents of the territory, Rob listed his father's home, Vinita, as his home, and Dill claimed Guthrie. Sharpe admitted the truth.

Like the New Mexico and Arizona Territories, the Indian Territory set up recruiting stations for anyone who wanted to volunteer. Capron recruited from the Cherokee and Creek Nations in Muskogee, while Robert Bruce recruited from the Choctaw and Chickasaw Nations in Ardmore. What made these troops unique was that Indians were recruited to serve in the same regiment as white soldiers. Yet, most of the members of these Five Nations had mixed blood when they migrated there at the early part of the century.

Thomas J. Isbell's father, Levi, had immigrated to the Indian Territory as a deputy marshal during its wild and lawless years when outlaws found refuge there. Levi was shot several times and severely wounded in the shoot-out with the Christy Gang in 1889. He had married a Cherokee woman, George Ann Lawther, which allowed him to acquire a plot of Cherokee land. Their son, Tom, grew into a superb horseman and crack shot. An accomplished cowboy, Tom would distinguish himself with his courage under fire and his incredible sense of humor. At 23 years of age, Tom Isbell was one of 24 men from Vinita to enlist in the Rough Riders, the most of any town in the territory.

Over several weeks, men arrived at the recruiting station from all over the territory and even neighboring Kansas, Arkansas and Missouri. Judge Thomas secured quarters for the volunteers at the Women's Christian Temperance Union where they slept on piles of hay strewn over the floor. The procedure for mustering followed that of Guthrie, but the two recruiting officers had to narrow 3,000 recruits down to less than 200. After 149 men passed their physicals, they were allowed to elect their officers.

Because of his immense charisma and professionalism, the Muskogee contingent elected Allyn Capron as their captain, Robert Thomas as the first lieutenant and 27-year-old Richard C. Day, a typist from Vinita, as the second lieutenant. Day's uncle was Navy Lieutenant Walter B. Cushing, who sank the Confederate torpedo boat *Albemarle*. The Ardmore contingent similarly elected their mustering officer, Robert Bruce, as captain, Ode Nichols, of Durant, as the first lieutenant and Albert S. Johnson as the second. Coincidentally, "Little Sidney" Johnson, of Oklahoma City, had previously failed to pass the mustering exam in Guthrie, but his influential father secured him a vacancy in the neighboring Indian Territory.

On Saturday, May 14, the Muskogee volunteers assembled at the depot wearing ribbons around their hats or on their coats, identifying them as the contingent from the Indian Territory. Each of the territories identified themselves this way. Lieutenant Thomas gave the first patriotic speech followed by words from Capron. Alice M. Robertson prepared a field kit for each man to take with him which contained a sewing kit and small Bible. Women had been making sewing kits or "housewives" for soldiers since the previous war. The citizens of Vinita presented a guidon to their volunteers, referring to them as the First Company of Mounted Riflemen. During the Civil War, the three Union Indian regiments had been referred to as mounted rifles. The men boarded the Missouri–Kansas–Texas Railroad bound for San Antonio. Judge Thomas, his personal secretary, David Dickey, and his daughter, Carolyn Thomas, accompanied the troop to Texas where they would remain until the men left for Tampa. Fair, young Carolyn became so popular with the troop that they would adopt her as their own daughter.

As the last two troops mustered in, the First U.S. Volunteer Cavalry took shape. This regiment recruited from the frontier represented the character of the West, and probably no other regiment up to that time contained such ethnic diversity. The intent had been to recruit the best riders and marksmen in the country, yet it produced a regiment where Whites, Indians and Hispanics would fight side by side without animosity. The last ingredient to this melting pot involved the introduction of the social elite to the working class of rural America. While Western men could overcome their prejudice against Indians or Hispanics, the privileged sons of millionaires would present a greater challenge.

CHAPTER 3

Make Yourselves Like
Regular Soldiers

The Santa Fe train carried the Oklahoma troop south, bypassing the washed-out bridges on their way to fame and adventure. Those fortunate 81 who met the physical qualifications had willingly walked away from the security of their civilian occupations to experience the hardship of military life ~~~~ ~~~~ ~rror of war. With the exception of Roy Cashi~~ ~~~~ ~~~~ cause they were about to risk their live~ ~~~~ ~~~~ ~ht and die for the liberty of people i~ ~~~~ ~~~~ for the love of liberty but the martial ~~~~ ~~~~ ~e of America. Every generation woul~ ~~~~ ~~~~ ~r any worthy cause, mostly because a~ ~~~~ ~~~~

To become a~ ~~~~ ~~~~ ld have to be transformed into a coh~ ~~~~ ~~~~ ~ had barely known each other a week, ~~~~ ~~~~ territories did not have much time t~ ~~~~ ~~~~ t these volunteers already had an ide~ ~~~~ ~~~~ as cavalry. As different as each of th~ ~~~~ ~~~~ ~nd: they proudly represented the Ter~ ~~~~

Twenty-five-ye~ ~~~~ ~~~~ ~ on yet another adventure. Born in ~~~~ ~~~~ aws as a deputy marshal in the lawle~ ~~~~ ~~~~ ~ Yukon, Alaska, during the 1890s attr~ ~~~~ ~~~~ out there, he returned to the Oklahoma Territory to wo~ ~~~~ ~owboy in Chandler. The prospect of a war with Spain provided one more opportunity for his insatiable appetite for adventure. Not a member of the Oklahoma National Guard, Paul took his chance and rode to Guthrie hoping to find a vacancy during the mustering. Successful in this endeavor, his promised letters to the *Guthrie Leader* would keep the folks back home well informed of progress of the troop.

At that time, the residents of the territory did not refer to themselves as Oklahomans, and, since at least the Civil War, soldiers have referred to themselves as boys, regardless of their age. So the volunteers referred to themselves as the Oklahoma boys.

The train arrived in San Antonio at 4 p.m. on Saturday, where Captain Huston fell the men into formation, and, as they came to attention, they yelled in unison, "Ray ray, First Troop A, Oklahoma Caval-ry."[2] Paul Hunter had come up with the troop cry, believing they had formed the first troop of the regiment. They then marched three and a half miles south of town to an oasis of trees in the Texas prairie known as the Riverside

[handwritten note overlaid:] united by a legacy of service and desire to continue it and being "Oklahoma boys" otherwise they were very different. — B/S about the men —

Park. To their surprise they were greeted by cheers from the Arizona contingent, which had arrived there the day before. As the third troop to arrive, the Oklahomans rounded out Major Alexander Oswald Brodie III's First Squadron. They were not A Troop, as they had originally believed, but were in very good hands.

Alex Brodie had graduated from the U.S. Military Academy in 1870 as a second lieutenant in the First Cavalry in time to see extensive action against hostile Apaches led by Cochise in Arizona. He even received a commendation from the secretary of war for his participation in an eight-hour skirmish against Apaches. His company later moved north to Fort Walla Walla, Washington, where he participated in the pursuit of Chief Joseph during the Nez Perce War in 1877. There, Brodie married Kate Reynolds but lost her during the birth of his daughter, who also died a few months later. Distraught, he then resigned his commission as a first lieutenant in September 1877. By that time, most of the warring Indian Nations had been subdued, and Brodie tried his hand as a cattleman in Kansas.

In 1882, the Chiricahua Apache, led by the medicine man Geronimo, fled the reservation and headed into their old haunts in Mexico, occasionally raiding back into Arizona. In August 1883, Brodie enlisted as a 33-year-old private in the Sixth Cavalry stationed in Arizona. He earned less than a common laborer. His M Troop patrolled the Mexican border against Apache raiding parties. In February 1884, just before his regiment moved into New Mexico territory, Brodie received an early discharge from his five-year enlistment. According to friend Tom Rynning, Brodie resigned because of an altercation with an officer over a young lady. He then became a mining engineer in Prescott, Arizona, and married Mary Louise Hanlon in December 1892. Their first child died in 1896, and his second son was born in 1896. For a man to change from one job to another there had to be something pushing and something else pulling. Regardless of what inspired him to leave civilian life behind, the prospect of war attracted Brodie to the military for a third time.

After the *Maine* sank, Brodie immediately began rounding up potential recruits for a possible war, anticipating the call for volunteers. Having mustered 250 men, enough to form a squadron of two troops commanded by Captains William O. "Buckey" O'Neill, of Prescott, and James H. McClintock, of Phoenix, he was appointed its major. A down-to-earth man, 48-year-old Brodie knew his business as squadron commander, and the Oklahoma boys came to respect him. Brodie and Huston took an immediate liking to each other.

Thirty-eight-year-old Buckey O'Neill was a very competent and charismatic leader. He had served as a lawman throughout the Territory of Arizona. His A Troop had plenty of veteran soldiers to choose officers from. He selected 29-year-old Frank Frantz for the position of first lieutenant. Frantz had only worked in Prescott a few years as a clerk for a mining company when recruiting began. Frank was born in Roanoke, Illinois, on May 7, 1869. He loved baseball and boxing. In fact, his brothers were accomplished baseball players. While Frank attended Eureka College in Roanoke, his older brothers settled in Oklahoma when the Cherokee Strip opened in 1893. Frank left college the next year and moved to Los Angeles, California, for a short period of time before moving to Arizona. Although he had not lived in Oklahoma, his family ties would eventually draw him there.

The Arizona contingent also brought with it the first of the mascots to the regiment. Thomas H. Rynning, a 33-year-old Herculean former cowboy and soldier from

Tucson, brought with him a young mountain lion he had lassoed a few weeks prior. Having served as a sergeant in the Eighth Cavalry, Tom quickly rose to sergeant in McClintock's B Troop. The Arizona contingent had adopted Josephine as their mascot, and eventually so did the regiment. The Arizona contingent, by the way, also provided their own national colors. Since the official regimental flag would not arrive until after the war, these colors served as the battle flag of the regiment and was placed under the care of Regimental Color Sergeant Albert P. Wright of Yuma, Arizona.

Colonel Wood, wearing a khaki uniform, waited for them upon their arrival. The sandy-haired, 37-year-old Indian campaigner was a bundle of energy. He had arrived the previous Wednesday evening with 11 freight cars transporting 189 mules, three horses and pack saddles he had picked up in St. Louis, Missouri. Wood brought 89 seasoned packers employed by the Quartermaster Department. Under the able leadership of chief packmaster Mickey O'Hara, they went about organizing into three packtrains, one for each squadron, and would conduct their own training. Tom Horn, who had served during the Geronimo Campaign with then Lieutenant Wood when he won his Medal of Honor, also served as a packmaster. The soft-spoken Wood greeted his men and informed them that they would most likely go to the front as soon as the rest of the troops arrived. Because of the difference in their duties, the soldiers and the "mule skinners" would have little contact with each other.

The War Department initially intended to drop the army off near Havana to join up with the Cuban *insurrectos*. The Spanish Army had three garrisons in the Caribbean: San Juan, Puerto Rico; Santiago; and Havana, Cuba. General of the Army Nelson A. Miles had proposed the strategy that the army first invade and secure Puerto Rico. A large force of cavalry with a light contingent of artillery would also land on the Eastern end of Cuba to train and assist the insurgents. Allowing the volunteers to train up during the rainy season, the combined forces of Regulars and volunteers would invade Cuba and assault Havana with the Cubans. Miles also suggested that if the Spanish fleet under Admiral Pascual Cervera held up at Santiago, the rest of the army should assist the U.S. Navy in taking that port city on its way to Puerto Rico. From Wood, the men learned that this regiment of cowboy cavalry would most likely screen as scouts ahead of the invading army of Cuba. As time passed, rumors in the press even made their destination doubtful. The men were anxious to go anywhere. Wood secretly feared that the war might end before he could move his command.

Wood had also received authorization to increase his regimental strength from 780 to 1,000 troopers. This would increase the regiment from ten to 12 troops. To do so, the ten troops from the four territories would reduce from 80 to 65 men. The excess from the two Arizona troops formed a third troop under the command of B Troop's First Lieutenant Joseph B. Alexander from Phoenix. The Oklahoma troop became D Troop of Brodie's Arizona Squadron. Their surplus men would then fill an additional troop, and afterwards each original troop would return to strength with individual recruits from the other states or territories. Many of these would come from Texas and Colorado. D Troop had to give up 12 of their own. The news came as a blow to the morale of the Oklahoma troop since they provided the smallest contingent. The men wondered who would have to go. The expansion of the regiment, however, also created two new captain vacancies.[3]

Lieutenant McGinnis's popularity increased daily with his men. George Telon wrote Huston from Guthrie describing Mac's leadership traits best: "If the animal exuberance of McGinnis can be kept in check, I fancy Mac has the grit all right.["4] Mac learned of the promotion slot to captain, but Alexander had date of commission on him by one day. While he aspired for the rank of captain, he was equally proud to stay with his troop. In consolation, he wrote, "I am for my home boys against the world. I am convinced that our boys rank any other troop here in physical make-up and intelligence, yet I am partial."[5]

The first four troops had unfortunately arrived before any of their equipment. In desperation, Wood went over to the neighboring Fort Sam Houston to request any supplies they could offer up. As the Fifth Cavalry was similarly preparing for war, they could only offer hand-me-downs—supplies condemned for destruction. The quartermaster officer issued Wood what blankets, mess tins and tin cups were available. Wood returned and gave out what little he had and checked the men into the spacious Exposition Hall at the fairgrounds. Some men borrowed horse blankets from the mule packers.

That evening, the hungry men shared a meal of stew with several men to a single tin plate. With no forks available, they just ate with their fingers. These hardened men of the frontier endured the inconveniences with little complaint. One fight did actually break out between two friends as one accused the other of hogging the choicest pieces of the stew. The offenders answered to their colonel. Wood scolded the two men in a manner that made them ashamed of their actions, and the two sullen men became friends again. The word quickly spread that the sharpness of Wood's tongue was far worse than any stay in the guardhouse. The selection process had been tough, and the men felt privileged to be a part of this unique organization. They were eager to please their commander. One of the belligerents was most likely John Rhoades, of Hennessey, whom Huston threw in the guardhouse under the grandstands that first day. While under confinement, a remorseful Rhoades passed the time by weaving hammocks for his three officers.

The men slept on the hardwood floor with as many as two or three to one ragged blanket. Since the Army did not train on Sunday, they were free to do what they pleased that day. Some played baseball, while others played jokes. This allowed the men to become better acquainted with those whom they would soon fight beside. Sergeant Webb hurt his knee playing baseball, and Huston had to take him to the hospital on the fort. Pollock passed his time drawing pictures.

A proud Roy Cashion had the time of his life. While there were several 18-year-olds, the idealistic Roy was the youngest man in the troop. He was a quiet boy who performed every chore cheerfully. He soon discovered that the government did not provide adequately for his every need. The troopers needed $5 to purchase additional items not issued by the government, such as rifle-cleaning equipment, toilet articles and knives. Someone was willing to loan them $5 on the agreement to pay $6 back on payday. Roy felt this interest was too high. Like many of the others, he wrote home asking for the loan from his family instead. Friends later asked Paul Hunter to write to the *Guthrie Leader* to see if there was an adventurous person who was willing to loan them money.

Many of the troopers visited San Antonio and marveled at the beauty of the tropical plants, narrow streets and old buildings. Many of the Oklahoma boys visited the legendary Alamo just across from the Menger Hotel. The 62-year-old scars of the battle were still clearly visible to them, an inspiration for the duty ahead of them. After a day of amusement, they retired to camp.

Reveille woke the volunteers up at 5 a.m. Monday. The Oklahoma men stumbled outside and lined up as First Sergeant Palmer called roll to see if anyone was absent. All present. From there they lined up for a breakfast of bacon, potatoes, bread and coffee. They would have to get used to this menu.

That began the first day of military routine for many of the volunteers. Palmer announced the names of the men assigned to fatigue detail: digging trenches, cutting and carrying firewood. In the afternoon, the four troops conducted dismounted drill. The Oklahoma Guardsmen already knew how to march, but this gave the new recruits time to catch up.

The men in civilian attire lined up by height in two ranks facing their commander. On command, the two lines of fours would turn around to form a column of fours and then march out onto the field. Four men or "fours" formed the smallest maneuver element of a cavalry troop. The fours comprised two pair of bunkies, or soldiers, assigned to share a bunk or two-man "dog" tent. Once matched, bunkies had to look out for each other, especially in battle.

According to the latest drill regulations, eight men formed a squad under the leadership of a corporal. Sergeants had their assigned positions in the company formation according to their numbered rank. The second and third sergeants lined up on the extreme right and left flanks as platoon guides, while the rest lined up from right to left according to rank behind the formation with the lieutenants. Depending upon the number of men, the troop was normally divided into two platoons under the leadership of the first and second lieutenants. If enough men allowed the formation of the third platoon, then the first sergeant would lead it. When the company was extending into open order for skirmishing, the sergeants assumed their places in the line as chiefs of sections, which consisted of two or three squads.

At various commands by the officers, the column of fours would change direction or pivot back into two extended lines. The two ranks would march obliquely either to the right or left, depending on the order. Once on line, the troop could then change direction like the swinging of a large gate and as desired return to a column in the similar manner as they had come. At Huston's discretion, the sergeants drilled their respective squads in a similar manner. This maneuver of lines and columns constituted dismounted drill. While the Oklahoma Guardsmen were proficient at it, Huston wanted to achieve perfection. The three Arizona troops had to start from the beginning. Drill continued until supper.

Colonel Wood's philosophy was to introduce the rugged frontiersmen gradually to military discipline. From his previous military experience in Arizona, he knew that men of the West possessed a strong, independent nature aside from their many other talents. This ability to adapt and think for themselves, he wanted to retain while instilling in them the discipline of acting in unison. He also knew they were highly motivated to become the best soldiers they could. With that in mind, he gathered them together and appealed to their desire to succeed.

"Make yourselves as much like regular soldiers as you can in the shortest possible time. If you think only of that you will be thinking exactly of the right thing and you will have enough to think about to keep you very busy. If you devote your time and attention to that, the regiment will be a success."[6]

Anticipating a common vice of the frontier, Wood prohibited the sale of alcohol in camp. However, local entrepreneurs, Quinn and Reiner, erected a saloon right outside the gate. Interestingly, the Rough Riders had few incidents of intoxication or delinquencies. Wood was lenient in other respects. At first, he permitted anyone with the slightest reason a pass to leave the camp. As the days passed, he began to tighten up on discipline by gradually reducing the number of passes that could be given out. Of course, the unfortunate regimental adjutant, who signed the passes, had to inform the men that they could not go to town when their troop had reached their limit. The unfortunate lieutenant who had to disapprove passes, after one of their officers had said they could go, was Lieutenant Thomas W. Hall.

Tom Hall, an 1887 graduate of West Point, had only served two years on the frontier with the Tenth (Colored) Cavalry when he resigned his commission to become a writer. As one of many young aspirants seeking a commission for the upcoming war, Hall was turned down by everyone except Colonel Wood. Wood commissioned him a first lieutenant as the regimental quartermaster just before he departed for Texas. When Hall arrived that same Saturday as Wood, he assumed the duties of adjutant, quartermaster and commissary—essentially all the regimental staff duties, until the two Regular Army officers arrived. In addition, Wood made him responsible for instructing guard mount. Walking their posts or standing guard at the exits around the camp offered a good way to teach military discipline. Guard mount was seen by the volunteers as the paramount performance of soldiering and would eventually become a source of pride.

While the men were eager and willing to learn the army way of doing things, Hall had to constantly remind the cowboys of the correct performance of their military duties. B Troop's Bill Owens, of Jerome, Arizona, stood guard one day when Hall passed by. With his right hand occupied holding his carbine on his right shoulder, Bill reasonably concluded that he should salute with his free left hand. "How are you, Captain?" The lieutenant came to a halt and barked out the command, "Pre-sent Arms!" Bill just looked at him a little puzzled. Again, the adjutant repeated the command with greater emphasis. Bill still had no idea what the lieutenant wanted. Hall advanced up to the guard. "Can't you Present Arms?" A confused Bill looked at him and then handed over the carbine. "Here, take her, Captain, but she is not loaded." Such comical scenes of adjustment to army discipline played themselves out throughout the regiment over the next few weeks.[7]

However, Hall's short, professional military experience limited his personal skills in dealing with men of the frontier. Unlike Hall, the two other West Point officers, Major Brodie and Captain Micah Jenkins, were more seasoned. These alumni had lived and worked among the men they were elected to lead. Hall came from New York. While meaning well, Hall tended to be strict in his interpretation of the regulations. He knew no other way than to do everything "by the book." Consequently, Hall earned the reputation as a martinet and grew quite unpopular among the men.

Meanwhile, that Monday morning, 18 men of the social elite sat down for breakfast in the finest hotel in San Antonio. Hamilton Fish, Jr., of New York City, looked around. He had fine company. These bachelors of privilege and wealth had descended from good stock and were the leaders of the New York cotillion scene. Most were members of the exclusive Knickerbocker Club of New York. These were the least likely men to don the army blue as privates.

Money was not the only requirement for admission to the social elite but a recognizable family name. The new rich retained the culture of their humble beginnings, while those born to a life of wealth and privilege were raised in an entirely different culture with expensive and refined tastes. Some of these not only had the money but long-established pedigrees. Reginald Reynolds was even able to break into the oldest established social scene of London.

Thirty-eight-year-old Woodbury Kane, of New York City, was related to the Astors and Chandlers, some of the wealthiest families in the United States at that time. He had played football at Harvard. He was an excellent horseman who played polo, rode cross-country and followed the hounds hunting foxes both in England and America. A devoted yachtsman, he had also participated in a number of yachting victories. On top of that, he was a member of the New York Knickerbocker Club and also a Harvard class-mate of Roosevelt. He was intimate friends with Roosevelt, whose nomination as lieu-tenant colonel of the cowboy regiment excited a similar martial spirit in many horsemen in the New York social clubs that he belonged to.

A little over 30, William Tiffany, also of New York City, was well known in New York for his kinship to the Belmonts and other aristocrats of the Newport set. His father founded the famous Tiffany Company. Willie had spent several years living on the plains in Montana. Just prior to enlisting, he had announced his engagement to Miss Mandy Livingstone. Thirty-five-year-old Craig W. Wadsworth, of Genesee, New York, was the best rider in the Genesee Valley Hunt Club. He had also ridden steeple chase at Princeton. Reginald Reynolds, another Knickerbocker, had played football at Yale. Another skilled horseman, he hunted fox, raced horses and played polo.

Many also descended from a martial tradition. Willie's granduncle Commodore Oliver Perry was the hero of the Battle of Lake Erie during the War of 1812. Wadsworth was son of General James S. Wadsworth of the Civil War, and Kane's brother was Colo-nel Delancy Kane, then "millionaire coachmen" who drove public coaches just for sport.

Ham Fish also descended from a notable family. He was named after his grandfa-ther, a prominent statesman of New York. Hamilton Fish, Sr., had served as the governor of New York, in the U.S. Congress and Senate and later as President Ulysses S. Grant's Secretary of State.

The others sitting at breakfast were superb athletes from Harvard, Yale and Princ-eton. Horace K. Devereaux, of Colorado Springs, Colorado, had played football at Princeton. Twenty-one-year-old Edward C. Waller excelled at high-jumping while studying at Yale. Ham Fish had been the captain of the Columbia crew. The war had inspired a martial spirit that swept across the campuses. Drilling had replaced sports in popularity. The men sat around that table representing the best stock of American man-hood in wealth, education and strength. That Texas morning, they had one more thing in common. They were privates in the First U.S. Volunteer Cavalry.

As they enjoyed the delicacy of the fine meal, they reflected on that fateful morning of May 5. They, among 1,500 others, had petitioned Theodore Roosevelt for permission to enlist in his regiment. Roosevelt, to his credit, did his best to dissuade them, but they persisted. After he received authorization to recruit two more troops, he selected about 50 to fill a troop just of millionaires and Ivy League athletes. He met with them in the Army Dispensary Building in Washington, D.C., and told them not to expect any spe-cial treatment. He gave them one last chance to back out:

> Gentlemen, you have now reached the last point. If any of you doesn't mean business, let him say so now. An hour from now it will be too late to back out. Once in, you've got to see it through. You've got to perform without flinching whatever duty is assigned to you, regardless of the difficulty or danger attending it. You must know how to ride, you must know how to shoot, you must know how to live in the open. Absolute obedience to every command is your first lesson. No matter what comes you mustn't squeal. Think it over—all of you. If any of you wants to withdraw, he will be gladly excused, for there are thousands who are anxious to have places in this regiment.[8]

For men accustomed to the privileged life, each would have to abandon all social distinction. They answered him with three cheers three times. None backed out. They would form K Troop, which the media referred to as the "dandy troopers" or "dude warriors." They picked up their issue of uniforms and left Washington on May 8.

Upon finishing their meal, they traded their fine woolen suits and derby hats for brown cotton fatigue uniforms, leggings, khaki felt hats and reddish-brown shoes which they had the privilege of picking up while in Washington. Once dressed they exclaimed, "It's all off after this,"[9] and that afternoon they walked into camp to a cheerful reception by the frontiersmen. They were the only uniformed men in the regiment. The physical quality of these volunteers from the East impressed the Westerners.

That evening arrived the contingent of 11 Harvard athletes: David M. "Dave" Goodrich from Akron, Ohio; Harrison J. "Harry" Holt from Denver, Colorado; Charles C. Bull from Belmont, California; L. Stanley Hollister from Santa Barbara, California; William M. Scudder from Phoenix, Arizona; William H. Saunders from Salem, Massachusetts; Locket G. Coleman from St. Louis; Guy H. Scull from Boston; William S. Simpson from Dallas; Summer K. Gerard from New York City; and Joseph Ogden Wells from St. Joseph, Michigan. They rolled up their underwear and toiletries in rubber blankets and left their dress suit cases at the train station. They headed for the Menger Hotel for an evening dinner before heading to the fairgrounds. After a civilized meal, they boarded a train for the fairground. As it neared, the college boys heard the Westerners cheering and were welcomed with hearty handshakes.[10]

During Monday night occurred one of the fiercest thunderstorms during their stay in Texas. The building leaked terribly, and many a trooper woke up soaked. Forty horses also stampeded during the night. The Tuesday morning air was still misty as the men fell into formation on the parade field that had turned into a shallow lake. The men ate soggy bread for breakfast as the wagons with the rations had fared no better than the men the night before.

The regiment had received its issue of medical equipment that first week and immediately established a hospital tent for the sick. Albert Thomas, of Guthrie, was the first Oklahoman to report sick to the hospital, where he would remain for a week. The hot Texas sun would soon take a greater toll on men's health. George Burgess from Shawnee, Oklahoma, had been a nurse and served as a hospital steward to care for the sick.

At 10:20 the Tuesday morning, 358 recruits from New Mexico arrived. Wood asked Huston to meet the train, receive the officers and escort them in. The First Squadron stopped in the middle of its training and fatigue duty to greet the new arrivals with cheers as they marched into camp. Major Henry B. Hersey brought four troops, E through H, which was enough to complete another squadron. This brought the regiment up to eight troops. They only needed the two troops recruited from the Indian Territory.

The New Mexico contingent brought with it the second of the mascots, Salisbury, their famous traveling dog. This dog was known throughout the Southwest because of his extensive travels. His owners renamed him Cuba. The Oklahomans, a little jealous, picked up a stray pup, which they adopted as their own mascot.

Thirty more Harvard and Yale athletes arrived from New York with similar fanfare. The Ivy League recruits asked to be distributed among the first four troops instead of going to K Troop. Huston picked up five of them. Three were among the first Harvard athletes to arrive: Harry Holt, William Simpson and Ogden Wells. They included a college baseball pitcher, the stroke on the crew, a quarter-mile sprinter, and brother to the great center rush.

Also, at 1:30 that afternoon, four or seven New York City policemen arrived. Remarkably, they would remain under full pay while serving their country. Himself a millionaire and once police commissioner of New York City, the regiment more and more took on the characteristics of Roosevelt. Each troop, however, identified with its territorial integrity. Collectively though, they saw themselves as Westerners. Consequently, the introduction of this social elite with their once-swollen egos was not entirely welcomed.

Not surprisingly, these "millionaire boys" or "Fifth Avenue Recruits" had to undergo their initiation into the "Ancient and Honorable Order of Cowboys"—with fatigue detail. That next morning, Woodbury Kane, dressed in his tweed suit and flannel shirt, dug drainage trenches around the headquarter's tents. His five Oklahoma coworkers let him do the easiest work of shoveling away the loose dirt after they had broken ground. Craig Wadsworth had the hardest labor in camp of carrying wood for the campfires. Willie Tiffany luckily missed fatigue but instead complained over the failure of the laundry man to bring him some clean shirts. He was the only millionaire to openly complain, which he did about nearly everything from laundry to food, work and media attention. Nonetheless, they were a hardy bunch. Where manual labor kept the men of the West physically fit, the privileged life allowed the rich the luxury to train in gymnasiums and health clubs. Both groups measured up physically to their duties.

Fortunately, all passed their initiation admirably. It impressed the Westerners to see those sons of millionaires perform manual labor side by side with men of lower social status. As it turned out, those rich athletes admired the quality of the plains man and came West to emulate them. Woodbury Kane aspired to become an expert at the fine art of lassoing under the tutelage of Tom Rynning. The well-dressed millionaire and the rugged cowboy worked side by side and gained a mutual respect for each other. Unfortunately, the newspapers watched their every move of the millionaires, and this special attention did not help improve relations. Since they had money, many also took to eating their meals at any dining establishment other than the army mess. Neither did this help bridge the social gap. But the one thing all had in common was that they could ride.

As soon as the regiment was authorized, the contract went out for the purchase of horses. Captain R.R. Stevens, the Quartermaster of Fort Sam Houston, quickly began purchasing mounts for the regiment. As soon as he had 25 to 35, he turned them over to several skilled horsemen of the regiment to herd back to the camp. Since the horses had arrived before the saddles, the riders mounted the tamest horses bareback. In cowboy fashion, they looped as many as ten of the wildest horses together with the makeshift lariats and then herded them through the streets of San Antonio to the regimental coral. Watering the horses then added to the list of fatigue details and provided a daily Wild West show. Herding the broncos was accomplished by great patience coupled with much profanity.

The contract for the mounts required that they stand 15 hands high, weigh 850 pounds or more and have been ridden. The demand for over 1,000 horses inflated the price anywhere from $75 to $125 for animals that would normally sell for $20 or $30. The need for mounts also stretched the interpretation of "have been ridden." To the horror of the Rough Riders, many of the Texas mustangs were wild and unbroken.[11]

That Tuesday, Troop B's Marshall M. Bird, from California, was escorting a herd of horses back to camp. His mount took off at a dead run, then came to an abrupt halt, catapulting Trooper Bird from its back. A tree stopped his flight and fractured his skull. The rumor quickly circulated that the throw had killed him, but he later recovered from his surgery in the hospital. He was discharged on August 8 with a disability.

The men anxiously wondered which unlucky troopers would have to ride the wild mustangs. Although the Easterners were experienced riders, Will Quaid, of Newburg, New York, remarked, "We all know how to ride, as we have followed the hounds and played polo a great deal, but the trouble is that we have never had any experience with Texas mustangs."[12] For that matter a multitude of Westerners had no skill in breaking mounts either, and none other than those detailed to herd the horses were allowed to ride them that first week as the saddles and horse tack had not yet arrived.

On Wednesday Huston finally announced the names of the unfortunate 12 Oklahoma boys who would transfer to Troop K. A number of the men had enlisted from the same town or county, hoping to serve together. The Kay County contingent lost Elisha Freeman and John Weitzel. This breakup of the troop came as a slight blow to the moral of D Troop. Their Oklahoma identity was for the honor of their territory. The three Arizona troops dumped only their millionaires into the two new troops. Huston later received seven Texans and two New Mexico boys to replace the ones he gave up. With five Harvard men already in their ranks, D Troop began to lose a little of its territorial identity.

It would take a week to organize the two new troops. Wood waited until Roosevelt arrived to determine which of the men would receive commissions. In the interim, Wood had Hall fill in as commander of K Troop. The troop, however, would not conduct its first military drill until Thursday of the next week.

The men of the other troops called this troop the "Clubmen," referring to the exclusive Knickerbocker Club. Edgar F. "Ed" Loughmiller, of Oklahoma City, wrote, "Troop K is made up of a lot of Fifth Avenue swells. The size of their heads will be reduced after a few days in the cook house, and that, like death comes to all privates without regard to color or age or who your papa is."[13] But in time everyone eventually agreed with Lieutenant Schweizer. "They are all fine fellows and are putting their shoulders to the wheel."[14] Bill McGinty and the other 11 Oklahomans soon discovered another advantage to being in the new troop. It was good to have rich friends.

Neither were the millionaires exempt from jokes. Since a soldier had to have a written pass to leave camp, a sentry with a sense of humor asked the unsuspecting K Troop "Clubmen" for their passes on their way out. When the men returned, the new sentry asked to see their passes, which they could not produce. These men of social prominence were then locked up in the guardhouse. Knowing that the papers scrutinized their every movement, they threw a fit before the real culprit came to their rescue.

By Wednesday, D Troop advanced from close order to extended order drill or skirmishers where the line of men spread out at a double-arm interval and advanced across the field as they would in battle. Those men not detailed to fatigue duty drilled. The time allotted for drill increased from morning until night and soon became burdensome. The camp was a bustle of activity all day. Huston wrote, "I am teaching the non-commissioned officers at night and have got them worked up to such a state that when we are called on for men, we are ready first."[15] His instruction included guard duty and drill regulations.

The Texas sun was unbearably hot. Many Oklahomans, as it turned out, were not accustomed to working out in the heat all day, which took some getting used to. After a week, their faces and hands took on the bronzed complexion. Although not the toughest-looking men in the regiment, after a week of drill they proved themselves the best drilled. When the bugle sounded, the Oklahomans were on line and in formation. The difference between them and the other troops became clearly evident. The three Oklahoma officers worked hard to make their troop stand out. One lady spectator wrote, "There is no doubt that Troop D will be the 'crack troop' of the 'crack regiment' of the present war. Viva Oklahoma."[16]

Brodie, on the other hand, had to instruct the Arizona officers on their duties. Since the major had to spend most of his time with the officers of the Arizona troops, the men of D Troop at first felt slighted and complained to their officers. It did not take them too long to learn why. Both Brodie and Wood lauded over the Oklahoma Troop at every opportunity. Wood even wrote Governor Barnes, praising him on the quality of the men from Oklahoma, boasting that they were the best in his command. The Oklahomans were proud, and by Saturday, Wood designated them the "color" or "base" troop of the regiment—a place of honor next to the regimental colors.[17]

Brodie with Wood marched his squadron out to conduct its first squadron drill for two hours on Thursday. Brodie did the same on Friday and Saturday afternoon. From observations of a local journalist, it appeared that it would take a minimum of two weeks to properly drill and discipline them for combat. The Oklahomans were proficient, so they quickly tired of marching around. Dismounted drill was the way the infantry went into battle. The Rough Riders were a cavalry regiment and planned to go to war mounted. They only needed their horses and equipment.

On Thursday, Captain Huston performed the duties of officer of the day with Lieutenant Sherrard Coleman of Santa Fe, New Mexico, as commander of the guard. That day, 12 more men lined up for guard mount at eight instead of nine in order to man three additional posts around the camp. Previously the guard had consisted of three reliefs of nine men each. They pulled two-hour guard shifts at various stations around camp. This increase was not just to keep soldiers in camp but unwanted visitors out. A few local citizens were caught stealing equipment. Lieutenant Hall read the order for the day, stating that one officer would remain in camp with each troop, one medical officer would attend any drill or parade and one medical officer would remain in camp at all times.

The logistics of building a regiment proved a nightmare though. Roosevelt had done well with his political influence to secure the items needed to go to war. He then loaded them early enough and shipped them by fast freight so that they should arrive in San Antonio the same time as the troops. Unfortunately, the railcars with the valuable cargo became separated and lost. With Roosevelt on one end and Wood on the other, the two burned off enough wire telegrams to move mountains. Eventually, a car would be found here and another there. By the first Tuesday, a load of saddles and Krag carbines had arrived. They were issued as soon as they were unloaded. The equipment was thrown out on the ground, and the men snatched them up as fast as they could.

The technicalities of making out requisitions and keeping accounts of the property initially fell in the hands of Quartermaster Sergeant Alfred E. Lewis. For whatever reason, Lewis deserted on May 5, just a couple of days after he had arrived. Lieutenant Hall had arrived just two days later as the quartermaster officer. Filling in for all the staff vacancies without any staff noncommissioned officers, Hall quickly became overwhelmed.

As a railcar arrived with an issue of some articles of uniform or equipment, it was immediately issued to the troopers instead of being held for one big issue. The next items to arrive were rubber ponchos and cotton undershirts. The troops received their issue according to first come, first served. Whenever the word went out, the troops ceased what they were doing and raced to the issue point. Finally, some order was established.

Captain Charles L. Cooper, of the Tenth Cavalry, who had mustered in the New Mexico contingent, provided an expedient and rapid means of distributing the supplies. Hall called off the name of a trooper from the troop muster roll. The man would step forward, guess his size and call it off depending on the item of issue. The experienced Cooper would then look the man over and call off his size. Fitting the item on the soldier, he would then make any necessary correction. Lieutenant William E. Griffin, of E Troop, would witness the issue, then the man would pass by the three officers receiving his appropriate issue from an open box until he reached Major George M. Dunn. Dunn, of Denver, Colorado, had been the Master of Hounds of some fox hunting club. He always provided himself a comfortable seat under the shade of a tree with a bucket of ice lemonade by his side. He would announce that the soldier had received his issue, then check him off. He was the only officer to find pleasure in this duty.

On Friday, May 13, enough horses were available to mount the ten troops on hand. Wood determined that the officers and noncommissioned officers would get first pick of the mounts, but the privates would have to draw lots to determine their order of selection; the lower the number, the earlier choice of the pick. Men with higher numbers were left to select from unbroken mustangs. Huston and McGinnis's horses finally arrived. From the selection available, McGinnis became the envy of the regiment, rivaled only by the charger of Captain William "Buckey" O'Neill, of Prescott, Arizona.

That Saturday, the ten existing troops drew their hats, leggings, underwear and chevrons to complete their uniform issue. The officers purchased their own brown fatigue uniforms and altered them to a nonregulation pattern by adding yellow collars and cuffs for cavalry. A one-and-a-half-inch yellow stripe down the side of their trousers denoted their commissions. Sergeants sewed one-inch and corporals a half-inch yellow stripe down the side of their trousers.

That day the men also drew lots for their pick of horses. Each trooper would pick his mount from the herd according to the color assigned to his troop. In cavalry tradition, the horses were issued according to color. D Troop would receive all gray mounts along with H Troop. A, F and K Troops drew the bays. B, E and M Troops would draw the sorrels. C, G and I were assigned the brown horses. L Troop, when it arrived, would draw the roan-colored mounts.[18] The men drew their numbers, and, not surprisingly, those with high numbers appealed to Huston for a new draw. Huston, of course, denied their requests. With numbers in hand, the troopers waited their turn to pick mounts, hoping there would still be tame horses left.

Fortunately, all the millionaires except for William Tiffany drew gentle mounts. All the unlucky men who drew unbroken ones had two days to break them. The rich did not have to worry. They had money. Tiffany hired broncobuster Bill Marvin, of Yuma, Arizona, to take some of the devilishness out of his horse. Marvin, along with other broncobusters, Sergeant Sam Rhodes, of Tonto Basin, Arizona, "Little" Bill McGinty and later Tom Isbell, when he arrived, became in great demand and could command any price they wanted. Ten dollars a horse was the going rate. Their Wild West exhibitions continued daily until all the horses were tamed, earning them a small fortune.

Bill McGinty had become quite a comical figure among the regiment, a regular "Mickey Free." His short legs caused him trouble on marches. He absolutely could not keep in step with the others. An accomplished horseman, he had never walked 100 yards if by any possibility he could ride. Little Bill assured everyone that he could keep step on horseback though.

Nicknames replaced common names. Very similar to the Indian culture, men's names changed from their birth to more colorful titles in their maturity to describe their features, occupations or celebrate their achievements. Known only unto themselves, the letters they wrote home rarely revealed their other identities. Some did leave a list of some of the more colorful noms de guerre: Cherokee Bill, Happy Jack, Hell Roarer, Admiral of the Hassayampa, Smokey Moore, Prayerful James, Smoke 'em up Bill Owens and Rattlesnake Pete.

While there were many men who were good cooks, no one wanted the job of troop cook because it would take them out of training. The First Squadron instead hired a cook and was the first to establish its own mess on Wednesday. Army rations, which consisted of meager rations of bacon, beef, cabbage, beans, coffee and bread, were the one constant complaint of men who could bear almost any inconvenience. Eventually, the rations improved with a regular issue of potatoes and canned tomatoes. On Saturday, Hall furnished the men a treat of an issue of onions. More often, the men combined these ingredients into a stew.

The officers and wealthy troopers ate their meals at a local restaurant set up within the camp. The rest of the troopers, being very popular with the locals, took every opportunity to visit picnics and dinner parties outside the camp. By Saturday, the camp came under strict military rule, and those still brave enough to venture off without a pass risked a night in the guardhouse.

Having motivated the proper railroad authorities to take action on the delivery of regimental property, Roosevelt's job in Washington, D.C., was finished. That Tuesday, employees of the different departments in the Capitol contributed to buy Roosevelt a silver-mounted cavalry saber. He then waited for a telegram from Wood inviting him to join the regiment. Roosevelt arrived at San Antonio at 7:20 Sunday morning with his African American valet, Marshall, a former Buffalo Soldier of the Ninth Cavalry. Colonel Wood and Major Dunn met him at the depot as he stepped off the train in his new khaki uniform. After a brief conversation, they escorted him to camp. Knowing the hard character of Westerners, it surprised Roosevelt to learn that there had only been one fight. Paul Hunter, however, remembered two fights that week. Roosevelt wrote, "I had been quite prepared for trouble when it came to enforcing discipline, but I was agreeably disappointed."[19] By that time, the men had adapted well to military discipline but still had a few rough edges to smooth off.

Wood introduced Roosevelt to his line of officers, remarking something about each of their talents. Roosevelt walked around with his big, toothy grin, shaking everybody's hand. When he reached the Oklahoma officers, Wood mentioned that they were the best drilled. Likewise, Roosevelt complimented them. Huston's spirits soared. Up until his arrival, few of the Westerners knew anything about their celebrity lieutenant colonel. Now they formed their first impressions. Huston remembered him as quite different from Wood. He "talks very emphatically and in a determined manner but very polished and polite."[20] Hall described him as "nervous, energetic, virile … polite almost to the extent of making one uneasy—most of the time."[21] B Troop's David Hughes, of

Tucson, Arizona, remembered, "he took the Western man at first sight, and the more they saw and heard him the more they liked him. His everlasting energy, his quick decision, 'yes' or 'no,' and he meant just what he said."[22] Roosevelt unloaded his luggage in the tent he would share with Lieutenant Hall.

Meanwhile, the men busied themselves cleaning the camp and preparing for inspection. Wood allowed no negligence in respect to camp hygiene. He ensured the men policed the camp of any and all debris. Wood had also scheduled a parade for the regiment that afternoon to ensure everyone knew how to wear their new uniforms.

Both Wood and Roosevelt reviewed the troops. Roosevelt remembered, "The uniform also suited them. In their slouch hats, blue flannel shirts, brown trousers, leggings and boots, with handkerchiefs knotted loosely around their necks, they looked exactly as a body of cow-boy cavalry should look."[23] They also carried their carbines and sabers for the first time.

When it came time to speak, Roosevelt brought the best news of all. The regiment was expected to move to Gal-

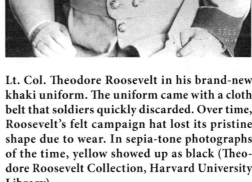

Lt. Col. Theodore Roosevelt in his brand-new khaki uniform. The uniform came with a cloth belt that soldiers quickly discarded. Over time, Roosevelt's felt campaign hat lost its pristine shape due to wear. In sepia-tone photographs of the time, yellow showed up as black (Theodore Roosevelt Collection, Harvard University Library).

veston on Thursday. This dispelled the existing rumor that they might leave on Monday or Tuesday. The two troops from the Indian Territory were also due in that night to complete the formation of the regiment.

That day, the neighboring Fifth Cavalry loaded up on railcars bound for Galveston. A crowd of nearly 5,000 citizens turned out to see them off. Their departure warned the Rough Riders that time was short. Wood, unbeknownst to others, knew that the War Department really did not need any volunteer regiments. So he secretly feared that they might still be left behind.

The officers had lunch with Roosevelt at their mess. Cadet Ernest Haskell, of Massachusetts, had also joined the Rough Riders while on a three-month leave of absence from West Point. Haskell figured that he could squeeze in a war during his summer vacation. Roosevelt naturally was the center of the conversation. Roosevelt admitted to Huston, "This regiment already has a great reputation and we must maintain it and every man must do his utmost to help."[24]

The two senior officers were entirely opposite. Wood was the quiet professional, while Roosevelt was the outgoing charismatic leader. Officers gravitated to each according to their own personalities. Paul Hunter wrote home about Wood, "He is kind and

Officer mess on day of Roosevelt's arrival. Standing, left to right: Cadet Haskell, Capt. Cooper (9th Cavalry), Dr. Church, Lt. Greenway. Sitting, left to right: 1st Lt. McGinnis, Lt. Carter, Capt. Alexander, Capt. Huston, Col. Wood, Lt. Col. Roosevelt, Capt. McClintock, Dr. Massey, Lt. Hall, Maj. Hersey, Lt. Frantz (Theodore Roosevelt Collection, Harvard University Library).

courteous to privates as well as to commissioned men and will listen to your troubles like a hero."[25] The men loved him for it. The Arizona men remembered Wood from his days campaigning in Arizona against Apaches. He was what they expected in a leader. He exhibited good judgment, was good-natured but could become stern when the situation demanded it. Hall remembered another side to Wood: "In moments of excitement he was stern, severe, and harsh."[26] Huston also favored Colonel Wood, the quiet professional. Wood gave him a couple of hymns that Sunday, claiming that he was not a singer. Huston prized them, believing that Wood would become famous one day. Roosevelt, on the other hand, was impulsive yet extremely charismatic, who more closely identified with other popular officers, like Capron or Buckey O'Neill.

Because of the celebrity of the regiment, the local citizens of San Antonio took great interest in them. Up to 2,000 locals visited that Sunday afternoon to view the ceremony and catch a glimpse of Roosevelt. Wood had excluded civilians from the camp except on weekends. Consequently, picnics spread out across the campgrounds that day. Pretty girls and soldiers strolled the grounds. The handsome Sergeant Sands, of Guthrie, had already developed a number of female acquaintances. The Texans were fiercely patriotic, and, whenever they would meet a Rough Rider, the Texans would wish him luck and remind him to "Remember the *Maine*."

Enlisted mess at San Antonio (Theodore Roosevelt Collection, Harvard University Library).

Dean Richardson, the "Fighting Bishop" from St. Mark's Episcopal Church came out at 4:30 to hold dinner services for the men. The white-headed old man stood on the bandstand in the front of the hotel in the midst of hundreds of people. In his sermon, he proclaimed that the men were fighting a holy war. "You should not feel that you are fighting for revenge, for vengeance belongs exclusively to the Almighty, but you are warring to redress wrongs, to correct evils."[27]

At 5:30, Mayor Callaghan and his party arrived at camp by horse-drawn streetcar. They walked directly to Wood's tent. The local band under Professor Carl Beck marched up and a choir of little boys, young men and women dressed in white from the church provided the evening entertainment. The band played a rendition of popular tunes: "Manhattan Beach," "Yankee Doodle," "Dixie," and "The Star Spangled Banner." Beck's band had previously entertained them the night before. Interestingly, whenever the band visited camp, it always played the popular tunes: "Goodbye, Dolly Gray," "La Paloma" and "There'll Be a Hot Time in the Old Town Tonight." At first, the recurrent song, "A Hot Time," became a joke among the troopers until eventually they accepted it as their regimental air.

The Indian Territory troops finally arrived that evening, and the Oklahoma boys turned out to welcome Captain Capron. Roosevelt met Capron and Thomas. Roosevelt seemed to be well read up on distinguished persons in American history. He remarked to others around him about the 19-year-old lieutenant, "I shouldn't like to be in that young man's shoes. He has eleven ancestors who were such brilliant fighters that I shouldn't like to live up to their records. But I think he'll do it."[28] The two troops then drew their issue of uniforms and equipment.

Rough Rider officers at San Antonio. Front row, left to right: 1st Lt. Hall, Maj. Hersey, Maj. Brodie, Col. Wood, Lt. Col. Roosevelt, Capt. Jenkins, unknown. Cpt. Rob Huston is standing in the second row between Wood and Roosevelt. Capt. Bruce is the second person to his left. Capt. Capron is second from right in the third row. Capt. McGinnis is standing on the left in the last row (Theodore Roosevelt Collection, Harvard University Library).

Capron's became L Troop and Bruce's M Troop. Bruce's troop, however, did not receive its horses or full issue of firearms. As Sunday came to an end, the majority of the regiment was fully organized, drilled and appeared ready for war. The next day's event would test their confidence.

Capron also provided a new format for muster rolls for the regiment. Huston wanted to be the first to have them complete. Huston wrote Vite, "This is my opportunity and I'm not wearing out the seat of my trousers sitting around."[29] He had First Sergeant Palmer and the troop clerk, Edward Johnston of Cushing, work all night on them. They finished three days later. Huston wanted his troop to be the best in every respect.

Right after breakfast on Monday morning, over 1,000 men lined up next to their mounts. Thus came the great day of reckoning. The command sounded, "Prepare to Mount!" The men anxiously stepped into the stirrups. The horses stirred. On the command, "Mount," men lifted themselves up into the saddles. At that moment 300 to 400 horses started to buck, kicking dust into the air.[30] Laughter rang out. Over 100 Rough Riders were tossed to the ground. Sergeant Rynning remembered, "It was more like a condensed cyclone or an earthquake than any kind of rodeo ever seen before or since." Some of the horses were so bunched up that they did not have room to buck and instead tried to climb over each other.[31] In cowboy tradition, they had to get back up and try again until they could remain mounted. Each of these men prided themselves on their horsemanship. This day provided a great comedy for those lucky or skilled enough to

Three Rough Riders preparing to mount (Theodore Roosevelt Collection, Harvard University Library).

stay in the saddle. Rumors flew as to how some performed. Several wrote back to the *Guthrie Daily Leader* to dispel any rumor that an Oklahoman was thrown.

Monday, May 16, also brought the second round of promotions for D Troop. Each cavalry troop was allotted seven sergeants and eight corporals. Huston had promoted Charley Hunter to quartermaster sergeant the previous Friday. He was considered something of a rustler, which might help improve their food situation. To rustle referred to the ability to acquire what one wanted through barter, trade or theft. Charley deserved those stripes. Scott Reay, of Newkirk, and Paul Hunter were also promoted to sergeants. Farrier Thomas Moran moved up to sergeant. Arthur Luther, of Pawnee, took his place. Lyman Beard, of Shawnee; Alexander H. Denham, of Oklahoma City; Henry Love, of Tecumseh; and Harrison Holt, of Denver, Colorado, also became corporals. John Brown became the second trumpeter. Brown and Wetmore, both of Newkirk, had to rehearse every bugle call so that each would sound distinct. In the roar of battle this would be the primary means of communicating military commands.

Albert Thomas finally returned from the hospital on Monday, while other troopers increasingly suffered from the effects of the heat. By Thursday, the regiment would have 18 men sick. Huston was having difficulty determining who was actually sick and who was just tired. By the next Saturday, five Oklahomans reported sick.

With Roosevelt in camp, Wood turned the supervision of the drill over to him. Roosevelt was a man of intense energy. Hall wrote, "He may wear out some day, but he

Mounted Rough Rider with full issue of equipment. D Troop mounted on grays behind regimental headquarters (Theodore Roosevelt Collection, Harvard University Library).

will never rust out." When he was not physically doing something, he read. Upon his arrival, he poured over the military drill manuals. He would read a paragraph while walking, then clasp the book in his hands behind his back as if contemplating its meaning, then bark out the commands. Roosevelt seemed entirely unconcerned about practicing within the presence of others. He did and learned everything with "ferocious earnestness." This lack of embarrassment about making a mistake in front of others made him unique.[32]

One afternoon, Roosevelt took Brodie's squadron out for a drill. He put them through the maneuvers from one formation to the next until he eventually issued an impossible order to carry out. The men did the best their formations could but became entangled in a mass of confusion. Roosevelt quickly called Brodie to take over. Brodie promptly ordered, "As you were!" The men resumed their original positions. Order was again restored.[33]

As the squadron returned from a hot day of drill, they passed a German beer garden. Roosevelt had sent Adjutant Hall ahead to make the necessary arrangements. When they reached the brewery, Roosevelt invited everyone in. "Men, this is a beer garden. Drink all the beer you want, but don't make fools of yourselves." Roosevelt's popularity with the men increased.[34]

Upon their return to camp, Wood reprimanded Roosevelt for his conduct as an officer and said he did not want Roosevelt filling the men up with beer. Theodore responded with something about "my regiment," which brought a sharp and icy response from Wood. "I'm still commander of this regiment." Roosevelt became very quiet. He had not meant any disrespect to his dear old friend by his remark. Roosevelt knew his place.[35]

A couple of days later the brewery presented M Troop with a couple of barrels of beer. Captain Robert Bruce walked up to Captain George Curry, of H Troop, who was the officer of the day, and asked what to do with them for Wood had a standing order that no intoxicating drinks were allowed inside the camp. Bruce and Curry went to Roosevelt with their dilemma. As Bruce started to make his request, Roosevelt threw up his hands. Still smarting from his reprimand, he said, "Nothing doing. Beer is a subject I do not want to hear about."[36]

Brodie's First Squadron in mounted drill. D Troop with gray mounts is third from the right (Theodore Roosevelt Collection, Harvard University Library).

The second week introduced a new phase of training—mounted drill. In this manner, the regiment expected to go into battle. Brodie took his squadron out for its first mounted drill on Tuesday. The Oklahomans found mounted drill considerably more enjoyable. The troops trained their horses to stay and move in line and perform the same movements as the troopers had practiced on foot. In this respect, the Westerners took keen pride in training their mounts. Hall wrote, "The ability of the men to ride saved many months of time, and the ease with which they learned the mounted drill was wonderful."[37] Roosevelt, however, admitted that their intervals were not always the correct distance and their lines were somewhat irregular, but the regiment quickly learned the essentials of the commands and movements.

Roosevelt had paid a Texas friend $50 apiece for two tough-and-hardy horses which his valet named "Little Texas" and "Rain-in-the-Face." During the training, the men of the West witnessed the superb horsemanship of their lieutenant colonel. Roosevelt put his horses through the paces with jumps and quick turns. Hughes remembered, "The men immediately recognized their master leader and after their talks, in groups that night after supper, they were ready to go anywhere at his command."[38]

During the second week, the troops still drilled on foot, but this time with carbines. They first practiced the manual of arms. They then began to rehearse fire and advance in skirmish order with one platoon pretending to fire while the other rushed forward. One platoon would drop to a prone firing position while the others rose up and advanced. Roosevelt admitted their plains craft skill and knowledge of weapons proved valuable during this aspect of training.

Training continued from dawn till dusk. The men adjusted well to military discipline and drill. By then, the newness of it had worn off, and soldier life became routine. The evenings were set aside for leaders' training. Since military drill was new to even many of the officers, they had classes the night before on subjects they would drill and rehearse the next day. The experienced officers led the training. Consequently, Capron trained the officers in guard duty, outpost duty, tactics, advance and rear guard.

Capron proved himself a demanding and most-able trainer. Like his father, he was a strict disciplinarian, yet he had a genuine love for his soldiers that in turn earned his men's devotion. No matter how demanding he was, they knew he meant it for their own good. There was also gentleness about him. Roosevelt described, "His ceaseless effort was to train them, care for them, and inspire them as to bring their fighting efficiency to the highest possible pitch."[39] Although his L Troop was one of the last to arrive and had missed a week of training, they quickly caught up with the others. Capron also took a keen liking to his young lieutenant, Rob Thomas, but would not openly admit it. He expected much out of him and was stern in his training, scrutinizing his every mistake.

Although demanding, Capron had a genuine concern for the welfare of his men. He saw William "Judge" Murphy, of Caddo, performing Sergeant of the Guard after herding horses for 20 hours. Even standing in the middle of a corral of horses, he had difficulty staying awake. Capron climbed over the fence and told him, "Go up and go to sleep on one of the boxes. I'll do your work for you. I don't want to kill my men—yet."[40] The men grew to love him. The First U.S. Volunteer Cavalry had some of the finest officers in the Army.

The increased training during the second week rarely allowed time for leisure or a pass to leave camp. Still some tested their luck. While trying to avoid the guards late one night, without a pass, Paul Hunter ran into the barbed wire fence surrounding the camp. The new scar on his nose provided fuel for jokes by his friend George Burgess of Shawnee.

With the myriad of duties, Hall needed help. Wood had sent it first in the form of Joseph A. Carr, of Washington, D.C., who would serve as the regimental sergeant major. Carr was the grandson of General Keith Walter Armistead of the first graduating class at West Point. His uncle, General Lewis Armistead, had died leading the famous Pickett's Charge at Gettysburg.

Hall had also been unable to make out receipts for items issued to the troops. Consequently, he was fully expected to go into bankruptcy when the government demanded its due. The regiment did not have the luxury of time for anyone to learn the complicated army supply system. Wood desperately needed someone with experience. The officers of the Fifth Cavalry from the nearby Fort Sam Houston knew the right man for the job. They had been impressed enough with their old quartermaster sergeant that they followed his post–army career. This was not difficult since he had created a legend for himself as one of the famous "Three Guardsmen" of the Indian Territory.

Chris Madsen had immigrated to America from Denmark after having fought with the French during the Franco-Prussian War and then with the French Foreign Legion in Algiers. He had enlisted in the Fifth Cavalry in 1872 and fought at the Battle of Warbonnet Creek in 1876. In 1880, his company was assigned to Fort Laramie, Wyoming, and he was promoted to corporal in September. Not long after that he was charged with stealing grain from the government and selling it to a civilian stage company. The court-martial acquitted him. Since the Quartermaster and Commissary Departments in Washington, D.C., determined the quantity of supplies and provisions the units out on the frontier needed, there were often shortages of some and surplus of others. The army functioned unofficially on a barter system to acquire the needed supplies that the government did not provide by trading off the excess. In this spirit of "horse trading" or "rustling," many succumbed to the temptation to line their own pockets with some of the profits and supplement their meager wages, hoping the army would not notice. One cannot be sure that this was the case with Chris Madsen, but this kind of trouble occurred throughout most of his jobs.

In 1881, Chris reenlisted for a third five-year enlistment. In June 1881, he was convicted by a civilian court of illegally selling government property. His officers placed him on furlough during his six-month incarceration in the Wyoming Territorial Prison, then had the confidence to reinstate him as quartermaster sergeant. Chris then served as an expert shot on the Fort Omaha Rifle Team from November 1881 to May 1882. By 1883, he was appointed in charge of the troop mess. He would have had responsibility not only for the preparation of the meals but for acquiring the food. From June 1884 to August 1885, he served as the Fort Washakie Acting Sergeant Major, after which, his Company A moved to Fort Riley, Kansas, and then to the Indian Territory where he became the battalion quartermaster sergeant. He also continued to compete in rifle marksmanship contests.

While at Fort Reno in the Indian Territory, Chris married the love of his life, Maggie Morris, in 1887. He obtained a little homestead outside the post during the 1889 land run. His meager pay of $29 a month was not enough to support his wife and two children, so he left the Army after 15 years of service. It took 30 years of service to qualify for military retirement. The officer mustering him out wrote of him, "Character good but not suited for the position of a quartermaster sergeant."[41] Evidently someone at Fort Sam Houston disagreed.

Chris became one of the three legendary deputy marshals under Marshal William Grimes. With his office at El Reno, Chris fought against some of the most notorious outlaws of the Indian Territory: the Daltons, Doolins, Starrs and Poes. He participated in the legendary shoot-out with the Doolin Gang in Ingles. His reputation carried him in employment to Kansas City, but the failing health of his beloved Maggie forced him to return to El Reno. On May 2, while the Oklahomans gathered in Guthrie to enlist for the war, Maggie died. Several days later, Chris heard a knock at the door. The telegraph messenger handed him a message from Colonel Wood asking Chris to come at once to San Antonio, Texas. Madsen wired back that it would be impossible for him to leave his two children and abandon his farm.

At the suggestion of the cavalry officers, Wood also sent telegrams to former Governor Abraham J. Seay and Madsen's former boss, Bill Grimes, to help persuade him to come. Again, Wood sent Chris another telegram. By this time, the widower began to inquire if neighbors could take care of his kids. Grimes and Seay met him and asked why he had not accepted. Chris explained his problem, and Seay answered, "Now you get ready to go on the first train. Bill and I will take care of your children and your other business. They need you down there in San Antonio or they wouldn't have sent for you." After 26 years of government employment, this immigrant decided that if there was anything he could do to help "win the war," he would go. Chris paid a family to take care of his children and hopped on a train for Texas.[42]

Upon arrival, Wood expressed his pleasure that Chris had finally accepted his invitation. "I want you to go to the quartermaster's office and check up on the invoices and receipts in the hands of Lieutenant Hall."[43]

"But Colonel, I have not been mustered in yet."

"I'll muster you in right here."

"I haven't been examined by the doctor," responded the 46-year-old war veteran. "I don't know whether I'm physically fit."[44]

The Regimental Surgeon, Henry La Motte of Williamsburg, Massachusetts, rode up, having overheard the conversation. The U.S. Navy had detailed Doctor La Motte as the surgeon to the Rough Riders with the rank of major. Without dismounting, he looked Madsen up and down and then pronounced him fit for military service.

Madsen reported to Hall. The lieutenant all but bit his head off. Hall then explained that if he had anything for the sergeant, he would send for him. With that news, Chris turned around and marched out. He had not been properly mustered in and officially was still a civilian. He could leave if he wanted. He walked up to the colonel and described his reception. Wood escorted Madsen back to the quartermaster's tent and explained that he had sent the sergeant for the papers and wanted them turned over immediately. Madsen straightened out the receipts, and Hall would not have to worry about owing the government a thing. However, the overbearing Hall and Madsen could not get along. Only one could run the quartermaster office. Wood would have to find a new quartermaster officer.

Meanwhile, Huston prided himself on his professionalism and the performance of his troop while both Schweizer and McGinnis's popularity increased. McGinnis was ambitious, and his opportunity to prove his talent came Monday of that second week with the assignment to shoe all of the regiment's horses. Mac raced to have all the horses shod before the quartermaster finished purchasing the rest of them. This was a tall task since the quartermaster already had a week's head start on him.

A good farrier might average about a dozen horses a day, but the regiment needed nearly 1,000 done. Hall later wrote, "But if you wanted anything done from the mending of a shoe to the building of a railroad you had but to raise your voice and ask for a man to do it. An expert would appear."[45] That was another advantage of the volunteer regiments. The men hailed from many professions.

McGinnis needed all the blacksmiths in the regiment and found three in his own troop. Even then the process did not proceed fast enough, so he hired a couple of civilian blacksmiths. The trick was how to shoe an untamed "bronc." This became a spectacle in itself. The blacksmiths had to throw the broncos down and tie them first. By Thursday, May 19, he finished the monumental task. Huston wrote, "All the horses of the regiment have been shod, and it was one of the biggest and most expeditious jobs in the horse shoeing line ever accomplished. Your own Lieut. S.A. McGinnis, of Troop D, had charge of the work, and has been highly complimented by the commanding officers for the manner in which he conducted it."[46]

To their disappointment the Rough Riders still had not deployed by Thursday. Wood and Roosevelt mentioned that the regiment might instead depart on Friday, although no arrangements for any rail transportation had been provided. Wood believed that they would move the first part of next week with a destination of Tampa, Florida. The men were not even sure whether they would sail to Cuba or the Philippines.

Tents had also arrived. A light rain fell that Thursday morning as the weather cooled. First Squadron abandoned the hard floor of the Exposition Hall to move out onto the parade grounds in pitched rows of two-man tents. By doctrine, the troop lined its tents up in a row behind its troop headquarter's tent on line with the other troop headquarters. The aisles between the rows of troops were known as streets, and in army traditions they were usually named. A Troop named the street in front of its tent openings "O'Neill Avenue"; B Troop named its "Arizona Avenue"; C Troop called its "Manila Avenue"; and D Troop named its street "Dewey Avenue." Riverside Park, or Camp Wood as it became known, with its tents in a rectangular grid pattern and horse picket lines finally took on the appearance of a military camp.[47]

Camp Wood at the fairgrounds outside the Exposition Hall in San Antonio (Fort Sam Houston Museum).

Roosevelt, Wood and Brodie in camp at San Antonio (Library of Congress).

There were quite a number of musicians in the regiment. Several choirs formed with the accompaniment of nearly a dozen talented banjo players. The familiar sound of music drifted through the air during the leisure hours every night after training. Music always played an important part of people's lives. In the time before radios, people gathered around the piano or other musical instrument to sing for evening entertainment. Before records, people collected song sheets. It was not surprising that talented soldiers would change the lyrics to scores or write their own songs about the regiment.

On Thursday, Roosevelt marched them several miles into the country for physical conditioning. First Squadron drilled on the campgrounds for an hour then marched several miles out of camp at 3 p.m. In time, Brodie had them executing complicated movements with remarkable precision. The riders handled their horses and kept them in line well. When it was over, both Wood and Brodie complimented the Oklahomans in a way that made them feel proud. That day also brought a round of promotions in the officer ranks.

Although Roosevelt had made the Easterners no promises, the new troops offered him the chance to promote some of them. Wood was inclined to commission the college graduates as officers. On Wednesday, May 18, John C. Greenway, of Hot Springs, Arkansas, became the first millionaire to receive a commission. He was made second lieutenant in I Troop. The next day, Roosevelt's friend Woodbury Kane was also commissioned to first lieutenant in K Troop. Cadet Haskell would become the second lieutenant. Both would train under the tutelage of Captain Micah Jenkins of Yonges Island, South Carolina. An 1879 graduate of West Point and son of a prominent Civil War commander from South Carolina, Jenkins himself had served on the frontier with the cavalry until his resignation in 1886.

Wood commissioned First Sergeant George Wilcox, of Prescott, as first lieutenant of B Troop. He had previously served in the Fourth Cavalry. Wood considered giving the second lieutenant vacancy to a Harvard athlete, David Goodrich. Twenty-one-year-old David was the youngest son of Benjamin F. Goodrich, who had built a rubber factory on the banks of the Ohio Canal in Akron, Ohio, in 1870. This would grow into the B.F. Goodrich Tire Company. After his father died in 1888, David's mother had moved the family to New York City where he led a privileged lifestyle. He left Harvard to join the regiment.

He was one of the Ivy League athletes who joined for the adventure and aspired to become cowboys. Upon arrival, he had asked to serve in the Arizona squadron instead of the millionaire troop. He ended up in B Troop and even had one of the cowboys teach him the art of throwing a lariat. Probably because David had been the captain of the Harvard Crew, Wood and Roosevelt saw something that would make him a good officer. The skills of leadership in one of the most prestigious sports in the Ivy League college at that time might translate into the leadership skills needed in combat. The cowboys, however, just saw a young, privileged college kid.

When the Arizona troopers learned of this, they put up a fuss. Wood called in Tom Rynning, newly promoted to first sergeant, and asked him his opinion. Tom had served as a mule packer with Wood when he chased Geronimo, and, evidently, the colonel respected the sergeant's opinion. While Tom did not disagree with the logic of commissioning college graduates, he mentioned that proven military experience should carry more weight. Wood commissioned Rynning as B Troop's second lieutenant instead.

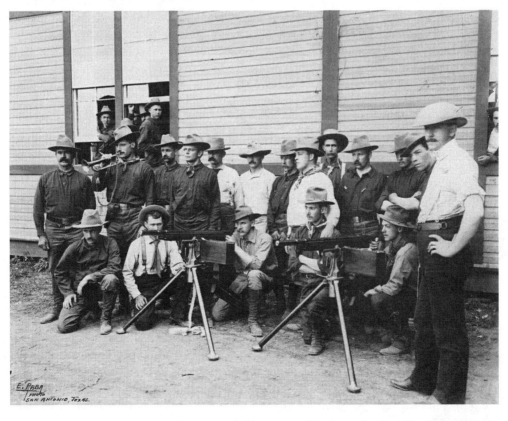

Tiffany's Colt rapid-fire guns (Theodore Roosevelt Collection, Harvard University Library).

Coincidentally, that Thursday morning two Colt rapid-fire guns and 10,000 rounds of ammunition purchased for the regiment by Kane and Joseph Stevens finally arrived. These belt-fed machine guns fired 480 rounds per minute and could hit a man at 2,000 yards. These 35-pound guns could be easily folded up and transported. Roosevelt set them up behind his tent and set about to learn all he could about them. He assigned several of the millionaires to the battery: Norman Maxwell, of Newport, Rhode Island, as the first sergeant; Ham Fish as the second sergeant; and Craig Wadsworth, the first corporal. The First U.S. Volunteer Cavalry would be the only regiment with automatic weapons in the U.S. Army. The promotions for this battery also opened some vacancies in the troop, so Willie Tiffany was made sergeant the next day. Nearly all the sergeants hailed from New York and the corporals from other Eastern states. Frank Wilson, of Guthrie, wrote home that they selected him as the first sergeant although he was never listed with any rank on the muster-out roster. The rank was either temporary, or he was trying to impress his parents.

That same Thursday, Huston also had duty as the officer of the day responsible for inspecting the guard mounts throughout the day and night. Wood and Roosevelt walked up to him and had a long talk about the quality of the officers from Oklahoma. They complimented him that they were the strongest and best officers in the regiment. Then they confessed the reason for their praise. There were still several promotion vacancies in the regiment, and they wanted to promote McGinnis and Schweizer. To ward off any objections, Roosevelt reminded Huston, "You have the best troop and you can get along without them."[48]

McGinnis's hard work had paid off. He was rewarded with the captaincy of I Troop. He signed over his company property to Huston and assumed his new command. Even though this is what he had strived for, he visited his old Oklahoma troop every day.

Schweizer was promoted to regimental quartermaster and commissary officer with the rank of first lieutenant, while Hall was relegated just to the duties of adjutant. Roosevelt tended to throw himself into his work to learn all he could about the function of a regiment, so he had little use for an adjutant. Once overwhelmed by his responsibilities, Hall found himself just a buffer between the headquarters and the regiment. Not an enviable position.

The promotion of Schweizer, however, did not improve Sergeant Madsen's morale. While in the Fifth Cavalry, Corporal Schweizer had served under Sergeant Madsen, not to mention that both had come from the same town in Oklahoma. Madsen had still not taken his oath of enlistment yet when he learned Schweizer would be his lieutenant. Chris complained that he might feel unpleasant serving under a former subordinate who knew nothing about the supply system. Wood said that the lieutenant would be the quartermaster in name only, and Chris would have a total free hand in running things. This did not improve Chris's morale. In essence, the Army would pay Chris $25 a month to do all the work and pay Schweizer $175 just to sign his name. Wood and Roosevelt promised Madsen that as soon as another officer vacancy opened, they would offer it to him. While the promotions of two of their own made the Oklahomans proud, it had its price.[49]

With plenty of good material to choose from in the Oklahoma troop, Roosevelt instead chose to commission some of his Ivy League alumni. Paul wrote to the *Guthrie Leader*, "The Acting Sergeant Major of the regiment was appointed our first lieutenant, and is a fair sort of a fellow—at least a Westerner. The second lieutenant is a Fifth Avenue Harvard college boy, who received his appointment by the powers that be, and from his big iron dollars." Sergeant Major Joseph A. Carr became D Troop's first lieutenant and Capron's First Sergeant, Earnest Stecker, took his place as the new regimental

Regimental Headquarters. Col. Wood and Lt. Col. Roosevelt are wearing khaki uniforms. 1st Lt. Hall is standing behind Roosevelt to his left and Surgeon La Motte to his left. Kneeling in front are Chief Trumpeter Platt, Commissary Sergeant, and Sergeant Major Stecker (Theodore Roosevelt Collection, Harvard University Library).

sergeant major. Sergeant David Goodrich replaced Schweizer as D Troop's second lieutenant. Goodrich's promotion in D Troop raised the same protest as it had in B Troop. Paul Hunter continued, "The boys are all righteously indignant and are on the point of a small revolution."[50]

To add further insult,

> He [Goodrich] even had to buy a gentle horse so he could ride it. He doesn't know anything about tactics or the men he has been appointed over. The injustice of the thing is we had a dozen boys who could teach him army regulations, shooting, riding and everything else that is essential to make a rough rider, and Troop D wants to say right here that she is sore, indignant and mad clean through, and registers her kick. We do not care to go out and win battles for some Fifth Avenue swell to reap the reward of our work, and don't mean to do it if it can possibly be avoided.[51]

To add to their fears, many believed their troop commander was also in line for a promotion. "If Captain Huston is promoted to a major's straps our identity will be lost and your 'Cholly' or 'Willie' will take the 'wough widers to the fwont.' … We want officers appointed over us that are capable of giving us a chance to uphold the 'honor of our country and territory and without that, Oklahoma may be disappointed in her representation in the Rough Riders.'"[52]

Paul appealed to the governor, calling on his earlier promise to help if they needed it. Barnes knew there was nothing he could do. The regiment belonged to the U.S. Army, and Colonel Wood commanded it. It did not matter anyway. Time later healed that wound.

When D Troop was finishing its dismounted drill on Friday, the next day, Huston lined them up in a skirmish line; then he gave the command to charge. The men raced a quarter of a mile across the field under the hot sun. At the finish, the men were permitted a short rest. Huston, having tested the stamina of his men, asked how they felt. George Burgess boastfully spoke up that he was ready to try it again.

Chris Madsen arrived too late to pick a good horse. The one he ended up with was not inclined to follow its rider's directions. Chris subsequently went over to Fort Sam Houston to look up one of his old lieutenants. He asked if the officer in charge of purchasing mounts was ashamed to see an old Fifth Cavalry man riding an old goat like the one Chris was trying to civilize. The captain laughed and directed him to the stable where the unassigned horses were kept. There Chris picked out a better mount. Chris again failed to demonstrate good judgment in horse flesh. While the one he picked was tame, it turned out to be slow and too tall for routine mounting and dismounting.[53]

With his tent right behind that of Wood's, the Colonel could not help but notice the tall horse. He complained that he himself could not find one as good looking as that. Chris told Wood he could have him. Wood responded that he really wanted it for Hamilton Fish. The tall Sergeant Fish had bought himself a tall horse but loaned it instead to the colonel. Wood was eager to repay Fish's generosity. Chris said that the captain purchasing horses was a former lieutenant, and he could just as easily get another. So works the loyalty between sergeants and their officers.

Ham Fish came to look at the horse. He took a fancy to the horse the moment he saw it. Fish apologized for taking such a fine stallion, but Madsen said he was welcome to him. Chris joked that if he wanted the horse back, he only had to wait until they went into battle. Since Fish was so big and ugly, Chris said the Spaniards would surely kill him the first time they saw him. Madsen would later regret what he had said. Unfortunately, they left for Tampa before he could choose another horse.

That Thursday another millionaire had arrived to take a look at the regiment. Hallett Alsop Borrowe, from Newark, New Jersey, was the superintendent of the Newark and New York trolley. He had also married the daughter of the late Austin Corbin less than a year before. Her inheritance made her the richest girl in America, providing him with more money than he knew how to spend. Hallett had unfortunately become entangled in the celebrated Coleman-Dayton divorce case. An accomplished horseman and swordsman, Borrowe talked with his Knickerbocker friends about their lives as soldiers. He stayed at the Menger Hotel and then decided to enlist on Saturday, May 21. He kept his valet at the hotel where he made daily pilgrimages for a shave and bath. This caused some resentment among the others.

The first incident of public rowdyism by any Rough Riders occurred Thursday afternoon. Henry Neal, an elderly dairyman, was driving home in his milk cart. He heard two horsemen approaching from the rear when one said, "Let's show him how we'll kill Spaniards in Cuba." Upon turning around, he saw two Rough Riders galloping toward him. One made a rush, and Neal's horse jumped, falling back in the cart, bruising Neal's limbs. The Rough Rider's horse also fell, knocking the wheel off the cart. The second trooper galloped up to assist his buddy back on his horse; then both galloped off.

Neal's son quickly arrived, fixed the wheel and gave chase in the cart. He pursued them as far as Lamm Brothers' store, then mounted a saddled horse and continued the chase down South Flores Street to Mitchell. As he neared the two troopers, his mount stumbled and fell, striking a barbed wire fence, cutting its throat. Neal was thrown, and his leg was almost severed on the wire. The horse died. The two Rough Riders were never identified.

The second weekend was typical except for church services on Sunday, May 22. It was conducted by the regiment's own chaplain. Thirty-four-year-old Henry W. Brown had been an Episcopalian rector of the Church of the Advent in Prescott, Arizona, when he received a telegram from Roosevelt on May 20 offering him the post of the chaplain of the First U.S. Volunteer Cavalry. He got his affairs in order and then bid goodbye to his wife. At that time, there was no qualification requirements for chaplains nor was there any definition of the duties of chaplains in the field. Brown would do what he felt an army chaplain needed to do to minister to the spiritual as well as physical and moral needs of his men. He would set the standard for others to follow.[54]

Monday of the third week came, and the men began to wonder why they still had not deployed, and another week of drill began. That week's drill put the finishing touches on the regiment. On Monday, the regiment conducted its second mounted regimental drill. The buglers sounded "Boots and Saddles" at 10 a.m., and in ten minutes the entire regiment was mounted with carbines slung over their shoulders. Still some spirited bucking took place, but the riders soon had their horses under control. The two

1st U.S. Volunteer Cavalry mounted with full issue at San Antonio. D Troop is the gray horse troop behind Col. Wood (Fort Sam Houston Museum).

new troops, L and M, drilled mounted for the first time. The column moved out in good order led by Colonel Wood, Lieutenant Colonel Roosevelt and his staff. A cloud of dust rose as the mounted cavalry in columns of four marched three miles southeast of camp to the prairie of the San Jose Mission. Wood and Roosevelt watched the columns put their horses through the drills for an hour. They went through the same paces as before. At first, they walked; then the bugle blew the command to trot and finally gallop.

At last, Roosevelt led a charge. There were still five or six unruly horses in each troop, and, consequently, dozens of troopers were thrown, leading to a stampede. The other riders howled with laughter. Paul Hunter admitted that the Oklahomans owed the credit of their performance to the skill of Captain Huston and the right guide, Sergeant Webb. The troops had just received their guidons, and Sergeant Webb was made the guidon sergeant of D Troop. A good and steady guide regulated the speed of march, which allowed everyone to stay in line. The rest of the day fell into its usual routine except for the evening. The regiment had progressed to regimental drill, which they conducted for three to four hours each day.

To acclimate the horses to gunfire, Roosevelt and about 20 noncommissioned officers rode around and fired blank pistol cartridges at the enlisted men while they held their mounts. Almost all of the horses pitched or bolted. Only after the horses had become accustomed to gunfire could the men ride them into combat. Believing that his regiment would be used against hostile cavalry, Roosevelt trained his men in shock tactics. From his readings, he believed that the horse could be used as a natural weapon. He trained his men to hit their adversaries with their own horses.

After they returned to camp that afternoon, Wood finally received a telegram from the War Department asking when he could move his regiment. He answered back that he could move within 36 hours. The War Department telegraphed back to be ready in that time. He had the order read to each troop and informed the men not to leave camp for more than five minutes without notifying their captains or first sergeants. The next day, the commissary issued the men three days of field rations, although Wood was not sure when they would leave. They were just waiting for orders. Even the previous rumors had numbed their optimism. Ira Hill wrote home that they could either leave in two hours or two months. That week, Wood also lifted the ban on visitors to the camp. The moment the gates were opened every evening, local citizens poured in to watch the drill and visit until dark.

That evening the Oklahoma boys sang a different tune about their new officers after a little informal celebration. Charley Hunter had traded flour to a baker for several baked pies. After a dinner feast, they listened to a concert provided by Professor Beck's band while Carr quenched everyone's thirst for alcohol and Goodrich provided the cigars. This successfully broke the ice so the men could get to know their new officers. With a drink in one hand and a cigar in the other, the Oklahomans had to admit that the "Swells" were not bad fellows after all. Paul Hunter changed his tone: "Our new lieutenants evidently know how to reach the hearts of Oklahoma's boys, and in a great measure have succeeded in gaining the respect of all the troop."[55]

With the increase in unit vacancies, the regiment began to take on more volunteers. Roosevelt had been flooded with hundreds of requests to join his celebrated regiment. Many showed up in Texas each week. He could afford to be selective about who he accepted. Among the multitude, he received a letter of application from Ben Colbert, a brakeman for the Southern Pacific Railroad working in Texas. Ben also mentioned that he was an Indian who wanted to join the fight. Roosevelt had read much on the history of the Cherokee and Choctaw Indians and recognized the name Colbert as one of the great Choctaw chiefs of the eighteenth century. That Monday, May 23, Roosevelt summoned him for an interview and determined that he would make an excellent recruit.

Ben was an adventurer from the Indian Territory. He had worked as a switchman on the Mexican International Railroad in Torreon during 1894. When he first learned of the Cuban struggle for independence, he sailed to Guatemala City to find a way to join the fight in Cuba. The American consul had him jailed to keep him out of the struggle, fearing that his participation might imperil American neutrality. Promising to keep out of the fight, Ben returned to Torreon. While a Katy switchman in Smithville, Arkansas, Ben learned of the sinking of the *Maine*. He later went to Texas where he found another chance to join the fight. He was assigned to Maximilian Luna's F Troop.[56]

At 8:30 that night, Professor Beck held another concert at Riverside Park for the regiment. Many believed that this would be that last public affair with the Rough Riders. The program was to begin with a popular John Philips Sousa tune, "The Stars and Stripes Forever," followed by "Light Cavalry," "El Capitan," "Cavalry Charge," "Grand Warriors' March," and Hattie Hymn from Riemst (third act). The rest of the arrangement included a coronet solo followed by more music and a series of cheers for the regiment. The newspapers posted the program, inviting the public to attend.[57]

Professor Beck was especially proud of his arrangement of the "Cavalry Charge." The sound of fife and drums represented the approaching infantry. Bugles signaled the cavalry arriving off in the distance, coming nearer and nearer until they charged upon the enemy. The accompaniment of cannon firing, bugles, fifes and drums would signify the melee of battle, defeat of the enemy and pursuit by the cavalry. This arrangement was his tribute to the Rough Riders.

One thousand local citizens turned out to what was the largest attendance at the park to that date. Around 9 p.m., at the conclusion of the performance, Beck sounded the cavalry charge, and one of the members of the band fired revolvers loaded with blank cartridges. Someone in the crowd yelled out, "Help him out, boys!" Several pistols started blasting away. At first a few people close to the bandstand began to move away. The firing grew into a fusillade of gunfire; then the rush turned into a stampede. Women lifted their skirts, screamed and fled. Men hid behind trees while the rest of the crowd dispersed as fast as possible toward the streetcar and any of the hundred carriages parked on the outskirts of the park. People aware of the gravitational effects on bullets shot in the air did not want to be there when they returned to earth.

The officers present instructed the first sergeants to assemble the men. The first sergeants shouted the orders, "Fall In!" In the calamity of the moment, the men were slow to find their appropriate troops and line up. At about 9:30, some "rowdy" with a malicious sense of humor cut the electric wire leading from the street to the park and turning the area into complete darkness. The firing continued with even more ferocity. Men stepped onto the dance pavilion and fired into the roof. Others gathered into groups and fired in all directions over the heads of the crowd. The next day, Carl Beck commented, "I was in the Franco-Prussian War and saw some hot times, but I was about as uneasy last night as I ever was in battle."

A local reporter, unfriendly with the Rough Riders because his paper was banned from the camp, blamed the troopers for the "flagrant exhibition of rowdyism." This sparked a journalist duel with rival papers friendlier with the regiment. Lieutenant Hall pointed out that none of the regiment could have been responsible since all the regimental pistols and carbines were under guard back in camp. An examination of the ground the next morning revealed that the cartridges were blanks.

On Wednesday, the regiment completed its issue of pistols. The single-action .45-caliber Colt was a familiar sidearm. It was a "cowboy style" pistol for which experienced men knew how to fan the hammer while holding the trigger to fire six shots in rapid succession.

For some reason that week, Captain Capron was not pleased with the performance of Dillwyn Bell, of Guthrie, as the first sergeant and replaced him with Frank P. Hayes, of San Antonio. Hayes had served in the Regular Army. However, Bell remained a sergeant.

Evidently, the time waiting in Texas was wearing away at the discipline and patience of a few of the rowdier troopers. While well motivated to go to war, not all were angels. At 6 p.m., C.H. Thompson from Arizona became drunk and disorderly on Main Avenue. He pulled out a butcher knife and chased everyone off of the street. Six policemen arrived and surrounded him at the White Star Laundry. They wrestled him down and carried him struggling out of the laundry. While being taken along the street, he grabbed a buggy in which two ladies were riding and nearly upset it. He even managed to abuse one of the assistant marshals when they forced him into the jail. The next day, the judge fined him $100 for being drunk and disorderly.[58]

Friday provided a culmination of three weeks of training. At 8 a.m., all the troops but M Troop formed up in line, then turned their horses to the right and again marched out to the mission. They drilled for three hours. Upon their return to the fairgrounds, the regiment again formed into a single line of battle that stretched from the grandstand all the way over the hill to the south. The single line of 1,000 mounted men covered with dust rode across the campgrounds, then wheeled around the field several times by fours. Then the battle line was again formed, and Wood gave the order to his bugler to sound "Charge." The troopers spurred their horses into a gallop. A few mustangs still became excited and threw their riders. However, the First U.S. Volunteer Regiment of Cavalry, as a whole, had mastered every maneuver needed for war.

That afternoon, half the regiment drilled in extended order. After dinner, the regiment held a parade in front of grandstands to a crowd of 600 people. Regular Army officers marveled at how fast these former civilians shaped up into skilled cavalry men. Roosevelt was astonished at how well the men adapted to military discipline and at their attention to military duties. He believed that guard duty and policing speeded up the transition. Ira Hill wrote home, "Just what we expected; it won't take a year to make soldiers out of western breed boys."[59] The combination of a lifelong skill with horsemanship and the gun combined with a great motivation to succeed produced these exceptional results. The regiment was ready for war.

That third week also took a harder toll on the health of the regiment. On Tuesday, two troopers from M Troop succumbed to heat exhaustion. William Cross, of El Reno, also entered the hospital for measles. Ogden Wells had been battling fever off and on, but by Wednesday, he had a 105-degree temperature, so the regiment sent him to the hospital in Fort Sam Houston. The doctor recommended that he stay under their care for two more weeks. On Thursday, Ira Cochran, of E Troop, died of spinal meningitis. His body was attired in a full-dress uniform and laid in a handsome black casket. This was the first death in the regiment, and his troop provided a mounted escort for his funeral the next day. Chaplain Brown held the services at 2 Friday afternoon.

On the previous morning, May 26, General William Shafter, Commander of Fifth Corps in Tampa, had received a telegram breaking the suspense as to when his expedition would embark. Secretary Alger instructed him to load around 25,000 men, including four batteries of light artillery, eight siege guns and one squadron of mounted cavalry. The expedition would sail on a date depending upon news of the location of the Spanish fleet.

That Friday evening at 5 o'clock, Wood assembled his regiment. Roosevelt stood before the men and read the long-anticipated telegram. The regiment had to be able to move within 36 hours' notice. It had finally received its marching orders to deploy to Tampa. That narrowed their destination to either Cuba or Puerto Rico. The men let out a cheer which lasted for several minutes. Cashion, who had been sick since Sunday, all of a sudden felt better. Wood and Roosevelt embraced each other like schoolboys, and excitement filled the air the rest of the day. They were going to war!

Major Brodie remembered that in accordance with army regulations soldiers going to war needed to know the Articles of War. Early the next morning, the regiment lined up, fully uniformed, in squadron formation in front of Colonel Wood's tent. Brodie read the Articles of War to all the officers. They, in turn, read the Articles to their companies in a process that took an hour and a half. They then prepared the camp for rail movement.

At 10 a.m. Saturday, Charles Hummel, the local sporting goods dealer, accompanied by friends, stepped off of the Edison electric streetcar and made his way past the guard to Roosevelt's tent. After introductions, Hummel presented Roosevelt with a

Rough Riders breaking camp at San Antonio (Theodore Roosevelt Collection, Harvard University Library).

custom-made Winchester Model 1895 carbine and leather holster on behalf of the Winchester Arms Company of New Haven, Connecticut. Roosevelt thanked them and said that he would use the best way he knew how in avenging the *Maine*.

After breakfast Sunday morning, the men marched to the great Fair Building for religious services. Twenty Western tenors from the regiment sang as the choir while A Troop's Trumpeter Emilio Cassi, of Jerome, Arizona, played the music. Cassi had actually been born in Monaco, Spain, and prided himself on his skill with the trumpet. During one of Beck's nightly concerts, Cassi asked to demonstrate his talent with the coronet. The professor warned him, "Now if you make a break you will have to set them up to the band."[60] Cassi accepted and took his seat with the other musicians. He played a very difficult solo. Upon completion, Beck patted him on the shoulder and admitted, "You are all right." That Sunday, the men united their voices to sing "How Firm a Foundation." Arthur Perry, of Phoenix, Arizona, stood up and sang solo, "Onward, Christian Soldiers." The emotion of the moment, whether the singing or the thought of finally going to war, moved a number of men to tears.

They had joined something bigger than themselves. Emotions stirred high over the last three weeks as they rushed themselves through training. They brought their own motivation. Their officers and noncoms only had to show their men how to become soldiers. They were in the company of great men, and war would test their mettle. Yet a slight doubt had crept in as to if they would even get a chance to prove themselves. They had come one more step closer to going to war. At that time, they probably had no thoughts about their own mortality. They just did not want to miss the big adventure.

Paul Hunter wrote the *Guthrie Leader*, "One thing D troop is proud over, is our captain. He is without doubt the best in the regiment, and there is not a boy in the troop that does not obey his smallest wishes."[61]

CHAPTER 4

Tampa: Hell Won't Be So Crowded

Saturday afternoon Captain Huston gathered his men and instructed them to get their gear ready and go to bed early. The regiment would depart early the next morning. After supper, the cook packed up the field kitchen. Quartermaster Sergeant Hunter then issued each man three days' field rations of hardtack, canned beef and coffee to sustain them over the next three days. The men, however, were too excited to sleep.

Reveille sounded at 3 a.m. Sunday on the 29th. In the cool morning air, each man fixed his own breakfast, then struck his tent and rolled his few belongings into his bedding roll to sling over his shoulder. As a veteran campaigner, Wood had instructed the troops to take the minimum possible luggage. He permitted the troopers to take only what they could carry on their backs and the officers very little more. Everything else they had to leave behind. Several of the wealthier troopers made arrangements to send their wardrobes back home. With this act, they shed one more aspect of their privileged lifestyle. From that day forth, all Rough Riders would live pretty much the same.

After breakfast, they went over to the rope corral to find their assigned horses. By 8 a.m., they received the order to saddle and bridle their mounts. Shortly afterwards, the First Squadron mounted their horses in unison. A column of four troops in brown cotton duck rode through ankle-deep dust back to the same railyard they had arrived at three weeks earlier. Their transformation complete, they left a barren camp. Each squadron had policed its camp of trash and burned all refuse. Except for the trampled grass, Riverside Park took on the appearance it had three weeks earlier.

In three weeks, the regiment had taken shape. While other regiments crowded into various camps, the Rough Riders had trained separately from the corps with which it would fight. Aside from the initial inconvenience of delays in supplies, they had been responsible for much of their own preparation and did not have to suffer under layers of bureaucracy. That Sunday morning, they were about to join Major General William Shafter's Fifth Corps. At Tampa, they would experience inefficiency on a grand scale. While isolated at San Antonio, they had feared that they might be overlooked. Their isolation, as they would later witness, had been a blessing.

The men dismounted their horses to load them onto the awaiting trains. To their surprise, the transportation was not ready. The Quartermaster Department had contracted the Southern Pacific Railroad to provide the men, animals and baggage good accommodations. It would take seven separate locomotives to pull sections of 100 cars each. Upon the Rough Riders' arrival at the railyard, five sections were not ready, and the other two had not yet been switched to the yards. Again, the men waited. In the rush to go to war, "hurry up and wait" was something they would become more accustomed to.

The officers of the regimental staff and First Squadron found their sleeper car on a sidetrack. They took the opportunity to brush off some of the dust and clean up. It also served as a buffet car, so they sat down for a civilized lunch.

As the railroad men moved cars about on the tracks and buckled them together, the dusty men removed the saddles and tack and then loaded all equipment into the available baggage cars. Leaving a guard on each car, the officers of each troop picked a dozen men to let the horses eat and drink their fill. They then led their mounts up the planks onto designated stock cars. Including the 150 pack mules, the regiment loaded 1,200 animals.

At long last, some men began to board their assigned day coaches. To no surprise the accommodations did not turn out to be so accommodating. Nonetheless, the men willingly crowded into their passenger cars, tolerating any discomfort in order to go to war. The men would sleep anywhere they could: on the seats, on the floor or on top of their baggage. Some sections had sleeper cars for the officers. Roosevelt, however, gave his up for the sick. Men crowded together in camp had provided a haven for the spread of disease. Charles Nicholson, of K Troop from Baltimore, contracted measles. It did not take long to infect others.

Sunday, Ogden Wells woke with a 103-degree temperature and read in the paper that his regiment was leaving for Tampa that morning. The major in charge of his ward would not let him leave, so after the major stepped out, Ogden offered the male nurse $5 to give him his uniform. He then sneaked out the back and returned to camp. He discovered his squadron had already left with the first train. Roosevelt assigned him to I Troop for the passage. When he reported to Captain McGinnis, an orderly reported that the train had been delayed and would leave in a half an hour. With hopes of catching up with his own troop, Wells raced to Roosevelt to acquire a pass so he could leave the camp for the train station.

Wells took the electric trolley to the railroad crossing where he planned to walk three miles down the tracks to the stockyard where they loaded the horses. Suddenly, he heard the sound of a train whistle as it approached the crossing. He knew it would slow down at the crossing, so he sat down and waited. As the train slowed, Wells recognized Marcellus L. Newcomb, Fred N. Beal, both of Kingfisher, and Lorrin D. "Lon" Muxlow of Guthrie in the stock car containing their horses. He jumped onboard. When it reached the station, Wells reported to Captain Huston, who relieved him of all duties under his sick condition. His fellow troopers were glad to see him, and even though the passenger cars were crowded two troopers to a seat, they freed up two so he could lie down. Muxlow attended him as his nurse. He drifted off to sleep, and when he awoke around noon, his fever was gone.

The first three sections departed in intervals with Colonel Wood in the lead pulling out at 2 that afternoon. The three sections contained all of Brodie's First Squadron and part of the Second. D Troop's train pulled out at 3 p.m. The citizens of San Antonio sent them off with a heartfelt goodbye. The ladies bestowed flowers on the troopers until flowers filled their hands, their buttonholes and their hatbands and were pinned to their coats. As each section of train passed from street to street, the Rough Riders heard the cheers of "Boys, Remember the *Maine!*" The Texans sent these men from all over the country off to war as if they were their own adopted sons. As such, the Rough Riders had developed a special place in their hearts for Texas.

Roosevelt remained behind to load the last four sections as the cars became available. The railroad men challenged his patience with their inability to get the cars arranged and connected into sections. With his usual energy and zeal, Roosevelt took charge to couple the stock cars to the appropriate baggage car of each section. He then waited for the passenger cars.

The passenger cars did not arrive until after midnight. By that time those cavalry troopers, not directly involved in the loading, had wandered off. Most had found their way into the drinking establishments bordering the stockyards. Consequently, Roosevelt sent out search details and had the buglers blow "assembly." Once each first sergeant accounted for his men, they could load. At dawn, the remaining passenger cars finally arrived, and the men then boarded.

Roosevelt assigned a senior captain in each section to depart once he saw that he had enough cars for his horses, troopers and baggage. Each section departed at a staggered interval so it would have time to unload, feed and water the horses at the station before the next section arrived. The long delay waiting for the passenger cars, however, had given Wood's three sections a rather lengthy lead over the remaining four.

Roosevelt chose to follow in the last section and had Capron take charge of the section just ahead of his. This would allow them time enough to talk together at stops. Capron took his business of training men for war seriously. His energy, skill and mastery over men had thoroughly impressed Roosevelt. Capron quickly became one of Roosevelt's favorite officers. The last section left with Roosevelt on the morning of June 30, a full day after it was supposed to. Nonetheless, the entire regiment was finally on its way. The quartermaster contract required the connecting railroads to deliver the regiment to Tampa, Florida, in three days. There Shafter's Fifth Corps waited for embarkation.

Through every little town in Texas, people gathered to cheer the passing Rough Riders. The lead section of train pulled into the Southern Pacific and the Louisville and Nashville Railroad Station in New Orleans to a cheering crowd on the second day. This was the first long stop to feed and water the horses.

The officer in charge of each section would also load hay for the horses to eat while in transit. He had also been issued 21 cents per day per man in his section to purchase coffee at each stop. At the end of the trip, he would turn in his receipts to the quartermaster for accountability. The first section pulled out of New Orleans as the second section entered. This process continued with the arrival of the train section with D Troop. Roosevelt's section would not arrive until late that night.

This trip beheld many new sights for the Oklahoma boys. Some of the younger ones had never before seen the great Mississippi River. Citizens crowded enthusiastically at the depot to greet them. The newspapers had kept the nation abreast of every activity of the regiment to include its trip. That was fortunate for Theodore Westwood Miller.[1]

Teddy, a son of a prominent and wealthy family in Akron, Ohio, had graduated from Yale in 1897 and entered New York Law School the next year. The sinking of the USS *Maine* had spurred on his patriotic sentiments, but reason prevailed during the first call for volunteers. If he had enlisted then, he would have lost his college credits and had to take the whole year over again. He resolved to wait until the second call for volunteers.

This occurred on May 25, in time for Miller to complete his first year of law school. With his father's blessings, Miller was ready to enlist. That next day, a friend suggested that Miller should call on his childhood friend from Ohio, "Dade" Goodrich, for a vacancy in the celebrated Rough Riders. He did, and on Friday, May 27, he received a telegram from Lieutenant Goodrich that he had a place for Miller in his troop, but he had to hurry. The troops were quickly filling up to their authorized strength of 80 men with new recruits. Miller quickly secured his train tickets, ate a farewell lunch with his closest friends and then departed that night from New York. Upon his arrival at St. Louis, Missouri, he read that the Rough Riders were to depart San Antonio on Sunday. He would miss them in Texas, so he exchanged his ticket for New Orleans.

Miller arrived in New Orleans at 9 a.m. on June 30. Wearing a dress coat and derby hat, he stepped out of the passenger car into a crowd of people. He spotted men in brown canvas getting on and off of railcars. This had to be his regiment. He then pushed his way through the crowd, searching for any colleagues who had already enlisted in the Rough Riders that he might recognize. He stumbled onto Sumner Gerard from New York. "Jerry" was a sergeant in Troop C. As luck would have it, Miller had arrived at the same time as the train section carrying D Troop. Jerry escorted Teddy over to meet Dade.

Lieutenant Goodrich was busy seeing to the feeding and watering of the horses but was glad to see that his old friend had caught up with him. Dade introduced Miller to Captain Buckey O'Neill and Lieutenant Frank Frantz, also standing nearby. Evidently, A and D Troops shared the same train section. Dade received permission to escort Miller over to Surgeon La Motte for a quick physical examination in the smoking compartment of the sleeping car. Miller passed.

Dade caught him up on the past three weeks as he escorted him over to D Troop's baggage car. The lieutenant introduced Miller to two Harvard men, Corporal Harry Holt and Ogden Wells, and then returned to his official duties. In that car, Miller also met Quartermaster Sergeant Charley Hunter, Corporal Henry Love and George Burgess.

The Oklahoma boys were not exactly pleased to have another son of a millionaire in their troop. They were still sore that they had lost 12 of their own and had the fear that their troop would soon lose its identity as the Oklahoma Troop. Paul Hunter had written, "We don't care to trade any more Oklahoma boys for Fifth Avenue boys, not-withstanding their notoriety."[2] Making fun of their accents, he referred to the wealthy Easterners as "wough widers." They politely welcomed Miller, nonetheless. For the rest of the journey, Miller was assigned to the hospital car. It also served as the commissary car, so he had plenty to eat.

Time came to depart. Along the outskirts of the town, cheering citizens lined the tracks, and others waved handkerchiefs from the windows of their houses. One old lady stood by the track and shouted, "God bless you, boys," to each car that passed. As Miller became more comfortable with his new acquaintances, he took off his hat and coat. He then stood up to search the train to see if he could find some friendlier faces. As he walked from car to car, he found an old Harvard chum, Stanley Hollister, of Santa Barbara, California. They talked for a while. Stanley served in A Troop. Miller wrote that he continued walking around and recognized another old friend, Edward F. Burke. He was in the company of two other civilians, Robert D. "Bob" Wrenn, a Harvard champion tennis player from Chicago, and William A. "Bill" Larned, another tennis player from Summit, New Jersey. Their common bond as new recruits made them fast friends. Typically, original members of any military organization do not warm up to new arrivals, so the recruits instead bond with other recent arrivals. While not yet members of the regiment, they still felt "out of sight" to have a chance to join such a celebrated unit.

Captain Huston had assigned Wells to the baggage car where he could rest better. There he met four new volunteers: Teddy Miller, Bob Wrenn, Bill Larned and Edward F. "Teddy" Burke of Orange, New Jersey. After the train pulled out, Ogden's friend Harry Holt felt sick and also reported to the baggage car.

The rest of the Rough Riders entertained themselves during the long, slow train ride by playing cards, singing or watching the passing scenery. The country along the Gulf Coast little resembled the vast prairie or desert that most were accustomed to. They observed large lakes and rivers which gave way to vast swamps. Singing helped pass the time. Along the journey to Tampa, each car resonated with melodies. Adjutant Hall remembered "John Brown's Body" was the favorite of the enlisted men in the journey through the South. The officers preferred "On the Road to Mandalay" and "The Little Black Sheep." The popular game among men was, of course, cards. It tested one's ability to read his opponents, requiring great focus. As money changed hands, it was not a sport to be taken lightly. A couple of Oklahomans had already won enough money off of two millionaires to send their families on vacations to seaside summer resorts.

Roosevelt read Demolin's *Superiorite de Anglo-Saxons*. Demolin argued that the English-speaking people were superior to the continental Europeans because militarism had deadened the individual initiative. The regimentation of military training completely suppressed individual will and atrophied his faculties of the continental European so that the individual soldier could become a cog in a vast military machine. Intrigued by this French man's argument, Roosevelt saw the complete opposite in the American volunteer regiment. Judging more from his own limited experience on training grounds of Riverside Park, he envisioned that the very nature of war would require his individual initiative and challenge all his resourcefulness. This would prove true for him, but he had limited experience with the Regular Army. Upon arrival at Tampa, he would see firsthand the war machine of an Army Corps. At San Juan Hill, he would witness how a lifetime of discipline in the Regular Army would stifle individual initiative and resourcefulness among career professionals. Roosevelt was an ambitious, amateur soldier who would be uninhibited by the discipline to wait for or follow orders implicitly. Contrary to what Roosevelt thought, Demolin was probably not too far from the truth.

D Troop's section arrived in Mobile, Alabama, the next evening just before dark for a two-hour stop. The usual gathering of local citizens greeted them. Ladies came by offering each soldier a drink of coffee. Young ladies marveled at the men in uniform. One officer entertained no less than 13 young ladies. However, one of his fellow officers spoiled his fun by informing the ladies that the officer was married. They quickly retreated to find another object for their affection.

Alabamans likewise bestowed flowers and gifts on the Rough Riders who, in turn, gave them mementos. Buttons, cartridges and hardtack were probably the most popular souvenirs from the regiment. Hardtack was flour and water baked into a hard biscuit. The men preferred to trade their meager field rations for real food. In some cases, a trooper might trade a couple of pieces of hardtack for an entire cake, and both parties would end up happy for the trade. Young Roy Cashion had a whole seat full of flowers.

Others entertained the visiting Rough Riders. Two old Confederate soldiers took Captain Huston to a saloon, treated him to cigars and drink, then talked his arm off. Paul Hunter took in some sightseeing of the torpedo boats and several large ocean steamers along the docks. Cashion and his buddies visited the torpedo boat *Dupont*, which had returned for repairs from the Battle of Matanzas. The Rough Riders learned from the crew that the Spanish fleet was bottled up in Santiago Harbor.

Nonetheless, this activity had little effect on the card games in the lead section. The belle of the town walked between her father and mother along the depot surveying the spectacle of uniformed men. The description of her beauty preceded her as the three walked alongside each car. The officers gambling in the sleeping car stopped long enough to take a look at her, pressing the face of the cards against their shirts so as not to tip their hands. The young belle saw the cards and, looking for approval of her parents, said in disgust, "Well, I don't see how any good can come from men who would do that."[3] As soon as the trio had passed the window, she slyly looked back to the little group with a smile, then threw them a kiss. They then continued with their game.

The troopers received a warm welcome traveling through the South, but the bitter memory of the war Reconstruction still burned among some. Someone shot at the train D Troop, which was 15 miles outside of Mobile. It hit the window four seats in front of Cashion. The troopers also discovered that someone had hamstrung four of their horses. They would have to take them out and shoot them at the next stop.

D Troop's section later stopped at Pensacola, Florida, for only an hour after dark on June 1. Nothing significant happened worth noting. D Troop then stopped in Tallahassee for about five hours, long enough to unload the horses to water and feed them for the first time since New Orleans. The men noticed the dried appearance of the land. They learned that this part of Florida had not seen rain in six weeks. Regardless, farmers brought plenty of fruit, watermelons and other food to sell. Those in D Troop, not on watering detail, searched for food. The guards had strict orders not to let any of the men off of the train, but everyone was hungry. By Tallahassee, Florida, their meager rations had run out.

The troopers climbed out of the windows and went into town. Those without money loaded up with as much provisions as they could stuff in their blouses, while others occupied the storekeeper's attention with stories of cowboy life. Upon their return, Cashion and his buddies ran into Major Brodie. He pretended to be mad at them but winked to let them know how he really felt. He warned them that they should not come back by a route on which he could see them since it was his duty to keep them from town. He said as long as he did not see them, it was all right. Several of the troopers visited chicken houses and liberated a total of ten chickens and two geese. One of the Stewart boys caught a rooster and settled under a tree to cook their ill-gotten trophies into a chicken soup. Teddy Miller, still a civilian, had not yet been accepted into the company of the men of D Troop and was not offered any of the soup. They instead sent the remaining broth to the patients in the hospital car.

The number of infirm increased. Sergeant Gerald Webb and Corporal James M. Shockey, of Perry, had both become sick by then. Huston considered them his best noncommissioned officers. Huston meanwhile went into town to get a shave and purchase some milk and eggs for the two men. There Huston ran into the Randolph family, who escorted him around in their carriage. Huston penned a quick letter to his wife, and the time soon arrived to depart. They pulled out, expecting to reach Tampa the next morning.

By this time, each section had a feel for how far behind the next section was. By talking with the captain in charge of the section behind his, Wood learned that the last four sections had caught up to within an hour's interval between each section. His regiment would close together at Tampa within a day.

The officers in Wood's section thought it would be a fitting occasion to sing "Suwannee River" when they crossed that celebrated river on their journey. It soon became apparent that this would not occur until the wee hours of the morning. This did not deter F Troop's Lieutenant Horace W. Weakley of Santa Fe, New Mexico. He woke everyone up in spite of their protests just before reaching the so-named river in time to sing. D Troop's train crossed that river made famous by the song at 10 p.m. Cashion stayed up to see it.

The first section finally reached Tampa on the afternoon of June 2, four days after its departure, one day longer than they had rations and coffee money for. B Troop's Sergeant David L. Hughes of Tucson, Arizona, summed up the experience: "Luckily for most of the troops that a number of boys of financial means belonged to these troops or we would have fared very badly, as we were out of food for three or four days, and they would wire ahead to some town where we were booked to stop to feed the horses and ourselves, and have coffee, bread and canned goods delivered to us going through the South at little country town stops."[4]

The train stopped behind a jam of other railcars a couple of miles outside the Tampa depot. Wood stepped off the train and found no one there to meet him. He had telegraphed his estimated time of arrival to Fifth Corps Headquarters. He had no idea of where to find facilities to unload his horses or where to go into camp. The afternoon passed until Wood lost his patience and walked into town. His little problem at the rail depot represented only a fraction of the chaos that confronted Shafter's Fifth Corps.

Stevedores at the Port of Tampa had begun loading coal and water aboard a collection of 32 ships purchased or contracted by the U.S. Army almost immediately after Shafter received the May 26 telegram from Alger. They had completed this by the 31st, so Shafter sent a telegram to Alger the next day that he expected to have all supplies and troops loaded and ready to sail by June 4. General Nelson A. Miles, the Commanding General of the Army, and his staff arrived in Tampa the next day to assist. Shafter had been way too optimistic in his estimate. He had no full grasp of the complexity of the problem until his men started to unload the railcars.

Tampa had been selected as the port of embarkation because of its proximity to Cuba, without regard to its facilities. Traveling across the sea, distance was the least significant issue. Any major Gulf port like Mobile would have sufficed. Prior to that, the Port of Tampa had served mostly for tourists on day trips to Key West or Havana. Secretary of War Alger had little patience with the delays and constantly urged Shafter to hurry up.

As the immensity of the problem revealed itself, Shafter reported to Alger on June 4, "The main cause for the delay [of the invasion] has been the fact that great quantities of stores have been rushed in promiscuously and with no facilities to handle or store them."[5] That same day Miles also reported to the secretary of war that over 300 cars, loaded with war material, were backed up on the railroads around Tampa.

To compound matters even more, contractors in their haste to deliver their goods had failed to include invoices or bills of lading. No one knew where the needed supplies were until one opened each car and broke open the crates. In one case, an officer discovered badly needed uniforms for one regiment in 15 cars 25 miles outside Tampa. The soldiers had, consequently, suffered without proper clothing for several weeks.

Five thousand rifles were not discovered until June 3. For this reason, the recently arrived volunteer regiments had drilled without weapons. Most, including the Rough

Riders, did not receive their ammunition until just before they boarded the transports. Miles reported that as many as 300 men in one regiment had never even fired a gun before. Several of these volunteer regiments would go into combat. What Wood and Roosevelt had encountered with their own supply problems in San Antonio multiplied itself in Tampa.

A single track from Tampa led ten miles to the port. Morton F. Plant had built the railway as a real estate speculation venture. It was not designed to handle heavy traffic, so only one train could drop off its cargo at the port while others waited their turn in Tampa. To compound matters, the traffic of civilian spectators and freight had not slowed down. The military did not have control of the rail system, so it could neither regulate nor prioritize traffic. The situation simply did not allow Shafter to expedite the loading.

Neither could the single wharf handle the volume of traffic needed to load a Corps. The track fed onto a narrow strip of land dredged only on one side, which could berth eight vessels and another two along a pier built at the end. The dock had no material handling equipment, so stevedores had to carry around 10,000,000 pounds of rations on their backs across 50 feet of sand up an incline into the ships. Since receiving the telegram on May 26, stevedores worked day and night to load the transports. Many were so exhausted that they simply slept where they fell at the end of their shift.

None of this allowed for proper planning in the order of loading supplies. The variety of supplies needed to complete the load of one vessel were scattered on different cars of other trains. Consequently, a transport would have to pull out into the stream so that another could take its place at the dock to finish unloading the same train. This docking and redocking only increased the delay in loading. Alger, with little sympathy for Shafter and Miles's problem, responded on June 6, "Twenty thousand men ought to unload any number of cars and assorted contents." Alger's form of encouragement only compounded the problem instead of helping.[6]

The U.S. Army had not conducted an amphibious invasion of another country since Winfield Scott's invasion of Mexico in 1848. The last invasion by sea occurred during the Civil War, when Major General George B. McClellan invaded the Peninsula in 1862. No institutional knowledge remained on how to conduct such an operation. Anything the Army may have learned in the past, it had long since forgotten. Wood approached Shafter's headquarters at the Tampa Bay Hotel on the afternoon of the second, angered that no one had met him at the railway depot. His volunteer cavalry regiment was assigned to the cavalry division of Shafter's Fifth Army Corps, commanded by Major General Joseph Wheeler, former general of the Confederate Army.

Not more than 20 years before, the Union Army had occupied the South during Reconstruction. This created bitter resentment in the Southern states that would not heal until that generation had passed. Since the war would take place in the Caribbean Islands off the southern coast, it was only logical that the American army should stage in the Southern states. In order to relieve any impression that this was another army of occupation, President William McKinley recommissioned three former Confederate generals in the U.S. Army.

Joseph Wheeler had graduated from West Point in 1859 and served in the Regiment of Mounted Rifles in New Mexico where he earned the nickname "Fighting Joe" for his actions against hostile Indians. When his home state of Georgia seceded from the Union in 1860, he resigned his commission from the Army. During his career in the

MG Wheeler (front) with (from left) two unidentified majors of the Cavalry Division, Chaplain Brown, Col. Wood and Lt. Col. Roosevelt (NARA).

Confederate Army, this wiry young officer who stood five feet five inches and weighed 120 pounds distinguished himself as a cavalry commander. He rose to lieutenant general and fought most of the rearguard actions of the campaigns in the West. Federal troops finally captured him in May 1865 and paroled him two months later.

After the war, he married a wealthy widow and settled down to running a plantation in Alabama. During his spare time, he studied law and passed the Alabama bar, then ran for Congress in 1883. He lost his first bid for election but won on the second attempt. The citizens of Alabama had elected him to that seat seven times by the time the Spanish–American War broke out.

On the night of April 26, President McKinley wrote Wheeler a message that he would like to see him at 8:30 that evening in his office. Wheeler reported promptly. There he saw the Attorney General, Secretary of War Alger, ex-Congressman Thompson, Major Webb Hayes and Major Hastings. After pleasant small talk, the president asked Wheeler if he wanted to go to war and if he felt able to go. At 61, Wheeler felt like 40 or younger and replied that he would love another chance to serve his country. There was little doubt of his loyalty. His son, Joseph Wheeler, Jr., had recently graduated from West Point in 1895. McKinley said, "I have got to appoint 15 major-generals; and it would have given you great pleasure to have heard the pleasant things said about you while we were discussing the matter yesterday."[7] On May 2, Wheeler received his appointment from the War Department to the rank of major general of volunteers, which was confirmed by Congress on the 4th. He received his orders on May 9 to report to Camp George Thomas in Georgia. Wheeler packed his bags and reported on the 11th. The next day, he was assigned to command the cavalry division at Tampa. He hastened to the railroad depot and arrived at Tampa the next day. He was rejuvenated to be back in the saddle again.

Shortly after Wood had left the rail depot, several officers from the cavalry division headquarters rode over to the depot to see what was going on. Upon discovering the Rough Riders, they concluded that it was far too late to move them to their assigned camp, so the cars were pushed back to a corral on the suburbs of town. They selected a campsite to the left of the corral, and the men of the first section disembarked. They quickly unloaded the baggage into their temporary campsite. They just as quickly unloaded their horses and then picketed them to ground ropes stretched between the stumps of trees. Fortunately, the men had some hay and grain left over with which to feed their horses. The horses had not fared well on the journey and showed it.

Section after section arrived and repeated the same process. D Troop's section made a short stop in Dade County for water and then arrived in Tampa around 7 that evening where they similarly unloaded their baggage and horses. Teddy Miller was amazed at how the Easterners worked like beavers alongside their Western comrades. The distinction between rich and poor, Easterner and Westerner was blurring. By the time the men had reached Tampa, all had become Rough Riders.

Details worked through the night. Anyone who still had money went into town to eat. Miller and his three friends went in and had dinner at a small restaurant. They had not been sworn into the regiment, so they were officially still civilians. Every meal they took outside the camp they considered their last civilized meal. They returned on a streetcar to the temporary camp in time for breakfast. Finally, the last section arrived with Roosevelt.

That morning, the men located their mounts in the corral and then loaded

Rough Riders unloading horses at Tampa (Library of Congress).

Rough Riders erecting tents at Tampa (Theodore Roosevelt Collection, Harvard University Library).

what regimental baggage they could onto the pack mules. They reloaded their rations and any other equipment back on the cars under the supervision of Sergeant Madsen. They would send back wagon transportation to bring it up later. Lieutenant Weakley remained in charge of the guard detail.

The rest of the regiment formed up and rode in a column of fours the eight miles into Tampa. A New York infantry regiment, standing on freight cars, cheered wildly as they passed. Because of Roosevelt, the Rough Riders were celebrities among the New Yorker regiments. They continued past Shafter's headquarters at the Tampa Bay Hotel as reporters and officers came out to watch. They reached the cavalry division headquarters where Captain Matthew F. Steele came out and guided them to a sandy clearing in the pines just west of town. The area was absent of any palmetto brush with its sword-like leaves that covered much of the Florida landscape. Adjutant Hall knelt down and checked the ground and noticed a covering of black charcoal as if a fire had recently burned away the underbrush.

The regiment halted in a column of fours and then formed into a column of troops by squadrons. First Squadron lined up in the order of A, D, C and B Troops. Under the supervision of Wood, the men dismounted and stretched out their picket line to which they tied their horses. Bunkies then buttoned their shelter halves together and erected their dog tents along troop streets behind the officer's quarters with the kitchen at the other end. Ogden Wells and Harry Holt agreed to take Westerners as bunkies. Wells

Rough Rider tent and picket line (Theodore Roosevelt Collection, Harvard University Library).

Camp at Tampa (Theodore Roosevelt Collection, Harvard University Library).

fastened his shelter half with Muxlow. Lon had been a preacher, ranch hand and prospector. The field officers and headquarters, on the other hand, had left their larger tents back at the rail depot awaiting further transportation. Their position on the right flank of the camp was marked only by saddles and bridles. In short order, rows of white canvas tents gave all the appearances of a disciplined military camp. This was a direct result of good leadership.

Wood and Roosevelt contributed their own unique talents to the success of the regiment. Wood was the disciplined soldier tempered with a deep understanding of men. Through him the men quickly became soldiers. Roosevelt's personality provided the glue that bonded such a diverse group of men together. In the confusion of the days to follow, Roosevelt's personal energy and political clout would ensure the regiment would go to war.

When they arrived, Madsen still did not have a horse. He was left at the depot on foot. After the regiment rode off, a bell mare from some packtrain wandered back to him. He mounted it and caught up with the regiment before it reached its new camp. The mare became like a pet to Madsen. Once he fed it sugar, every morning she would stick her head in his tent for her breakfast treat of sugar. He finally found his mount.

There had been no water for the men and horses at the depot that morning. Neither was there any at the camp when they arrived. Colonel Wood and Quartermaster Schweizer set about hustling water and food for the men. Meanwhile, several officers with the financial means rode into town and purchased food for their men. The Regulars, camped nearby, saw the predicament of the Rough Riders and invited some of them over for meals until their rations arrived. Each troop would only send a few men over at a time so as not to put too much of a burden on the Regulars.

Wood and Schweizer did not locate any wagons until the afternoon. Then they sent them back to the depot for the rations. By the time the wagons arrived, the engineer on the train had received orders to move the cars since they blocked traffic. Lieutenant Weakley drew his revolver and in no polite terms convinced the engineer to wait. The wagons, loaded with food, consequently returned to Camp Alger late in the afternoon. Some of the baggage, however, still remained at the depot, so the field grade officers and headquarters staff had to sleep in the open under their horse blankets using their saddles for pillows.

The Rough Riders had their first day in camp off. The regiment went to Tampa Bay to go swimming. For many of the Westerners, this was their first time seeing the ocean and the curiosities in the water. Corporal Shockey, having just recovered from the hospital, and Forrest L. Cease, of Guthrie, were both stung by a stingray while in the surf, and they joined the other sick at the regimental field hospital. Unfortunately, they did not receive any better treatment in the field hospital than they would have resting in their own tent. They ate the same food as the rest of the camp. Any other food they received came from any extra money they had to buy food or what friends brought them. The surgeon administered to them the same pain medicine used to treat colds, rheumatism, sore throat or eyes, fever or any other illness. Needless to say, medical treatment was poor. To no surprise, Huston had been unfavorably impressed with Henry La Motte while back in Texas.

Meanwhile, Miller and his three civilian friends went to the Tampa Bay Hotel as soon as they were released. The Tampa Bay Hotel was an oriental Victorian brick structure that stood out among the wooden houses surrounding it. Another business venture of Morton Plant, it caused one cavalry officer to comment, "Only God knows why Plant built a hotel here, but thank God he did!"

That hotel provided the only decent place to reside. So it abounded with sightseers, war correspondents, artists, photographers, celebrities, foreign military attaches as well as Shafter's own staff. Everyone of importance was there. Presidential hopeful William Jennings Bryan had even accepted a colonelcy in an Illinois regiment to join the war effort in Tampa. Roosevelt's wife had also come down to stay there while he waited to go to war. The Tampa Bay Hotel was the center of activity and information. Those not busy with work lounged around in the numerous rocking chairs drinking lemonade.

Since William Randolph Hearst and Joseph Pulitzer had played a major hand in trumping up the war, they sent their best journalists to cover it. As the four young recruits entered the hotel, they saw war correspondents Richard Harding Davis and Caspar Whitney. Both recognized Bob Wrenn and let out a yell. Bob introduced them to his friend Teddy Miller. As the four prospective troopers worked their way through the crowd, Burke recognized a number of other acquaintances. Burke introduced Miller to the legendary artist Frederic Remington. That day, Miller rubbed shoulders with men he had only read about.

The four recruits finished their meals and then returned to camp. They tried to enlist, but no senior officers were available. So they spent the night with their respective troops sleeping in the open. Wrenn and Larned were assigned to A Troop, while Miller and Burke joined D Troop.

Roosevelt talking with Richard Harding Davis with Rough Rider camp in background (Library of Congress).

The sound of reveille woke everyone up at 4:30 a.m. Saturday the 4th. The Rough Riders ate breakfast and then began skirmish drill in the woods an hour later. At 9 a.m., they discontinued drill and set about doing the odd chores of camp fatigue. The regiment resumed its routine of drill four times a day and guard duty. They allowed the horses 36 hours to recover their strength from the long journey. Several had already died of distemper. Once the horses had rested, the troops would resume mounted drill and even conduct a few regimental drills. After drilling in the afternoon, the riders would unsaddle their mounts and then ride them bareback to the bay for a swim in the bay for about an hour. The horses seemed to enjoy the surf as much as the riders.

As the only volunteer cavalry regiment in the cavalry division, they camped adjacent to the Regular cavalry. The Regulars did little drill since they already had plenty of experience. Instead, they scrutinized the drill of the volunteers. The purpose of the drill did not serve as much to improve their skill as to refresh their memory. The unwanted attention by the Regulars, reporters and foreign military attaches caused its share of stage fright as the Rough Riders appeared to have forgotten much of what they had learned in Texas. It seemed the critical eye of spectators was more intimidating than the fear of going into battle. However, in a few days they were back to their regular form.

The Regulars seemed to live the life of luxury in comparison to the volunteers. Not only did they drill less, but they had their own bands. Every evening the band of each regiment would play a concert for its soldiers. The Rough Riders were surrounded by bands on all sides at night, and the men would drift off to sleep to popular tunes of the day.

Meanwhile, supply problems still persisted. One day, Madsen reported to the Depot Quartermaster for some equipment that his regiment still needed. The captain turned the old sergeant down and told him that the Regulars had to be outfitted first, and the volunteers could have anything that was left over. It did not matter to Madsen that the volunteers were low on the priority of issue, but the way in which the officer had said it insulted him. Madsen remembered having to show that same officer where to sign his name on forms when he was a lieutenant fresh out of West Point.[8]

Madsen reported the incident to Roosevelt, who then wrote out a long telegram to the president. He told Madsen to take it to the telegraph office and wait for an answer.

When he handed it to the telegraph operator, the latter told him to return in a week. It seemed that every officer had sent a telegram to the president, and few received replies. So Chris walked around town, then returned to find an answer waiting for him. The old sergeant took it to the quartermaster and told him to read it. The unimpressed captain replied that anyone could write a telegram, and he did not plan to pay any attention to it until someone verified it.

After Madsen told him the response, Roosevelt ordered Chris onto his horse, and the two paid a visit to Major General John J. Coppinger, the commander

Roosevelt's tent at Tampa (Theodore Roosevelt Collection, Harvard University Library).

of troops. Roosevelt was not about to let anything or anyone prevent his regiment from going to war. Chris did not listen in on the conversation but talked with the chief clerk who had been a sergeant with him in his old company. The old supply sergeant seemed to have friends everywhere in the Army. No wonder he was good. After the conversation ended, the general sent his aide with them to visit the quartermaster. From that time on, Madsen had no trouble getting anything he wanted for his regiment. Roy Cashion wrote home, "We joined the right regiment when we joined this, as Roosevelt can take us most anywhere he wants to."[9]

Water pipes did not extend into the Rough Riders' camp until the night of June 4. Earlier details had to escort the horses to the troughs of the Regulars. After the pipes were installed, the Rough Riders had plenty of water for their animals and field kitchens.

On the morning of the 4th, Roosevelt finally administered to Miller and his civilian friends their oaths of enlistment. Upon completion, they asked permission to go back to the hotel for one more square meal. As they entered the crowded hall, they ran into Wood, Roosevelt and General Miles, with whom they had a pleasant conversation. None of these officers had any air of superiority over the enlisted men but treated them with dignity. After getting their personal property in order, the four privates returned to camp at 5 that evening to receive an issue of a pup tent and blankets for them to sleep in that night.

Another late arrival to enlist in D Troop was 24-year-old, red-headed William Franklin Knox from Grand Rapids, Michigan. Unlike the others, Frank did not come from a wealthy family. His father ran a grocery store. Frank had delivered papers at the age of 11, and then after high school, he left home to work as a shipping clerk for $5 a week. He lost that job during the Depression of 1893 and returned home to work as a grocery clerk for $2 a week. He then earned less than a private's wages in the Army. At the recommendation of the Rev. Thomas G. Smith, Frank entered A.B. Alma College in Michigan, although he only had completed three years of high school. Through hard work, he paid his way through college while earning good grades and distinguishing himself on the football field. The war broke out during his last year.

Frank rode his bicycle 60 miles to Camp Eaton, Michigan, and talked with Captain John L. Boer. Frank decided to enlist in Boer's Company E, Thirty-Second Michigan Volunteer Infantry. The captain asked if there were any other

Chaplain Brown giving services at Tampa (author's collection).

Alma boys like Knox who would enlist. Frank pedaled back to his college that same day and recruited 15 of his friends. On the day that they were sworn in, Frank had to return home because of an illness in the family. Determined not to miss the war, he returned and accompanied the company to Tampa with no more status than a camp follower. He could take his oath of enlistment later. While in Tampa, Frank realized that the Rough Riders had a greater probability of going to war than his regiment. So he walked over and talked to an old acquaintance from St. Joseph, Ogden Wells. Wells had just returned from a bath, a large bowl of soup and milk at the Tampa Bay Hotel that Friday.

Frank admitted he had been in Tampa with the Thirty-Second Michigan but would like to join the Rough Riders. He added that he could ride and shoot. "Gosh, you're lucky to get into this famous regiment, with horses to ride and a great chance to get into action early." Frank Knox asked, "What do you think of my chances of getting in with you?" Wells replied, "I do not see how you can transfer, but maybe it could be worked." With that Frank confessed, "I'm not on the rolls of my company because I was absent when they were sworn in and I'm just a camp follower, more or less." Frank remembered Odgen responded, "Well, I'll take you to Dave Goodrich, lieutenant of our troop. He was a Harvard crew captain and knows Roosevelt. If anybody can fix it he can. The Colonel has just promoted him from the ranks of B Troop." Ogden wrote in his diary that he would speak to Roosevelt.[10]

As promised, Wells talked to Roosevelt about Knox. Roosevelt admitted he still had nine vacancies to fill and wanted to reserve them for Regulars if possible. He then told Wells to bring Knox around the next morning. Saturday morning, June 4, Roosevelt interviewed the hardy young Knox about his college and sports. Roosevelt was impressed and said, "You'll do. Hold up your right hand." Frank Knox became a trooper in D Troop. Frank drew his brown uniform, revolver and unruly bronco and then rode back to his Michigan camp to turn in his infantry issue. His friends were envious of his new status. Wells and Muxlow made room in their tent for Knox. The two Harvard men liked to sit around and discuss literature.

On Sunday morning of June 5, First Sergeant Palmer assigned the duties for the day. Miller and Burke heard their names called out for stable police duty. They were finally in the army. Palmer also reminded the troop that Chaplain Brown would hold services under the pines at 9 a.m. He also announced that no one could leave the camp without the permission of their captain.

Chaplain Brown ascended the pulpit made of a bale of hay under the shade of a large pine tree precisely at 9 a.m. A large portion of the men and all the officers attended. He opened the service with "My Country 'tis of Thee." Brown delivered an able and instructive sermon from his text, "Put ye in the sickle for the harvest is ripe," then closed with the hymn, "God be with you 'till we meet again."

No one drilled on Sunday. During their time off, the Rough Riders played a football game since they had a number of college athletes. James Hamilton, of Deming, New Mexico, had just returned from town as Major Hersey's orderly. A big man, he could not resist getting into the game. During a play, he jumped to tackle William Ricketts, of Phoenix, Arizona, and Charles E. McPherren, of Caddo, Indian Territory, who had played for the University of Pennsylvania. Hamilton had unfortunately forgotten to take off his spurs before entering the game, subsequently wounding the others in the fray. Otherwise, the rest of the men just sat around and talked.

Rumors abounded throughout Camp Alger almost immediately upon arrival. There was talk that only one squadron would get to sail, and then it increased to two. One rumor had it that only 50 men from each troop would get to go while the remainder stayed to guard horses. The main topic of conversation during those first few days in Tampa was who would go. The Regulars often teased the volunteers that they would not get to go at all. After all their fears in Texas of being left behind, their arrival in Tampa did not assuage that anxiety. As with any rumors, they developed out of events unfolding at the docks and conversations around the Tampa Bay Hotel.

H Troop preparing for mounted drill (author's collection).

By May 31, coal and water had been loaded upon the transports. The next day, Colonel John F. Weston, chief of commissary, had been directed to load enough rations for 20,000 men for six months. Because of the delays and the need for haste, Shafter reduced this order to two months of rations.

Loading continued. The wagons and guns of the light artillery began loading on June 1, the day before the Rough Riders had arrived. The siege guns and their ammunition were not located until June 4 and then not assembled until that evening. The stevedores had loaded the rations, ammunition, forage, wagon transportation, medical supplies and animals by 11 a.m. on June 6. Shafter then gave the order at noon for troops to begin boarding, but transportation would not deliver the first troops until 2:30 a.m. on the next day. To expedite the matter of loading troops, transports would moor two abreast. Shafter had discovered on June 1 that, by some miscalculation, the fleet of 32 transports which was supposed to accommodate 27,000 troops could only carry 18,000 to 20,000. It became clearly evident that some of the units would have to remain.

Alger's May 26 orders also stated that he could only take one mounted squadron of cavalry. That honor fell to Major William A. Rafferty's squadron of the Second Cavalry. Even with the original capacity for troops, Shafter did not have room for more horses. His corps included 13 regiments of volunteers. The order did state that he could take dismounted cavalry as infantry in lieu of untrained volunteers. He had five regiments of Regular cavalry and considered the First U.S. Volunteer Cavalry a unit which showed great promise. He believed that the Regular cavalry would fight better as infantry than the volunteer infantry.

Remington, a longtime fan of the cavalry, saw Miles sitting at the hotel. Thinking it a great misuse of the cavalry to not take their horses, he asked, "General, I wonder who is responsible for this order dismounting the cavalry?" Miles looked up from a note and asked, "Why, don't they want to go?" He had probably heard that complaint before. A little taken aback, Remington responded, "Oh yes, of course! They would go if they had to walk on their hands!" With that he retreated whence he came.[11]

Shafter's Corps included 16 regiments of Regular infantry, five regiments of Regular cavalry, a company of engineers, four light artillery batteries and two heavy batteries. The only volunteer regiments that Shafter included were the Second Massachusetts Volunteer Infantry, the Seventy-First New York Volunteer Infantry and the Rough Riders. The Rough Riders would have to go dismounted, and David Hughes later wrote, "that almost took the starch out of the boys. We had been planning things we would pull off on the Spaniards on our horses and as a cowboy is almost as helpless on foot as a fish is out of water."[12]

Not only did the decision to leave their horses come as a blow, but the worst of the rumors proved true. The first report allowed only one squadron of each regiment to go. The disappointing news later came at noon on Monday, June 6, that only three troops would go aboard ship. The Rough Rider camp was all astir. Wood went to meet with Shafter to fight for more. Huston anguished in a letter to his wife over whether his troop would even get to go. He had worked hard to make them the best troop in the regiment. In his mind, he must have known that Roosevelt clearly favored Capron and O'Neill. While Huston was penning his worries, Brodie walked into his tent and informed him that eight troops could go. Shafter had increased the number of squadrons to two. One squadron of four troops, and the packtrain would remain in Tampa. Wood and Roosevelt's decision as to who would remain seemed to have been made by what would have been fair to each of the territories as well as which troops were the best.[13]

Of the Arizona troops, Wood initially decided to leave behind James McClintock's B Troop. Upon hearing the news, Lieutenant Tom Rynning rushed to Colonel Wood as fast as he could. Wood confirmed the rumor that Rynning's troop was to remain behind and cited insufficient drill as the reason. Captain James McClintock, commander of B Troop, had seniority over Captain Joseph Alexander of C Troop. Rynning challenged Wood on that point and claimed that his troop was as well drilled as any other. Wood confided in secret that there was another reason. Rynning protested that he was going to resign and enlist as a private in O'Neill's A Troop. Wood scolded the lieutenant: "That's no way to talk! A good soldier is supposed to perform whatever duty may be assigned to him."[14] Rynning did not back down. He added that Wood would need every experienced veteran he had. Wood told him to drop the issue for the time. Within an hour, Wood announced that C Troop would remain behind instead of B Troop.

From the New Mexico squadron, Wood selected William Llewellyn's G Troop and Muller's E Troop to go. Wood called Captain Max Luna and George Curry to break the bad news. Wood, Capron and the squadron commanders were standing under a large pine tree when the two captains arrived. Wood informed them, "I am sorry I cannot take you both, but I must leave one of your troops here." Luna protested to Wood and Hersey not to leave his command. As the only officer of pure Spanish blood in the Army and with most of his men having Spanish blood in their veins, he demanded the privilege of proving in a war with Spain that his race was as loyal to the United States as any other. It was a sound argument.

The First U.S. Volunteer Cavalry represented an almost entirely integrated regiment in a time when the Army segregated African Americans, Indians and Whites into separate regiments. Men of different ethnic backgrounds and extremes of the social spectrum would fight side by side. Luna's appeal made sense to Wood, but it was Capron who suggested a solution. He recommended that Luna and Curry toss a quarter to see who would get to go. Luckily, Luna's F Troop won the toss. So Curry's H Troop agreed to remain behind. He later told a friend, "I felt bad in having to stay behind, especially on account of my men, all of whom were eager to see action. It was orders. There was nothing we could do."[15]

The two troops of the Indian Territory had arrived a week later than the others and had the least amount of training. Clearly, Capron had impressed Roosevelt in his ability to train up his troop in the short time. His L Troop would go instead of M Troop. Since the Oklahoma Territory had provided only one troop and had earned the honor of being the color troop, it was included on the list to go. Only one other troop had to remain behind.

The two troops recruited from millionaires were the last formed and the least trained of the regiment. It was obvious that Wood would not leave behind the Colt rapid-fire guns. His was the only regiment with automatic weapons. Sergeant Tiffany and his guns had a guaranteed place on the troop transport for Micah Jenkin's K Troop. This troop included the 12 men from Oklahoma. In a way, this could be construed as the only case where the millionaires had bought their way into the war. Tiffany, to his credit, could have never known this ahead of time. The cost, unbeknownst to him, would prove higher than he could have perceived. Instead, I Troop would stay behind. Schuyler McGinnis's promotion to captain cost him participation in the war. His old D Troop with its two Yankee lieutenants would see action instead.

Lieutenant Colonel Roosevelt and Major Brodie, the two senior field grade officers, would command the two squadrons. Majors Hersey and Dunn would stay with the squadron left behind. Hersey was particularly grieved as he had brought from New Mexico the largest contingent of troops. The decision was based clearly upon seniority and military experience.

For those selected to go, there was great celebration. Roosevelt also remembered what a great disappointment it was for those selected to stay and that more than one officer broke down in tears. Others were speechless with disappointment. Everyone had made tremendous sacrifices to join this regiment. To have come this far and not get to go to war would for many be a big disappointment for the rest of their lives. Many who did go to war would never be the same afterwards. Many of those left behind would regret that they would never know the experience.

In presenting the unfortunate news, Wood and Roosevelt stated that those who stayed behind were entitled to the same honor as those who went. Each man was doing his duty and "the hardest and most disagreeable duty was to stay."[16] Credit should go to those who performed their duty regardless of what it was and not to accidental valor in combat. Interestingly, one of the most decorated men in the U.S. Army would rise out of the ranks of those left behind. No telling how the others would have performed. Only a handful of brave ever find themselves in the circumstances to prove their valor. None of this alleviated the sadness of those left behind. As far as Roosevelt was concerned, every Rough Rider went to Cuba, and he would not refer to anyone otherwise. He and Wood believed that the rest of the dismounted regiment would follow later as more transports became available.

Capt. Capron and Capt. Bruce (courtesy Oklahoma Historical Society).

This was not the end of the bad news. Each troop could only take 70 men. By then D Troop had a total of 90 officers and men. Those who remained would guard the horses of their troop. Men quickly jockeyed for positions to go.[17]

That same day, Dade Goodrich had hustled Miller and Burke around to get them clothed and equipped. By 4 in the afternoon they still had very little. Burke and Miller talked it over and agreed that if only one of them could go, Miller would go. At five, Captain Huston called a formation to see who had all their equipment. Only 69 answered the roll. Huston turned to those standing aside: "If any man can find a gun, he may go."[18]

Quickly, Teddy Miller remembered where Saddler Dick Amrine had left his carbine. As the saddler, Amrine had to stay with the horses. By that logic, Wagoner Lon Muxlow would have also remained. Miller "rustled" Amrine's carbine and reported to his commander. Just as quick, Amrine came up to reclaim his firearm. Miller returned it to him.

To his surprise, Huston said he could take the place of a weaker soldier. Miller had a great sense of fairness. He did not want to wrestle with his conscience for taking advantage of anyone. He passed the privilege off on another trooper who he felt had a better right to go. Miller had only been in the troop a few days. Miller did not want to do any man injury by stealing his rightful place. The other man reported to his captain, and, upon learning he could go, jumped in the air yelling. Because of his sense of fairness, it looked like Miller would not get to go.

The next day, Huston walked up to Miller and handed him a carbine and cartridge belt. They belonged to a trooper who had fallen asleep on guard duty the night before. Goodrich wrote Miller's mother that Huston ordered Miller to take the man's place. He was going to war! His friend Dade Goodrich had some influence in this.

Later that day, Miller was sitting under a tree with his friend Burke, Corporals Holt and Simpson and others when Lieutenant Carr walked over. He told them that Henry S. Crosley had to go back home to Guthrie on account of the expected death of his ailing wife. The muster-out roster, however, lists Crosley as a deserter, discharged on July 8. Teddy Burke would take his place. While on sentry duty one night, a corporal relieved Frank Knox, telling him to report to Sergeant Ira Hill. Hill informed Knox to get his gear ready, that he was going with the troop. Knox originally had been selected to remain behind. Dade Goodrich had been a little anxious himself because he had heard an order that the second lieutenant of each troop would stay behind in charge of the horse detail. His spirits lifted when the order was rescinded. The recent recruits had not undergone any military training. However, their college status had considerable influence as many who had trained with the troop all through Texas would remain behind.

The sick would obviously not go. William Tauer and Jacob Haynes happened to be sick in the hospital, so they also remained. In fact, quite a number of men were coming down with malaria. Forty-five out of 83 men in C Troop would not be able to travel to New York the next month because of the illness. Neither had Shockey and Cease recovered from their injuries. Cease later became sick with malaria. Shockey's pain and health grew worse daily. Not only would he remain behind, but he wrote a letter on June 9 to Captain Huston pleading with him to help him get out of the Army so he could go home and seek better treatment. He received his discharge on July 1. Arthur A. Luther, for some reason, was discharged the same day. He most likely numbered among those left behind. Paul Hunter wrote that seven of the men who had enlisted at San Antonio also remained to guard the horses. Second Lieutenant Hal Sayre, Jr., of C Troop assumed command of the remnants of A and D Troops. He was a Pudding man from Harvard who hailed from Denver, Colorado.

Some men in the troops left behind immediately sought transfers to other troops, especially the swells. Sergeant Ham Fish was not about to remain behind. He asked for a transfer into L Troop. He had as much admiration for Capron as the captain had for him. Capron made Fish the sergeant of a squad from Muskogee, Indian Territory. Fish's reputation could not allow him to stay behind. Some may have seen him as a bully for he was intimidated by no man. Those may have asked whether he would be just as brave under fire. For this reason, he had to go. Of all the millionaires, Ham felt that he had the most at stake. He was a hero on the field of sports, and he had to prove himself a hero on the field of battle.

Rough Riders loading ammunition in cartridge belts (author's collection).

On Wednesday, June 6, infantry men came over to show the cavalry troopers how to roll bedrolls into packs. They would lay the shelter half on the ground, put the blanket on top of it and then extra clothing and other articles rolled up inside and the ends folded together in the shape of a horse collar or horseshoe. They would wear it over their left shoulder and under their right arm. They would also hang their mess kit and tin cup on the saber hooks of their cartridge belts. With the exception of their carbines, they would look and fight like infantrymen.[19]

Just before leaving, Shafter sent word for the Rough Riders to assume responsibility for the dynamite gun bought by Khedive of Egypt. This artillery piece would propel sticks of dynamite at the enemy. Both the dynamite gun and Colts were cumbersome and could only be used in the defense. This tasking fortunately allowed a few more men to go. Wood appointed Hallett Borrowe the acting sergeant in charge of the dynamite gun and Sergeant William R. Reber his assistant. Both came from McGinnis's I Troop.[20]

With the selection complete, there remained one more task. Normally soldiers were scheduled to be paid every two months. For the Rough Riders, payday should have occurred upon their arrival. Unfortunately, the paymaster had run out of money by the time they arrived, and the Rough Riders might sail before more arrived. Most of the men who previously had any money, aside from the millionaires, had already spent it by then. Even Huston was broke. His wife pleaded with him regularly for money as his bills still accumulated during his absence. Embarrassingly, she had to borrow money from relatives.

Wood and Roosevelt talked with the paymaster about their predicament and learned a way that he could secure enough funds to pay the regiment for one month's service. The regiment would have to pay the cost to transfer the money by telegraph. In a few minutes, the officers with money had collected the required amount. Again, the wealthy members of the regiment came to its rescue. On the evening of June 7, the Rough Riders marched two miles to the grounds of the Tampa Bay Hotel to receive one month's pay.

Meanwhile, the men made preparations to depart. Huston could find no time to mail his pay to Vite. Instead, he trusted Lieutenant Sayre to mail the money since he would remain behind. First Sergeant Palmer assigned both Miller and Burke to guard duty while the troop waited to depart. Of the 12 posts around the troop camp, Miller guarded Post Number 8 right next to C Troop. That evening Miller could hear celebration all over the rest of the camp, but it was very quiet in C Troop since they would remain behind.

At 1 p.m. on the 7th, they had received their first order to strike tents and prepare to embark. They would board a transport that night with destination unknown. Huston guessed that they were bound for Puerto Rico. The level of excitement increased. It turned out to be the first of several false alarms during the day.

That day, Alger sent a telegram to Shafter to sail immediately. The Navy had prompted this urgency. The fleet had assembled at Key West on June 7 to escort the expedition. Admiral William T. Sampson had also sent an optimistic telegram to the president, stating, "Bombarded forts at Santiago 7:30 to 10 a. m. to-day, June 6. Have silenced works quickly without injury of any kind, though stationed 2,000 yards. If 10,000 men were here, city and fleet would be ours within 48 hours."[21] All delay of ending this war seemed to be placed squarely on the shoulders of Shafter. This overly optimistic message would have dire consequences for the soldiers. Fifth Corps had to stop loading supplies and equipment and sail with what it had.

The first regiments began boarding the transports that afternoon. However, the confusion of moving troops to the docks and boarding them on the transports resembled the same confusion as occurred with the supplies. There were not enough trains to move everyone in sufficient time. Alger lost his patience with the slow progress and sent a telegram at 8:50 in the evening: "Since telegraphing you an hour since, the President directs you to sail at once with what force you have already."[22] Shafter sent word that

D Troop, 1st USVC as dismounted cavalry with horse collar bedrolls. Pollock is seen standing seventh from the left (Fort Sam Houston Museum).

each regiment had to find its own transportation to the dock, or the transports would sail the next morning without them.

Regiments overlooked no means to get to the port and not be left behind. The Ninth Infantry stole wagon trains from the Sixth Infantry. The Seventy-First New York sent out an advance party to find any transportation. At about 11:30 that evening, they heard a train coming up the track which was for the Thirteenth Infantry. They captured and held it at bayonet point until the rest of their regiment joined them. By 8 in the morning, the Thirteenth had located an empty train of cattle cars. With a little searching, they found a locomotive, then woke up an engineer, and by 10:30 in the morning, they had reached the pier.

At 9 nine that night, an officer from Shafter's staff informed Wheeler of Alger's order and that cars would be ready at 11 to take his cavalry division the nine miles to the Port of Tampa.[23] That same warning had reached the Rough Riders at 10 o'clock. The men selected to go lined up by troops in the light of the moon. They stood in brown cotton duck, red bandannas around their necks and tan broad-brimmed hats. They wore "horse collar" blanket rolls, canteens and haversacks over their shoulders like the infantry. They marched over to the railroad and unloaded their wagons. The men could see off in the distance other trains backing down and cavalry regiments loading. One officer of the Regular cavalry passed by and remarked with a sneer, "Oh you needn't worry. Your regiment is not going. You're not wanted."[24] There seemed to be no end to the fear of being left behind.

The unloading had not quite finished when word came that they would embark on another track. The work stopped; then the men lay down on their equipment and slept while Wood, Roosevelt and several other officers wandered about seeking information. They even questioned general officers, yet no one knew anything about their train. The remaining officers stayed awake, smoked and talked. They were beginning to get nervous, fearing that they might actually by accident be left behind.

At 3 a.m., they received orders to march back to an entirely different track, also crowded with infantry. They reloaded the supplies on the wagons which had arrived at the new track just before daylight. When reveille woke those left behind, they saw their comrades a short distance away, still waiting. The four troops prepared coffee and brought it over to their comrades.

By coincidence, the Fifth Cavalry also marched by. It was the very same regiment which had left the Rough Riders at Fort Sam Houston thinking it would go to war first. It had just arrived from Mobile, Alabama, and now feared missing the boat. The night before, the Second Cavalry Regiment had also arrived from Mobile and went into camp just north of the Rough Riders. Several Regular Army regiments had been delayed at Mobile while waiting for transports. It appeared that not enough regiments would go to war because of poor planning and coordination coupled with the urgency of the secretary of war, who had no grasp of the complexity of the situation.

The transportation was as fouled up as everything else. Roosevelt had not come this far to miss the war. It became clearly evident that the Rough Riders would have to hustle their transportation like they had everything else in Tampa. At 6, a train of coal cars came by heading away from the port. By various means of persuasion, Wood and Roosevelt convinced the engineer to back the train to the port with their men inside. Along the way, they passed the Seventy-First New York in a train going the

Rough Riders waiting for train to take them to port of Tampa (Theodore Roosevelt Collection, Harvard University Library).

K Troop riding coal cars to the port (Theodore Roosevelt Collection, Harvard University Library).

Port of Tampa (U.S. Army Transportation Museum).

same direction. The New Yorkers yelled to Roosevelt standing on one of the baggage cars occupied by the officers, "Show us your teeth, Teddy!" Roosevelt, standing in the door in his khaki uniform and blue polka-dot bandanna, bowed. Everyone laughed. Covered in coal dust the Rough Riders reached the pier at 10 a.m. After all the fears of being left behind, the Rough Riders had finally reached the pier. Their all-night marching and countermarching jokingly earned them the new name, "Wood's Weary Walkers."[25]

Again, there was no order to the chaos on the pier. Railcars lined one side of the pier and transports the other. Men and supplies crowded the space in between. K Troop's Sergeant Thaddeus Higgins, of New York City, eloquently described the scene: "Hell won't be so crowded on the last day than this dock is now."[26]

The trains unloaded their passengers and equipment wherever they stopped without regard to the location of the vessel to which the soldiers might board. While the men unloaded the equipment, Wood and Roosevelt immediately set out to find which transport was theirs. They asked everyone from the highest general down, and no one seemed to have the answer. Someone suggested that Colonel Charles F. Humphreys, the Depot Quartermaster, might know.

They located his office and inquired as to his whereabouts. His assistant did not know but thought he might be asleep aboard one of the transports. The two officers then returned to the crowd of soldiers on the dock in their search for Humphreys. After an hour's search, the two separated but located the elusive quartermaster at about the same

Soldiers arriving at the Port of Tampa (U.S. Army Transportation Museum).

time. From him they learned that the Rough Riders would sail on the *Yucatan*. She was a fast ship commanded by Captain Robinson that could do 16 knots.

Roosevelt also learned that she had also been allotted to both the Second Infantry and the Seventy-First New York. Each transport had a capacity of 750 men. The Seventy-First had more men than that. There were not enough transports for all the men at the dock. The race was not over.

They also learned that the *Yucatan* waited out in the bay. Roosevelt ran full speed back to his men. He gave them about nine minutes to gather up what they could carry, then rushed them at double-time a half mile to the other end of the quay where the *Yucatan* would dock. He left a guard on the baggage. Meanwhile, Wood commandeered

Rough Riders waiting to board transport (U.S. Army Transportation Museum).

a stray launch with 11 of his men and Surgeon La Motte and steered it to the transport with the number "8" painted in white on it. They took possession of the *Yucatan* and forced it to the quay just as Roosevelt arrived with his two squadrons. Again, they waited. They stood in the burning, hot sun while someone erected the gangplank. Ben Colbert recorded that the weather must have been 100 degrees in the shade. Most important, the Rough Riders had taken physical possession of the transport by the time the two other regiments arrived.

Only enough room remained for four companies of the Second to board. The rest, along with the Seventy-First, had to find other transports. Fortunately for them, they found adequate room aboard other ships. The Seventy-First loaded onto Transport Number 23, the *Vigilancia*. The rest of the Second was split between Number 32, the *Clinton,* and Number 18, the *San Marcos.*

For the rest of the day, the Rough Riders walked the half mile distance back to their baggage, food and ammunition, which they carried the same distance back to load aboard the ship. They finished loading by the end of the day. Exhausted and hungry, most had not eaten since the day before. With everything loaded, they could finally relax.

As darkness fell at 7:30 that evening, the *Yucatan* weighed anchor. Paul Hunter wrote home, "as the big ship began to move slowly around the boys felt for the first time that at last we were about to start on the long looked for voyage."[27] After all the earlier fears, most of the men attributed that but for the untiring efforts of Roosevelt, they would have been left behind. In their minds, there was no turning back now.

The *Yucatan* anchored in midstream, eighth in the line according to its number. Each of the 32 vessels anchored 800 yards apart, forming a line of transports 20,000 yards long. The adventurous Roy Cashion climbed to the top of the 120-foot mast and surveyed the scene around him. He wrote, "It is the grandest sight I have ever seen!" For him everything was new and a learning experience. They waited for orders to sail.[28]

As soon as he had unloaded all the supplies, Madsen returned to camp. He would not go with the first expedition but instead get the rest of the troops and horses ready to deploy with the next. Wood and Roosevelt's horses were loaded on another vessel.

Accommodations on board ship were cramped. A little over 1,000 men crowded into a vessel designed to hold 750. The transport had three decks. Ammunition and supplies were stored in the lower deck. Bags of oats, hay, coal and water filled part of the hold. The crudest of bunks had been hastily constructed for the men in the hold with little room between them. The heat down there was almost unbearable. The officers, fortunately, were assigned to more comfortable quarters in the state rooms. Wood, seeing the problem of overcrowding and poor ventilation, assigned as many men as possible to sleep on the deck. At night, it became almost impossible to walk about without stepping on bodies. One trooper hung a sign, "Standing Room Only." Not too much later another added, "And damn little of that."[29]

D Troop was assigned to the starboard side of the upper deck. While aboard ship, the troop was divided into six squads, each under the supervision of a sergeant. Miller and Burke were assigned to Sergeant Ira Hill's squad with John Rhoades as its corporal. Most of the other squad members: David McClure, Marcellus Newcomb, Fred Beal, Albert Russell, and Robert L. McMillan, came from Oklahoma. For some reason, McClure had lost his corporal stripes. A commanding officer could promote and demote at whim. John Schmutz hailed from Germantown, Ohio; Fred Wolff from San Antonio, Texas; and Frank Knox was born in Boston, Massachusetts, although raised in Michigan. Hill was a fair leader and took good care of all his men. He identified with and became fast friends with Frank Knox.

That Wednesday, June 8, most of Shafter's regiments were aboard the transports. They had not boarded by daybreak, as he had promised Alger in an earlier telegram, but the work of loading was nearly over. At 2 in the afternoon, the worn-out corps commander took a launch out to his headquarters ship, *Seguranca*. It slipped out into the stream and anchored. Finally, he had his chance for a well-deserved rest. No sooner had his head touched the pillow than an aide brought him a telegram. "Here, General, this is important."

Shafter sat up, rubbed his eyes and read the words, "Wait until you get further orders before you sail. Answer quick."[30] It was from Alger. Shafter responded to his aide's comment, "God, I should say so!" After all the rush, they were not going to sail. It was the navy's turn to delay the expedition. Commodore George C. Remey had cabled the Secretary of Navy from Key West on June 7 with bad news. Lieutenant W.H.H. Southerland aboard the *Eagle*, a yacht converted into a gunboat, had spotted an armored Spanish cruiser and torpedo boat destroyer in the St. Nicholas Channel, off the northeast coast of Cuba. Fearing the Spanish vessels might intercept and sink the transport fleet, Sampson wanted to verify the report. He sent scouting vessels toward the area of the sighting and also Lieutenant Victor Blue into the Santiago Harbor to verify that all of Cervera's fleet were in fact bottled up and accounted for. In the meantime, the army, which had been rushed on account of the navy, would then wait aboard ship because of it. The First Volunteer Cavalry soon became the "Woeful Waiters."[31]

Rough Riders aboard the *Yucatan* (U.S. Army Transportation Museum).

Capron cried like a baby upon hearing the news. When he had the chance, he pleaded with the general to let them take their chances and run past the Spanish ships. Shafter had his orders. Capron wrote, "I am nearly wild for fear the Spanish government will cry peace before we get started."[32] Like his father, Capron was a professional soldier, and war was his profession. He had joined the Army too late to see any action, and this might be his only chance. In a warrior culture, no one becomes a great warrior without a war. Capron had prepared his whole life for this opportunity.

Shafter ordered the transports which had moved out into the bay to return and anchor in columns three abreast. Secretary Alger also asked if Shafter thought the troops should disembark since they may have to wait quite a while before leaving. After all the chaos of trying to get them loaded, Shafter had no intention of going through that ordeal again. The men would stay aboard their transports but could go ashore in small detachments. Shafter issued the order that each command allow the greatest liberty in passes, but the soldiers could not go beyond the port except those on important business, and they had to be back aboard at 9 p.m. Each transport would hold roll call at that time every night. The animals were taken ashore during the wait since it did not take but a few hours to load them, and a prolonged stay aboard ship would weaken them.

Aboard ship, the men fell into their routine. Wood ordered the troops to conduct a manual of arms drill aboard ship at 7 every morning and at 4 every afternoon. The ship was washed every morning, and the men hung their clothes to air out. Officers held inspection at 10:30 every morning and guard mount at 6:30 in the evening. Each troop continued to hold noncommissioned officers' school while Capron still taught classes on tactics to the officers.

Capron was critical of the section of the book of tactics relating to retreat. He felt that too much attention to it had a bad effect on the men. "If you go into action you want to go in to win. I have heard officers say in the presence of their men that soldiers cannot live in the face of a direct fire from the modern rifle. You had better impress upon your men that the only way for them is to charge through, and to charge through it quickly."[33] This would be the first time that Americans had faced the new high-velocity bullets fired from bolt-action, magazine-fed, smokeless powder rifles. The American army since 1873 had issued an inferior, slow-loading weapon so that the soldiers would not fire off all their ammunition too fast. No one was certain what to expect fighting a European army with modern weapons. Capron just felt retreat was not an option.

The first mounting of the guard discovered two stowaways, both young boys, one no more than 13 years old. They had traveled far to get there. Dabney Royster had traveled from Tennessee and the other from the West. One brought plenty of money, and the other had hustled with a great businesslike sense to earn enough money to buy his rifle. Both were fully equipped for war. Royster had a .22-caliber rifle with three boxes of ammunition. By then both were also "dead broke." They expected to earn their passage by doing errands for the men. As they stood there, looking pitiful between their tall guards, the officers felt sympathy for them, wishing they could stay, but the thought of four worried parents decided the matter. The weeping boys were put ashore. Royster was fortunately adopted by the squadron left behind and given a small Rough Rider uniform.[34]

General officers also inspected the state of discipline aboard the vessels. Miles inspected the regiment, and upon reviewing L Troop, he asked what troop it was. Capron's pride swelled in his chest when the general responded, "L Troop is the best I have seen in the volunteer forces." His hard work was paying off. He wrote to his friend Judge Thomas, of Vinita, about this accomplishment and the progress of Lieutenant Thomas.[35]

"Rob is doing well. I have been very strict with him, indeed, and if he has an idea that I am a little more severe with him than with any other officer or man, I would prefer to have him keep it. He is a good officer and will make his mark if we can but get the chance. Do not let him know how much I think of him, as I would prefer to have him imagine that I intend to hold him to a strict account, as indeed I do." Capron's serious exterior could not always hide his true nature.[36]

The Second Infantry band also played two programs each day for the entertainment of those aboard the *Yucatan*. Capron usually displayed nothing but a businesslike attitude, yet one particular song revealed his comical side as he sang along with an *ad lib* chorus, "de monk, de monk, de monk, de monk." Nearly every boat had a band, and the bay echoed with concerts that played popular tunes every evening until dark.[37]

During the wait, the dynamite gun and its load of explosives came aboard the *Yucatan*. Accompanying it was the son of the inventor and a Cuban major. Evidently, the Cuban had developed a dislike for the officer commanding his first transport, so he transferred ships. Shafter assigned him to the Rough Riders as an interpreter. Upon his arrival, he did not hesitate to express his ill feelings about the former commanding officer as he walked about the deck. It was to his shock and horror that he was spun around to face the anger of the Herculean captain. Unknown to the Cuban, the commanding officer whom he openly criticized was none other than Captain Allyn Capron of the Artillery, the Rough Rider's father. The Cuban, henceforth, kept his distance from the son.

The major, in addition, displayed a form of contempt for the men who would fight for his countrymen's freedom. One officer approached him with a warning that if his attitude did not change, "he might feel hurt at the action that would be taken by the officers." He became a polite little guest for the remainder of his stay. Unfortunately, he had won the disrespect of the Rough Riders, and he represented their first impression of the Cuban army.

Aside from the drill, guard mount and cleaning, the men had plenty of time to fill. Some of them fished off the deck. Swimming in the morning and evening provided them another diversion aboard ship. Many explored the ship out of curiosity. It rained at least once a day, so the boys on deck had to hustle to keep their gear dry. The rest of their time the Rough Riders spent hustling for food.

The men had to eat canned rations while aboard ship. The ship had no provisions to cook for those aboard except the ship's crew. Each troop mess had to wait its turn to cook coffee in a single barrel with steam from the boiler. The main course was always canned fresh beef. The meat was stringy and tasteless. Many did not eat it. Some preserved meat was brought aboard, but it had a sickening odor. Consequently, Wood ordered the spoiled meat tossed overboard.

The ship's baker soon realized that some men could afford to pay for extras such as bread or pies. The entrepreneur went into business for himself. Demand quickly outstripped the supply. Of course, inflation set in. The prices started out at 25 cents a loaf or per pie. The baker made $200 the first day. The price for pies then inflated to 50 cents, then 75, and finally $1. Other luxuries included sandwiches, ice and ice water. A glass of ice water sold for ten cents. Keep in mind a private's monthly salary was only $13. A soldier without other income means could go broke waiting aboard that ship. His alternative was to subsist off of a diet of "horse meat," beans and coffee or wait for a friend going ashore.

Whenever a launch went ashore, the men sent money with those aboard to purchase extra food, condiments and catsup to improve the taste of the daily ration of hash. Miller, never quite having made the crew team at Harvard, did know enough to serve as the stroke of the troop crew on his turn to go ashore. He rowed Wood to visit the flagship, *Seguranca*. His crew then went ashore, where he enjoyed the luxury of ice cream and bought cookies for his friends.

As time progressed, money ran out, and food became even scarcer. The men had not intended to remain aboard the vessels that long. They scrounged for food everywhere, using every connection they had with people working in the ship's mess. Teddy Burke finally purchased a loaf of bread and brought it back to share with his squad mates. That helped break the ice with the rest of the squad. To Teddy Miller, accustomed to a life of luxury, it was the best-tasting bread he had ever eaten. Routine aboard ship, however, passed into boredom.

It did not take Roy Cashion long to tire of the routine. He wrote home, "I am tired of being on this boat. I have not been ashore in three days. There is so little room to get around.... There is nothing new here, just the same old thing. We eat three times a day and lay around the rest of the time. We have plenty of swimming, but that is the only thing we have plenty of." Roy's other problem was that he had no safe guaranteed way to mail the $5 he had borrowed from his brother Carl. The censor opened every letter and held them for five days. Even Huston advised him against mailing it home.[38]

Cramped life aboard the ship must have produced tensions. Boredom combined with whiskey (sold at $5 a bottle) or beer (sold at 25 cents a bottle) added the spark. On June 11, a trooper in Luna's F Troop, under the influence of liquor, disobeyed a swimming regulation. This in itself was a minor offensive, but a second lieutenant of the Second Infantry was the officer of the day. The lieutenant, fresh out of West Point, tried to enforce the regulation. The trooper became angry and made threatening speeches to the lieutenant. The latter drew his pistol on the Rough Rider, which only angered him even more, so the guard accompanying the lieutenant subdued the man.[39]

The next day, the lieutenant brought court-martial charges against the trooper. Lieutenant Tom Hall was the judge advocate, and Captain Huston served as one of the officers of the board. The man, then sober, was penitent and pleaded guilty. He received 30 days hard labor and forfeiture of pay. He was the only man court-martialed in the regiment.

Another breach of discipline occurred within D Troop. While at sea, Miller discovered two $20 bills missing. He narrowed the suspicion down to Fred Wolff, who was in his squad. Previously broke, he mysteriously had turned up with a similar amount of money. He claimed to have won it in a game of dice. Miller reported his discovery to his commanding officer. Huston then sent two sergeants to apprehend Wolff. He asked Wolff the show him his money. He produced $4.50 and held out that it was all he had. Huston then searched him and found $50 hidden inside a tobacco sack. The captain asked Miller to identify the bills. Miller said one was a brown back but could not be certain if that one was his. Huston believed the man had stolen the money. He brought charges against Wolff on June 18 and placed him in the guardhouse. If found guilty, Wolff would have spent two years in prison and been dishonorably discharged. Wood called in Miller, Cliff Scott, of Clifton, and Edgar L. Wright, of Guthrie, to recount their testimonies. Evidently, the evidence was not strong enough as Wolff mustered out with the rest of the regiment. Otherwise, discipline remained good.

While waiting in anchorage, the officers speculated on their destination. They poured over maps, analyzing the situation. Newspapers claimed they were bound for Santiago. The officers could not believe that the War Department would permit accurate information to leak to the press. As such they believed it had to be any place but Santiago. By an inadvertent slip from a naval officer aboard ship, Hall learned that their destination was in fact Santiago. Roosevelt and Huston, along with some of the other Rough Riders, still had their doubts. They finally heard a rumor that they would sail on June 13.

Sampson finally became convinced that the report by the *Eagle* was wrong. Shafter received his orders at 1 p.m. Sunday, June 12, to immediately put out to sea. Fifth Corps had lost valuable time that they could have loaded more supplies and equipment. Shafter ordered the animals back aboard and for the transports to make final preparations to depart. The work of loading took the rest of that afternoon and continued on into the night.

Ben Colbert's turn to go ashore came at 2 p.m. that Sunday afternoon. He only had four hours but did not make it back in time to get back aboard his transport. So he just found himself an empty boxcar to sleep in. A heavy downpour blew up that night between 6:30 and 9 p.m. The men raced down into the lower deck, but the wind blew a number of hats and blankets overboard. White caps sprayed foam over the deck. Everyone was drenched. Woodbury Kane moved about the deck in the middle of the storm, giving orders to save the baggage. He displayed great nerve while soaked as "wet as a rat." Ben had picked a good night to stay ashore.

The next day, Miller discovered an empty room on the stern of the ship. It was for prisoners, but since there were none, Miller asked Wood for permission to sleep there. He then invited his friends Bill Larned, Bob Wrenn and Teddy Burke to join him. The next day, others found out about the room, and it quickly became crowded. A day later, it was converted into a hospital in response to a recent outbreak of measles.

Meanwhile, Monday morning, half the vessels signaled that they were in need of fresh water. Each transport had two or three signal men with a set of signal flags and the International Code of Signals for communicating between ships. An investigation revealed that their unintended delay had in fact depleted a considerable quantity of each ship's water supply. Shafter ordered those that could to sail out of the mouth of the bay and anchor while a lighter brought fresh water to the rest.

At long last, the *Yucatan* weighed anchor and began to steam out of the bay in its turn. Ben Colbert wrote in his diary, "We had been penned up in suspense so long that we had lost heart and had been disappointed so many times with rumors that we cared but little whether we had finally started on our Cuban Expedition or not." They were happy to go anywhere. The bands played, flags flew and the men cheered. While the bay was large, the channel was narrow and tortuous. It was becoming dark when the *Yucatan* slowly steamed for the channel. Each ship gave a slight lead to the other. Huston reported to the bridge as the duty officer of the day to watch the activity.

The captain of the *Yucatan* proposed to follow a bit to the right of the lead ship. While the Second Infantry band played and the men cheered, the pilot could not hear the instructions from the captain and steamed straight for the other ship, which unfortunately ran aground. The pilot suddenly reversed the engines, and the ship's crew dropped the anchor, stopping the vessel within six feet of the other. Everyone else on both decks stood frozen. The fact that the dynamite gun and all its explosives were stowed in the bow of the vessel would have brought an abrupt end to the career of the Rough Riders had the two vessels collided.

The *Yucatan* then backed up and slowly steamed ahead, passing within inches of the stranded vessel. Tom Hall claimed that the men of one vessel could have handed a newspaper to the men on the deck of the other. In time, the *Yucatan* took its place in the column with the other vessels and waited for the rest to join up. Although they had orders to sail, Huston shared the same fear as Wood and Roosevelt that the war might still end before they arrived at their destination.

At 6 a.m. on June 14, Shafter ordered all ships to sail at once, regardless of loading. By 9 a.m., the remainder of the army transports, with the *Seguranca* in the rear, sailed for the mouth of Tampa Bay to rendezvous with the other vessels. The convoy finally put underway. The officers and men of the Rough Riders alike were spellbound at the spectacle of the armada sailing for the Gulf of Mexico. Transports steamed in columns three abreast for as far as the Rough Riders could see. From their vantage point, the convoy stretched from horizon to horizon. The flagship, *Seguranca,* with Shafter and his staff aboard, pulled off to one side of the flotilla as the ships passed in review. At about 5 that evening, the sight of Florida faded away.

The vessels steamed at seven knots an hour, although many could do better. They had to travel as slow as the slowest vessel or towed barges. They passed Key West the next night, and, on June 16, they steamed 20 miles off the coast of Cuba. Huston could see the faint outline of land through his binoculars. When they awoke that morning, the battleship *Indiana* and a number of torpedo boats had joined them for escort. The captain of the *Yucatan* told the officers that he expected to reach Santiago de Cuba in four days.

Being at sea changed the monotony of the ship routine. Roy Cashion, however, could find excitement in even this. This was his first time at sea. He wrote home, "This is the dandiest trip I have ever taken as we do not stop at any stations at all, and there is nothing to see but water around you. Once in a while you see land, but you do not know where it is or what it is."[40]

The officers lounged around on the open deck behind the bridge. As they would lean out under the canopy to stare out to sea, nearly everyone made the mistake of hanging onto a taunt line which stretched from the bridge to the smokestack. To the hilarity of the others, the unwitting officer, high or low in rank, learned that it was the line by which the captain blew the whistle. In the evening, the band would play until the sun set. Then the men marveled at the stars against a pitch-black sky and searched to see the Southern Cross for the first time.

As the transports sliced through the waves, the men reminisced of home. Time was one thing they had in plenty surplus. The Rough Riders discussed the past and contemplated their future. Roosevelt and Huston shared pictures of their children and talked about family. Brodie mentioned to Huston that his brother-in-law owned several vessels that cruised between Halifax and South America. If the regiment remained in Cuba for the winter, he would have him bring his wife down. She was from New York and planned to spend the summer there. Huston liked the idea and said he would like to also bring his wife down. Brodie agreed.

As it turned out, Vite Huston had decided to leave her home and move back in with her parents in New York anyway. The pressure of paying bills and living alone was too much for her. She had been critical of McGinnis for leaving his wife with no means of support, requiring her to move in with her parents. Vite would leave their house in the hands of Miss Florence Hadley and friends while she likewise moved away. Renting their house would provide some steady income while Rob was away. Meanwhile, the transports steadily plowed through the waves to their destination.

Because of the slow pace, most of the Rough Riders did not suffer sea sickness until they hit rough seas on June 16. While at sea, Peter H. Byrne, of Guthre, and James V. Honeycutt, of Shawnee, both came down with the measles.

On June 18, the transport, *City of Washington*, towing a boatload of ammunition, fell behind. Another transport towing another load had fallen behind earlier only to be picked up by Captain Clover's gunboat, the *Bancroft*, which guarded the rear of the convoy. Shafter ordered the *Yucatan* to fall back and keep her company. Huston could not figure out why, other than his boat had the dynamite gun and two rapid-fire Colts. To him a Spanish war vessel could stand off at a mile and a half out of range of his weapons and sink all the vessels. The *Yucatan* gradually fell 60 miles behind the main flotilla, and that night at 5:30 Cashion remembered seeing five battleships on the horizon. Fearing the worst, Roy and his friends thought the Spanish fleet had discovered their vulnerable little convoy. Fortunately, they turned out to be part of Sampson's fleet, which had turned back to protect them.

The convoy rounded Cape Massie on Sunday, June 19. At 10 in the morning, Chaplain Brown preached a sermon that day on the subject of respect, reading from Psalm 119. The service was well attended as men became more religious the nearer they came to war. Three band musicians played the music while others sang in the choir. Colonel Wood sang in the choir every chance he could get. Miller wrote about the pleasure of singing right beside his colonel.

That morning, Roy had finally learned of their destination. Up until the night before, he thought it was Puerto Rico. The next day, Miller pulled his guard down in the hold where the dynamite was stored. Lieutenant Goodrich came down, and they chatted. Evidently, Miller was feeling ill. On Monday, June 20, Dade invited his old friend up into his stateroom for lunch. The hospital steward took care of Miller, and a couple of good meals put him back on his feet again. There Miller learned about the invasion plan. The expedition would land in three columns, six to seven miles apart, then unite outside Santiago. There they would seize the water supply and starve the Spaniards out, then advance upon the city.

That day, the gunboat *Helena* and transport *Olivette* joined the fleet. By noon, they passed Guantanamo. The *Bancroft* steamed over and back to report that the U.S. Marines had just finished a small battle which had begun the day before. It reassured them that the Spaniards still intended to fight.

Shafter had sent a vessel ahead the night before to warn Sampson of their arrival. Sampson dispatched Captain Chadwick in the *New York* to guide the transport fleet to his location. Around 4 p.m., they neared the mouth of Santiago Harbor. Cheers rang out from the decks of the warships of Sampson's Mosquito Fleet at the sight of the transports. The soldiers returned the cheers, signaling that they had arrived. Roy Cashion wrote home, "Hurrah! We can see and we are 60 miles east of Santiago. I must close as we have to pack up to disembark, our first battle will be in the near future." The invasion was about to commence.[41]

Sampson boarded the *Seguranca* to discuss his plans with Shafter. The admiral wanted the army to storm the coastal battery at Morro Castle, then place fire on the Socapa battery on the opposite hill so that the navy could steam into Santiago Harbor and destroy the anchored Spanish fleet as Dewey had done in Manila. The flagship traversed the coastline so that Shafter could gain an appreciation of the terrain. Shafter saw no other way to storm the fort than frontal assault. In essence, his troops would pay the price in casualties so that the navy could become the heroes.

Thirty-four years had passed since the Civil War, and Shafter assumed that Americans would not tolerate large casualties in this small affair with Spain. He did not want to take the blame for high casualties. Instead, he proposed that his corps invade inland, surround Santiago and force the Spanish Army to surrender. He wanted to win a bloodless victory. Shafter knew that malaria and yellow fever would cause more casualties than bullets, so he wanted to get inland as quickly as possible. He just needed a safe place to land to support his operation.

Sampson invited Shafter and some of his staff to transfer to the *Gloucester* so they could meet up with General Calixto Garcia at Aserraderos at the head of 4,000 Cuban insurgents. Shafter explained his plan, and Garcia recommended landing at Daiquiri. Daiquiri was a mining village built by the American-owned Spanish–American Iron Company. The village had a short steel dock and a shorter wooden one for loading iron onto small vessels. The coastal plain stretched about a half a mile to the hills that rose abruptly to 2,000 feet behind it. Garcia estimated that only 300 Spanish soldiers occupied the town. It was the weakest defended of all possible landings.[42]

The leaders agreed to a plan. The navy would begin the bombardment at daybreak on June 22. They would bombard Daiquiri, Siboney, Sardinero, Aguadores and Cabanas so as not to alert the Spaniards to the exact location of the landing. Several transports, with the last of the troops to land, would also sail under the navy's protection to Cabanas as a feint, while General Jesus Rabi with 500 Cubans would stage an assault from the rear. General Demetrio Castillo would move a regiment of 1,000 guerrillas behind Daiquiri to intercept the escaping Spaniards and assist in the landing.[43]

On June 21, it had begun raining, and the seas kicked up at 5 that morning so the fleet sailed further out to sea to prevent the storm from driving the ships aground or into the bay. The rain continued until noon. For men accustomed to tornadoes, they marveled at the formation of a waterspout that twisted its way through the fleet. The

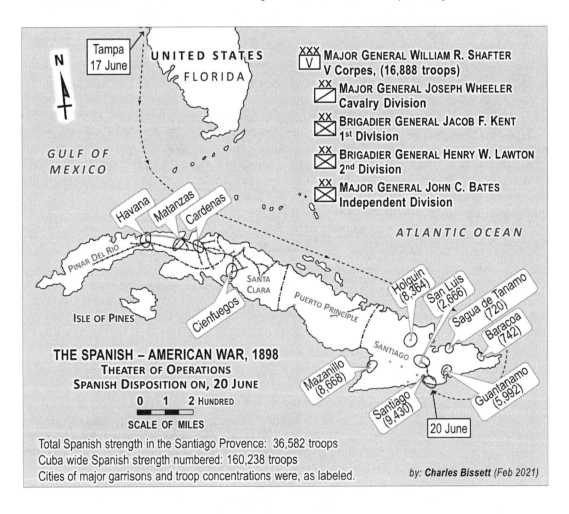

ships had scattered so far apart that Shafter could not assemble his division and brigade commanders on the *Seguranca* until 4 in the afternoon to issue his orders.

Late in the day, Captain Tyree Rivers, of Young's brigade staff, came aboard the *Yucatan* and passed on the orders for the landing. Brigadier General Henry Lawton's Second Division of infantry would land first with the Gatling gun detachment and establish the perimeter directly in front of Daiquiri. Brigadier General John C. Bates's brigade would disembark second and form the reserve behind Lawton. Wheeler's dismounted cavalry division would then land and form up to the left of Lawton. Next, Brigadier General Jacob F. Kent's First Division would prepare to land at Demajayobe or Juragua. Rafferty's cavalry squadron would disembark last.[44]

When the Rough Riders learned that they would land under naval bombardment the next day, they let out a hearty cheer. Shafter's instructions stated that they would land with their blanket rolls, three days' field rations, canteens filled and 100 rounds of ammunition per man. They then began to fill their canteens with water and packed one day's ration in their haversacks in preparation for the landing.

What they were about to do next others would write about in history. Everything they had done up to that time had been closely monitored by their hometown press mostly through their letters. The local hometown papers leaned towards one of the two major party persuasions. They had paid scant attention to the Cuban struggle for independence until their own sons entered the fray. Starved for news about their local heroes, they solicited family members to publish letters from the Rough Riders in the papers. When the invasion fleet set sail, it would take several weeks for those letters to reach home. Starr Wetmore's mother, whose son wrote home every day, and the friends and families of other Rough Riders would have to rely on the national press for news releases until then. Yet in time of a popular war, many wanted to contribute.

CHAPTER 5

Baptism of Fire

The Rough Riders awoke before dawn to observe the spectacle. The preliminary bombardment began before the sun rose on the morning of June 22. The *New Orleans*, *Detroit*, *Castine*, *Wasp* and *Suwanee* fired their guns in unison on the town of Daiquiri and the surrounding hills. Fires broke out on the buildings on shore. Meanwhile, Eighth and Twenty-Second Infantry soldiers climbed down into small boats alongside their transports.

The army had no suitable surf boats but instead counted upon the small launches of the transports, three steam lighters, a tug, and two light-draft steamers. The tug and two of the lighters, for some reason, had failed to arrive with the fleet. During the planning, the Fifth Corps Quartermaster had hoped that the force would land in a protected harbor with a deepwater pier. He had no such luck. Realizing that Shafter could not land his corps very quickly with the type of vessels he had on hand, Admiral Sampson offered the use of 52 additional small boats and a number of steam launches manned by navy personnel. Shafter accepted. These launches had left before dawn in search of their respective transports still scattered about in the sea. The navy possessed the expertise for such operations, and Shafter gladly turned the supervision of the landing over to them. Sampson, in turn, assigned an officer in charge of the amphibious landing and another as the beachmaster on shore.

To compound the problem, the army transports did not want to venture in too close to the shore for fear of running aground. The commander of the larger transport, *St. Louis*, steamed as close as one and a half miles from the steel pier to instill confidence in the others. It did not work for most remained far out at sea. This made the work of landing all the more time consuming.

By 9:40, one of Lawton's brigades had climbed into the boats towed by the steam launches. A naval officer gave the signal for the formal bombardment to begin. For 25 minutes, the infantry bobbed up and down in the waves. At 10:15, the navy ceased its bombardment, and the infantry-laden boats raced for shore. All eyes on the *Yucatan* strained to see if the Spanish would contest the landing. Lawton's infantry climbed out on the slippery beams of the wooden pier and walked onto Cuban soil. Someone on the *Yucatan* exclaimed, "Why, they're forming by companies."[1] Indeed, the infantry formed up to march inland. The Spanish had evidently fled the area without a fight, saving the American army a disaster. The fires, as it turned out, were set by the evacuating Spaniards. The Spaniards had also pulled up the planks on the wooden pier and stacked them on shore.

The nearby steel pier was of no use. It was crowded with cars filled with iron ore and much too high for troops to climb onto. It had been built high above the water so

Steam launches towing empty launches back out to the transport fleet from Daiquiri (Theodore Roosevelt Collection, Harvard University Library).

the railcars could dump iron ore into awaiting lighters. For the rest of the day, small boats put men ashore. Crews rowed their boats and then threw out guide ropes to men on the wooden pier. So the men on the wooden pier had to pull the boats up alongside. Waves lifted the boats till a man's head rose above the pier and then dropped them down six feet below it. The passengers waited until a wave lifted them up; then they tossed their weapons, blanket rolls, canteens and haversacks on the structure. They waited for another wave to reach up to grab someone on the dock. Consequently, much equipment was lost in the surf, and some unfortunate men inadvertently slipped into the water.

Roosevelt and Wood interpreted the confusion of the landing as they had everything else associated with this expedition. To them it was once again every regiment for itself. Luck again favored the Rough Riders as the gunboat *Vixen*, a converted yacht, returned from its bombardment of Cabanas. Its captain, Lieutenant Alexander Sharpe, had been Roosevelt's aide while he was the Assistant Secretary of the Navy. Sharpe steamed alongside and offered to help put the Rough Riders ashore.

The regimental staff and a few of the officers and men of Capron's L Troop boarded her. The higher standard of living of the sailors on the gunboat impressed Adjutant Hall. He also learned from the naval officers that 20,000 Spanish soldiers occupied Santiago with reinforcements on their way. So much for the navy's boast that they could take the city with 10,000 infantry.

The *Vixen,* with a Cuban pilot, steamed to within a few hundred yards of the pier, and the *Yucatan* followed right behind her. Other transports began to follow. The Rough Riders then disembarked on launches from the *Massachusetts* and *Marblehead* ahead of their sequence and ahead of the rest of the cavalry.

Captain Buckey O'Neill and E Troop's Corporal Charles E. Knoblauch, of the New York Stock Exchange, saw their opportunity. Both good swimmers, they remained on the pier to assist in the landing. They stripped down and dove in the water to retrieve lost weapons and equipment. On one occasion two troopers from the Tenth (Colored) Cavalry slipped and fell into the water. Neither could swim, burdened by the weight of their heavy equipment, and disappeared under the waves. O'Neill and Knoblauch made repeated dives to save them, but, unfortunately, the troopers drowned.

There were no means to land the horses and mules other than for them to swim. Men just pushed the animals overboard, and others in boats tried to guide the frightened animals into shore. Still, many confused animals swam out to sea and eventually drowned. With ground transportation assets limited, this did not help the situation. Both of Wood's horses made the swim, but one of Roosevelt's drowned. Texas made the swim. Once ashore, men and animals moved further inland to the foot of the hills.

The blockhouse on top of Mount Losiltires had remained untouched by the naval bombardment. It had a steep tin roof, cupola and flagstaff. Edward Marshall, reporter for the New York *Journal*, and William Bengough, also an artist from the *Journal*, climbed up the crest of the hill to erect a little American flag on top of the blockhouse. In war after war the flag symbolized the identity of the unit or the nation. Civilized warfare was a contest for real estate. A battle was won when a man could plant his flag on the hill, and the enemy could not push him off. The flag flying over the enemy works symbolized victory. Similarly, that day, the two journalists saw an historic opportunity. In the rush to get ashore, no one else had planted the American flag on Cuban soil.

Once on top, Marshall looked down the hill to see Surgeon La Motte, Color Sergeant Wright, and Chief Trumpeter Clay Platt, of San Antonio, also scaling the hill. Platt brought up the American flag presented to the regiment by ladies of Arizona. Major

Landing barge bringing some horses ashore at Daiquiri (U.S. Army Transportation Museum).

General Wheeler, wanting to outdo Lawton's infantry, had ordered Wood to have a man climb to the top of the hill and hoist up their regimental colors.

Wright and Platt looked around and found a ladder by which they climbed up into the cupola. From there, Platt crawled out onto the roof through the firing loopholes. He could not keep his footing on the steep roof and fell off. The little group was beginning to give up hope when a sailor joined them. He observed Platt's difficulty, then offered to complete the task. Gracefully, he crept out through the loophole like a cat, climbed up the roof and stood erect. He then lashed the flag to the pole.

The proud men then relaxed to enjoy their accomplishment and the view. A cheer began to resound from the beach as men looked up. Ships then began to blow their whistles. From the deck of the *Yucatan*, D Troop, still waiting its turn, recognized the American flag flying over the blockhouse. Everyone began to cheer. After everything they had been through, the sight of "Old Glory" waving over the Spanish blockhouse was their first major accomplishment of the war.

Wright and Platt found an abandoned case of wine in the blockhouse to celebrate their victory. They were about to take a drink when La Motte came up. He snatched the opened bottle away from them and smelled it. He told them it was poisoned and began to break every bottle with the copper binding of a six-inch shell. They then climbed down to the beach.

Other than their experience with the Cuban major, this day was the first time the Rough Riders saw the Cuban army. Although a few Cubans had been injured by the naval bombardment, they presented the most pitiful sight that the troopers had seen. Ranging in age from 13 to 70, most wore no other clothing than a groin cloth. Some wore sandals made out of local plants, and many were armed with nothing more than a machete or cartridge belt. The few rifles they had represented a wide variety of types and makes. By the time the last of the Rough Riders finished landing, the Cubans, however, had received their new issue of magazine-fed Lee rifles along with ammunition.

The Cubans looked so emaciated that many of the Rough Riders began to give them their rations. They had received orders not to since the Cubans would receive an issue of rations when they were off-loaded, but the troopers ignored the order out of pity. One Rough Rider after another began to unroll their blanket rolls to pull out and give their extra underwear to the nearly naked Cubans. In a short time, the Cuban regiment was uniformly clothed in army-issue, cotton long underwear. The returning civilians did not look much better off.

Although most felt sorry for the Cubans, Adjutant Hall, always with a critical eye, saw something different. He noticed how the officers were much better uniformed and arrogant. To him the soldiers also appeared lazy or not in much of a hurry.

Finally, D Troop disembarked at 6 in the evening. The entire regiment with its rapid-fire guns and dynamite gun stood on dry land by the time darkness fell. As each boatload of Rough Riders landed, Wood marched them a quarter of a mile to the valley of the Daiquiri River. There they went into camp behind the Tenth Cavalry in a dusty, brush-covered flat adjacent to the jungle. The grass grew taller than the dog tents, so Wood allowed the greatest liberty in erecting shelters. The men gathered broad, leafy palm leaves to construct impromptu roofs. This is where the men of the frontier exhibited their great skill and creativity at fieldcraft. The nearby stream provided the men their first chance to bathe since boarding the transports two weeks before.

They also discovered an abundance of large land crabs and the largest tarantulas.

Rough Rider makeshift shelters at Daiquiri (Theodore Roosevelt Collection, Harvard University Library).

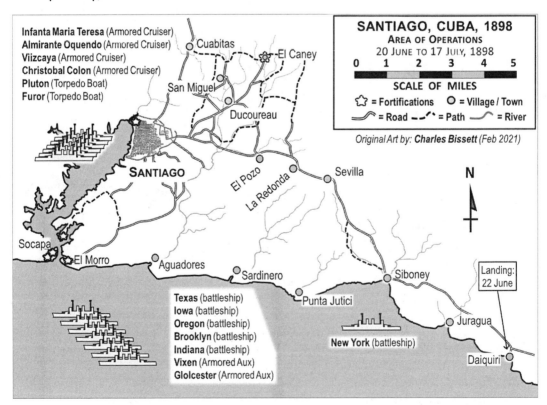

Burr McIntosh, an actor and writer for the *Journal*, had organized turtle races while back in Tampa. He decided to give it a try racing tarantulas. Unfortunately, one bit him. He, Ham Fish and Major Brodie searched the camp for whiskey, which was considered a remedy for snake and insect bites. All the while, La Motte did the best he could for McIntosh's pain, but it was not enough. Finally, they discovered a storehouse down at the dock full of Jamaican rum and demijohns full of sweet Spanish wine. The rum was too raw to drink, but they brought the wine back to camp. The next morning, McIntosh and his companions awoke with intense pain of another sort.

That morning the Rough Riders returned to the beach to help unload their additional rations, ammunition and field kitchens from the boats onto shore. A detachment of Rough Riders also attended the funeral for the two drowned cavalry men. While the men labored at the beach, the campaign proceeded.

Lawton's division had started down the coastal road the same day they arrived and went into camp. The road followed the railroad and then turned toward Santiago at Siboney. Shafter wanted Lawton's division to seize Siboney so the corps could finish landing there. From there Fifth Corps would march inland toward Santiago. All morning, the Rough Riders watched infantry marching toward Siboney while they waited. The regiment of Cubans also marched by.

By 1 in the afternoon, Wood received orders to be ready to move at a moment's notice. Brigadier General Samuel B.M. Young, to whose brigade the Rough Riders were assigned, realized that his brigade had arrived out of turn and planned to take advantage of the fortunate situation. The men rolled up their gear and made ready to march.

Troops forming up at Daiquiri for a march to Siboney (Theodore Roosevelt Collection, Harvard University Library).

Roosevelt's horse finally arrived but without a saddle. Shafter had promised the journalists plenty of room for their horses, but, at the last minute before loading, changed his mind. The journalists' saddles had arrived nonetheless. So Edward Marshall, who had attached himself to the Rough Riders, gave Roosevelt his.

What few mules had swam ashore were not enough to fill every need. The Rough Riders would again have to hustle. They needed mules for their rapid-fire guns, dynamite gun and field kitchen. Wheeler located some horses for the dynamite gun, while Major Joshua W. Jacobs and Sergeant Borrowe managed to find some harnesses. They spent the afternoon adjusting them so as to pull the gun. Captain L.S. McCormack, of the Seventh Cavalry and assigned as liaison from Wheeler's staff, found a mule for the regimental kitchen. Wood also gave up his beautiful Kentucky thoroughbred for it. It broke his heart to see his faithful mare used as a beast of burden. He just turned away as the cook led her off.

Thirty minutes after the warning, Wheeler ordered Young's calvary brigade forward. Fighting Joe Wheeler could not wait to engage the enemy. Young's brigade contained a squadron each of the First and Tenth cavalries and two of the First U.S. Volunteer Cavalry. This was all the cavalry Wheeler had at the time, and, having arrived out of turn, he wanted this brigade out in front as soon as possible. The Rough Riders closed up the brigade rear.

Capron's L Troop led the regiment as the advance guard. Wood led the regiment on his charger while Hall and Color Sergeant Wright followed on foot. A small Cuban boy on a native stallion preceded them. Their little headquarters included two Regular Army officers dressed in blue wool attached as liaison. Captain Rivers represented Brigadier General Young's staff and Captain McCormack Wheeler's. Marshall also accompanied this little group. Roosevelt followed with the hospital corps in the rear to police up any stragglers. The machine-gun detachment would catch up after it found enough mules.

The road was nothing more than a trail through a jungle of coconut and date palms leading up and over a rocky mountain. Monkeys scampered from tree to tree along the trail. The hot tropical sun bore down on the dismounted cavalrymen carrying heavy loads on their backs. When they halted, most simply collapsed on their packs. After each break, the Rough Riders got up and pushed on. Not two miles out of camp, the Rough Riders began to pass infantrymen prostrated from heat exhaustion. As they advanced even further, they would pass one or two more soldiers about every quarter of a mile or so.

One trooper of the Tenth Cavalry learned that his enlistment had run out at 5 p.m. Halfway through the march, he demanded his discharge. A happy man, he then quickly turned over his gear in spite of the jeers of his friends and turned to walk back to Daiquiri. As he crossed the path of Capron, the captain collared him like a "yellow dog" and passed him down the line of Rough Riders who stripped him of his uniform, leaving a few bruises in its place.

When the Rough Riders reached a cool, clear stream, Wood passed the word back, "You can fill your canteens here, if you don't foul the water yourselves."[2] Some started to fill their canteens, then saw troopers of the Tenth Cavalry swimming upstream. They changed their minds and were not very impressed with the Tenth.

The sun set quickly, and the march continued on after dark. Sentries lined the railroad embankment on the left of the road. For fun, they yelled out warnings to the passing soldiers of imminent danger of Spanish attack and sudden death at the next thicket.

The Rough Riders finally reached Siboney at 8:30 that night, having only lost 20 to 30 men on the march, all of whom caught up later. They had only marched eight miles in as many hours. Two weeks cooped up aboard the transport combined with the tropic heat had weakened them. Huston noted that two of his men nearly died after getting into camp. Teddy Burke became sick and delirious with typhoid. Teddy Miller had received permission from Captain Huston to fall back and help his friend. Carrying Burke's pack, Miller arrived very ti[...]oned house established as a hospital. [...] harnesses, so the dynamite gun depa[...] dark, an infantry commander stopped[...]

The exhausted [...] ely upon arrival. Small fires cooked [...] houghts and conversations turned t[...] mark as a writer before the war, four [...] rrespondent Marshall. Marshall con[...] d to write.

No sooner had [...] wed to seek shelter or sleep in the hous[...] d vermin, the men endured the pouri[...] t their brown canvas uniforms to dr[...]

Shortly after t[...] d Young had occupied the finest hou[...] lerate cavalry man had a scheme to ge[...] e Shafter remained aboard his flagshi[...] ground.

Wheeler explained to Wood and Young their situation. Apparently, Lawton's troops had entered one end of the town as the Spaniards retreated out the other, firing the first American shots of the Santiago Campaign. No one was wounded, and 100 Cubans then pursued and engaged the enemy's rear guard on the Santiago Road. They returned with eight of their men wounded and reported that the Spaniards waited in prepared ambush positions at the intersection of two jungle trails this side of Seville.

Upon his arrival, Wheeler rode out to reconnoiter the enemy. He discovered the Spaniards in the strong defensive position about three to five miles from Siboney and also saw one dead Cuban on the road. With the help of General Castillo, Wheeler prepared a map of the area. He laid this out before Wood and Young. A mountain trail on the left intersected with the valley road to Santiago about five miles inland at a place known as Las Guasimas (mistakenly referred to as La Quasina by some). There the Spaniards had prepared a strong defensive position with two blockhouses and trenches. Wheeler expected 1,500 Spanish soldiers to put up a good fight. Hall similarly learned from a classmate in another regiment that the Cubans had never been able to drive the Spaniards from that position in three years of fighting.

Wheeler planned to sneak his cavalry out ahead of Lawton's infantry at daylight the next morning and strike the first solid blow against the Spaniards. Since they had failed to oppose the landing, Wheeler wanted to follow up on Lawton's and the Cuban attack to keep the Spaniards on the run. Wheeler did not want to lose the momentum. Shafter, on the other hand, had planned that his regiments go into the defense and wait until the entire corps was ashore before it attacked. He had instructed Lawton to lead the advance, but, since Shafter was still on his flagship, Wheeler had seniority in rank over Lawton. This veteran of numerous battles against the Yankees felt it was his privilege of rank to alter the plan. He would send Shafter a message the next morning explaining his intentions to press on to Seville when it was too late for Shafter to stop him.

Young discussed at length with Wood, who was second in command of the brigade, how they would attack the position. By doctrine, an attacking force needed a three-to-one advantage. Young's Brigade of around 1,000 men would attack against an entrenched enemy with superior numbers, who knew they were coming. These were bad odds.

Young decided that he would advance up the main road with the two squadrons of Regular cavalry, about 464 men, and the Hotchkiss battery. Two hundred Cubans under Castillo would follow. Wheeler sent instructions for the dynamite gun to catch up and also go into action. Meanwhile, a couple of Cubans would guide Wood, with around 534 Rough Riders, on a detour over the mountain trail on the left to attack the enemy's flank. The two forces would go on line at a place where the two roads were about 700 to 800 yards apart and then drive the Spaniards from their position.

After Wood had gone off to see Wheeler and Young, Roosevelt strolled over to visit Capron. Capron stood around a fire with Lieutenants Thomas and Day, Sergeant Ham Fish and two other soldiers. Capron discussed his plans for the fight the next day, while Fish asked questions. Both longed to prove their mettle in battle. Roosevelt marveled at the physical prowess of both Capron and Fish. To him there were no two finer specimens of fighting men in the army.

Roosevelt had laid down just before midnight when Wood returned. Wood summoned the troop commanders together to outline the plan for the next day. He issued the order for each of the troop commanders to have their men ready to march at 5:30 a.m. He added that the men were not to fire their carbines unless they saw a Spaniard, nor were they to stop during the fight to help any wounded. A seasoned veteran, Wood had good reason for both orders.

Reveille sounded at 3:45 a.m. This gave the men time to eat a breakfast and pack their gear. Fish's bunkie shared part of a can of tomatoes but wanted to save the rest of it for later. Fish said to him, "Oh, let's have some more, it's my last breakfast."[3] Many men going into battle often have a premonition of their own fate. Fish, evidently, had his. He also gave away his extra underwear and shirt, cheerfully claiming that he would not need them for dead men do not often change their clothes. Foreseeing his own fate, he would meet it as bravely as he could.

Wood and Roosevelt had not had any time to sleep that night. Walking around in his yellow slicker, 37-year-old Wood looked worn and haggard. His voice cracked and was hoarse. Roosevelt in his slicker was still "as lively as a chipmunk."

Buck Dawson, the chief packer, and the cook had difficulty getting the mules packed. Hall had developed disgust for the colored regimental cook. Keep in mind that no one ever had anything good to say about Adjutant Hall either. The running of the regimental mess had always been a bother to Hall, and he referred to Roosevelt's valet disdainfully as the "Ethiop prime minister." He had even ranked among the stragglers the night before. The time to depart came, and they were still not ready. This delay infuriated the already-worn-down Wood. He told them if they were not ready in ten minutes, he would leave without them. They were ready.

At 6 a.m. on July 24, the Rough Riders marched in single file up into the jungle looking for a fight. Roosevelt told the men that they would meet the enemy before the day was over. They passed on instructions for the men to shoot only when they saw the enemy.

The first part of the journey was a steep climb up 600 to 800 feet. They passed outposts of men of the Twenty-Second Infantry guarding the heights overlooking the camp. The sentries warned the passing Rough Riders that they had heard the Spaniards preparing their positions all night. Once atop the mesa, the men were exhausted. Marshall turned to survey the scene below. He could see transports and warships in the bay and hear bugle notes floating up the hill. While the camp stirred to life below, the cavalry marched into harm's way.

From then on, the pace of the march picked up. The trail was eight feet wide, lined with a barbed wire fence on both sides. Dense jungle of Spanish sword, cacti and palm trees bordered the right side, and a chaparral of waist-high grass and scattered trees bordered their left. Wood rode out in front. Behind him followed his little entourage. The Cuban major and Adjutant Hall walked on foot. Wheeler had sent Captain McCormack as his liaison officer while Young had sent Lieutenants Tyree Rivers and W.R. Smedburg, Jr., all three mounted on mules. Two journalists, Marshall and Richard Harding Davis, also accompanied the regiment in search of a story. Davis had fortunately found a mule to ride. Behind them followed Capron at the lead of L Troop. His troop had again been assigned as the advance guard. Roosevelt rode ahead of his squadron of G, A and K Troops in that order. Next followed Brodie at the lead of his squadron of D, E and F Troops. B Troop followed in reserve. Sergeant Tiffany brought up the rear with the Colt guns. The dynamite gun had still not caught up. Wood had sent the two Cubans out in advance as scouts.

About a mile to a mile and a half inland from the brow of the hill, Wood ordered Capron's troop to march out ahead of him as the advance guard. Along the march, the men heard the call of the wood cuckoo. Wood and McCormack mentioned to Marshall that Marines had told them that when they had landed, the Spaniards had used the sound of the cuckoo as a signal. They then began to peer through the thickets searching for Spanish sharpshooters. They heard the signal five or six more times along the march but saw nothing suspicious. The advice proved correct. Spanish sharpshooters camouflaged in the trees kept them under constant observation and signaled the progress of the Rough Riders back to their commanding general. They held their fire until after the Americans entered the kill zone of the ambush.

The Rough Riders halted several more times. Along the right of the trail they passed a deserted mansion with a palm tree which had grown up through the roof. Roosevelt rode up to check it out. Marshall puzzled over why he picked up two shovels and fastened them to his saddle.

The men again rode or walked carefree through the Cuban jungle. They marveled at the strange vegetation and sounds of exotic tropical birds. Some men of B Troop sang, "There'll Be a Hot Time in the Old Town Tonight." The journey reminded Davis of a hunting excursion out West. He and McCormack pointed out the unfamiliar fauna and flora of the tropics to Roosevelt riding just behind them. McCormack said it reminded him of Southern California, while the well-traveled Davis said it looked more like the trails of Central America. Roosevelt, an avid hunter, commented that it looked like good deer country.

After an hour and a half into the march, the main column had crossed the summit 500 yards from the intersection. There the trail narrowed and descended sharply downward. Wood spotted Capron walking back up the trail. Wood stopped the column and rode ahead to confer with him.

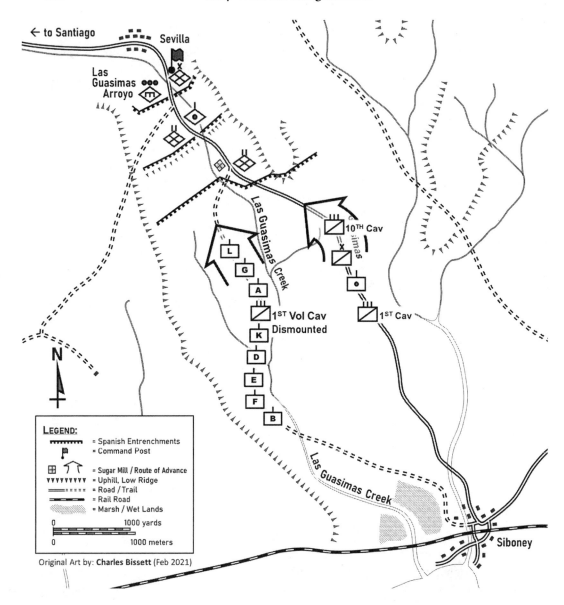

The Cuban scouts had reported that the Spaniards were in force just up ahead and then headed back to Siboney. Wood warned Capron that, at a certain point, he would come across the body of a dead Cuban killed in the fight the day before. If he did not see the corpse a little further ahead, he would see the remains of a campfire. Wood returned and ordered, "Pass the word back to keep silence in the ranks."[4] He explained that the advance guard had located a Spanish outpost. His instructions echoed back down the trail. The men were also told to load their carbines. Wood then rode forward about 7:10 in the morning.

Wood had also sent Smedburg[5] off into the jungle to report this information to General Young. Unable to ride his mule through the thick vegetation, Smedburg offered his mount to a grateful Marshall. Marshall heard that someone had seen the dead body, further back. He then rode back to examine the body of a dead Cuban. Marshall could not locate any wound and determined that the man had been dead for some time.

Marshall then rode further back along the line. He saw men lying carelessly in the grass by the side of the trail with their rifles beside them. Some had taken off their blanket rolls. The men appeared unconcerned. They did not believe that they would make contact with the enemy that day. Their conversations covered about any subject but the Spaniards. One trooper in B Troop declared, "By God! How would you like a glass of cold beer?"[6] His comrades answered by throwing sticks at him. Having reached the end of the column, Marshall then turned back to the command group.

After coming across the Cuban corpse, Capron called for volunteers to reconnoiter the enemy position. Tom Isbell volunteered first followed by five others. Capron set out with six skilled scouts as point, leaving the rest of his troop 250 yards behind on the small knoll kneeling with their carbines at the ready. Because of the dense jungle, he deployed no flankers. Tom Isbell led the little scouting party. Ten or 15 minutes after starting, Tom reached a turn in the trail about 250 yards out from the main body. There the young Cherokee spotted several Spaniards off about 300 yards through the woods. He was certain that they did not see him. He then crept up to within 50 or 60 yards of them. Edward Culver, another Cherokee from Muskogee, followed a few feet behind to his left with Corporal Bud Parnell, also from Muskogee, to his right. Sergeant John Byrne, of the New York Police Department; J. Wylie Skelton, of Trinity Mills, Texas; and Trumpeter Thomas "Tom" Meagher, of Muskogee, followed behind them at about 30 feet apart.

Observing no other Spaniards, Tom Isbell raised his carbine. He fired and dropped a Spaniard. No sooner had he fired than it seemed as if the whole Spanish Army opened fire on him. Two rounds knocked him to the ground. Refusing to leave the field, he kept on firing. Exposed and alone as he was, he was hit five more times for a total of seven times: twice through the left hand, twice through the neck, twice across the back of the head and once through the right hip. Years later, he recounted to Bill McGinty that upon being hit with the first volley, he joked, "You know, I think someone over there is shooting at me."[7] Isbell had earned the honor of killing the first Spaniard in the fight and also was the man with the most bullet wounds.

When the first shots were fired, Adjutant Hall looked at his watch to note the time.

At 7:20, the battle had begun in earnest. The enemy occupied a crescent-shaped position behind breastworks with L Troop in the center of it. The little group came under such intense enemy fire that they thought the enemy had machine guns. The rest of L Troop came up at a dead run with Ham Fish in the lead. Capron deployed them into a skirmish line through the woods. Fish came up and laid down beside Culver. "Culver, have you got a good place?"[8]

Looking up from behind a rock, Culver answered, "Yes."

Fish fired a few shots, then sank to the ground at the foot of a tree and exclaimed, "I am wounded." The same Mauser bullet that had passed through his chest had also struck Culver under the left arm through the lung and lodged in the muscles of his right side. Culver answered back, "And I am killed."[9]

Believing his wound was fatal, Culver wanted to kill as many of the Spaniards as possible before he died. At first the wound had dazed him, but he soon began to recover and could take aim. By the time friends carried him from the field, he had left 45 spent cartridges in his place. Samuel "Cherokee Bill" Davis, of Waggone, also came up behind Fish. Of the point element, Meagher was also wounded in the left forearm.

About 30 minutes into the fight, Capron came along and stood over Fish. Others had rallied around their fallen comrade. Capron knelt down beside Sergeant Dill Bell and said, "Give me your gun for a minute."[10] Bell did not remember seeing Capron flinch once from the enemy fire but instead fired two quick shots in succession. He saw a Spaniard fall with each shot. Meanwhile, Bell picked up Fish's carbine and fired steadily alongside his captain. Suddenly, Capron fell to the ground. A bullet had struck him in the left shoulder and exited out his abdomen.

Men attempted to carry him from the field, but he insisted, "Let me see it out, I want to see it all."[11] Capron knew he was dying. In the midst of the fighting, Capron passed on to Bell parting words for his wife and father. Tilden Dawson, of Vinita, was then shot through the head next to Capron. Command then fell to the ranking first lieutenant.

First Lieutenant Thomas had learned everything he knew about soldiering in the last month from his mentor, Captain Capron. Capron was 15 feet away from the lieutenant when mortally wounded. Thomas realized that he was the next in command of the troop, and L Troop was the center of the line. They just had to hold the enemy's attention until the rest of the regiment came on line. This meant they had to bear the brunt of the fighting until the others reached a position to attack.

Thomas moved along the line, ordering the men to spread out to their proper intervals of six feet apart. As he moved down the line, Fish heard his voice and raised to his elbow. Evidently in great pain, he said, "I am wounded, I am wounded." Thomas could not stop to attend to Fish's wound but gave him words of encouragement that someone would come by to take care of him. Fish smiled, then lay back down. It broke Thomas's heart to have to leave him, but the lieutenant had a whole troop to attend to. Fish died minutes later.[12]

Thomas had no thoughts of fear or heroics. He focused on his duties. About 20 minutes after he had assumed command, the regiment had come on line, and Thomas prepared his men to charge. He suddenly felt as if a baseball bat had struck him across the lower right leg. He fell to the ground with his leg paralyzed. Surprisingly, he felt no more pain.

Sergeant Joe A. Kline, of Vinita, came over and cut off Thomas's trousers to inspect the wound. A bullet had passed through the tibia. Kline then tied a tourniquet around the leg with Thomas's canteen strap and a stick to stop the bleeding. After 15 minutes, the pain had become intense. Following Capron's example, Thomas refused to be carried from the battlefield but lay there cheering his men on. Capron had trained Thomas well. Second Lieutenant Richard C. Day then led the troop from there on.

While lying there, Thomas saw a bullet hit Schuyler Whitney's carbine. The round splintered, with one piece cutting his scalp and the other his neck. He fell to the ground and was covered with blood from the neck down when men later carried him from the field.

Kline, also wounded in the leg, was ordered to the rear along with several other wounded. Along the way a Spanish sharpshooter fired at him. Kline returned fire and dropped the Spaniard from the tree. Kline went over and picked up a silver-mounted revolver as a souvenir, which had fallen from the dead man's clothing.[13]

Sergeant Dill Bell was wounded in the back by an exploding shell and was ordered back to the hospital but quickly returned. Again, he was ordered to the rear, but, after a few minutes, he was again seen firing away on the front. Ordered to the rear for a third time, he returned this time to the cheers of his comrades in arms. He remained on the line until the end of the fight.[14]

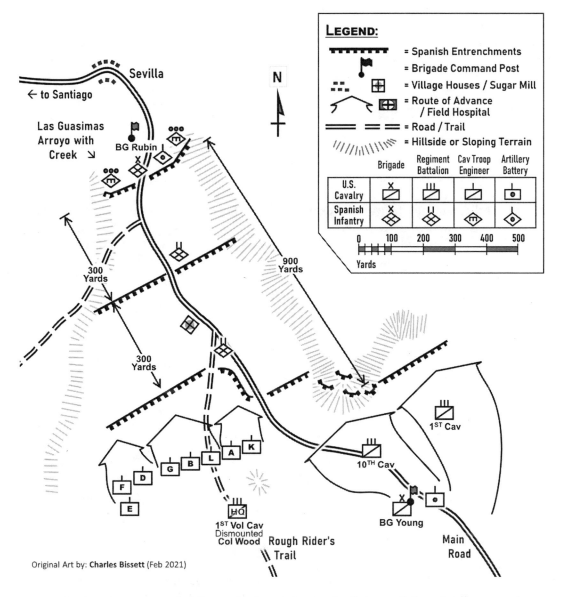

Original Art by: **Charles Bissett** (Feb 2021)

As the advance guard, L Troop had to maintain the fight until the other two squadrons came on line. Consequently, it took the heaviest casualties of the regiment, with three men killed and eight wounded. When the battle opened, it caught the other troops completely by surprise.

Action on the Right

After Marshall had joined up with the command group behind L Troop, he saw everyone lying in the grass except Wood and Roosevelt. Men chewed on blades of grass or fanned themselves with their hats, grateful for the halt. Everyone was completely unaware of how soon they would enter combat. Richard Davis thought it seemed unlikely that the Spaniards would oppose them there since they had failed to oppose the landing. He doubted that they would encounter any Spaniards until they reached Santiago.

Roosevelt walked over to Marshall and talked about a luncheon he had had with Randolph Hearst in the Astor House back in New York. They stood next to a barbed wire fence. Roosevelt casually glanced at it and noticed that the wire was cut. He reached down and picked up a strand. Upon examination he exclaimed, "My God! This wire has been cut today."

"What makes you think so?" asked Marshall.

Handing the wire over to Marshall, Roosevelt responded, "The end is bright, and there has been enough dew, even since sunrise, to put a light rust on it, had it not been lately cut."[15]

At that moment, La Motte rode noisily up on his mule. Roosevelt headed toward him, reprimanding him to be quiet. Just then they heard the first shots fired up front. Wood returned as cool as ever and ordered the men to load and chamber their carbines.

Men reacted differently. Roosevelt literally jumped up and down, as Marshall witnessed, "with emotions evidently divided between joy and a tendency to run."[16] Davis thought it was just a false alarm. He figured that Capron's scouts were firing at random, trying to get the enemy to disclose their positions.

Wood had instructed that in case of attack, Roosevelt would take G, K and A Troops into the jungle to the right, and Brodie would deploy D, F and E Troops into the open field on the left. Adjutant Hall suggested placing the Colt guns in position on the left to support the action. Wood ordered it done. However, the mule packers hurried off for the rear with the rapid-fire guns, while the mules stampeded into the jungle. Hall claimed the regimental cook also fled to the rear with the field kitchen.

At the sound of battle, the men cut the strands of wire with nippers. Marshall observed that a dozen men had crossed the wire while Roosevelt stared at the end of the strand in his hand. He seemed transfixed on the wire.[17]

"It was as if that barbed-wire strand had formed a dividing line in his life, and that when he stepped across it he left behind him in the bridle path all those unadmirable and conspicuous traits which have so often caused him to be justly criticized in civic life, and found on the other side of it, in that Cuban thicket, the coolness, the calm judgment, the towering heroism, which made him, perhaps, the most admired and best loved of all Americans in Cuba."[18]

Roosevelt then stepped across that wire and "from that instant, became the most magnificent soldier I [Marshall] have ever seen." Marshall followed Roosevelt into the jungle to witness his transformation into an American hero.[19]

Llewellyn's G Troop pushed its way through the dense vegetation with Jenkin's K Troop to its right and O'Neill's A Troop on the extreme right. The underbrush and vines for most of the time hid the men from each other. The officers had no control over their formations. The troopers could only keep in line by the sound of twigs breaking, heavy breathing or the crash of someone falling down. Without any urging, they continued to move in the direction of the sound of the fighting.

The air snapped with the sound of Mauser bullets. The Spaniards preferred to fire in volleys rather than as individuals. The Rough Riders were unfamiliar with smokeless powder. Accustomed to looking for that puff of white smoke emitted each time a rifle fired, they found the enemy virtually invisible. Consequently, the Rough Riders saw no targets to fire at. Fortunately, the Spanish fire initially was high. After a while, they found the correct range and took their toll on G Troop. Henry Haefner, of Gallup, New Mexico, fell to the ground shot through the hips. His friends dragged him behind a tree for protection. Haefner asked for his canteen and rifle and kept firing. The men advanced through the jungle, leaving him alone. They later found him dead.

Roosevelt advanced between Llewellyn's G Troop and Jenkin's K Troop and heard the sound of Hotchkiss cannons indicating that the battle of the Regulars had already begun on his right.

At 7:30, Captain Albert L. Mills, with patrol of two men, had discovered the Spaniards entrenched at the intersection of the valley road and mountain trail. The Spaniards had erected stone breastworks flanked by two blockhouses along the ridge that paralleled the road. Their fortifications overlooked the intersection of the two trails. The way the road curved to his left placed the ridge to Young's left front. To the right lay a ruined hacienda building.

Young rode forward to examine the Spanish position. He then returned and placed his Hotchkiss battery in concealment 900 yards from the enemy. He deployed the squadron of the First Cavalry, under the command of Major James M. Bell, on line in ground as difficult as the Rough Riders negotiated. Behind them he placed the squadron of the Tenth Cavalry, under Major Stevens T. Norvell, in support. He then waited, knowing that Wood's regiment had the hardest climb to get into position.

During the wait, Wheeler rode up. Young explained his plan, and Wheeler approved it. At 8 o'clock, Young's Hotchkiss battery opened fire. The Spaniards quickly answered with an intense volume of fire that shocked Wheeler. He had never witnessed musketry like that during the Civil War. They could fire at a rate of five times faster than muzzle loaders that he was used to in the last war. That was the effect of bolt-action rifles. He also heard similarly intense gunfire to his left, indicating that Wood was just as heavily engaged.

The fighting continued for an hour, with the Spaniards stubbornly defending their position with volley after volley. The two squadrons of Regulars merged into one line but could no longer advance. Casualties increased: three officers and eight men killed and at least 20 wounded. Wheeler then began to have doubts about his ability to drive the enemy from the field. Major William D. Beach, his engineer officer, suggested, "We have nine big regiments of infantry only a few miles back on the road. Let me send to General Lawton for one of them and close this action up."[20]

Wheeler hesitated since he had stolen ahead of Lawton. It would be an embarrassment to call on him for help, but there seemed no other choice. Beach scribbled down the message for the courier to deliver. To the major, time did not fly while waiting under fire. It crawled. It seemed as if the sun stood still in the sky.

Over on the other trail, the men of G Troop broke through a wall of vines into a clearing overlooking a ravine with a small ridge on the right. Beyond that ridge lay the valley road. Entering into the open field, they dropped either to one knee or a prone position and returned fire. There, the Spanish fire more accurately took its effect on G Troop.

Rifle fire came not more than 80 yards away from G Troop's left front. Since they could not see through the brush in that direction, Roosevelt assumed that L Troop had swung around to their own right and mistakenly fired on them. Roosevelt ordered the men to cease fire. With all the firing, G Troop did not hear the order. Llewellyn and

Lieutenant Greenway ran along the line swatting the men with their hats to get them to stop firing. The men, in turn, began to shout at those they thought were L Troop to cease firing. Upon later investigation, they realized that they were at right angles with L Troop, which faced in a completely different direction. The spent cartridges of Mauser rifles along the trail verified that the Spanish had fired on G Troop.[21]

Roosevelt lost contact with his two other troops, so he sent Lieutenant Greenway, Sergeant Marcus J. Russell, of Troy, New York, and George Roland, of Deming, New Mexico, down the valley to find them. They had to expose themselves to extremely heavy fire. Greenway and Roland returned with information that K and A Troops had descended blindly into the valley. They fared much better in the fight by taking far fewer casualties. Unfortunately, Russell, who served as a colonel on the governor's staff, was killed.

The other two returned to their places on the firing line. Roosevelt then noticed that blood trickled out of Roland's right side. Roland did not seem to pay any attention to it. Upon examination, Roosevelt discovered that the wound was slight, but Roland had a broken rib. He ordered the trooper to report back to the hospital stewards for treatment. After some grumbling, the trooper consented and left. Fifteen minutes later, Roosevelt saw Roland again on the firing line. The trooper said he could not find the hospital. Roosevelt doubted this but let him stay anyway. Roosevelt secretly admired every wounded man who refused to remain out of the fight. He usually cited these men for bravery.

Roland had actually reported to Assistant Surgeon James R. Church, who had established his field dressing station where the first wounded had fallen. Church told him there was nothing he could do for him at that time and to sit down until he could be taken to the division hospital at Siboney. After a short while, a restless Roland protested, "I don't seem to be doing much good here."[22] He picked up his carbine and returned to the fight.

About the time that Greenway and Roland had reported the location of the other two troops, Lieutenant Woodbury Kane walked up smiling with a platoon of ten men. He was evidently comfortable in this environment. Roosevelt lay down in the grass and conferred with Llewellyn and Kane about the lay of the land and where the enemy might be. Llewellyn told Kane that he did not need his men and to return to his own troop. Kane, still with a smile on his face, disappeared with his platoon over the edge of the hill to the right, not even stooping over to avoid the bullets.

To G Troop's front, Roosevelt recognized Richard Harding Davis acting like an officer, exposing himself to fire. Davis studied the ground across the valley with his field glasses and discovered a force entrenched on the ridge. He recognized that they were Spaniards and not Cubans by the cockades on their hats. He yelled over to Roosevelt and pointed across the valley to their right: "There they are, Colonel; look over there; I can see their hats near the glade."[23]

In a minute or two, Roosevelt finally recognized the enemy. He estimated the distance at 500 yards and called it off to three or four of the best shots nearby. They adjusted the rear leaf sights on their carbines and fired. Roosevelt did not see any effect of the rounds. He increased the range each time, getting more men to fire. Suddenly, the Spaniards broke from their position and ran to another where Roosevelt identified even more enemy. He brought as many men as he could find on line and had them fire as fast as they could. After a few minutes of accurate firing, the Spaniards retreated into the jungle to the left, and the Rough Riders lost sight of them.

They saw another large body of soldiers follow the retreat of the Spaniards. Since Roosevelt could not recognize them, he could only assume that they were Cubans and had his men hold their fire. Unknown to him, the Cubans had failed to participate in the battle, and he later learned that those men had been Spaniards. These were the only Spaniards that the three troops would see all day.

Again, they saw more troops advancing across the ridge to their right front. Studying them through his binoculars, Roosevelt recognized their blue uniforms as that of the Regular cavalry. Anxious for the Regulars to recognize them, Roosevelt ordered K Troop to signal them. Jenkins sent First Sergeant Frederick Lie, of Organ, New Mexico, back up the ridge. There he climbed a tree and waved his troop's red and white guidon. He came under instant enemy fire but continued to wave his flag. Very soon the Regulars waved their guidon back in recognition. The Regulars extended their line to connect with O'Neill's troop.

Roosevelt's squadron had established contact with the Regulars, and the enemy had been driven from his front. A tangle of vines and brush flanking G Troop's position prevented any further advance forward. Nor could they see 20 feet into the jungle. Neither could Roosevelt determine where the enemy nor his own lines were. Not sure of what to do, he decided to turn Llewellyn's G Troop around and join up with Wood. He would tell Roosevelt what to do. Roosevelt left Jenkins and O'Neill's troops with instructions to maintain the communication with the Regulars.

The fire from the left was still intense. Besides the two men killed, G Troop had five wounded. Jenkins and O'Neill's troops fared much better down in the valley. K Troop had not lost a man, but A Troop had two killed: George H. Doherty, of Jerome, Arizona, shot in the head, and Edward Liggett, also of Jerome, shot while back at the road, just above the heart. Tom Hamilton, of Jerome, held him until he took his last breath.

On Roosevelt's order Llewellyn's men crawled back slowly on their hands and knees, dragging their wounded with them for fear of leaving them behind for the buzzards. G Troop crossed the trail at the same cut in the wire where they had first entered the jungle. They saw that the site had been converted into a dressing station. They left their wounded in the care of the hospital stewards, then spread out in open order and moved forward to join the left wing of the attack. Upon reaching the trail, Roosevelt ran down the path littered with the wounded of L Troop in search of Wood. He heard the battle raging a half a mile ahead.

Dressing Station

As Davis stepped out onto the trail, he saw a tall young man with a Red Cross brassard on his arm coming back down the trail carrying a wounded man much heavier than him over his shoulders. The stooped man raised his head and nodded to the war correspondent. Davis was sure he had seen that face covered with blood, dirt and perspiration before but had trouble placing it. Then the memory of a young Princeton football player came to him. It was none other than Bob Church. La Motte had evidently returned to the hospital at Siboney. This left Lieutenant Church the senior surgeon on the field. Church would carry three more men from the battlefield that day.

As soon as the fighting began, Church, with the rest of the regimental hospital corps, ran forward to treat the wounded. The trail at the top of the knoll, where the fight had begun, made a logical site for a field dressing station for the wounded. Edmund S. Norris,[24] of Guthrie, found a man wounded in the left lung and carried him back up the hill. Carrying 150 pounds uphill under fire seemed agonizingly slow. Fortunately, the wounded began to come in on their own at a rate where Ed did not need to go out again.

After the fight had advanced past him, Tom Isbell walked on his own back to the dressing station. His fatigues were so soaked in blood that he joked when discarded they stood by themselves in dried blood. He later joked, "Every time I move I hurt and every time I hurt I move and hurt again."[25]

Davis walked down the trail. Only the clatter of crabs walking across the stony path or the whistling of bullets broke the deathly silence. Along the narrow, descending path, he saw blood spattered on rocks and matted grass. Blanket rolls, haversacks, canteens and an occasional carbine littered the way. To the veteran war correspondent, the signs resembled an army in retreat, but this path led to the enemy.

Suddenly a hospital steward burst out of the bush. "Lieutenant Thomas is badly wounded in here, and we can't move him. We want to carry him out of the sun some place, where there is shade and a breeze."[26]

Davis followed him off the trail. There he saw Thomas, half naked and covered in blood, tossing and raving wildly in pain. They lifted up the corners of a blanket holding the lieutenant. He sat up and cried out, "You're taking me to front, aren't you? You said you would. They've killed my captain—do you understand? They've killed Captain Capron. The _ _ _ Mexicans! They've killed my captain."[27]

The stewards assured him they were, but he did not seem convinced. Carrying him toward the trail, they stumbled forward, leaving a dark streak of blood where the blanket brushed against the ground. Again, Thomas sat up, clutching at one of the stewards with his bloody hands. "For God's sake, take me to the front. Do you hear? I order you; damn you, I order—We must give them hell; do you hear? We must give them hell. They've killed Capron. They've killed my captain."[28]

Again, he fell back and fainted from the loss of blood. The tourniquet was the only thing holding life still in him. Davis left him on the trail in the care of the stewards. Fifty feet further down the trail he again ran into Church. Bob cradled Capron against his knee with the captain's handsome head resting on his shoulder. Davis remembered that some had said Capron was the most soldierly looking officer in the army. The surgeon had cut away the tunic exposing his broad white chest and shoulders, then pecked away at the dark wound. In spite of Church's efforts, an hour and a half after receiving his wound, Capron's life ended. Tragically, it was his 27th birthday. Shelby F. Ishler was lying next to Capron in his final moments of life. The captain "asked if the boys were retreating." They told him no, to which he replied, "Thank God. He sank back into his cot and breathed his last breath."[29]

Fifty yards farther down the trail, Davis came across a wounded boy lying behind a rock. A dark hole between the eyes marked where the bullet had entered. Still the boy's chest heaved with short, hoarse breaths. Davis knelt down and gave him water from his canteen, but the water would not pass through his clenched teeth. Davis laid him back down and found a pocket New Testament with the name Tilden Dawson on it. As he was writing the name in his notebook, another young man came up from behind.

"It's no use. The surgeon has seen him; he says he is just the same as dead. He is my bunkie; we only met two weeks ago at San Antonio; but he and me had got to be such good friends—But there's nothing I can do now." The young man dropped down on the rock, staring down at his friend, tears running down his cheeks. Davis left them.[30]

Not seeing any more abandoned field equipment, Davis assumed that he neared where the fight had started. There the body of a sergeant stretched across his path. He noticed, "after death the bodies of some men seem to shrink almost instantly within themselves; they become limp and shapeless, and their uniforms hang upon them strangely." The man who had died farthest in the line of battle was Ham Fish.[31]

Davis borrowed a carbine from a wounded man and joined up with L Troop. There he saw Lieutenant Robert Day walking around directing his troop's fire. Sergeant Byrne actually seemed to enjoy himself. The action on the left started out about the same way as it had on the right.

Action on the Left

Colonel Wood wrote in his report that he had initially deployed two troops each left and right while keeping three troops in reserve. When he realized that the Spanish line exceeded his, he ordered two more troops on line, one to extend the left and the other the right. This made his line equal in length to the Spaniards, and then he advanced.[32]

D Troop had been the first troop in line of march of Brodie's squadron when the fighting began. Teddy Miller heard a few stray shots followed by volley after volley. The distant thunder removed all doubt that they would see action that day. At that moment came the word to load their magazines and advance. Huston climbed through the fence to the left. His men followed.

Odgen Wells and Frank Knox had marched together. After the shooting started, Wells remembered moving through a gap in the wire while Knox remembered climbing over the barbed wire fence, and his pants snagged on the barbs. While struggling to free himself, a bullet passed through his hat. Frank tore his trousers in his escape from the wire. He ran into a hard-faced George Doherty of A Troop, who told him he would stay as long as he had a cartridge to fire.

When the battle started, D Troop advanced a few paces into an open coconut grove with waist-high grass. They swung around and spread out in a skirmish line, then dropped to the prone position. Wells recorded that he was the extreme left flank of D Troop with George Burgess and Roy Cashion to the right of him. Everyone in D Troop heard gunfire constantly from their left front but could not see where it came from. They fired a couple of volleys in return. Unaccustomed to smokeless powder, they fought an invisible enemy, which proved the most frustrating aspect of the battle. But Wells admitted that after his first round, his nervousness left him, and it was like shooting quail.

Remembering Wood's instructions not to fire unless one saw the enemy, Huston ordered his men to stop shooting. In all the excitement, it was hard for Miller not to fire. Under Huston's orders, they again advanced, this time on the run downhill to join up with L Troop. Huston had divided his troop into three platoons. Lieutenants Carr and Goodrich led the platoons on the left and right flanks while First Sergeant Palmer led the center platoon. Wells remembered that Goodrich walked up and down the firing line like a veteran. Palmer, who had never received much mention in letters before, impressed his men by leading that advance on a dead run while under heavy fire from their left and front.

Running through high grass, they pushed their way through vines and creepers with their carbines. Panting for breath, D Troop finally came on line with L Troop. The men dropped behind the cover of scattered trees and brush, then returned fire with a vengeance. F and E Troops followed in columns around to D Troop's left rear. Wells heard firing from his left rear and assumed it was F Troop. He and Burgess called for them to cease fire. It only increased.

When Edward Marshall later joined them, he observed that other than the indentations in the grass where Rough Riders had lain or the presence of a few officers walking around, only the sound gave any indication of a battle. The grass waved back and forth as if blown by a breeze, but there was no breeze. Marshall described the passing bullets as making a "zeu" sound. First Sergeant Palmer wrote that the Spanish bullets made a distinct sound like little firecrackers on the Fourth of July. Roosevelt said that they sounded like the humming of telephone wires. William Palmer, of Shawnee, just wrote "the bullets came thick and fast."

Edward W. Johnston, of Cushing, wrote that the bullets passed over them "like a swarm of bees" cutting the trees and ground around them. Sergeant Scott Reay, of Newkirk, wrote that bullets had cut the grass within a foot of his head, and branches fell from above. He later walked over the battlefield and saw trees as big as his arm cut down by enemy fire. He thought it looked as if a tornado had passed through the area. That contest for the first Spanish trench proved to be the hottest fighting of the battle.

Most of the men of D Troop had found cover on the forward slope except six. Because of the five- to six-foot interval between men, they were left in the open. From left to right: Marcellus "Sell" Newcomb, of Kingfisher; William F. Palmer, of Shawnee; Fred N. Beal, also of Kingfisher; Johnston; Corporal Rhoades; and either William Bailey, of Norman; or one of the Stewart brothers from Pawnee lay in the open. In less than five minutes after they had dropped down into position, three of them were hit. Newcomb was shot in the right knee, Beal in the leg and Rhoades also in the leg. Realizing the danger, the officers ordered the six to take cover. Designated the company first aid man, Burgess left Wells to treat the wounded.

Corporal William S. Simpson, of Dallas, Texas, and Teddy Miller had lagged behind the troop during the rush. As they came downhill, Miller spotted Beal and Newcomb to his right. Beal was twisting around on the ground, clutching his knee in pain. Since both were in Ira Hill's squad, Miller realized that he was in the right place. Beal looked up and asked for help. Miller stopped to bind the wound above the knee. He then recognized Lieutenant Carr, took a position on line and waited. At that time, firing became intense from the left rear.[33] Most thought another troop was firing on them by mistake. Johnston volunteered to run over as a courier to tell them to stop firing. Wood walked over and told Huston they were Spaniards, and F Troop had been ordered to advance upon them.

The exchange of fire continued. Under the direction of their officers, the men answered each volley with their own firing in the direction of the sound of the enemy guns.

About that time, Roosevelt and Edward Marshall joined up with Wood. Captain McClintock's B Troop was already on line. The men had only hesitated long enough to pile their haversacks by squads before they rushed up the road. B Troop squeezed in between the left of L Troop and D Troop's right.

When Wood realized that Luna's F Troop had fallen behind, he ordered Lieutenant Tom Rynning, of B Troop, back to bring F Troop up on line. Rynning took off running backwards, stumbling several times. When he found L Troop, Luna walked up and asked what the matter was. Rynning told him, "Get your troop up on the firing line, you're way behind." With that Luna rushed his men forward.[34]

When Rynning returned to the front, Wood asked him why he had run backwards. The Arizona cowboy and former cavalry man answered that if he were shot, he did not want to get hit in the back.

Meanwhile, two bullets struck McClintock's left leg just above the ankle. He staggered a little, slightly caught his balance, then fell to the ground with his gun waving over his head. The fallen captain then calmly called to Lieutenant George B. Wilcox, of Prescott, Arizona, to assume command. Six-foot, two-inch William Proffitt, also of Prescott, came over, reached down and placed his captain on his shoulder, then carried him to a safer place out of the line of fire. Lieutenant Rynning came over and asked, "Any orders you want to give, Captain?"[35]

McClintock answered, "Just give 'em hell."

Sergeant Charles Utling, of Phoenix, lit his captain a cigarette. Marshall also walked over and asked if there was anything he could do for him. McClintock, in great pain but cheerful, responded, "Not a damn thing, except get out."[36] A private who had been sick for several days recognized his wounded captain. He crawled over and leaned back against the tree between McClintock and the enemy, saying, "Never mind, captain, I am between you and the firing line. They can't hurt you now."[37]

G Troop finally caught up, and Wood squeezed it in between D and B Troops. During the last advance, Wells lost contact with D Troop and fell in with G Troop. Captains William Llewellyn and Huston walked by, and Wood noticed that Llewellen carried an ax on his shoulder and Huston had picked up a shovel. Wood stopped them and jokingly asked them, "What are you going into the fight to do? To dig holes in the ground?"[38]

Neither had an answer. Both had absentmindedly picked them up just as Roosevelt had earlier. They said they had no idea why they picked them up. The colonel then asked them to repeat their orders for the battle to him and then let them return to their troops.

Wood, with his sandy mustache and bronzed almost the same color of his khaki uniform, walked around fully erect on the enemy side of his sorrel horse. Marshall observed that the grass moved about his legs from passing Spanish bullets. Wood admitted to Marshall later that he felt that he was the only person in the fight with nothing to do. His troop commanders controlled their part of the action. All he could do was walk around and convince his men that he was not afraid. However, he regretted that he had not taken out that $100,000 life insurance policy, for he had his doubts about whether he would survive that engagement.

Near Wood stood Adjutant Hall and Captain Rivers. Roosevelt and Major Brodie also joined the little group. Roosevelt could not see how Wood had not been hit as exposed as he was. Even more incredibly, Roosevelt could not see how Wood's horse, a much bigger target, had not been hit. Roosevelt had left his tied up back on the trail and regretted that he had not left his saber there too. It kept getting tangled up between his legs.

Brodie also brought his adjutant, Lieutenant Frank Frantz, from A Troop. The two adjutants looked at each other with a grin. They had absolutely nothing to do but stand around and look unconcerned while bullets sliced the air and grass around them. Sergeant Wright walked close to Wood proudly displaying the regimental colors. Two rounds clipped his hair and another three passed through the flag, scratching his neck.

The officers of the regiment inspired confidence by deliberately exposing themselves to fire. Ed Johnston wrote, "Wood sauntered around and looked quite at home. Roosevelt stood beside me in the hottest fire and seemed as cool as a cucumber."[39] Corporal Denham remembered seeing Huston "two or three times directing his men as quietly as if he was on parade."[40]

This war marked the transition between nineteenth- and twentieth-century warfare. Bolt-action, magazine-fed rifles no longer required men to stand shoulder to shoulder to fight while their officers stood next to them. Soldiers could then load and fire from the prone position. Since the Franco-Prussian War in 1870, armies had adopted the advance and fire tactics used in that fight. Smokeless powder had also increased the range and accuracy of the rifles. Exposing oneself deliberately to enemy fire would prove suicidal in the next war. Probably because they were beyond the range of the pinpoint accuracy of the Spanish Mausers, the Rough Rider officers took no greater risk against volley fire by walking around than they would have by lying down. In this case, it improved the morale of the men. From then on Roosevelt would follow Wood's example and not seek cover again during a battle.

While the officers continually exposed themselves to fire, that was their duty as seen in nineteenth-century warfare. This risk was not expected of the surgeon. La Motte had turned to Tom Rynning, of B Troop, and said, "This is no place for me," and moved further back to establish a hospital.[41] Church, on the other hand, recovered several seriously wounded men from the firing line while under fire and returned them to a secure position on the road. Doctors were not expected to take this kind of risk. It qualified as courage displayed above the call of duty.

After an hour of waiting under intense fire, Huston received the order to advance. Evidently, the enemy had abandoned their first line of trenches. Huston's men raised up from the grass and ran downhill. Miller did not let Simpson out of his sight. Miller's sum total of training consisted of nothing more than guard mount while in Florida and on the boat. He had no concept of the battle drills, advance and fire. When the troop ran forward, he followed. When it dropped to ground in the tall grass, he was alone.

Fear creates tunnel vision, and the peripheral vision depends upon the individual's understanding or tolerance for fear. This did not mean that Miller was a coward. All men in combat get scared. Because of his unfamiliarity with the actions of the troop, he just did not know what was going on. Combined with the enemy's intent on killing him, Miller's peripheral vision became very narrow. In his mind, he was lost all the while he followed behind the left flank of D Troop.

Simpson and Miller ran into a trooper shot through the arm from Luna's F Troop, which had fallen in on D Troop's left. He helped him back to a tree where an "emergency man" could look after his wound. Soon they recognized their own captain walking around. They ran over to Huston and decided not to leave his side for fear of losing the troop again.

Wood and Roosevelt walked up and talked with Huston under some trees. After some discussion, the troop advanced a short distance further. Miller spotted Bob Wrenn and one of the Stewart brothers. Miller then saw some men lined up behind entrenchments across the valley to his right and asked Huston if they were Cubans or Spaniards. Huston called over to Wood to see if he could identify them. Meanwhile, Stewart had decided for himself that they were enemy and started firing anyway.

Edward Marshall saw about 300 Spaniards break from cover and "run away like rabbits." On Huston's orders, D Troop opened fire on the fleeing enemy. The Oklahoma boys let out a wild whoop since they had advanced a half a mile without seeing one single enemy. They finally had targets to aim at. Marshall saw a dozen enemy drop with the first volley, attesting to the Americans' accuracy. Wood then yelled out, "Don't shoot at retreating men."[42] The firing, however, drowned out the sound of his voice. He called trumpeter Cassi over and told him to blow "cease fire." Hearing the bugle notes, the men finally stopped. While some may have thought it a mistake, they did not know that Wood feared another flank attack. He did not want the men to waste their ammunition. Brodie also ordered Captain Frederick Muller's E Troop to fall in behind F Troop to protect the left flank.

The Rough Riders captured the trench line and a small blockhouse. The Spaniards fell back 300 yards to a new trench line that Wood estimated extended 800 to 1,000 yards in length.[43]

Wood's fear proved correct. They again received flanking fire from the left. Wood shouted, "They're on the run!"

A man nearby proclaimed, "Things seem to be coming our way."

Another quipped, "Yes, bullets."[44]

Suddenly, Brodie spun around and fell to the ground like a wet rag. He looked down and saw blood flowing from his right forearm. He was shocked. He got up and walked over to Wood and said, "Great Scott, Colonel, they've hit me."[45] At first Brodie tried to remain at the front, but the pain became too intense, and the loss of blood made him faint. Wood ordered him to the rear, then directed Roosevelt to take command of Brodie's squadron on the left. Wood would personally lead the three troops on the right.

Hall wrote that Wood then ordered him to go back to the field hospital to pick up a first aid package for Brodie. No sooner had he crossed the open field than Hall heard the sound of gunfire from the regiment's right. He looked back and saw from a distance the body of a man in khaki fall wounded. Having expected his exposed commander to get shot at any minute, Hall assumed it was Colonel Wood. He found Bob Church and told him to hasten over to help both Brodie and Wood. Hall claimed he then continued to the rear to try, without any success, to report to General Young that Wood was wounded.

There was no love lost between the men and Adjutant Hall. To them he was a martinet. It later became known that someone, possibly an unwounded officer, had fled all the way back to Siboney and reported that the Rough Riders had been cut to pieces in an ambush. Lawton dispatched the infantry to hurry up to the Rough Riders' rescue only to discover that the report was false, along with the claim that Colonel Wood had been killed. B Troop's farrier Frank W. "Barney" Harmsen coming up the trail ran into Hall heading the other direction. He incorrectly assumed that his troop had been annihilated. Hall wrote that both a mule packer or the colonel's cook and valet had fled to the rear at the outset of the battle. Hall did not like the veteran Buffalo Soldier any more than Roosevelt liked Hall. One packer, wounded through the neck, did return to the rear and hollered, "Come on, boys, help us out!" While the men did not see the other two flee, many did see Hall go to the rear. In their mind, he was the man who "turned yellow" and ran back to Siboney screaming disaster. Sergeant Paul Hunter phrased it more objectively: "He took a notion to go to the rear and couldn't stop."[46]

The khaki-clad figure on the right-hand side of D Troop that Hall had seen fall was Edward Marshall. Burgess had been designated D Troop's aidman. He bent over to examine Marshall's wound. The round had passed through his body near the spine. Burgess removed a flask of ammonia from his brown medical pouch and revived Marshall to consciousness. The first thing the journalist saw was the quiet blue eyes, thin straight lips of his benefactor. In a calm, quiet drawl, he told Marshall that he thought the wound was mortal and not worth dressing. He apologized and then ran over to check on other wounded men. Marshall watched the man fearlessly walk erect about the wounded while under fire. Every now and then he would stop to fire his carbine.

Two minutes later, Burgess ran back to Marshall and asked if he wanted to be carried to the shade. He then picked the wounded journalist up in his arms and carried him to a tree where he dropped him, "murmuring wild and Western oaths." He then sped back to the front. Wood had ordered his troops on the right forward. The enemy had abandoned their second line of trenches.

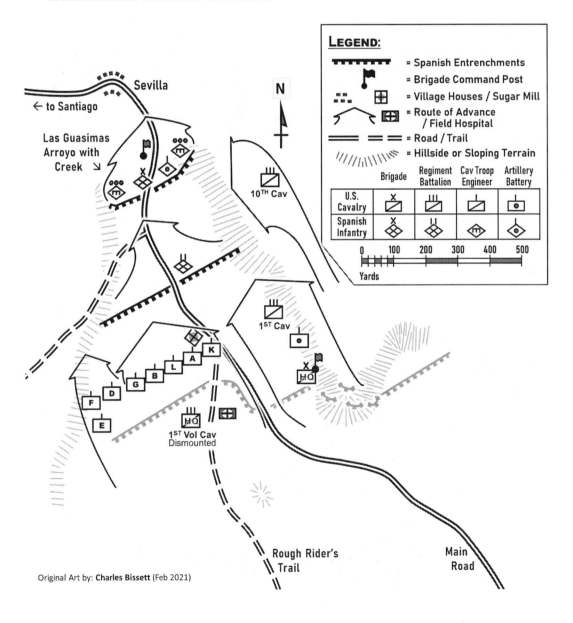

Original Art by: **Charles Bissett** (Feb 2021)

Marshall slipped in and out of consciousness but all the while writing what he saw. Dedicated in his profession to what he thought might be the end, he was probably the most observant person on the battlefield. His peripheral vision was wide. He noticed that upon hitting, the bullet made the sound of a "chug." The men went limp and fell quickly like clods, making no moan but the thud of the human body and the metallic jingle of canteens and carbines. He could hear it 100 feet away. But he did not hear the one that hit him.

As the Rough Riders advanced, the forest became thicker. With Roosevelt in command of the left and Wood on the right, neither could see more than 30 men at a time. The two field grade officers had to rely on the initiative of their subordinate officers. Roosevelt saw Dade Goodrich march along behind the men of his platoon, constantly reminding them to watch their intervals and fire slowly with careful aim. He picked up a carbine and joined the D Troop line. Lieutenant Goodrich reminded him, "Keep your interval, sir; keep your interval and go forward!" Like a disciplined soldier, he did.[47]

On the right, Davis observed that the men advanced in short, stubborn rushes. The men did not fire "at will" but waited patiently for the signal from their officers to fire in volley. The men moved through the vegetation in the manner they were previously accustomed to. On the command from their officer, the Easterners broke in a dead run for the next tree "like men trying to get out of the rain." The Westerners "slipped and wiggled through the grass like Indians; dodging from tree trunk to tree trunk and from one bush to another."[48]

The fight had lasted an hour, pursuing after an enemy which had retreated up a slight incline to their third line of trenches on a wooded ridge. The Rough Riders could see a ruined plantation house with a red-tiled roof surrounded by several outbuildings for making sugar, at the edge of the woods. It had been a former distillery for *aguardiente*. Both Wood and Roosevelt recognized that the distillery was central to the enemy position. Others directed their squadrons toward it. D Troop then made a wide swing forward to the right across a large patch of palmetto plants.

Alexander Denham suddenly felt as if he had been hit by a sledgehammer. He took another step and fell while bullets rained around him. He lay there for an hour. Shelby F. Ishler, of Enid, was also shot in the right forearm.

Wood ordered his squadron, "Cease firing and advance!" The troops rose and began their advance with a cheer. Davis observed that the first cheer wavered, but it invigorated them. It let the men know where the others were. It gave them confidence. The second cheer sounded like a "howl of triumph." With a wild cowboy yell, the men rushed forward.

Roosevelt had lost sight of the right wing, so he stopped his squadron. The day was becoming hot, and, after two hours under fire, his men exhibited signs of exhaustion. He saw through the distance Spaniards firing from plantation houses. He had picked up a carbine from a wounded trooper and fired at the buildings himself. Soon after, he heard cheering on the right. Assuming the other squadron had charged, he ordered his three troops to charge the buildings 500 yards away. Screaming like fiends, the Rough Riders ran full speed. At that same time, the First and Tenth Cavalry also advanced upon a ridge from the American right and placed it under heavy fire. This combined final assault completely unnerved the Spaniards, who broke and ran. Whatever misgivings the Rough Riders may have had about the fighting abilities of the Tenth had been rectified. The men from Oklahoma wrote home about their newfound respect for the quality of the "colored" cavalry men. 🎇

D Troop and the rest of the squadron reached the plantation house panting, nearly out of breath, and continued about another 200 yards down the other side through the thickets into a ravine. The firing finally stopped, and Miller heard a bugle sound "recall." The men then walked back down the ravine and found where D Troop had reorganized. Teddy Miller located Sergeant Ira Hill and his squad. Wells left G Troop to find his own and came across Doherty shot through the head. His chest wheezed in short gasps. He called for the surgeon. Church and Wells carried the mortally wounded soldier back to the dressing station, Wells becoming lightheaded and nearly collapsing until Church caught him. The surgeon then opened his case and poured sprits of ammonia down Wells's throat and told him to report to the hospital in the road. He had nearly suffered heatstroke.

Wells walked down the trail and found D Troop. He reported to Captain Huston, who instructed him to go back on line. Wells found Frank Knox and Harry Holt. There he learned of the men wounded in D Troop. Wells again began to feel faint, and Lieutenant Carr told him to report to the temporary hospital established in the stone distillery. Cashion asked Wells for his tin cup so that he could fetch him some water, but it had a bullet hole, rendering it useless. Wells had no idea he had almost been hit.

In the end, the Rough Riders occupied the Spanish ground as the Spaniards had beaten an orderly retreat back to Santiago. The American maneuver against a vastly superior, entrenched enemy became known as "Wood's Bluff." Triumphantly, Wood walked across the battlefield leading his horse with his left hand and carrying the regimental colors in his right. As the Spaniards vacated their entrenchments, Young's Regulars similarly advanced and occupied the trenches. Some would claim that Wheeler in his excitement supposedly exclaimed, "Come on, boys. We've got the damn Yankees on the run!" About that time, the Ninth (Colored) Cavalry came running up the road behind the Rough Riders with Lawton's infantry in tow. One cavalryman eagerly exclaimed, "Show me a Spaniard, I am rarin' to go." Sergeant David Hughes, of B Troop, pointed over to a dead Spaniard about 25 feet away in the tall grass. "Take a look there, but his troubles are over."[49]

Fortunately, Young's cavalry brigade had carried the day on their own. Neither the dynamite gun nor the Cubans participated in the fight. Sergeant Borrowe, still delayed by the infantry, could hear the battle in the distance. Major Beach looked down at his pocket watch, and it was just 10 a.m. He was astounded that only two hours had elapsed, and it was not even the afternoon.

Roosevelt then sent out pickets to his left flank and placed the rest of the squadron in the sunken road leading to the intersection. D Troop deployed as advance skirmishers forward of the plantation buildings. Roosevelt had the wounded and those who had suffered from heat exhaustion placed inside the abandoned distillery. He learned that there was water down in the ravine, so he sent details down there to fill canteens.

Corporal Henry Love was among those sent out on a water detail down into the ravine. He walked back up the trail with heavy canteens strapped over his shoulders; all the while, hot, thirsty soldiers of other regiments marched to the front. They begged for water, which he shared. He returned to the stream and refilled the canteens for another trip. On his return, he ran into the Second Massachusetts Infantry. Once again, he shared his water. Realizing he could not turn down the requests of thirsty soldiers, he returned with empty canteens. One of the other corporals whose canteen he had carried failed to find sympathy with his explanation and looked at him with contempt. Teddy Miller just said, "That is all right, Love, I am just as much obliged."[50]

First Sergeants became very busy after the battle. First Sergeant Palmer checked the status of food, ammunition and water like all other first sergeants. He had personally fired off 35 of the 50 rounds he carried in his cartridge belt. He learned that most of the others were also low on ammunition as well as water.

At 10:45 that morning, Palmer then led a detail of ten men back to find where they had dropped their haversacks and blanket rolls. The troopers kept their food and extra ammunition in their haversacks. Sergeant Hughes, of B Troop, had the foresight to have the men in his squad strip down everything except their canteens and cartridge belts at the outset of the battle. They then consolidated their gear into a pile and memorized the location. Palmer was not so lucky. His men had discarded their field gear anywhere from the road, or like Teddy Miller, to their last assault position.

Since all haversacks looked the same, they identified Palmer's by the picture of his wife and daughters, which he must have shown to everybody. Palmer's detail found nothing to eat but hardtack. Most of the contents of their packs had been ransacked, they assumed by the passing infantry. They were not permitted to eat any of the captured beans or chickens in fear that the Spaniards had poisoned them. Fortunately, the passing Second Massachusetts Infantry offered them all the canned beef, tomatoes and other food they wanted. Other Rough Riders later saw Cubans, who would camp behind their position, wearing the American tunics and blanket rolls and assumed that they had pilfered the dead. Some Rough Riders then regarded them as nothing more than the land crabs that also scavenged off the dead.

Elisha Freeman was by that time the cook for D Troop. He went down to the spring where they got their drinking water and saw a Cuban about to take a bath in it. Freeman warned the Cuban not to since it would foul up the water. The Cuban ignored Freeman's warning and started in anyway. Having lost all regard for the Cubans since the battle, Freeman drew his pistol and shot the Cuban dead.[51]

K Troop's Fred Herring, of San Antonio, Texas, also set out through the woods to track down the scattered pack mules that had carried off the rapid-fire guns. He successfully rounded them up by following the trails they had left in the grass.

While looking for his own squad's haversacks and blanket rolls, Sergeant Hughes ran into none other than Adjutant Hall. Hall asked him where to find the regiment, and Hughes told him. Hall found Roosevelt and incorrectly reported that Wood was dead.[52] Believing he was then in command of the regiment, Roosevelt walked toward the other squadron to organize their defense. To his delight, he ran into Wood, who was still alive and well.

Wood informed Roosevelt that more regiments were coming up the road. They then met with Major Eugene D. Dimmick, in command of the Ninth (Colored) Cavalry, and discussed their next course of action. They decided that the Ninth would take a position out front so as to let the Rough Riders rest.

A Regular Army officer came up and reported to Huston that Brodie had been wounded and that he had instructions for Huston to take command of the left wing. This appointment as acting squadron commander assured his standing in the regiment as the senior captain in line for promotion. His men took the appointment with the same sense of pride. Huston was essentially recognized for their accomplishment. So this was something many wrote home about.

Huston lined the rest of D Troop up and swept through the mill and thickets beyond. Finding no enemy, the troop returned to their former position to discover

Wood, Roosevelt and other officers waiting for them. While the men rested, the officers decided upon a plan for security.

D Troop advanced again to the mill with E Troop on the right and F Troop on the left. They remained at the mill for another two hours. Each of the officers—Huston, Goodrich and Carr—continually walked about the line inspecting the security. Roosevelt then called back Huston's squadron to the intersection of two trails. By 5 p.m., D Troop was withdrawn back to the distillery where they watched infantry regiments pass along the road ahead of them. The cavalry could then relax. The Battle of Las Guasimas was over.

Immediately after the fight, the first sergeants also took an accountability of their men to determine how many were killed or wounded. They then sent back details to recover the eight dead and carry the 34 wounded back to the hospital. Frank Knox was assigned to the squad detailed to find the dead and recover the wounded. This was the worst duty as he saw the gruesome effects of the war. The vultures and land crabs had found the dead before their comrades did. The mutilated bodies of the dead were gathered up and laid in a row under a tree along the road. One trooper then stood guard over the bodies to protect them from further desecration by scavengers.

Palmer checked the roll and learned that D Troop had only five men wounded. Of the action on the left flank, B Troop had only three men wounded, E Troop had only one, but F Troop, which had attacked the flanking movement, had seven wounded and one killed. William T. Erwin, of Austin, Texas, was shot in the head.

Palmer then sent details back to find his men. Ed Loughmiller and Ed Johnston found Denham and Shelby Ishler, of Enid, who were lying where they had fallen for over an hour. Tears welled up in Ed's eyes when he found his wounded friend, Alexander Denham, from his hometown of Oklahoma City. Denham wrote that to see those tears in his eyes hurt worse than the pain of his wound. Loughmiller and Johnston picked him up in a blanket and carried him back to the field hospital. Burgess similarly carried men back to the field hospital. The other troops did likewise.

After bandaging Newcomb's leg, Church gave him the choice of riding back to Siboney or waiting for a litter to carry him the next day. Newcomb preferred to start at once. So the stewards lifted him up on a large Mexican saddle on a stray mule. Church asked, "Does it pain you? Can you stand it?"

"Stand this?" Newcomb quipped, "Why, this is just like getting money from home."[53] Calmly he rode back down the trail smoking a cigarette with his bloody leg dangling from the mule. He bragged to the passing infantry, "Damned near stepped on the son-of-a-bitch; then he got me—but I got him! Now you go and get yours!" The infantry racing to the front cheered him.

Covered in blood, Church and the rest of the hospital stewards patched up as much damage to the wounded as they could in the matted grass under the shade of a mango tree. The open-air hospital initially consisted of one tent with the medicine, but pack mules eventually brought up more tents.

Captain McClintock and Marshall lay near Brodie. Rumors spread that both Wood and Roosevelt had been killed. Church reassured them that it was not true. A little later, Wood personally came back to the hospital to check on the wounded.

Wood walked over to the journalist. "Hello, Marshall! How are you now?"

Marshall drifted off into unconsciousness, but when he awoke, Wood still stood over him. "I was awfully sorry that I couldn't go to you when you asked me to. I tried to, but it was the turning point of the battle." Marshall suddenly realized the absurdity of the idea of the commander leaving in the middle of the battle to see him. He laughed. Wood started laughing too.

"Won't you have a drink?" Wood offered Marshall a five-ounce vial of Scotch whiskey. After taking a drink, Wood then offered it to McClintock, who exclaimed, "By God! That's good!"[54]

Once word of the fight reached Siboney, other journalists joined the flock. Stephen Crane and Richard Harding Davis paid Marshall a visit. Davis offered to file Marshall's dispatches and then brought up a stretcher to carry him back down to Siboney. The wounded remained at the field hospital until the next day.

Meanwhile, a corporal and seven men had been left to protect the field hospital. Throughout the day and night, the fear of Spanish sharpshooters caused seven alarms. The first resulted from a single shot that hit one of the wounded. Each time, they sent the squad out to investigate. The other six times had resulted from the noise of land crabs walking. Fear began to set in. At one point, a wounded man exclaimed, "Great Scott, Major! There come a lot of Spaniards."

Brodie, who was walking about, looked but could see nothing.

The man told him, "Get down here and you can see them through the bushes and grass." Upon closer investigation, Brodie recognized that they were just 200 Cubans a few hundred yards away.[55]

As they later learned, the Spaniards had left 200 sharpshooters behind concealed with leaves and brush in the trees. They were released prisoners issued rifles and told to

Division Field Hospital at Siboney (Theodore Roosevelt Collection, Harvard University Library).

kill Americans and not to return under the pain of death. Some surrendered, but most did not. They shot mostly at returning wounded.

No one in the field hospital could sleep because of the pain and moaning.[56] That night they sang songs. Someone started singing, "My country, 'tis of thee, Sweet land of liberty, Of thee we sing." Then the others picked it up. As they finished, Marshall remembered hearing one lone voice struggling to continue. "Land—of—the—Pilgrims'—pride—Let—freedom…" He died, unable to sing any further.[57]

Most of the Rough Riders were too exhausted to erect shelter tents that night. Wood and Roosevelt felt it appropriate to relax discipline after what they had been through that day. There was none of the usual conversation or singing. The Rough Rider camp was unusually quiet as the men contemplated the events that day. Most reflected on their own performance. In a way they were happy. The question that had nagged many of them going into battle was how they would perform under fire. Almost all could write home with confidence that they had passed the test.

Many troopers searched the battlefield for souvenirs to send home. Many collected spent Spanish Mauser cartridges. Some sent home pieces of a Spanish uniform. Edmund Norris found Marshall's pocketbook containing $700, which he returned to its rightful owner. The grateful journalist rewarded Norris in return with his pistol, some Spanish money and three pieces of silverware. Norris sent these treasures home along with other souvenirs, a pair of gauntlets and a Cuban machete. Norris's thoughts turned to after the

Wheeler's council of war after the Battle of Las Guasimus (Theodore Roosevelt Collection, Harvard University Library).

war, and he wished he owned a herd of cattle. He mailed $50 home and asked his father to buy some calves for him. He also included seed for a kind of bluegrass he had found, which he hoped to cultivate for his herd to graze on.

Late that afternoon, the sentries captured a Spanish soldier in a tree armed with a revolver. He claimed to be a Cuban, but, upon investigation, his papers identified him as an officer. He was handed over to the Rough Riders for questioning. Nearly everyone in the regiment who heard about it dropped by the headquarters to take a look at the prisoner. The poor, bewildered soldier dropped to his knees and clasped his hands in the air, praying that they would not kill him. The troopers laughed at the idea and walked away.

Captain Luna, who spoke fluent Spanish, interrogated him for the officers. They learned that the Spaniards had lost about 200 dead and many more wounded. The official report claimed that the Americans buried 42 Spanish dead. Roosevelt and O'Neill walked the battlefield and only counted 11, which his men had buried. The Spanish prisoner complained that he did not understand how the Americans fought. They did not fight the way they should. Every time that the Spaniards fired, the Americans rapidly fired back. They kept coming and did not stop. This story circulated the entire camp, which the Rough Riders took as a compliment. Wood ordered him hung as a spy. Two or three Rough Riders then escorted him over and turned him over to the Cubans. While walking him through the woods, three Cubans cut his head off, propped his body against a tree with his head replaced and then spat on him. Tom Rynning, who was officer of the day, ran back and kicked one, chased down and kicked another, but the third escaped. The cruelty of the Cubans dropped them one more notch on the popularity list of the Rough Riders.[58]

The greatest praises of any unit's fighting abilities often come from those whom the unit has fought. After the surrender of Santiago, another popular story circulated through the camps. A resident of Santiago asked a Spanish soldier returning from the Battle of Las Guasimas how the Americans had fought. He replied, "They tried to catch us with their hands!"[59]

Roosevelt walked around trying to encourage his men. The men were tired and hungry. Roosevelt sensed the feeling around the camp. He knew what men needed to boost their morale. They were short of rations, and a packtrain intended for them had been ordered for use by another regiment. He found instead a load of Spanish beans on a dead Spanish mule. A number of mules had been killed during the fighting while the Spaniards were loading them with supplies. Ignoring the warning against eating contraband food, he issued the food to his men.

Meanwhile, Chaplain Brown was unloading supplies at Siboney. Brown had been left behind at Daiquiri to help unload regimental stores; then the *Yucatan* moved to Siboney. Upon learning of the fight and that Adjutant Hall had seen Wood get killed, he hustled a mule, loaded it with provisions and what Rough Rider mail he could find at the newly established post office and then headed up the trail. The Rough Riders would not get the rest of their mail until June 30. Brown rejoined his regiment just after supper. He was disappointed that he was not with his men during their time of need.

If any man had had any doubt about his mortality, the battle removed it. One man from E Troop felt that was a good time to be baptized. At Chaplain Brown's request, Captain Muller and Huston stood as witnesses.

Hall's animosity toward the regimental cook grew even worse that night as he slept out under the stars without his yellow slicker or tent which the cook had taken with him back to Siboney. Being unprotected against the tropical climate brought about a return of the symptoms of malaria that Hall had contracted in his earlier military career.

That night, in culmination of the battle, an orderly from a brigade asked for the casualty reports and the trimonthly returns for the past two periods of ten days. Hall submitted the list of wounded and killed but was completely unaware of the requirement for this report. All he had was a vial of watery ink and an old pen. Fifth Corps had ordered him to leave all administrative supplies behind before they left Tampa. Evidently, someone at corps headquarters believed that the paperwork would stop on account of war. He was wrong. The orderly offered to loan him one form and allowed Hall the luxury of waiting until he returned to the states to complete the required triplicates.

The next morning, Wells felt much better and joined the detail sent in search of dead and wounded since a few men were still unaccounted for. He came across several dead Spaniards and a few packs. What impressed him most was the damage done to the trees during the fight. The bullets had cut them to pieces. The detail returned in time for the burial ceremony.

At 10 a.m.,[60] Chaplain Brown, standing in a gray shirt and coveralls, held the burial services for the slain Rough Riders. He had been unable to find his surplice among the baggage. Eight bodies wrapped in their shelter halves were buried right beside the road where they had fallen. They were laid to rest side by side in a long trench with their feet pointing to the east. The burial detail, comprised of men from each troop, had been too tired to dig separate graves. Frank Knox served on the burial detail and picked up the Westerner who had confronted him at the barbed wire fence. Counting the rounds in his cartridge belt, Doherty had only fired five rounds before a Spanish Mauser round drilled clean through his head. The bottom of the grave was lined with blades of long, thick, green guinea grass, and broad palm leaves as long as the grave covered the bodies. The regiment and guests turned out.[61] Brown read from the burial service book of the Episcopalians: "I am the Resurrection and the Life, saith the Lord..." He then said, "Let us pray," and without any directions, every man removed his hat, knelt and prayed. Brown realized that these were religious men accustomed to going to church. With bared heads the men of the regiment sang "Rock of Ages."[62] Someone threw a clod of dirt in the trench; then Cassi blew taps. That ended the short ceremony. The position of each body was recorded, and Colonel Wood, Lieutenant Hall and Chaplain Brown each kept a copy of the memorandum. The burial detail marked the graves with wooden boards. Later, the Cubans erected crosses of stones. Eight months later a tombstone with "To the Memory of Eight Unknown Soldiers" would mark their grave.

The men offered Capron's few belongings to his father, still aboard ship, but the old, grieving battery commander refused. Instead, they sent his campaign hat and shoulder straps wrapped up in a newspaper tied with Spanish barbed wire to his widow.

Captain O'Neill began to make arrangements for a raffle for Capron's horse. This was an old army tradition to raffle off the belongings of a deceased comrade or a deserter to raise money for the family or unit. In this case, Buckey planned to raise money for Capron's widow and still give her the horse. He would not finish the task before someone would have to arrange a raffle for his belongings.

That afternoon, comrades in arms began to carry the wounded in litters down to Siboney. Most of the wounded Rough Riders found a porch or hut to rest in. Denham stayed in an abandoned store until it came time for them to transport him home. The

Rough Rider graves at Las Guasimus (Theodore Roosevelt Collection, Harvard University Library).

army sent men back on the hospital ships. Edward Marshall, to everyone's surprise, would recover from his wound.

By then, typhoid and malarial fever began to deplete the ranks of the regiment as four to five Rough Riders a day came back to the hospital at Siboney. Leroy E. Tomlinson, of B Troop, even died while aboard a hospital ship on June 23. He would not be the last. As many as 20 Rough Riders would die of disease, including a number of men from the troops left behind in Florida. Only 25 would die of wounds. Surprisingly, Oklahoma's D Troop, the Indian Territory's L Troop, and McGinnis's I Troop recruited from different territories were the only troops not to lose anybody to disease.

At 10 in the morning on June 26, the Rough Riders moved their camp a few miles further in a marshy area near a beautiful stream. As the days passed, so did packtrains and other regiments. Canvas "dog" tents did little to protect them from the daily torrential downpours common to the tropics. The men rested and waited anxiously for the next fight.

One night it rained especially hard. After it had been pouring for about 30 minutes, Goodrich looked out from his little tent and saw a sentry walking up. The man was thoroughly soaked. Goodrich offered the trooper his rubber raincoat. The trooper came to present arms and looked up with a smile from under the sagging brim of his dripping hat and said he did not mind getting wet. He then walked along. Goodrich recognized the happy face of his friend Teddy Miller.

The Rough Riders had only salt pork and hardtack to eat during their wait and little to nothing else except mangos or any other fruit they could find. Everything was scarce. One man auctioned off two ounces of tobacco for $47.50, more than two months' pay for a sergeant.

The Army issued salt pork and hardtack not because of their taste. These proven army marching rations could survive almost any condition without spoiling. Salt pork was nothing more than a square slab of fatty bacon soaked in brine. Hardtack was flour and water cooked into a square biscuit, so hard that some soldiers joked that it could bend a bayonet tip. The latest attempts since the last war at preserving canned beef had gone bad, as the Rough Riders experienced during their voyage. The Army had wholly inadequate means for preserving perishables at that time. Any other rations of potatoes and onions depended upon their availability. So the Army fell back on its old, tried-and-true rations of salt pork and hardtack.

Soldiers had to survive with those two ingredients every day in the field. To get the hardtack soft enough to eat, one had to soak the hardtack in water either whole or broken in pieces until it became doughy. One common recipe was to fry the bacon in a mess tin. When done, add salt to the dough, mix in coffee and then fry in the bacon grease. Once finished, put a little sugar on top. If the Army provided vegetables, then all the ingredients could be tossed into a pot and cooked into a stew. Some of the cooks either boiled the mangos in sugar to something similar to applesauce or fried them in sugar to something that tasted like a sweet potato.

Roosevelt, consequently, led a detail of his cook and two of the best walkers from I Troop, leading the officers' horses and a stray Spanish mule or two back to Siboney. Through great exertions on his part and the help of Colonel John F. Weston of the commissary, Roosevelt secured rations of beans and canned tomatoes. He also purchased with his own money a bushel of potatoes at $60 and onions at $30. Within an hour or so after their arrival, the aroma of a beef stew filled the air. Morale picked up. Soon the men were summoned to a big boiler at the mess tent. As the mess personnel dished out the stew, the Rough Riders could hardly believe their eyes. Everyone laughed when one New Yorker exclaimed, "And it's got real onions in it too!"[63] There was no limit to what Roosevelt would do for his men. Neither was there any limit to what they would do for him. He led several more expeditions back to Siboney after that.

On a return trip carrying a heavy load through a downpour, Sherman Bell, of Colorado Springs, Colorado, slipped, fell and reopened an old rupture. He crawled and walked, when he could, the rest of the way back to camp. Surgeon Church closed it with a spike bandage but informed Bell that he would have to return to the states on the next boat. Until then, he would have to wait in a hospital tent. The ambulance did not arrive until the night of June 29. As soon as he heard it coming, he crawled out into the jungle and lay there the rest of the night. It left without him. The next afternoon, his friends in K Troop carried his bedding roll, cartridge belt and carbine while he staggered behind the column on the march to Santiago. When Roosevelt discovered him that next morning of July 1, Bell told his colonel that he preferred to die fighting. Impressed, Roosevelt did not have the heart to turn him back. His rupture opened two more times, but Church patched him up each time, and he survived.

On the afternoon of June 30, Captain Mills rode up to Wood's tent to inform him that Wheeler and Young had both fallen ill to fever. Both had to relinquish their commands to subordinates. Brigadier General Sumner took command of the cavalry division, and Wood took Young's brigade. Command of the First Volunteer Cavalry passed to Roosevelt. Wood had accomplished what Roosevelt had expected of him. He had not only organized and trained the regiment but had trained its lieutenant colonel as well. It was almost as if fate had destined this army surgeon to move on to greater challenges so that Roosevelt could fulfill his own destiny of leading into battle the regiment that his personality had inspired.

Right after the battle the men scribbled letters home, letting their parents know that they were all right. However, they knew the letters would arrive weeks after the fact. Families back home would first read about the battle in the papers. The Oklahoma newspapers received the bulletins with the list of killed and wounded on Sunday night, the 25th. Excitement crowded around the telegraph office as people waited for the names. The next morning, the list was compared with a roster of enlistees at the Adjutant General's Office in Guthrie, and it was learned that it had mistakenly listed only four of the Oklahoma boys as wounded but in Troop B. It left off Alexander Denham's name. Family or friends scanned the names in the list of the wounded in the papers. "CAPRON, the Gallant Rough Rider, Killed in a Battle at Playo Del Este" read across the front page of *The Guthrie Leader* on June 25. Oklahomans mourned his death as one of their own sons, although they had only known him for a short while. Hamilton Fish's death similarly attracted the interest of readers. Starr Wetmore's mother worried herself sick waiting. His father penned a letter after the battle, wishing belatedly that he had not enlisted.

The Battle of Las Guasimas served as the Rough Riders baptism of fire. It had tested their mettle and not found them wanting for courage. Colonel Wood proved himself a skilled tactician. Trained as a surgeon, he had earned the Medal of Honor as a lieutenant, and Wood's Bluff turned out to be the decisive maneuver to break the enemy's hold on the important intersection. He had undoubtedly earned his star. This left the command of the Rough Riders to his subordinate, Lieutenant Colonel Roosevelt. Roosevelt had deferred the command of the regiment to his friend because he did not feel that there was enough time to organize and train the regiment for war. That turned out to be the wisest move. Wood had accomplished that task and had trained his subordinate as well. As fate would have it, Wood, an army surgeon, would go on to command a cavalry brigade so that Roosevelt could rightfully command his regiment in its last and climactic battle.

What they had accomplished at Las Guasimas is still debated. The volume of fire put out by the Spanish defenders caused the Rough Riders to estimate that the enemy had between 2,000 and 4,000 soldiers with two machine guns. Considerable speculation remains about the exact count. The *New York Times* ran an article on July 1, claiming that the Spaniards had 4,000 men at Las Guasimas and had lost 265 killed and wounded. Wheeler later asked the civilian governor of the province how many men General Linares had on June 24. The governor informed Wheeler that Linares had 4,000. General Jose Toral y Velazquez said that they had fewer than 2,000 and had lost 250 men. When Wheeler asked about the 265 casualties, Toral admitted that the number included the fight with the Cubans the day before. General Linares told Wheeler that he had engaged the Americans with a force of 1,400 that day, and General Frederico Escario claimed they had lost 200 men. Regardless of whose count, fewer than 1,000 men drove a superior force from an entrenched position. This defied the three-to-one odds required for such a maneuver.

Some historians have argued back and forth over the merits of Wheeler's attack on Las Guasimas because General Linares had planned to evacuate the position. Had Wheeler not attacked, the same results would have occurred. The Spaniards would have evacuated the road junction, but no lives would have been lost on either side. Shafter had hoped to win with minimal loss, but even he recognized the morale effect that the battle had on the army. However, he did issue an order for Wheeler to engage in no more battles until the entire corps was in place. Those historians, however, did not view the battle from the perspective of the participants.

This was war, and the soldiers did not enlist to sit around and wait. They yearned for combat. Each man had something to prove. For them, Wheeler was the man of the hour. This veteran of numerous campaigns shared the same eagerness for battle as they did. The consequence of this battle for the Rough Riders was the loss of eight lives. Two of them were the most popular men in the regiment and probably the country. Both eagerly sought combat. Hamilton Fish did not have to go but actually had to persuade Capron to take him. Capron was a professional soldier through and through. He cried at the thought that war might end before he arrived. These men were great losses to their nation and those loved ones they left behind. But they willingly took that risk. They died far out in front of others. All men have to die someday. These two chose the ground upon which to die and the way they would meet their fate.

Capron refused to be withdrawn from the field. At that moment there was no greater love than that which he had for his own men. People who have never commanded men cannot understand this relationship. In his dying moments he wanted to see if his men performed to the level that he had trained them. His young lieutenant,

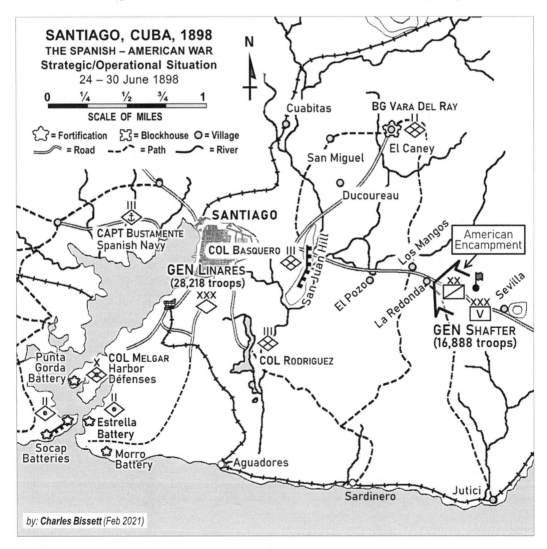

Robert Thomas, similarly was willing to make that same sacrifice. Other privates on the line made similar selfless sacrifices, such as that made by the private who guarded Captain McClintock.

The Rough Riders enlisted for but one reason—to fight in combat. This celebrated regiment was an experiment. Rarely had any regiment been recruited along this line. Men were specifically selected on their ability to ride and shoot rather than from just the same hometown or state. The Army rushed this unit into service with so little training. Only a battle would provide the test as to whether this volunteer regiment was as good as any Regular Army regiment with years of training and decades of heritage. Las Guasimas answered that question. Their final charge upon the last entrenchment not only proved they were as good as the Regulars but may even have been better. They proved it not only to all critics but most importantly to themselves. This would become very crucial for the test of courage that the next battle would provide. To the Rough Riders, they could have served under no better division commander than that old Confederate cavalry man, Fighting Joe Wheeler.

CHAPTER 6

A Crowded Hill

Finally, by the 30th of June, the Rough Riders received orders to march against Santiago. Shafter had unloaded sufficient rations for daily consumption plus three extra days. By noon, the regiment struck camp and drew up in line behind the First Cavalry as the last regiment in the brigade. There they waited for hours as other troops and pack mules marched past them. Each man carried three days' rations of salt pork, beans, coffee and hardtack. By this time, Borrowe and Tiffany had rounded up enough mules to transport their dynamite gun and Colt rapid-fire guns. Captain Albert L. Mills, who had distinguished himself at Las Guasimas with the Regulars, and Lieutenant William E. Shipp accompanied Roosevelt as liaison officers. First Lieutenant Carr commanded D Troop since Captain Huston commanded Brodie's squadron of D, E, F and G Troops. Captain Micah Jenkins assumed command of Roosevelt's squadron of A, B, K and L Troops, having turned his K Troop over to First Lieutenant Woodbury Kane. By midafternoon, the Rough Riders moved out in their turn.

The column of soldiers slogged their way along the muddy road like an accordion, extending then contracting as the men bunched up. During these frequent halts, the Rough Riders in blue flannel shirts and brown canvas trousers rested on their khaki canvas haversacks and bedrolls. They waded through two knee-deep streams. As they neared a camp of an infantry regiment on the left, it squeezed in ahead of them, separating the Rough Riders from the First Cavalry. More infantry regiments began to squeeze in and separated the Rough Riders further from their brigade.

A division staff officer rode up and informed Roosevelt that he could take another road to the south of the main road to catch up with his cavalry brigade. He did. The Rough Riders passed the corps headquarters and First Division Hospital along their way. As they marched, they caught glimpses of the Signal Corps balloon looming in the sky off in the distance. Lieutenant Colonel George McClellan Derby in the basket underneath reconnoitered the enemy trenches along the heights around Santiago.

Accompanied by Lieutenant Colonels Edward J. McClernand and John D. Miley, General Shafter surveyed the ground for the next day's battle from El Pozo Hill. He could see San Juan Hill and the country around El Caney. General Lawton, along with one of his brigade commanders, Brigadier General Adna R. Chaffee, joined them at noon. Shafter then summoned his two other division commanders, Brigadier Generals Jacob F. Kent and Samuel S. Sumner, Jr., to develop his plan of battle.

Wheeler had previously reconnoitered the neighboring town of El Caney before he became ill and had learned that about 500 Spaniards under General Joaquin Vera de Rey occupied it. He had recommended that Shafter attack it with either a division of cavalry or infantry. The aggressive Wheeler felt optimistic that they would catch the Spaniards

Infantry marching to Santiago (Theodore Roosevelt Collection, Harvard University Library).

retreating out of Santiago. The conservative Shafter, on the other hand, had heard that Lieutenant General Luis Manuel de Pando y Sánchez was advancing from Manzanillo with 8,000 reinforcements for Santiago and would arrive in a few days. He feared that reinforcements down this road would threaten his right flank. Shafter gave the task of taking El Caney to Lawton. Lawton, who as a captain had chased down Geronimo with Lieutenant Leonard Wood, boasted that his division could take the town in two hours. Shafter instructed General Garcia to block the approaches to El Caney with his 3,000 Cuban insurgents. Doctrinally, he would seal off all approaches and escape routes to Santiago.

Shafter also estimated that General Arsenio Linares commanded the high ground overlooking the San Juan River with 12,000 soldiers at his disposal. This was three-quarters of his own strength. So even with all three divisions, Shafter would not have the needed three-to-one advantage for a successful attack. Actually, only about 500 to 750 Spaniards defended the entrenchments on the high ground that Shafter intended to attack. The rest waited in the city below.

Shafter planned to attack with three divisions abreast. Sumner and Kent would advance down the main road. Sumner's cavalry division would cross the Aguadores and San Juan Rivers, then turn right, while Kent's infantry division would cross it and turn left. Upon reducing El Caney, Lawton's infantry division would join up on Sumner's right, and then they could attack. The assault positions where the divisions would wait were 700 yards in front of the enemy. This had been a safe distance to line up in battle during the last war when they fired black powder muzzle loaders. The old Civil War veterans did not have an appreciation for the range and accuracy of the new weapons. That

Shafter holding war council (Library of Congress).

oversight and timing the attack on Lawton's arrival would prove the costliest mistakes in Shafter's decision process.

Meanwhile, the Rough [Riders] [ag]ain rejoined the main road but came upon two regiments of infantry halted [...] [in]fantry to give way and pushed his reg[...] road, the rear of his regiment separate[...] [m]arching. By 8 p.m., under the cover of [...] [o]f El Pozo Hill and finally received the [...] [n]oon with heavy traffic to walk about f[...] [...] in camp cooking their meals. The re[...] [T]he Rough Riders rested where they fel[...] [co]nfident the next day would bring battl[...] Mills and Shipp, after extending his [...]

While Hall may not [...] [w]as a stickler to duty. He immediate[...] guard. No sooner had the bugler sig[...] member of his staff rushed down to a[...] [with]in one and a half miles of the enemy [...] the general that bugle calls were not s[...] [th]en passed a glance around at what he considered half a dozen [...]

"Of course, they can see the fires," growled the officer. He then continued to "light

(handwritten note)
— civil war tactics verses what was happening
— Power play
* Rough Riders no longer as proud and boostful *

into" the lieutenant for mounting the guard in the presence of the enemy. Realizing that the conversation with the general officer had become one-way, Hall considered it useless to defend his acts. Hall did not bother to respond that the camp guard so near the enemy was probably more necessary than at any other time. "Keep your old guard on," relented the general.[1]

Ever faithful to the regulations, Hall remembered that it was against the Articles of War to keep a man on guard duty for more than 24 hours. But he knew the futility of arguing with this general officer who had already passed judgment on him because of the bugle call. Hall promptly gave orders to dismiss the guard.

The general then settled down and admitted, "Well, as long as you have got them in ranks go ahead and mount them."[2] He then ordered Hall to reduce the size of the guard for the night. Meanwhile, Roosevelt had ordered O'Neill to set up an outpost down the road with his A Troop. He also sent Lieutenant Rynning, Goodrich and two others out to reconnoiter the enemy positions. They spotted the artillery and approached close enough to hear the soldiers speak Spanish. The little party returned with sketch maps of the enemy positions.

Attitudes had changed since the last battle. No longer did Rough Riders boast, "Aw, them Spaniards won't fight," or "Dagos can't shoot, anyhow."[3] Veterans of one battle, the Rough Riders had an edge over most of the other regiments going into battle. Their conversations did not have the same levity as before. They did not brag about their own invincibility but wondered who would get shot. Las Guasimas had taught them the reality of war.

Their late arrival, followed by cooking supper, did not leave the Rough Riders much time to sleep for those that could. All night, other regiments marched by while some went into camp next to the Rough Riders. Hall still felt the effects of malaria, and Lieutenant Haskell felt even worse. In fact, Haskell was too sick to eat that morning, concluding, "Well, they ought not to be able to hit me in the bowels"—a nearly prophetic statement.[4]

Roosevelt and Wood did little talking. Neither knew the plan for the next day. Both curled up under their slickers and slept on their saddle blankets. They would sleep soundly except for the times they had to wake up to make the rounds to check the sentries.

At 4 a.m. on July 1, the men awoke to a breakfast of hardtack, coffee, salt pork and beans. No bugles sounded reveille this time. Ogden Wells remembered Captain Huston shook his shoulder and told him to get something to eat. When the sun rose, 490 Rough Riders fell in ready to march into battle. Besides the eight killed and 34 wounded, they had lost seven more sick or injured since the last battle. Corporal John Rhoades, of D Troop, numbered among the sick in the hospital. The Rough Riders stood in a grassy basin, a mile and a half long and a half mile wide, just north of an adobe ranch house and abandoned sugar factory on El Pozo Hill. All around them waited another 7,000 Regulars. The Rough Riders knew very little about their role in the upcoming fight.

Roosevelt had still not received any orders as to the battle plan other than Lawton would lead the main attack against El Caney. He believed his regiment would participate in a diversion. Rumors circulated about the plan for attack. From what little the Rough Riders had learned about the plan for that day, they knew the battle could not proceed until Lawton took El Caney. When they heard that the Cubans supported Lawton's attack, they let out loud, derisive cries.

At 6, Captain George Grimes's horse-drawn battery of howitzers wheeled up onto a small hill just southwest of them which provided a forward command post and observation point of the heights surrounding Santiago. At 6:15,[5] the Rough Riders heard

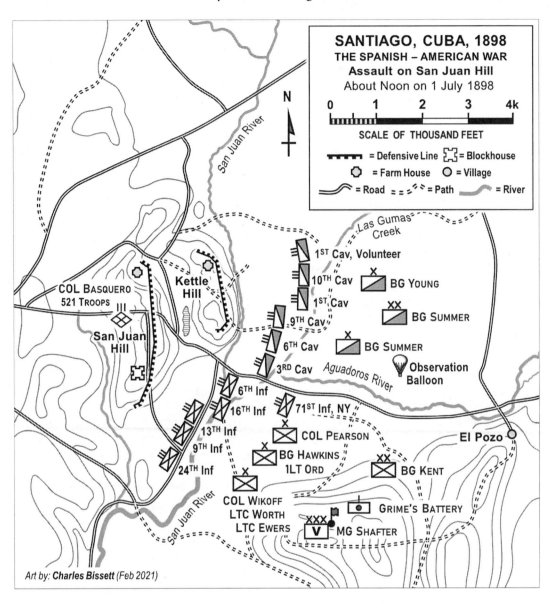

Art by: **Charles Bissett** (Feb 2021)

Capron's battery signal the beginning of Lawton's fight for El Caney. The sound of small arms fire in the direction of El Caney caused Colonel McClernand to believe that Lawton's attack was well underway. Shafter, from his command post further to the rear, then ordered Grimes's battery by phone to open fire. At 8, the Rough Riders heard, "Gun Number One, Ready—Aim—Fire!" followed by a roar of cannon.[6] The signature of white smoke in the distance verified that the round had indeed hit the red-tiled blockhouse on the Spanish position. The Rough Riders let out a cheer. The battery began its cannonade on the Spanish positions, hoping to draw the Spanish battery into a fight.

The battery fired several more shots, receiving the same enthusiastic response from the Rough Riders. Each time the battery had to wait a minute or two for its smoke to clear. Richard H. "Dick" Stanton, of Phoenix, who was sitting on several bricks, predicted to David Hughes, "In a few minutes you are going to hear some yelling on the other side." Another soldier commented, "You can bet your life, those Spaniards know the exact distance to this hill and they'll fire right into us."[7] Hall remembered that a number of officers also expressed similar concerns.

After 20 minutes of cannonading, Kane ordered every eighth man in K Troop to go behind the house and pick up boxes of shells for Tiffany's rapid-fire guns. Roosevelt and Wood sat next to each other, watching the spectacle. Wood mentioned to Roosevelt that he wished he could move his brigade to another position out of the line of any answering enemy fire, since they rested within a hundred yards of the battery.

No sooner had he uttered those words than the Rough Riders heard the faint sound of a distant cannon followed by whistling overhead. The cheering ceased. A few men cautiously started to seek cover. A staff officer put down his field glasses. "Here, what's the matter with you? That's only a shell."[8] The first burst harmlessly above the building. Some men laughed while the staff officer looked proud of his guess. The first round affirmed the range.

A distant thud heralded the arrival of another round. The second burst directly over K Troop of the Rough Riders. It was a canister. Men scattered in every direction for cover to escape the rain of balls and shrapnel. Four wounded Rough Riders remained where they fell. Bill McGinty returned from his ammunition detail to discover that three men who had been standing near him were wounded. He had escaped their fate by luck. The shrapnel had wounded Sergeant Samuel G. Devore, of Wheeling, West Virginia, in the left forearm; Mason Mitchell, of New York, in the left arm; and Benjamin A. Long, of New York City, in the left thigh, all of K Troop. A piece of shrapnel also hit Wood's horse through the lungs. One of the balls from the exploding shell left a welt across Roosevelt's wrist. A third round hit Grimes's battery, killing two of his men.

Immediately after the second round, Roosevelt and Wood leaped to their feet and mounted their horses. The regiment scattered down both sides of the center slope. With difficulty, Roosevelt rounded up his regiment, then rushed them 100 yards over the crest of the hill into the thick underbrush. They watched from safety as the shelling flew back and forth for another 15 to 20 minutes.

Hall ran to his horse, which was tied to a nearby bush. As he started down the hill, he heard a man quietly cry out, "Please get me out of here."[9] He turned to see a wounded man. A piece of shrapnel had ripped his leg wide open, which bled profusely. Two or three other Regulars were also wounded. Hall told him that he would help but did not know what to do. To his relief, he saw Surgeon La Motte and two hospital stewards running his way. They went to work on the man. Roosevelt later claimed that the man lost his leg.

While others treated the wounded, the American black powder dueled at a disadvantage with the smokeless powder, which made the enemy almost invisible. One round hit one of Grimes's guns square in the muzzle, causing it to tumble back several times. His men rushed to upright the carriage and place the gun back into action. At 8:45, the enemy battery quit firing. Grimes's battery fired with a few more shots, concluding that it had won the duel.[10] Suddenly, a bugle sounded, and riders raced teams of horses up the hill to hitch up to the guns. They then sped back down the hill out of sight with the guns in tow. It was a sight that David Hughes would never forget. With the artillery duel complete, the ground battle could commence.

Suddenly, blue-clad infantry regiments raced to the front while the Rough Riders began to hear the cracking of small arms ahead. At 9, McClernand directed Sumner to march his cavalry division to the edge of the woods and wait. Wood ordered the Rough Riders to fall in behind Colonel Henry K. Carroll's cavalry brigade which had already started down the road. The Rough Riders, having learned from their last battle, left their tunics, haversacks, bedrolls in a pile and even left the Colt rapid-fire guns behind so as not to slow them down. The rest of Wood's cavalry brigade followed behind the Rough Riders. Capron's L Troop, under the command of Lieutenant Richard Day, led the regiment down the road, ten feet wide at its narrowest part, as it squeezed past several infantry regiments, each waiting its turn to advance. Jenkins's squadron followed in the order of march, A, K and B Troops, with Huston's squadron behind. After a half an hour of marching, Frank Knox heard the order to keep silent trickle back. All the Rough Riders knew what that meant. Knox could hear all around him the sound of cartridges slipping into the magazines on the side of their Krags.

Signal Corps balloon launching near San Juan Hill (Theodore Roosevelt Collection, Harvard University Library).

For some reason Colonel Derby launched the aerial balloon over the main road right above the Rough Riders. He had followed right behind the cavalry division. As if the enemy had any doubts about which route through the jungle the Americans were following, the balloon removed it. In their effort to down the balloon, Spanish artillery and rifle fire rained down on the advancing columns. By 10 a.m., the Rough Riders reached the crossing of the Aguadores River, which was little more than a stream, and had entered within the range of enemy rifle fire. Sumner ordered Carroll's brigade to cross and then turn into position. Because of traffic jams, the Rough Riders halted several times before reaching the next two-foot-deep ford.

While the enemy could not see the Americans, they knew the range to that crossing. The tropical sun was getting hot, and the enemy fire was getting hotter. Again, the men felt frustrated as fire rained down upon them from an enemy masked by the jungle they marched through. Bullets popped through the air, and shrapnel intended for the balloon rained down upon them. It sounded like the Fourth of July. Men dropped to the ground as if they had tripped, some never to get back up. Some of the heaviest casualties of all regiments were taken at that area, which became known as the "Bloody Ford" or "Bloody Bend." Dead and wounded lined the road to Santiago. Around 1 p.m., Major Valery Harvard, chief surgeon of the cavalry division, would later select this as the logical location for the ambulance and dressing station since they would not have to go very far to collect most of the wounded. The medical personnel would adjust or apply bandages. Ambulances would shuttle the wounded back to the First Division Hospital at Siboney.

Near the ford, Colonel Miley consulted with General Sumner when Captain Robert L. Howze, of Carroll's staff, rode up and reported that the First Brigade was in place.

6th Infantry crossing San Juan Creek under fire (Library of Congress).

"They are waiting to go at 'em." Howze was an energetic officer who seemed to be everywhere on the battlefield without regard for his safety.[11]

After further consultation, Miley gave in, "Well, you gentlemen are older than I am."[12] With that, Sumner sent word to Roosevelt to cross the Aguadores at about 50 yards; then turn to the right to link up with Lawton's division. A few minutes later, Roosevelt received the orders. He hurried his men across the ford to minimize their exposure to the intense fire. Another orderly from Sumner rode up and instructed Roosevelt for each troop to also throw out flankers and warned them not to fire on the Regular cavalry in front. Hall remained at the ford to pass on the instructions to the following troops.

Most of the Rough Riders had not filled their canteens since before the last day's march. They went into battle with empty canteens and felt muddy water was better than nothing, so many tried to stop in the ford to fill them. Sumner told Hall not to let the passing troopers stop to refill their canteens. The ever-unpopular Hall once again had to enforce another unpopular order. He knew the men despised him and figured that they would assume he was the author of that order. The soldiers had to hurry up and get into position so they could again wait. Dehydration would result in dire consequences for the regiment.

For some reason, the Rough Riders again halted. Sumner told Hall to send an officer with the message to have Roosevelt move them further ahead. Hall looked around and saw Lieutenant Haskell. He sent Haskell with the message to Roosevelt. As the last troop cleared the ford, Hall rejoined his regiment.

About noon, the volunteer cavalry marched out of the jungle and then turned to the right after crossing the Aguadores River and followed the western bank of the Las Guamas Creek through a field of tall grass. Roosevelt halted his regiment about three to 400 yards from the Santiago Road and moved his men to the cover of a sunken road. Hall remembered it was about three feet deeper than level ground, and the regiment's right was anchored on another road that led up to the top of the hill. A barbed wire fence lined the right side of the road. Roosevelt ordered his men to lie down on their bellies. The forward troops, which included L and A Troops, lay down behind the cover of the three-foot bank of the sunken lane, while others, to include D Troop, waded into the knee-to-waist-deep Las Guamas Creek and hid behind its bank that was nine feet high in some places. The rest laid down behind patches of brush and waist-high grass.[13] All the Rough Riders except those in the river could see the enemy in the trenches but could not fire with the First and Ninth (Colored) Cavalries ahead of them. The cavalry division lined up with Wood's Brigade behind Carroll's, awaiting the order to attack. The Rough Riders were held in reserve with the Ninth to their front and the Tenth Cavalry further off to their left.

Looming before them across a field of grass dotted with small scrubs was a ridge of hills. A blockhouse and Spanish flag topped the one to their left. The center hill with large ranch houses extended out a little to the right of the cavalry, the base of which was just 200 yards from the San Juan River. The Spaniards were well entrenched on top, and Mauser fire from these positions intensified. The American army waited, helplessly exposed within full view and range of Spanish marksmen. The bullets whirred and popped overhead with ferocity. Spanish guerrillas fired on the Rough Riders from the trees behind them. Lawton was still heavily engaged with a stubborn enemy at El Caney and, unknown to everyone, would not join them that day. At that point, Shafter's plan began to unravel. Everyone knew that to wait further meant death.

San Juan Hill (Library of Congress).

Casualties mounted. Roosevelt was also losing a number of his key officers. A bullet had hit Lieutenant Devereaux in the forearm and arm while his K Troop had waited at the ford. Lieutenant Shipp, Wood's aide, had also been killed. B Troop's commander, First Lieutenant George Wilcox, of Prescott, Arizona, lay prostrated by the heat, turning the leadership of B Troop over to Lieutenant Tom Rynning and Sergeant William "Billy" Davidson, of Phoenix. Rynning walked up and down the riverbank to make sure his men kept their heads below it. Waiting under fire was probably the most fearful experience of the troopers' lives. Goodrich later wrote, "There we had to stay knee deep in the water with Mauser bullets whistling as near our heads as the banks of the stream would allow and shrapnel bursting over us higher up. It was certainly trying to hear the fighting all around us and not be taking part in it." Only assaulting the enemy entrenched on the hill would end the carnage, but they had orders to wait.[14]

The always impatient and demanding Roosevelt felt even more frustrated by his vague instructions. The cavalry was to simply turn right and link up with Lawton. None of the brigade or division commanders had reconnoitered the area. No information about the enemy strength or his position had filtered down to the field commanders. They were blind as to what opposed them on the hills or to the support of infantry on their flanks. In spite of being the regimental commander, he knew as little about the plan as the average soldier.

While the Rough Riders had moved into their attack position, the riddled balloon descended to earth with news that another trail led off to the left. By this route, infantry regiments still on the road could move to the front without waiting for the rest of the cavalry to get out of their way and line up on the right. Kent, without forethought, pushed the next regiment in line down the trail—the Seventy-First New York. He sent word to Hawkins that this would put them on his left quicker. Pushing their way down the narrow jungle trail in the lead against galling enemy fire, the lead battalion of the New York Volunteers recoiled in fear. This caused the column to halt. Kent ordered the panic-stricken men to lie down while others passed. The Regulars behind them tried to encourage them with insults and jeers but to no avail. With the exception of two companies, the Seventy-First ceased to exist as a regiment during that battle. Individuals picked up and joined the angered Regulars who stepped over them on their way to the front. Brigadier General Hamilton S. Hawkins, meanwhile, waited with two infantry regiments of his brigade under fire for arrival of the Seventy-First, his reserve. Shafter's plan was rapidly falling apart.

The calamity was further compounded. Heat exhaustion had prostrated General Shafter in his headquarter's tent five miles back from the fight. He planned to control the battle by telephone through his aides at El Pozo and then by runners to his aide Colonel Miley on the front line. What Shafter knew of the battle, he determined from the telephone calls and the distant sound of gunfire. He had no real clue as to how dangerous the situation had become.

Waiting under fire immensely angered Roosevelt, not a patient man to begin with. Probably his greatest frustration resulted from his inability to do what he knew was obvious. He could not take charge as he had always done in the past. He had two layers of disciplined commanders between him and Shafter. Roosevelt's regiment was only one of six cavalry regiments which lined up between him and the top of the hill. He had no choice but to wait for orders. He stood next to A Troop.

While the adjutant's place was supposed to be by the side of his commander, Hall started down the hill, away from the fighting. Trumpeter John Foster, of Bisbee, Arizona, saw this and asked, "Do you want your adjutant, Colonel?"[15]

"Certainly!" boomed Roosevelt, and off ran Foster. He slapped his hand down on the lieutenant's shoulder, spun him around, then told him that Roosevelt wanted him back. Rynning, standing nearby, remembered that Hall reported to his colonel white faced and trembling like a leaf. Hall asked and received permission from Roosevelt to place a picket of six men on the extreme right flank. While the job of the adjutant was to carry the commander's messages to senior officers, Roosevelt had not forgotten Hall's performance at Las Guasimas. If he sent him to seek the brigade commander, the message might get distorted and Roosevelt might never see Hall again. Instead, he had to rely on others so his terrified adjutant would not leave the battlefield.[16]

Roosevelt sent messenger after messenger searching for Sumner or Wood to get permission to advance. In the absence of orders, he was fully prepared to march toward the sound of the guns. All the while, the situation continued to worsen.

William Saunders, a Harvard man from Salem, Massachusetts, served dutifully as Roosevelt's orderly, running messages on foot while under fire and the hot, blazing sun. He finally collapsed from a combination of fever and heat exhaustion. While sitting on the road embankment, Roosevelt turned to another nearby trooper to go and find any general and ask if he could advance. When the trooper stood up to salute, a bullet severed the carotid artery in his neck. He then pitched forward over Roosevelt's knees. Henry P. Bardshar, of Prescott, Arizona, offered to take his place. He served faithfully by his colonel's side from that day forward.

When Hall returned, he saw his colonel bending over Haskell. The West Point cadet had been shot in the stomach, contrary to his prediction. Roosevelt praised him for his bravery under fire. Haskell shook Roosevelt's hand. "All right, Colonel, I'm going to get well. Don't bother about me, and don't let any man come away with me." His wound, however, would disqualify him from continuing his education at West Point. Roosevelt promised him a commission in the Regular Army as consolation.[17]

Meanwhile, Captain O'Neill confidently walked around smoking a cigarette. His A Troop was 75 yards ahead of K Troop with Capron's troop ahead of it. Lieutenant Kane, of K Troop, called to him from the riverbank: "Captain O'Neill, you are drawing fire. Why don't you come down here, under cover, till we get orders to move further along?"[18]

O'Neill answered, "I am going to go to my troop."

Kane then said, "Bring your troop down here. Mine is here."

O'Neill walked over to Kane, who stood in the bottom of the creek behind the bank, four or five feet below the captain. A sergeant warned him, "Captain, a bullet is sure to hit you."[19]

Buckey removed a cigarette from his mouth and blew a puff. "The Spanish bullet has not been molded yet that will kill me." He laughed and put the cigarette back in his mouth, turned and walked away.[20]

In B Troop, Jerry F. Lee, of Globe, Arizona, let out a cry. A bullet struck him in the top of his head and came out his ear. Billy Davidson and First Sergeant David "Dave" Logue, of Leavenworth, Kansas, carried their wounded comrade down to the creek to wash off the blood.

Suddenly, First Lieutenant Frantz, of A Troop, came running back asking for a doctor. His hands were covered in blood. Kane and Davidson asked him if he was hurt. He answered no, but Captain O'Neill was. Buckey had been talking with Captain Howze about the direction of enemy fire. As O'Neill turned around, a bullet struck him in the mouth and exited the back side of his head. He stiffened, then collapsed to the ground. Everyone in the immediate vicinity ran to him, but the bullet had killed him instantly. They returned to their positions while two troopers dragged his body under shade and covered his face with his hat. Unable to find medical help, Frantz returned to the side of his captain. The loss of their beloved captain unnerved A Troop as they were momentarily at a loss as to whom to follow. Neither Frantz nor Second Lieutenant Joshua D. Carter, of Prescott, commanded the proper confidence to rally their men's spirits. A Troop ceased to function as a cohesive unit. Almost an hour had elapsed, and, of the eight troops, only three of the eight original commanders remained in command of their troops: Muller of E Troop, Luna of F Troop, and Llewellyn of G Troop. Besides the two dead and one wounded, Huston and Jenkins had been promoted to squadron commanders.

Since the last battle, Wheeler had supervised the placement of troops and selection of campsites. He also reconnoitered the enemy positions. Evidently, after 33 years out of uniform, Wheeler had forgotten very few of the details of his former profession. He had ridden under the hot sun for six days and slept without the benefit of a tent in the cool, damp air. He finally succumbed to fever, like several of the other officers, on the last day and retired to his tent, taking the medicine that the doctor had prescribed. Wheeler claimed he actually felt better, but Shafter probably gauged the magnitude of his fever based upon his own and reported it accordingly. Quite possibly Shafter did not want Wheeler interfering in his plans like before.

The distant sound of battle that morning had brought Wheeler to his feet. Although

Shafter had told others not to tell Wheeler about the battle that day, the old rebel would not stay out of a fight. He quickly dressed and rode forward to El Pozo Hill. There McClernand asked him to carry a message to Kent that Shafter wanted the whole command to move forward. Wheeler then rode forward and passed the instructions to Kent. He rode further and found Sumner and Miley. In spite of how Wheeler felt, he clearly appeared sick to the others, but they were glad to see him. Wheeler later wrote, "My former instructions and the general custom of the service made it proper that I should exercise this control over the whole line, which was fully appreciated by General Kent." Once again, Major General Wheeler was the senior officer at the front.[21]

The situation did not look good. Only two regiments of Hawkin's infantry brigade waited on line, having lost the Seventy-First. Colonel Charles A. Wikoff's brigade pushed its way down the trail to get on line while the third still waited on the road. Even though a third of Kent's division were in position, Wheeler knew what he needed to do. He summed up the situation: "After the line was formed it was quite evident that the enemy had our range very accurately established, and that it would not increase our casualties to charge; but would shorten the time spent by our troops subject to galling fire." He directed Sumner to advance. Sumner personally rode forward to direct the movement of Carroll's brigade.[22]

At last, lieutenant colonel Joseph H. Dorst rode over and passed instructions for Roosevelt's men "to move forward and support the Regulars in an assault on the hills in front."[23] Roosevelt immediately leaped on his horse, waving his hat in hand and ordered his men into a column of troops. The men rose up, and each troop of about 60 men stretched out into a line about a double arms' distance apart, ready for skirmishing. Their right was anchored on the barbed wire fence of the sunken road that led directly to the house on the hill. D Troop waded to the road, then marched about 300 yards further on and deployed into line. The officers moved about, aligning their troops. Like many of his officers, Roosevelt felt weak from the heat. He chose to ride exposed on his horse, Little Texas, for fear that he might not keep up with his men.

Captain Jenkins, his eyes jumping with excitement, led the first squadron and Captain Huston the second. Huston was also feeling ill. Roosevelt later wrote that he responded to each man according to what motivated him. He swore at some and joked with others. Hall remembered him in a "fine Berserker rage" as he rode along the regiment getting everyone into line to move forward. This time, without his sword, his blue polka-dot bandanna fastened to his campaign hat floated in the air.

Captain Mills reported to Roosevelt with additional instructions: "The red-roofed house yonder is your objective."[24] Roosevelt sent his liaison officers, Mills and McCormack, off to also get his men moving. Mills rode to the rear to keep the men in line and close the ranks. Roosevelt realized that whenever men had been lying in wait for any length of time, they became hesitant, each looking at each other to see who would move first.

After the skirmish line had formed, Roosevelt shouted, "Well, come on," but not a man moved.[25]

"What are you cowards?" he screamed.

A tall man brought his carbine to port arms and responded, "We're waiting for the command."

Roosevelt realized that he had not given these disciplined soldiers the correct command. "Forward, March!" And they went forward into battle. Along the way they passed the lifeless body of Captain Buckey O'Neill with his hat over his face as if he were resting under a shade tree. His reputation had earned him the admiration of everyone in the regiment. The squads of A Troop fell in with the other troops.

Roosevelt rode along the line, passing on instructions to his officers and calling men forward. "We'll have to take that hill." A bullet that scraped Little Texas also grazed Roosevelt's elbow. He raised his arm for his men to see that he too had been wounded: "I've got it, boys! I've got it."

He came upon a man hiding behind a bush. He ordered him up. The trooper looked up with hesitation. Roosevelt provoked him, "Are you afraid to stand up when I am on horseback?" While he spoke, the man fell forward; a bullet had passed through the full length of his body. It dawned on Roosevelt that there was too much chance involved in who was killed. That man had been killed while hiding, yet Roosevelt rode his horse in full view of the enemy.[26]

Huston stood with his bugler, Starr Wetmore, and another orderly by his side. He ordered his squadron to advance. After blowing the command, Wetmore then collapsed, a bullet having shattered the bone in his right thigh. In consolation, Starr would claim that he blew the charge that led the men up the hill. Huston's other orderly was partly shot through the knee, while another round pierced Huston's hat. In the hail of bullets, Huston continued to do his duty.

On the way up, the hot-tempered Tom Holmes felt something hit his left knee, knocking him down. He turned to Sel Newcomb and angrily asked why in the thunder he had hit him with a rock. Tom then looked down at the bloody pant leg and realized that he had been shot instead. The rest moved forward.[27]

Roosevelt took a position in the rear of his regiment. The purpose of the military training was to keep the formations straight. The lead troop advanced more slowly under fire than those behind them. The next troop soon ran into the one before it. This process continued as the lead troops merged into one confused line, losing their unit integrity. There was no advancing by the book. There was no advance, support or reserves. Neither was there any advancing by squads or sections. The aligned column of troops gradually became one mass that resembled no formation that they had rehearsed on the parade fields. The other regiments experienced this same phenomenon. Advancing over broken terrain and under fire, their attack resembled nothing they had rehearsed in Texas. As Sergeant Thomas P. Ledwidge, of Santa Fe, remembered, "There were no great masses of troops charging with waving flags and sword pointing officers in the lead. Instead there was a succession of squads of men hurrying towards the hills, pausing to shoot and then rushing on again."[28]

This was the first war where the Americans could test their Emory Upton tactics of fire and maneuver against a modern European army. Instead, the men advanced by short rushes. All foreign observers and correspondents watched in horror at what appeared to be too small a force to assault an entrenched enemy.

Roosevelt rode along, encouraging his men. He came upon Jenkins who had stopped his men to realign their ranks. Roosevelt snapped, "Let the formation take care of itself. The thing to do just now is to take the hill. Lead your men forward." Jenkins obeyed.

The Spaniards had evidently expected the Americans to advance up the road. Consequently, Jenkins's squadron took the heaviest casualties advancing up that lane, with L Troop, in the lead, suffering the worst. L Troop finally cut the wire and with a cheer ran across the road to advance up the right flank of it.

Captain Henry A. Barber, walking along the line of the Ninth Cavalry in the sunken road, suddenly saw a skirmish line advancing through the tall grass from his right rear. Ahead of it rode Roosevelt. Barber heard someone yell to the Rough Riders not to fire. Seeing Colonel Carroll, Barber ran over and reported to the brigade commander. Carroll instructed the captain to meet with the Rough Riders and caution them as to the location of Barber's regiment so as to avoid shooting into the Regulars.

The Rough Riders advanced behind the right wing of the First Cavalry and the left of the Ninth, which had crowded into the sunken road which made a long snake-like bend perpendicular to their advance. The men were lying down while their officers walked about giving instructions. That was as far as their orders had called the Ninth to advance.

Roosevelt realized that they were already halfway up the hill. In the fury of the battle, he explained to Barber that they could not take the hills by just firing at them. They had to attack. Barber explained that he had orders not to advance any further and asked if Roosevelt had any such orders to advance.

Roosevelt then asked where the captain's commanding officer was. He did not know, so Roosevelt told him, "Then I am the ranking officer and I give the order to charge!" Barber hesitated. The angered Roosevelt demanded, "Then let my men through, sir!" He turned around and yelled, "If any man runs I'll shoot him myself." After a little thought, he added, so Barber and his men could hear, "And I won't have to shoot any of my own men either."[29]

The Rough Riders kicked down the eight-strand barbed wire fence and moved under fire the rest of the way up the hill. Roosevelt then rode along the line to the end of the left wing of the Ninth. Barber ran back over to Colonel Carrol and his Squadron Commander Captain Dimmick to report that Roosevelt had given the order to assault. A few moments later the word came down that Captain Charles W. Taylor was about to lead a charge of his own on the left in support of the Rough Riders. Captain John F. McBlain called out, "We must go in with those troops; we must support Taylor." Barber passed this on to Dimmick. The two then ordered the charge. A cheer rolled down the line as men heard instructions to assault.[30]

The Regulars joined in on the charge. Roosevelt crossed the fence where Lieutenant Michael M. McNamee had directed a couple of his Regulars to knock down the wire. Roosevelt then rode forward, waving his hat in his hand, and gave the order to charge.

The men were caught up in the excitement of the assault. They yelled and fired their way up the hill. Clare Stewart, of Pawnee, later wrote home, "I never heard such a yell in all my life, and I hope I will never hear another."[31] At that point, the attack became a race to the top. Instead of leading, the officers boasted that they had to run to keep up with their men. Roosevelt rode over to help Goodrich get his D Troop across the road. D Troop, evidently still intact in the rear of the column, had heard someone shout, "The Ninth is on the hill and can't hold it; they are motioning for help."[32] Roosevelt encouraged them, "Boys, charge that hill and kill or capture every damn Spaniard on it. Don't shoot until you catch up with the Ninth, and then give them hell." D Troop ran over to reinforce the Ninth Cavalry's right flank. Goodrich calmly issued out commands as if leading his men on a football field. Where they had once protested his commission, the Oklahomans then responded to his every command. Roosevelt observed Pollock leading the charge stripped to the waist. Roosevelt then wheeled his mount around and charged up the hill.

Captain Mills, at the direction of Lieutenant Colonel Ernest A. Garlington, had already thrown a troop across this road on the left, and two others followed. At this point Huston collapsed from heat exhaustion; then Captain Mills led his squadron. Hall had also fallen out from the heat. Hall claimed that a total of six officers succumbed to heat exhaustion that day. A shot between the eyes dropped Mills while he gave orders. It destroyed the sight permanently in one eye and temporarily in the other, but he would live.

Mounted on horseback Roosevelt reached the top ahead of the others. Bardshar ran up the hill and remained close by his side the whole way. Bardshar dropped two Spaniards with well-aimed shots. B Troop's Sergeant Campbell, Dudley Dean of Boston, Sergeant Edward G. Norton and his brother, Oliver B. of Phoenix, followed close behind him. Forty yards from the top, Roosevelt ran into another barbed wire fence. He dismounted and turned Little Texas loose, never expecting to see his trusted warhorse alive again. The Rough Riders took the hill from the right while the Ninth and Tenth stormed it from the left. The Spaniards likewise took flight.

Men rushed to be the first to plant their flags on enemy soil. Not surprisingly, the troops commanded by the three original captains—Muller, Luna and Llewellyn—advanced from the rear to plant their guidons on top of the hill first. Although troopers from A and B Troops also reached the top first, their guidons followed later. Captains Taylor and McBlain, of the Ninth, also claimed to have planted their guidons on the hill first.

Color Sergeant Wright jumped up on one of the three large copper kettles that would give "Kettle Hill" its name and began waving "Old Glory." Soon that gift from the ladies of Arizona was riddled with holes. Color Sergeant J.E. Andrews, of the Third Cavalry, was shot in the abdomen and tumbled back down the hill clutching the regimental colors. Sergeant George Berry, of the Tenth (Colored) Cavalry, snatched up the flag and carried both his and the Third's colors up the hill. He kept yelling, "Dress on the colors, boys, dress on the colors!"[33] Lieutenant Colonel Charles D. Viele personally planted the colors of his First Cavalry. General Sumner also rode up to join his cavalry division on the hill. By 1:30, the hill abounded with the waving red and white guidons, yellow regimental flags and the red, white and blue of the national colors.

After 15 minutes from when the advance began, six regiments of cavalry crowded on top of a small hill, losing all identity as regiments. The men became so mixed that troopers from different regiments fought in the same squad, following any officer or noncommissioned officer they saw. As Roosevelt remembered, it was a troop commander's and almost a squad leader's fight. Rough Riders fought gallantly side by side with the famed "Buffalo Soldiers" on that crowded hill. Many things had changed. Despite earlier prejudices, many would later swear that they would drink out of the same canteen with any of the black cavalrymen. Clare Stewart wrote, "I will tell you one thing though, our boys are proud to be classed with the 8th and 10th, and they are proud to be classed with us."[34]

Suddenly, the cavalry received artillery and rifle fire from the next ridge about 300 to 400 yards from their right. Most dropped to the ground, while some sought cover behind the kettles. During that delay, the cavalry took more casualties. Among those killed and wounded were more key leaders. Colonel John M. Hamilton, commander of the Ninth Cavalry, was killed and Colonel Carroll and Captain Taylor wounded. A bullet hit Lieutenant Day, who had gallantly led Capron's troop up the hill, through the left shoulder and arm. He had to return to the rear, turning the command of his troop over to his sergeants. Captain Llewellyn, a large, heavyset man, finally collapsed from the heat but would remain with the regiment.

Roosevelt walked around conspicuously encouraging the men. He ordered the wounded to the rear. When he saw the bloodied head bandages on David Hughes and Fred Bugbee, of Lordsburg, New Mexico, he asked, "Didn't I order you back?"[35]

Bugbee responded, "You go to hell, we are not going back."[36] Roosevelt turned away and continued moving about the men, secretly admiring their determination. Shortly thereafter, Hughes became weak from the loss of blood and had to find his way back to the hospital. In his usual form of gallantry, Assistant Surgeon Church again roamed the battlefield dressing the wounds of his boys.

Meanwhile, the cavalry on the hill could see the infantry advancing on their left up the steep hill toward the blockhouse. The cavalry provided supporting fire on the Spanish trench line. Rough Riders obeyed the orders of any officer who took charge. Suddenly, the men heard an unusual drumming sound. The men yelled that it was the Spanish machine guns. Roosevelt listened and noticed that the sound came from the flat ground below them, not from the Spanish positions. He jumped to his feet, hit his fist on his thigh and shouted, "It's the Gatlings, men, our Gatlings!"[37]

Lieutenant John H. Parker, with the four horse-drawn Gatling guns, had raced across the ford. "Where in the Hell are the Spaniards?" he asked. "I've been fighting all day and haven't seen a one."[38]

A captain graciously pointed to the top of the hill. Parker thanked him, then swung his guns into action. At 1:15, the booming sound of his multibarreled guns kicked up yellow plumes of clay dust along the Spanish trenches with tremendous effectiveness. The enemy return fire was just as intense as they tried to silence the Gatling guns. Spontaneously, the infantry regiments moved forward. Parker advanced his guns alongside the infantry. After nearly 40 years of their existence, Lieutenant Parker had figured out how to properly employ Gatling guns as suppressive fire weapons. At half past one, 15 minutes from the time the charge had begun, the infantry had stormed the blockhouse and hauled down the Spanish colors.

First Sergeant Palmer had somehow become separated from his D Troop after they scattered back at El Pozo. He moved forward to the river and found himself in water up to his armpits. He cooled off while waiting for another line of troops to enter the creek. By then, only the wounded and stragglers lined the banks of the creek. Soon, he heard the sound of the Gatling guns. Realizing that the battle was on in earnest, Palmer decided to make a break for the front. He crawled from cover and ran up the steep hill.

Lieutenant Goodrich had waited next to his old friend Teddy Miller. With a little more experience behind him, Miller seemed to enjoy himself during this battle. D Troop had fared pretty well so far. About that time, Roosevelt had his men on Kettle Hill cease fire then turn their attention to the enemy in the trenches on the hill across to their right front. He drew his revolver, called to his men, "Who'll follow me?"[39]

Goodrich was sent over to order the troop on his right to charge. At the same time, Carr ordered D Troop to advance. As they crossed over the crest of the hill, a Spanish volley dropped four men of D Troop. Edward Johnston was shot through the right thigh. A bullet entered one of Corporal Henry Meagher's shoulders and came out the other without touching his spine. Robert McMillan was shot through the left shoulder and arm. Goodrich's friend Teddy Miller also fell wounded.

Corporal Henry Love said, "Miller, I'll come to you in a minute."

Miller replied, "That's all right, Love, don't bother about me."

Corporal Holt and another trooper remained with him. Miller lamented, "I'm going, Harry, but it's a good cause, isn't it?"[40]

Roosevelt jumped over a wire fence, but only five followed, and three of them were quickly wounded. Roosevelt only recognized Henry Clay Green, of Santa Fe, who was mortally wounded, and Winslow Clark, a Harvard man from Milton, Massachusetts, who was shot through the leg. The four lay in wait while Roosevelt returned to the hill. He climbed back over the fence to scold the others: "I thought you would follow me."[41]

His men innocently responded, "We didn't hear you, we didn't see you go, Colonel; lead on now, we'll sure follow you." Roosevelt wanted the help of the other regiments, so he ran over to Sumner asking for permission to lead the charge. The general told him to go, and he would ensure men followed.[42]

About that time, Goodrich returned and found Miller. Upon the initial examination, Goodrich only found a wound in Miller's right shoulder that did not look too serious. Goodrich asked Miller if he was hurt badly. Miller smiled and said he did not think so. Miller, however, was paralyzed from the shoulders down. Upon further examination, Goodrich discovered the exit wound in the left shoulder. The bullet had skipped across both shoulder blades, severing the spine.

Miller urged his friends to go on without him but whispered to Dade that it was hard for him to breathe. Otherwise, he felt no pain. Goodrich put something behind his head to make him comfortable. Contrary to orders, Goodrich detailed six men to carefully carry his friend in a blanket back to the dressing station at the ford. Goodrich said goodbye to his friend and then joined Roosevelt in the charge across to the next hill. He did not know that he would never see his friend again.

With Jenkins at Roosevelt's side, about 50 of the Rough Riders and another 250 officers and men from the different regiments ran down the hill and up the next.[43] Captain Dimmick led the Ninth Cavalry forward. Captain McBlain also accompanied him. Major Henry W. Wessel, Jr., led his Third Cavalry. Some men splashed through the shallow lake between the two hills.

The long-legged John Greenway, William Proffitt, of Prescott, Arizona, Lieutenant Milton F. Davis, of the First Cavalry, Goodrich and a few others outraced the rest of the men. Several of Goodrich's men, to include Ira Hill, Roy Cashion and Frank Wetzel, kept pace with him. Greenway, along with John Beissel and John Fitch, both from G Troop, reached the blockhouse first. They searched the dead and found one Spaniard playing possum. He begged for mercy, and Greenway sent him to the rear while the others searched for souvenirs. Fitch picked up a Spanish bullet and took a bayonet off of a Mauser. As soon as others joined them, they ran over the hill and down into the jungle below.

Frank Knox had become intermingled with the Tenth Cavalry and lost contact with his troop when they reached the summit of the first hill. He fought shoulder to shoulder with the black cavalrymen, gaining great admiration for their courage under fire. With a yell, they leaped to their feet and charged the next hill, yelling all the way. Knox saw that the Spaniards began to flee the trenches with the first yell. When he reached the next trench, the dead and wounded Spaniards littered the trenches. Knox and his new comrades in arms dropped to their bellies and began to shoot at the fleeing enemy.

First Sergeant Palmer reached the top of Kettle Hill and joined up with the Tenth

Kettle Hill as seen from San Juan Hill. This was the ground over which Roosevelt led the last charge (Library of Congress).

Cavalry. The officers were just forming their men to rush the next ridge. He could see a line of men, led by Roosevelt, down in the valley ahead. His group fired into the next trenches over the heads of their advancing comrades. Palmer heard an officer yelling out commands. He turned around and saw General Sumner. Their turn came to run down the hill and up to the next. Sumner held the rest of the cavalry in reserve on Kettle Hill under the command of Major Jackson of the Third Cavalry.

Roosevelt's group swept over the next line of hills before all the enemy could flee. Roosevelt shot at two Spaniards with his revolver at a distance of ten yards as they ran from the trenches. He hit one, killing him "like a jack rabbit." Roosevelt thought he was the only man to have killed a Spaniard with a pistol until he found out weeks later that First Sergeant Clarence Gould, of the First Cavalry, also had shot a Spaniard not far from where Roosevelt killed his.

When Palmer reached the next hill, he saw the Spanish dead in their blue and white striped uniforms. One dying soldier lay breathing heavily on the bodies of two others. He saw cavalrymen from every regiment mingled on that hill. Some foraged through the blockhouse for wine, food and as usual, souvenirs. Many like Ira Hill picked up Mauser cartridges as souvenirs. The Spaniards had abandoned the line while their meals still cooked. Roosevelt drew his revolver and ordered the hungry men forward, threatening to shoot any man who disobeyed him.

As Roosevelt stood on the hill, one shoulder strap bearing his rank was held onto his blue flannel shirt by a thread, while the other had been entirely lost. He was the senior officer in command of the right flank. He set about reforming the troopers from more than six different regiments into a defense. He had his motley command move down the forward slope and lie down.

After the entire ridge was in American hands, Wood rode up and asked Rynning if he had any packers in B Troop. The Arizona lieutenant said he had many. Wood told him to go back and find them some ammunition. Wilcox had also recovered once the charge started and again commanded his troop. Wood failed to mention to Roosevelt that he had sent Rynning off on this errand, so Roosevelt did not number Rynning or Wilcox among the officers who had reached the top of the hill.

Rynning then took several men and a bunch of mules not too far back before they

Roosevelt after the charge. His polka-dotted bandana is tucked into his weather-beaten campaign hat (Theodore Roosevelt Collection, Harvard University Library).

ran into a pile of ammunition belonging to the Tenth Cavalry. They rustled ten boxes of ammunition at the protest of the sergeant guarding it. Rynning saw Colonel Wallace A. Downs, of the New York infantry, running away from the battlefield. He tried to stop him, but the frightened commander was determined to flee to the safety of the rear. He let the colonel go. Rynning's detail then diamond hitched the crates on the mules when Captain Matthew F. Steele rode up. The staff officer was about to stop Rynning's theft of the Tenth Cavalry's ammunition when he recognized the former Sergeant Rynning of his old Eighth Cavalry. The two exchanged pleasantries. Rynning then returned to the front with his boxes of ammunition.

Meanwhile, Captain Howze rode up to Roosevelt with instructions from General Sumner to hold the position "at all hazards." Roosevelt scolded Howze for exposing himself by riding his horse too high up on the ridge. Howze thought it an odd reprimand since Roosevelt walked around exposing himself to enemy fire. Completing his task, this staff officer was in no hurry to return. He remained at the front for some time, rendering any service he could to Roosevelt and his command. Roosevelt then sent a request to General Kent for additional infantry. Kent sent over the Thirteenth, which Roosevelt placed on the extreme right next to the Ninth Cavalry. Captain William H. Beck, of the Tenth Cavalry, commanded small groups of men from different regiments on the extreme left next to the infantry.

Somehow infantry men from the fight on the far left had mingled with the cavalry in the last charge. Evidently, they had not been satisfied with just taking their assigned hill. On that forward slope the men lay flat as bullets and shrapnel flew overhead. About eight or ten soldiers of the Twenty-Fourth (Colored) Infantry began to drift to the rear either to help the wounded or seek out their own regiment. Those black infantrymen had fought bravely taking that hill, but, in the

Packtrain bringing up supplies (Theodore Roosevelt Collection, Harvard University Library).

absence of their own officers, felt inclined to leave the front. Roosevelt jumped up in full view of the enemy and walked a few yards to the rear, drew his revolver and halted the soldiers. He could not afford to lose even those few men. He praised them for their gallantry, but he would shoot any soldier who for any reason withdrew to the rear. "Now I'll be sorry to hurt you, and you don't know whether or not I will keep my word, but my men can tell you I always do."[44]

By that time his Rough Riders had sat up to watch. They resounded in chorus, "He always does, he always does." Broad grins spread across their faces as the infantry returned to their lines. They accepted Roosevelt as their leader.[45]

Taking an assessment of the line, Roosevelt learned that he had about 20 to 30 men trapped forward of his trenches. Jenkins, Greenway, Goodrich and a number of other men had pursued the Spaniards down the hill 350 yards beyond their lines. The cavalrymen had not stopped until their party reached the safety of the next trench line at the base of the hill. Those Rough Riders then became trapped under fire from the next Spanish line. Frank Weitzel, Ogden Wells, Henry Meagher, young Roy Cashion and several other men from Oklahoma and about a dozen men from G Troop numbered among that group.[46]

Lieutenant Hugh Berkley, of the First Cavalry, with a sergeant and two troopers had also reached another exposed position on the downhill slope. The sergeant and one trooper were killed. Those Americans hid in the forward trenches under intense fire from rifle, machine gun and artillery, but they held their ground.

Jenkins's party occupied the salient less than 200 yards from the Spanish hospital identified by the red cross painted on the roof. Roosevelt ordered First Sergeant Palmer to lead a platoon of men to recover Jenkins's men with covering fire. They advanced only a short distance before enemy fire forced them back.

Somehow Roosevelt got a messenger through. Around 2:30, Goodrich reported to Jenkins that Roosevelt had ordered them back. They retreated 50 yards back toward their trenches. When they reached the open space by the wire, they came under heavy fire. The withdrawing Rough Riders returned fire and saw an officer in a white uniform riding a black horse behind the Spanish trenches. Disappointed that they had missed him, Jenkins, a crack shot, borrowed a carbine from a nearby trooper and aimed at the mounted officer. As he pulled the trigger, the officer and his horse disappeared in the trench. They later learned that he had wounded none other than General Linares in the left arm.[47] When Jenkins turned to hand the carbine back to the trooper, the man lay at Jenkins's feet with his face bathed in blood. Jenkins assumed that he was dead.

They continued to work their way back under heavy fire. At about 4 p.m., Roy Cashion raised to fire his carbine but was struck in the forehead and killed instantly. He was also the only Oklahoman killed in action. Ogden Wells was just two feet from him, and Corporal Henry Meagher on the other side was shot in the shoulder. In the retreat to their lines that night, the Rough Riders had to abandon Roy's body. While each had his own personal reason for signing up, the idealistic Cashion had joined to fight for Cuban independence. When the word of his death later reached the Oklahoma volunteers, nearly everyone wept at his tragic loss. The older troopers had become very fond of him and grieved his loss.

Once safe on the other side of the crest, Ogden Wells raised his head to peer over the other side and saw three Spanish officers riding their horses. He then asked Lieutenant Carr for permission to engage. He crawled forward and fired at them. On the third shot he had elevated his sights to 500 yards and dropped the officer in the center.

Late that evening, a packtrain with provisions of canned tomatoes and hardtack arrived. At 7 p.m., the men had their first meal for the day. Although the attack was delayed until all the regiments had three days of ammunition and rations, it remained in their haversacks, back at El Pozo Hill. They could not abandon their trench line to go back and get them.

The Americans had won control of the heights around Santiago. The meager cavalry brigade under Roosevelt commanded the extreme right of the American line. The Spaniards massed in preparation for a counterattack that afternoon. A few seconds of fire from the cavalry dissuaded them from their futile effort. During the fight, Roosevelt also heard the same drumming sound that he had heard during the infantry assault on the blockhouse. He walked over to the right of his regiment and discovered Lieutenant Parker blazing away with his Gatling guns. Roosevelt welcomed the machine guns on wheels. Parker remained on the Rough Riders' right for the duration of the siege, and they struck up a friendship. Roosevelt remembered that as the only serious attempt by the Spaniards to retake the hills.

As darkness fell, the enemy ceased firing. Those men held in reserve at Kettle Hill rejoined their regiments. Some of the troopers returned to the buildings in their rear to forage for food. They found meals in the officers' mess still cooking, which they brought forward. By then, they had ignored the standing order not to eat any food or provisions left by the enemy: three big pots, one of cooked beef stew, one of boiled rice and another of boiled peas along with loaves of rice bread, small cans of preserves and a few salt fish. Palmer finished off a meal of the beef stew and cooked dried peas. Others did likewise. Ben Colbert ate a meal of pea soup, beef and corn bread.

That night Captain Charles Morton and Daniel H. Boughton, of the Third Cavalry, approached Roosevelt with news of a rumor that they had to withdraw from the hill. They protested any withdrawal, but there were others not so confident. They had far fewer men than the enemy, and their flanks were exposed. Finally, General Wheeler arrived on the hill. The general also heard petitions from some officers to withdraw. If this fear took hold of the leaders, then they would lose all that they had achieved that day. Wheeler knew the importance of leaders on the morale of fighting men. Although Shafter had returned him to just command of his cavalry division, Wheeler acted in the capacity of senior officer on the field. He set the tone of confidence. He reminded the officers that they had driven the enemy from the field at Las Guasimas and again successfully driven the enemy from a strongly defended position that day. He reminded them, "These facts will convince the Spaniards that we will continue our attack upon their next line and with that expectation it is unreasonable and not to be expected that they will return and attack us in the strong position we now hold."[48] Wheeler sent his staff officers along the line to reassure the officers and men that there was no need whatever of retiring from their positions. He also reassured them that reinforcements would arrive. Nonetheless, he feared that they might send their fears straight to Shafter. At 8:20, he sent a message back to Shafter confirming that his thin line could hold.

Wheeler discussed the situation with Roosevelt when one of Shafter's orderlies delivered the order to withdraw. Shafter had given in to the fears of men. Without ever having seen the position or what it took to take it, he felt that the Americans had too few soldiers to defend it. Wheeler instead sent for the two infantry division commanders, Generals Bates and Kent, so he could establish his command authority and confer with them about the order. Roosevelt protested, "Can't you countermand the order?"[49]

Wheeler responded, "Yes." Once again Wheeler asserted his authority as senior officer on the battlefield. He sent back his reply, concluding that to fall back would result in a great loss of prestige. The day would end with the Americans in control of the heights around Santiago. While Wheeler may have been selected to serve as a peace offering to bring the loyalty of the Southern states back into the Union, he was proving over and over again that he was more than a token former Confederate general. He would have another opportunity to prove his importance.

CHAPTER 7

The Siege

It is upon reaching the heights of San Juan Hill that most histories of the campaign end or skip to the surrender. Unfortunately, the most casualties and the greatest ordeal of the war would be faced in the next few weeks. While Roosevelt had displayed great heroism, he probably displayed his greatest leadership during the most trying time of his regiment's existence.

To confirm his intentions to stay, Wheeler issued instructions to start entrenching. The enemy trenches lay in the jungle outside the city of Santiago just 500 to 700 yards from the Rough Riders' position on the hill. Two parallel rows of barbed wire with six to seven strands each had been strung by the enemy to slow down any attack so that the machine guns could cut down the attackers. It was a method of warfare that would reach fruition during World War I. Shafter would still stick to his plan of strangling the Spanish garrison into submission. The American navy had bottled up the Spanish fleet so nothing could come in by sea. Shafter would arrange his additional regiments around Santiago to cut it off from supplies by land. He would also cut the freshwater supply into the city as planned. This siege would become a war of waiting. The greatest enemy that the Americans would face was not bullets but disease.

During the lull in fighting, Lieutenant Greenway had searched the buildings and found entrenching tools. Roosevelt had his men retire 50 yards back up the hill where they began digging three lines of entrenchments on the forward slope facing the enemy. The men just dug deep enough to provide protection from rifle and cannon fire, and the dirt was thrown out on both sides instead of to the enemy side. None of the Rough Riders who reached the top of the hill had any experience in the science of earthworks. The trenches were not constructed according to doctrine but were sufficient for protection. Since there were not enough shovels for everyone, Roosevelt moved the remainder of his men into the valley to the right behind the Gatling guns. As artillery burst overhead, it took an hour or two of repositioning the men in hollows and depressions for him to figure out where was the safest place from enemy artillery and rifle fire. He also had the men begin a lateral trench to connect with the forward trench abandoned by Jenkins. The men would throw up a double row of sandbags 25 feet long and five feet high to provide a Cossack outpost for eight to ten sharpshooters. During this pause they needed more men and supplies.

Corporal Thomas Moran of D Troop selected Orlando C. Byrnes of C Troop, Walter M. Cook and Ogden Wells of D Troop for the Cossack outpost. They collected the picks and shovels and then silently moved forward. Moran and Cook pulled security while Byrnes and Wells dug a pit large enough for three men on the crest of the ridge. They then dug another pit large enough for a single sentry 15 yards forward. They then

Infantry trenches on top of San Juan Hill (Theodore Roosevelt Collection, Harvard University Library).

Infantry trenches below Kettle Hill (Theodore Roosevelt Collection, Harvard University Library).

took turns manning the forward outpost for an hour each during the night. They shivered in the cool night air, listening to the sounds of movement below them.

Wood sent Rynning back around dusk to round up stragglers. The lieutenant had rounded up 42 men at the hospital with superficial wounds. Upon his return he slipped on the mud and slid into the San Juan. Completely soaked, he crawled out of the chilly water "cussing a blue streak." He saw a man on a horse silhouetted against the night sky who asked, "Did you get wet?" A little irritated, Rynning said he sure had and asked who in the hell was he.[1]

"I'm Wood. I came to escort you back to the trenches. Your outfit has changed position since you left." Wood then offered the embarrassed lieutenant his horse, but the soaked Rynning preferred to walk in order to keep from freezing in the night air.[2]

About 11, Rynning returned to the trench line. Captain Muller called over to him that his B Troop was nearby. Under the cover of darkness, the scattered men had sought out their respective regiments and troops. The regiments realigned that night, with the Rough Riders occupying the center crest of the hill with Carroll's brigade on the left and the First and Tenth Cavalry of Wood's brigade on the right. Right after Rynning arrived, the Spaniards opened fire and made another assault to within 100 yards of the Cavalry but were again driven back. All through the night the tired and hungry men continued to dig in details since there were not enough tools for everyone. Those without shovels tried to sleep.

That night Frank Knox also rejoined his troop. There was total confusion on the battlefield with very little unit integrity. Knox, who had fought with the Tenth Cavalry, had no idea that many of his comrades were not too far away. By the middle of the afternoon, he learned that part of his regiment was back at Kettle Hill. So he left the line to find them. As he walked to the rear, he witnessed the horrors of war. The dead and the wounded littered the hillside. He found some of his comrades under the brow of the hill where they waited the rest of the afternoon without firing a shot. Evidently, someone located them late that night, and they joined the rest of the regiment forward. They spent the rest of the night digging trenches.

First Sergeant Palmer assisted Goodrich, who had rejoined his troop from the forward position, in supervising the work. Meanwhile, two Oklahoma men tried to go out under the cover of darkness and recover Cashion's body. Enemy pickets opened fire, forcing them back to where they had come from. The Rough Riders finished their trench line just after midnight. The tired men simply collapsed upon the completion of their work. Sweat-soaked flannel shirts provided little protection from the cool night air as a heavy dew settled in. A few men found blankets left behind by the Spaniards. Palmer found a dirty and bloodstained one. He figured that it had lice but did not care as it would provide some protection from the night chill. Roosevelt and his new orderly, Henry Bardshar, moved up behind D Troop and shared a blanket with Goodrich that night. Goodrich had become a member of a small group of young Ivy Leaguers that Roosevelt favored.

Unknown to them, General Bates's infantry brigade arrived and reinforced Kent on the extreme left at 1:30 that morning. The brigade had marched up from Siboney during the day and joined Lawton at El Caney. Lawton finally took the hard-contested town by 4 that afternoon. He released Bates's brigade and then later marched his own men down the El Caney-Santiago Road. As darkness fell, he did not want to venture into unknown territory. Lawton doubled his division back to the more familiar road by El Pozo. This detour cost them much time. They did not arrive that night, which left the cavalry brigade right flank open.

About 3 in the morning, Spaniards opened fire on the trenches again. Knox had just lain down under a tree to sleep. An alarm woke everyone from their slumber. Those in the rear jumped to their feet and scrambled to trenches. Soon the gunfire died away, and the men returned to their slumber. In an hour, dawn broke, and the Spaniards resumed their firing.

At dawn, Palmer led a detail which slipped into the trenches. Roosevelt felt that he had to change details occupying the trenches every six hours. Roosevelt had no training in entrenchments and knew very little about them. He had failed to have his men dig traverses or approaches. Without a zigzag approach trench, Roosevelt had the relief party wait behind the hill until there was a lull in the Spanish fire. Then on command, the men rushed up over the crest of the hill to where they were exposed. They then dropped to their bellies and crawled the rest of the way down to the trenches. The detail in the trenches ran up over the hill. Each time the Spaniards responded with a terrific fire. Once the men were safe, it eventually died down.

Knox described the cramped ditch as having only enough room to sit up. The hot sun cooked the men inside the trench. About 1 p.m., Knox and his comrades crawled out of their trench as the relief party came crawling back in. This was not safe during the day, so the next day the troops would change details at dawn and dusk.

Knox was weak, and, on the run back, he stumbled and fell under the heavy enemy fire. Roosevelt rushed forward and asked, "Are you hit?"

The trooper replied, "No, I stumbled and fell."

At that point Roosevelt asked, "Are you hungry?" Knox thought that was a foolish question under the circumstances, but Roosevelt was continually looking out for the welfare of his men. He told Knox, "Stop at my tent and get something to eat. Just help yourself." Knox went back to find the same diet of hardtack, salt pork and a few beans. After his meal, Knox dropped off to sleep.[3]

The long-range enemy machine-gun fire dropped far behind the hill into the American reserve. That morning, an artillery shell burst right over the regimental headquarters just behind Palmer's trench, where Roosevelt had established his headquarters under a tree. Goodrich, Roosevelt and his newly appointed adjutant, Second Lieutenant Maxwell Keyes, of San Antonio, were lying in the open. The shrapnel surprisingly hit none of the officers but wounded five enlisted men nearby, mostly from A and B Troops. Roosevelt, who had never once sought cover since Las Guasimas, again escaped injury. As if by divine providence, he had risen to command at the time of the climactic battle, and that same providence similarly spared him for the challenges ahead.

The second day of fighting established a routine for the defenders. The men waited either in the trenches or behind the ridge. Those in the trenches fired only when they saw targets, trying to conserve their ammunition. As the sun rose in the sky, it baked the wet clay of the newly dug trench into a hard surface, making further digging difficult. The men had no idea of how long they would wait nor what they would do next, but they were in no hurry to do otherwise.

That same morning Ben Colbert thought about the bullets as they flew over his head "like hail." He would have never believed it if someone had told him he would sit and listen with little concern as bullets zipped closely by. But as he looked around, others seemed just as unconcerned. The enemy fire had become constant. A few close ones could still make one respond like a turtle. Lieutenant John L. Barbour, of the Ninth Cavalry, paid a visit to Rynning shading himself under a section of canvas. At the sound of bullets cutting the air around his head, Barbour instinctively ducked. "Dammit, I thought I'd got used to those things."[4]

In the Cossack outpost, designated sharpshooters picked away at the Spanish officers. W. Lee Snoderly, of Bisbee, Arizona, took aim and shot the horse out from under its rider at the range of 1,000 yards. One Spanish soldier kept jumping up and down, challenging the Americans to hit him. Finally, he stood still long enough to wave his hat at them. Rynning, who had joined them for a while, took aim and shot, breaking the soldier of his bad habit. Returning enemy fire tore up the sandbags, spilling out their contents. Soon they offered little protection.

Similarly, the Spaniards employed sharpshooters well concealed to their front. Their smokeless powder did not betray their positions. They continually harassed the American line. Rynning talked with a retired captain in civilian clothes working the Gatling guns. The manufacturer of the guns had sent him there to make sure that the weapons worked. The man mentioned that he thought the sharpshooters were hidden in the palm trees. Upon Rynning's suggestion, the multibarreled guns tore up the palms, and a couple of snipers tumbled out of them. Roosevelt also picked his best marksmen to shoot at where they thought they were. That was the advantage of having recruited from the frontier territories. There was no shortage of skilled marksmen among men who grew up in the gun culture of the frontier.

The next detail relieved Palmer's men in the same manner about 1 p.m. so his platoon could return to the reserve. Shortly after, a packtrain with coffee, hardtack, salt pork and canned tomatoes came up that afternoon. There, Palmer distributed food and ammunition to his troop. Each man would have to cook his own meal. The threat of artillery bursts prevented a consolidated troop mess. That was their only meal for the day. The starving men said no meal ever tasted so good. After the meal, most settled in for a rest as best they could with the few blankets the Spaniards had left for them. Until the line was reinforced, they could not go to the rear to recover their gear.

Roosevelt felt sympathy for those hungry troopers who had just entered the trenches. They would not get even a meager meal of hardtack until relieved that evening. Roosevelt asked for volunteers to take some canned tomatoes, hardtack and coffee to them. Bill McGinty volunteered. Roosevelt said he would also go. Woodbury Kane responded that the regiment could not afford to lose him, so he would go in the colonel's place. McGinty replied that there was no reason to risk either of their lives.

He threw a box of canned tomatoes on his shoulders and tried to stay as low to the ground as he could while rounds whizzed close overhead. He reached the men without a scratch but was dripping with tomato juice. Later Dick Shanafelt reached them with a big can of coffee.[5]

The men were still hungry, and hunger heightens the memory of the taste of food. As a joke one black trooper of the Ninth came up to talk with one of his buddies a few feet from the lines of the Rough Riders. He told his buddies about how great the Rough Riders had fought so that the volunteer cavalry men would pay attention to his conversation: "Nossuh! Dey's suah regulahs. You-all c'n tell by de way dey-all fights."[6] The Buffalo Soldiers then went on to discuss different kinds of food so as to accentuate the sense of starvation. He began to discuss in excruciating detail and length every aspect of his mother's award-winning recipe for strawberry shortcake. Every description worsened the Rough Riders' hunger. Finally, the officers cursed him to shut up and go away. He chuckled in his deep Southern accent, "I figuahed you-all 'ud shuah be inte'ested in strawbe'y sho't cake."[7] In spite of the respect that the Rough Riders had developed for the black cavalry men, that evening they joked that they were tempted to kill one of their newfound brethren. Most accounts described that the black soldiers exhibited the best humor and morale during those trying times.

Soldiers had a way of telling about their experiences that took on a life of their own. The Rough Riders and the troopers of the Ninth developed quite a camaraderie. Both Rynning and David Hughes remembered the same humorous account told by one old gray-headed sergeant that had become quite popular among his friends.

After the others had recounted their feelings about the fight, they asked old Sergeant Bivens, "Where were you at? Didn't you-all get into this scrap a-tall?" "Huh, did I? Did I?" The old sergeant responded, "I shore did." They would persist, "Well, how did you-all feel when they was shooting at you?" Bivens answered, "Say, did you know that bamboo thicket way down there by the balloon?" His buddies nodded. "Well, when them there little ones came by me, p-sst here and p-sst there, I didn't mind them much—didn't pay much attention to them, they was too trifling, but, boy, when I got near that old sugar mill and they began to send the big fellers [artillery] over, what keep sayin' 'Wha' is yuh? Wha' is yah?' I'm jes' a-diggin' mah grave eve'y time I heahs dem."[8] Bivens's eloquent gift at storytelling had widely become a favorite. Someone else remembered him finishing with "But de shrapnel, dat's different. Dat say, 'Oo-oo-oo; I want yeh, I want yeh, I want yeh, mah honey! Dat's w'at makes a man's head kinda shrink like between his shouldahs."[9] What makes a war story good is not just the delivery of the punch line but the language.

When First Sergeant Palmer checked roll, he learned his troop had eight enlisted men wounded and one killed. Two were wounded that second day. The enlisted wounded included Corporal Henry Meagher shot through both shoulders, trumpeter Starr Wetmore shot through the right thigh, Edward Baily accidentally shot by himself through the right foot,[10] Warren Crockett shot through the leg, Tom Holmes shot through the left leg, Edward Johnston shot through the right thigh, Robert McMillan shot through the left shoulder and arm, and Teddy Miller shot through the shoulder and paralyzed from the neck down. Palmer did not think Miller would live either.

At 6 p.m., Palmer scribbled a letter home, like the few others who were lucky enough to find paper, to let folks back home know he was still alive. He described in detail the events of the last two days. The entire experience had been an adventure for him. For most of the other Rough Riders, the charge up that hill remained a terrifying blur that most would rather forget. They would describe it in their own letters with a line or two, entirely omitting the details. Corporal John Rhoades penned the sad news to Cashion's parents that their son had been killed in action since he was also from Hennessey and had been next to him when killed. So did Captain Huston. Their letters would arrive a few weeks later. Palmer's commander, Lieutenant Carr, also ranked among the wounded.

Lieutenant Carr had numbered among the 50 Rough Riders who had reached the last hill with Roosevelt, but when Ogden Wells came off duty that morning from the Cossack outpost, he saw a half-naked Carr sprawled out on the ground with his swollen tongue protruding from his mouth, a sign of extreme dehydration. Finding Carr's canteen full of rum, Wells offered him some of his water. About that time, Captain Frederick Muller of E Troop walked by and ordered Wells and Byrnes, who was nearby, to take Carr back to the hospital. They lifted him up and supported him on both sides. As they walked down the hill with the lieutenant's arms around their necks, they saw a Spanish mule they hoped to put the lieutenant on, but Carr did not think he could stay in the saddle. So they carried him further down the hill, passing other wounded. After crossing the same barbed wire fence they crossed at the beginning of the battle, Carr exclaimed, "My God. I'm shot!" and collapsed to the ground.[11] Rounds and artillery had been passing over the battlefield all day, but Wells thought the lieutenant was mistaken. Upon examination, they discovered an entry wound in his groin. So the round had been fired from behind the front lines, and they supposed it was a stray American round.

They carried Carr to the road to dress his wound while Byrnes sought help. A surgeon walked up and examined Carr's wound. He said it was from a Spanish Mauser, as sharpshooters hid in the surrounding trees. The surgeon properly dressed the wound, and another round barely missed Wells. Since he could not see from where it had come, he stood up to draw fire again. When the next round missed, he dropped as if hit, then lay there looking for the sharpshooter 300 yards away. About that time, Harry Holt and Campbell E. Babcock of K Troop came up after carrying the seriously wounded Teddy Miller back on a shelter half. Wells pointed out the location of the sharpshooter, and all began firing. Wells hit him on the first round, but the sharpshooter remained on the branch, and Wells fired three more rounds. The sharpshooter rolled off the limb and fell to the ground.

The men rolled the shelter half around their carbines into a makeshift litter and carried Carr the rest of the way to the field hospital at the base of El Pozo Hill. They waded across the San Juan River and finally found Surgeon Church. Having delivered the lieutenant to proper medical care, they then went in search of their packs to find something to eat. They then headed back when Holt collapsed in Wells's arms from heat exhaustion. Unable to continue, they camped there for the night.

Carr had made the greatest sacrifice for his country, short of death. A bullet went through both of his testicles and came out his left thigh. Command of the troop then descended upon Second Lieutenant Goodrich.[12]

When Roosevelt took an assessment of his own regiment, he had gone into battle with 490 men and lost 15 killed, 76 wounded with four missing that first day and lost eight more wounded the second day. His regiment then only numbered about 387, and heat had also prostrated another 40 of them.[13] He only counted a few officers who had reached the top of the hill. Huston's name was not among them. After Las Guasimas, Huston was the senior captain in line for major. Sickness and heat took him out of the battle at the critical moment, while Jenkins charged on farther than any other officer. One hour had changed the fate of both officers.

With Huston in command of a squadron and Carr wounded, command of the Oklahoma Company fell to Second Lieutenant Goodrich. With no other officers left in D Troop, sergeants then led the platoons. As men sat around the campfires over the next few days recounting feats of heroism, they spoke highly of their Harvard lieutenant and how he had calmly led them up the hill.

No doubt the biggest hero of the fight on the cavalry side was Roosevelt himself. He was the only officer to ride mounted during the charge. Although one of a few regimental commanders to reach the top of Kettle Hill, he took the initiative and led an assault on to the next hill. There he organized its defense and commanded the right wing of the fight, which repelled the only major Spanish counterattack. General Hawkins received official recognition for similar work in the infantry attack, but he did not lead the charge. Without a doubt, the success of the cavalry attack resulted from the leadership of one amateur soldier: Theodore Roosevelt.

Throughout the previous day's fighting, Chaplain Brown had attended to the wounded. On July 2, he led a detail of walking wounded to bury the dead and said final prayers over each body. Details hunted out the dead hidden in the tall grass. The sky, however, had filled with circling buzzards. Search parties just waited for the buzzards to land to locate their fallen comrades. The details then shoveled dirt over the dead, leaving their toes sticking out of the ground. They found the body of one dead Rough Rider sitting under a tree with a picture of his wife and children in his hand. Many of the mortally wounded had crawled off to some shade to die.

Having no more need for Hall as his adjutant, Roosevelt sent him back to bring up Tiffany's Colts. Shafter's headquarters had become the forward supply depot for his corps. A steady supply of wagons pushed ammunition and food up from Siboney and Daiquiri. Returning wagons hauled back wounded. From there, packtrains and a few wagons carried supplies to the divisions' rear. A heavy rain fell that afternoon, making that steep road in front of Siboney almost impassable. The shortage of transportation severely limited the quantity and type of supplies brought forward to the troops. That second day, ammunition took priority over rations. All the while, the Signal Corps strung telephone line forward to the division headquarters.

At El Pozo, Hall ran into Colonel McClernand, who provided him four horses for the guns. In Hall's search for ropes, he found war correspondent Richard Davis resting in the adobe house using Buckey O'Neill's bedding. The correspondent also had the captain's saber and other personal effects, which he promised to turn over to either the Corps Headquarters or First Division Hospital so they could mail them back to O'Neill's family. A week later, Davis casually informed Hall that he had left O'Neill's property in the same house. Hall located the personal effects but developed a loathing for Davis.

The two professional writers were the exact opposite. Hall focused on the little details but failed to show courage. Davis showed courage but did not care about little things. Consequently, Davis had won the admiration from the Rough Riders and Roosevelt that Hall desired. As a result, Hall found an object for his hatred. Meanwhile, Hall located what he needed, and the Colts joined the trenches. Borrowe's dynamite gun also joined the front. Hall delayed for a while around the First Division Hospital at El Pozo.

He saw wounded crowding the road to the First Division Hospital at Siboney. During the fight, those who could either walked, hobbled or crawled the three miles through swamps. Dead horses, mules and men lined the road. Some had their heads shot off and some with holes through them big enough to see through. Once at the field hospital, the wounded waited until one of the surgeons treated them. Three large tents housed the operating tables, pharmacy and dispensary. Another quartered wounded officers while a dozen smaller wall tents provided shelter for the wounded enlisted men. In all, the First Division Hospital could provide shelter for 100 wounded men without the comfort of any cots, hammocks or mattresses. The Army Corps had suffered 1,071 dead and wounded on that first day of battle alone.[14] Four surgeons under Major Marshall W. Wood had to operate on their wounds. Consequently, most of the wounded lay out in the open. The numerous "dog" tents provided shelter for about 20 hospital stewards, litter bearers and other attendants.

Many bloody and sweat-stained bodies with ashen faces waited in pain for hours

Sergeant Borrowe's dynamite gun (Theodore Roosevelt Collection, Harvard University Library).

to come under the surgical knife. Some gasped for air while others vomited blood. The war correspondent George Kennan heard neither a groan, murmur nor complaint from the soldiers. Occasionally, he might hear one swear under the pain of the surgical knife or the crying of a beardless Cuban boy for his mother. Most merely accepted their fate. He saw numerous times where when one soldier's turn came for treatment, he would say, "Take this one first—he's shot through the body. I've only got a smashed foot, and I can wait." Later one of the surgeons with tears in his eyes confided to George, "When I look at those fellows and see what they stand for, I am proud of being an American, and glory in the stock. The world has nothing finer."[15]

Late that night, the regimental and division surgeons returned from the dressing station at the Bloody Ford to help out, bringing the number up to ten. They treated the wounded on tables outside the crowded tents illuminated by candles held by the stewards. After 21 hours of continuous work without food or rest, they had treated 154 wounded that had come in. The hospital staff could retire to their own tents for a well-deserved rest.

The morning revealed many wounded soldiers lying out on the ground without any cover. The rising sun brought intense heat and thirst. Unable to walk about, many of the wounded cried out for water and food. As more wounded started returning from the front, the medical staff had to turn their attention to those in greater need of immediate medical treatment. The wounded lying on the ground had to depend upon their comrades to erect shelters and fetch food and water. George Kennan was touched by the fact that when he offered water from his canteen to some parched soldiers, instead they asked him to give it first to a comrade who had either suffered longer or had a worse wound.

Kennan telephoned Clara Barton back at Siboney to send up blankets, clothing, malted milk, beef extract, tents, tent flies and other comfort items. The next day, she arrived with an army wagon load of supplies accompanied by two physicians, Dr. Julian Hubbell and Dr. Joseph Gardner, and two other Red Cross representatives, Mrs. Gardner and Mr. McDowell, to do what they could to help. They set up a Red Cross emergency station but could only cook enough cornmeal gruel, hot malted milk, beef extract, coffee and a beverage known as "Red Cross Cider" to satisfy a fraction of the men. The next day Barton and Hubbell returned to Siboney for more blankets, pillows and the rest of the supplies the wounded needed. Meanwhile, those who could walk scrounged.

David Hughes ran into an old friend, Tom Peppers of Packtrain Number 13. Tom mounted his friend on a mule and took him 400 yards back to the bounty of the supply depot. Tom introduced David to his cook and told him to give Hughes all the food he wanted. Eating and drinking his fill, David then spent the rest of the day carrying cans of tomatoes and coffee to his wounded comrades.

After treatment, most of the wounded awaited evacuation by mule-drawn wagons over eight miles of rocks and gullies back to the field hospital at Siboney. There they waited for a hospital ship. To pass the time, most looked around to see who among their friends had joined them at the hospital. Tom Holmes had only his hat and a pair of trousers with one leg cut away. He knew Starr Wetmore had also been wounded but could not see him. In the previous war, the surgeons would have had to amputate his shattered leg, but they knew more about preventing infection now. Wetmore's thighbone had been shattered, so the surgeons merely fused Starr's thighbone together. However, there was very little they could do for Theodore Miller but make him as comfortable as possible. He died on July 8.

All the while, men behind the heights of San Juan Hill still came under fire. Even surgeons and hospital stewards with their Red Cross brassards came under fire. They assumed it came from guerrillas hidden in the trees. Convicts had been promised amnesty if they would remain behind the lines, sniping on the Americans. They made a seat in the palms with rope and leaves, hauled up a three- to four-foot-long bamboo pool filled with water and enough food to last several days. They were virtually invisible in the palm leaves.

A company of infantry and a mounted troop of cavalry were detailed to hunt down the snipers. They found none, leading Colonel Miley to conclude that the long-range Mauser fire from the front lines was falling far to the rear, wounding soldiers. Not satisfied with that conclusion, Roosevelt picked his own detail of 30 sharpshooters that afternoon to hunt down guerrillas.

The men worked in pairs. One would work his way around, occasionally exposing himself to a suspected Spanish sharpshooter, while the other lay in wait. When the guerrilla moved to shoot the decoy, he gave away his position to the other American sharpshooter.

Richard E. "Dick" Goodwin, of B Troop, paired up with a black sharpshooter from the Tenth Cavalry with orders to take no prisoners. The Tenth had also received the order to go hunting. They said that it resembled a "coon hunt" or "squirrel shooting bee" from back home. Goodwin and his companion stealthily maneuvered around in the undergrowth for several hours listening to the guerrillas shooting until they identified two palm trees where they suspected the shooting was coming from. They crawled to within 50 yards of the palms and definitely identified one of the guerrillas. The black trooper wanted to shoot him and take their chances on the other. Dick wanted to spot the other so they could both get a kill. The sharpshooters fired a few more times, and the black cavalryman said, "Let's drop this bird before he kills a good man."[16] They both took aim and fired simultaneously, and the guerrilla fell out of the tree like a dead squirrel. At the same time, they saw a rifle fall out of the other tree and a guerrilla climb down. The two American sharpshooters ran over to wait for him when he reached the ground. The man pleaded for mercy in broken English, but the black trooper cut his throat. Soldiers in battle tend to show no mercy to those they feel do not fight by the same rules as they abide by. They gave no quarter, as ordered. Roosevelt considered Goodwin and William Proffitt, both from Arizona, the best at hunting down guerrillas that day.

The designated sharpshooters hunted down the guerrillas all afternoon and the morning of the next day and killed 11 Spanish sharpshooters in that manner.[17] It is not enough to teach a man to shoot, which is what the army does on the firing range. To become skilled to the point where one can move through unfamiliar terrain, all the while alert to his surroundings, then instinctively take aim and hit his target, that is a skill acquired over years of practice with a gun. The work performed by that detail of American sharpshooters proved the merit of recruiting men already familiar with firearms and hunting. The Tenth Cavalry became known as the "squirrel hunters."

The second day, Lawton's division finally marched up from behind the cavalry and finally took up a position on their right. The Americans commanded the heights, forming a horseshoe around Santiago. Still, Shafter had his doubts about holding it.

Conflicting reports came from the front. Four light artillery batteries, which had occupied the trenches at night, found their positions untenable during the day. Major John W. Dillenbeck returned them to the safety of El Pozo by 3 in the afternoon. From there, however, they could not support the men in the trenches. Shafter then received several reports that the enemy had brought up siege and field guns so as to place enfilading fire down the trenches. Several infantry officers again urged Kent to withdraw. Some even went over their commanders' heads and reported directly to Shafter, urging him to withdraw. Shafter also feared that if the rains continued, he would not be able to supply his corps with supplies over the muddy roads.

At 6 p.m., Shafter directed Colonel Miley to summon Generals Wheeler, Lawton, Kent and Bates to El Pozo at 7 that evening. For two hours, they discussed their options and the methods by which they would withdraw if necessary. Of course, Wheeler protested any withdrawal. Shafter consented to let the troops remain in their positions for the next 24 hours until the general officers conferred again. Just as Shafter returned to his headquarters at 10 p.m., the Spaniards again opened with a horrendous fire which lasted an hour. Shafter feared that the Spaniards had attempted to break through the American lines. He eventually learned the truth.

Right after dusk, Roosevelt had sent out pickets and outposts well forward for early warning of any enemy attack. This time he had dug approach trenches. Roosevelt saw watch fires appear on the mountain passes far to his right. He assumed that it was some signal to Spanish reinforcements or the guerrillas. This put everyone on alert. Meanwhile, the same two Oklahoma boys went back out searching for Cashion's body. They had just located it when suddenly the Spaniards in the jungle to their front opened fire, seriously wounding one of the pickets. Another trooper brought him in. Meanwhile, this sporadic firing spread to a fusillade of rifle and artillery fire from across the Spanish line. The Americans answered back with equal intensity. The two Oklahomans quickly abandoned their task and snuck back under heavy fire.

Roosevelt ran up to the trench line to see what was happening. He instructed his men to fire low, cutting the grass to their front. In the dark, he could clearly see the muzzle flashes of both sides. He realized that the Spanish fire had come from their trench line and scattered outposts in the jungle between them. There clearly was no evidence of movement indicating an attack.

Since there was no Spanish attack, Roosevelt felt that the men were simply wasting their limited supply of ammunition. Officers of other regiments felt likewise. Roosevelt ran down the trench line from left to right, ordering his men to cease firing. The exchange of artillery and rifle fire that Shafter heard actually lasted about 20 minutes before the order came down the line to cease fire. As Roosevelt ran down his line, he similarly heard the booming voice of Captain Charles Ayres, commanding the trenches of the Tenth Cavalry, issuing the same order. They continued their early Fourth of July celebration. Soon a voice far away yelled out, "Cease firing in the First Volunteer Cavalry." The firing continued on their right. The voice repeated the order several times more, each time angrier. At last, an insulted Roosevelt shouted back, "You ass, we are not firing!" It offended him that the officer in the Regulars automatically assumed that his volunteers lacked discipline.[18]

The Rough Riders laughed and cheered as Captain Ayres scolded his men: "I am ashamed of you, ashamed of you! I wouldn't have believed it! Firing when I told you to stop! I'm ashamed of you! Why you're no better than Spaniards. Get out of there, every one of you."[19] The night soon became again quiet except for the chuckling by the black cavalry men as they walked back to their places in the rear.

Just before daybreak on Sunday, the third day of the siege, the Spaniards once more attempted a charge toward the American trenches. The biggest nuisance came from the sharpshooters hidden in the palms to their front. The only casualty the Rough Riders suffered that day resulted from a hidden sharpshooter. Roosevelt planned to send out a few expert woodsmen with only canteens and a little food into the jungle to hunt down those sharpshooters. When word got out, he had plenty of volunteers and a good selection of prospects. He selected 20 men, many of whom had hunted down guerrillas the day before.

Desultory firing continued until noon when the Americans ordered a cease-fire and raised a white flag. The firing ceased on both sides. This put an end to Roosevelt's hunting party. Shafter sent Colonel Dorst into Santiago with a letter to the commanding officer of the Spanish forces, demanding their surrender. If the Spanish commander did not meet Shafter's demands by 10 the next day, then he would shell the city. They had 24 hours to evacuate the civilians. The Spaniards flew a white flag over their positions so that their troops would know the truce was in effect.

At the same time, Shafter had Colonels Miley and Derby reconnoiter good positions for the artillery to bombard the city. He also waited for Admiral Sampson to meet him at his headquarters. The day before, Shafter had asked Sampson to force his way into the harbor. The admiral replied that he could only if Shafter would storm the harbor fortifications from the rear. Both planned to meet that morning of July 3 to work out their differences.

As the sun rose on July 3, Wells and Byrnes awoke and headed for the front line. Along the road, they saw discarded blankets, canteens, uniforms and other unnecessary equipment for fighting. They saw wounded and dead at the Bloody Ford and then came across a burned-out Gatling gun with three dead soldiers and a disemboweled horse nearby. On their walk up the hill, they passed more walking wounded returning to the rear and the dead bloated beyond recognition, some still holding their carbines. Upon reaching their position, they reported to Captain Huston.

Meanwhile, Shafter again considered withdrawing his corps from the heights around Santiago. He sent a message to Secretary Alger the morning of the 3rd informing him that he had already lost 1,000 men to date and expected to lose more due to illness and the heat. He mentioned that the rains made the roads difficult to supply the troops on the line. Shafter secretly feared the Spaniards had a considerable number of forces within reinforcing distance at Manzanillo, Holguin and Guantanamo, and their combination would outnumber his force. Fortunately, Alger advised Shafter that although he was the best judge of the situation, it would be better to hold the present position than fall back.

As usual the Rough Riders learned about the surrender demands through rumors. They were in no hurry to fight again and welcomed the truce. They took advantage of the quiet to lie out in the sun and write letters home. Spanish officers requested permission to enter American lines to police up and bury their own dead. This was granted, and Huston sent out a party to recover Cashion's body. Sergeant Joseph Randolph and Corporal Henry Love wrapped his vulture-ravaged body in his shelter half and buried it under the shade of a tree on the hill that he had sacrificed his life to take. Chaplain Brown held a short service.[20]

Infantry men relaxing during a truce above Santiago (Library of Congress).

Around 9:30, they heard firing off near the mouth of the harbor. They could only speculate what had happened. A troop of mounted cavalry under Captain Henry Allen on the extreme right of Lawton rode over to discover that the Spanish fleet had made a break for open sea. Allen rode back and reported this news to Shafter at 1 p.m. Allen had no news of the outcome. By this inopportune coincidence, Sampson missed the naval battle he had waited so patiently for. His second in command, Commodore Winfield Scott Schley, would destroy Cervera's fleet and win glory for himself.

The army transports sailed out behind the navy to witness the battle. Late that afternoon, they returned with the news. At first, the word circulated that the U.S. Navy had beaten the Spanish fleet with the loss of some Spanish vessels. The *Colon* and a few other Spanish vessels had escaped. Within an hour, a thundering cheer rose in the trenches to their left and worked its way toward the Rough Riders. They soon learned that the American fleet remained unhurt yet sank all enemy vessels except the *Colon*. Wild pandemonium broke out as men danced and cheered in celebration of the naval victory. They would learn the next day that the U.S. Navy had also sunk the *Colon*. The Americans had achieved both a naval and military victory.

Roosevelt's heart swelled with pride in the performance of his regiment. In less than 60 days the regiment had been organized, equipped and fought at the forefront of two battles. His men accounted for themselves equally to or better than the Regulars. Colonel Dorst complimented them with the title of "Eleventh United States Horse"[21] since there were only ten Regular cavalry regiments. They had brought with them from the frontier skills that it took the Regular Army years to train recruits. The frontier had hardened them physically and made them resourceful. They were all good shots and aggressive in battle. Roosevelt knew his men, and they had grown to trust and have confidence in him as their leader. He would do everything in his power to see that they were fed, sheltered and spared any undue hardship. In return, he knew he could expect them to suffer any degree of hardship and perform any kind of fatigue without a murmur or fearlessly face any danger. He and his officers shared the same hardships and danger as their men. The regiment had become everything that he had ever expected. He had proven to be a brave leader in battle, but the challenges over the next few weeks would prove the quality of his leadership. His success would grow from a genuine love for his men.

CHAPTER 8

Paper War

The war entered its negotiation phase. Neither side cared to fight anymore, yet neither side knew the full extent to which the other suffered. Shafter did not know how much Toral had to lose by surrendering, so he had to negotiate from a position of power—while disease sapped away at the strength of his corps. That third day, Shafter and Sampson conferred upon their strategy.

With Cervera's fleet destroyed, Shafter suggested that if Sampson would force his way into the harbor, the city would surrender without any further sacrifice. Samson replied that the fortifications guarding the harbor entrance were still formidable, and he did not wish to endanger the fleet. Shafter would have to stick to his original plan to strangle the Spanish garrison. By the night of July 3, Shafter's Fifth Corps had completely surrounded Santiago from the bay on the north of the city to the San Juan River to the south. General Pando was marching from Holguin, but Shafter felt confident that the Cubans under General Garcia would keep him out of Santiago.

With bullets no longer falling in the rear during the truce, Shafter instructed the soldiers to gather up their abandoned clothing and rations. The Rough Riders sent details to recover the jackets, haversacks and bedding abandoned back at El Pozo. Roosevelt organized a packtrain with the officers' horses, two or three captured Spanish cavalry horses, a few Cuban ponies and two or three abandoned mules. The details passed the carnage of war as dead men, horses and mules were littered everywhere. Ben Colbert and four others carried all their troops' gear the three miles from El Pozo, what seemed like five, back to the hill. He wrote that their burden would have given credit to any donkey. D Troop left men to guard their equipment while others carried it forward in several trips.

No longer dodging bullets, the men shifted their attention to food and shelter, the basic needs of survival. The men then erected their shelters. Fortunately, there had been little rain over the last three days. When Roosevelt's personal baggage arrived, he took the opportunity to shave for the first time since the morning of the battle. Many of the men would take the opportunity to walk down to the streams and bathe.

A packtrain led by Tom Horn finally arrived carrying food by 6 that evening. Each Rough Rider drew a ration of three hardtack biscuits, a piece of bacon and a handful of coffee. After three days without much to eat, those rations tasted delicious. Rations of coffee, sugar, meat, and hardtack began to arrive regularly. Other supplements such as tobacco were rare, again causing inflation. One 20-cent bag of tobacco sold for $10.

Some troopers went hunting for the few scarce guinea hens they might see. There were plenty of mangos to eat, but the fruit gave the troopers diarrhea. No longer did the troopers have to prepare their food individually under fire. This interlude of peace offered the cooks the chance to once again practice their trade. However, they needed ample amounts of firewood. Since soldiers do not like to walk very far to do their duty, they stripped the nearby farmhouses and buildings of their lumber.

Roosevelt was not about to rely entirely upon the corps' packtrain for the welfare of his men. He sent the ever-resourceful Rynning back to coast to pick up the mail since he still had his mule. Along the way near Las Guasimas, he saw an elderly man digging up one of the graves where the Rough Riders had buried their fallen comrades of the first battle. Rynning approached the man and asked what he was doing. The old man turned out to be none other than Hamilton Fish, Sr. He showed the lieutenant an order that authorized him to dig up the body of his son and that of Capron. He had two metal caskets that would transport both of them back to the United States.

When Rynning arrived at Siboney, he asked the whereabouts of the mail. When he found the mail shack, he learned that the postmaster had died of yellow fever and his body was kept in the shack with the mail. The medical authorities did not know that the disease was transmitted by the city-loving *Aedes aegypti* mosquito. They believed that it was contagious, and fear of an epidemic soon followed. The first definite case of yellow fever in Siboney was diagnosed on the 6th, but a week later a total of 38 cases would be recorded.

The sentry from the Thirty-Third Michigan Volunteer Infantry paced back and forth in front of the shack and informed Rynning that mail would be burned. The Michigan regiment had been assigned to stevedore and supply duty at Siboney. The lieutenant acted uninterested. When the sentry reached the end of his beat, Rynning slipped through the window and discovered a total of three corpses in there. He rustled around until he found two sacks of mail marked "Colonel Roosevelt's Command." He tossed them out the rear window and carried them a distance of 400 or 500 yards away, where wounded Rough Riders waited for hospital ships to take them back to America. There Lieutenant Day gave him Captain McClintock's typewriter. From then on, Rynning spent most of the truce on detached duty.

The rains started again, and the ground began to emit a sickly smell. While rations piled up at Siboney and Shafter's headquarters, the shortage of pack mules restricted the quantity that went forward to the soldiers. In addition to that, the rain washed sewage and decay from the dead bodies into the water supply to their rear. Men weakened by poor rations increasingly fell ill due to the hot climate and foul water. The sick lay under shelters on the slopes below the trenches. The sun beat down, making all water almost too hot to drink. Church had set up a field hospital on the shoulder of the hill. He had very little medicine and was even sick himself. The sick unfortunately could not eat a diet of hardtack and salted pork and only got worse. D Troop had lost 20 men to fever by the third day, leaving only 30 effective fighting men. Huston numbered among the sick.

At 6:30 that evening, General Toral, who had replaced the wounded General Linares, sent his reply that he would not surrender. The British, Portuguese, Norwegian and Chinese consulates, however, accompanied Dorst, requesting that Shafter delay his bombardment until July 5 since the city had some 15,000 to 20,000 citizens to evacuate. They also asked if the civilians had permission to go to El Caney. Shafter agreed and said that he would not shell the city until July 5 under the condition that the Spaniards made no assaults upon the American lines. They agreed. No one was eager to begin fighting again.

Meanwhile, the Rough Riders could see the Spaniards bringing up their siege guns. They placed one immense gun that flanked the entire cavalry line of entrenchments.

During the lull, an engineer officer inspected the trenches and informed Roosevelt of their problems. Roosevelt did not hesitate to ask how he should have dug them. His training in Texas was offensive maneuver; now he would learn how to properly defend. Roosevelt then set about with the usual zeal to make his trenches first-rate. Roosevelt had his men dig bombproof shelters and communication and approach trenches in anticipation of the cannonade at the end of the truce.

If the healthy troopers were not on duty digging, they were put on some other detail or they could sleep. They usually pulled between six and seven hours duty in the trenches. The truce allowed the troops to fall into old military habits of standing muster formation every day for accountability. Those too sick to stand were excused, and those on guard the night before could sleep as late as they wanted except for the fear of missing breakfast. Roosevelt was not one to slow down nor did he let his men remain idle. He kept improving his position in anticipation that the fight would begin again.

That night Roosevelt picked up a detail of 60 men from the First, Ninth and Tenth Cavalries along with a detail of 60 of his men. They extended a zigzag trench from his lines out to a knoll which overlooked the Spanish trenches. There, with the helpful supervision of Greenway, Goodrich, Parker and Stevens, Roosevelt had the men dig bombproofs and a semicircle trench with sandbag walls complete with firing loopholes. He placed pickets well forward in the jungle to prevent the Spaniards from interfering with the digging. Parker dismounted two of his Gatling guns and placed them in the bastion along with Tiffany's two Colt rapid-fire guns. The Gatling men dubbed the bastion Fort Roosevelt.

Parker's Gatling guns in trenches (Theodore Roosevelt Collection, Harvard University Library).

Roosevelt rotated the men in the trenches as usual but permitted three out of every four men to sleep. He inspected the line once a night except when either Wilcox, Kane, Greenway or Goodrich was on duty. He trusted their leadership and would even take his boots off and sleep the night through.

Men not digging could relax and for the first time enjoy the scenery. They noticed how beautiful the surrounding countryside was. Palm trees silhouetted the night sky. Cubans off to their right burned the abandoned blockhouses. A rocket rose from the Spanish lines, exploding then sending a shower of balls of fire down onto the palms. It signaled their sharpshooters to come in from the palms. All this added to the spectacle of the tropic night.

The next day was Monday, the Fourth of July. An order was read to the men that General Miles was on his way with reinforcements, assuring that the outcome of the campaign would be victorious. Roosevelt wrote his report of the battle to Wood. He called a conference of his leaders for their recommendations. Since the Army only had one medal for gallantry, the Medal of Honor, most heroism of the time was recognized by the mention of names in the official report. Huston and First Sergeant Palmer recommended Roy Cashion and Corporal John Rhoades, both of Hennessey. Rhoades had been wounded in the hospital on July 1. The sound of the distant battle had brought him to his feet, where he escaped to join his D Troop in the fight.

In Roosevelt's report, he cited Captains Llewellyn, Muller and Luna for leading their troops and Lieutenants Kane, Greenwood and Goodrich for taking charge of their troops under fire. He praised Jenkins for his gallantry but did not mention Huston. Roosevelt admired men who refused to abandon the fight after they were wounded. He cited 14 such troopers. Of the Twin Territories, his list included Corporal Rhoades and Trumpeter Frank R. McDonald from Oologah, Indian Territory. He cited 11 troopers for coolness and gallantry under fire. The most conspicuous gallantry he praised was George Roland's.

Meanwhile, Shafter sent three letters to General Toral, first offering to release the wounded Spanish soldiers the Americans had captured if they agreed not to raise arms against the American army, unless exchanged. Shafter had learned that the Spanish soldiers believed that the Americans would shoot them upon capture. He concluded that if he released the wounded, they would tell a different story about their treatment by the Americans. His next letter offered to exchange his prisoners for the crew of the *Merrimac* and any soldiers the Spaniards might have captured. Toral sent a message thanking Shafter for the offer of releasing the wounded back to his care but stating that an exchange could only be authorized by his Captain General Ramón Blanco y Erenas. He requested that Shafter send the names of the three captured Spanish officers so that he could select the one he would trade for Lieutenant Richmond Hobson. He also agreed to exchange the seven sailors for seven of his soldiers. The third letter agreed to conduct the exchange between the lines with one commissioner from each side at 2 p.m. on the 6th.

On July 5, emaciated and sickly Spanish citizens paraded out of the city on their way to El Caney. Old men, women and children struggled under their burdens and the hot sun. It rained at two that afternoon, the last time for many days. The Rough Riders waited for the impending hostilities that would follow, but both sides extended the truce for another 24 hours. Toral sent a message to Shafter that Blanco had accepted the proposition for an exchange of prisoners.

Meanwhile, the Rough Riders continued improving their trenches and bombproofing bunkers. The men in the Cossack outpost believed that the Spaniards were

G Troop bombproofs behind San Juan Hill (Theodore Roosevelt Collection, Harvard University Library).

preparing for an attack at 3 a.m. on the 6th. Everyone was ready, but the attack did not materialize.

General Shafter learned that at 10 p.m. on the 3rd, Lieutenant General Luis Manuel de Pando y Sánchez had fought through the Cubans under General Garcia and marched into Santiago with 5,000 reinforcements down the Cobre Road. Shafter realized that he could not count on the Cubans to hold their line but had to depend entirely upon his own troops. To take Santiago would require 15,000 more men. On the 5th, Shafter urged the president to direct Admiral Sampson to force his way into the bay. Shafter felt that the city would fall within hours. However, based upon Shafter's earlier report that his line was weak, Alger recommended that Shafter wait for reinforcements. Shafter received a telegram that day that Brigadier General Wallace F. Randolph had departed Key West with 3,500 reinforcements and six batteries of artillery board, the *City of Macon, Gate City, Hudson, Comanche, Unionist* and *Specialist*. Shafter sent the news to Wheeler to pass on to the men in the line.

Rynning finally collapsed in the mud one day from exhaustion, so Wood ordered him down to the coast for a few days' rest. Roosevelt then sent Hall back with his improvised packtrain to Siboney and Daiquiri for wagons to bring up extra food. Unlike Rynning, Hall went through appropriate channels. Hall reached division headquarters and begged convincingly enough to receive one wagon. He then reported to corps headquarters and made the same appeal. Shafter, who was discussing war plans, turned to Hall and said, "You are not going to take any tents to the front are you?" Hall answered, "No, sir."[1] He then received an order from the quartermaster for a wagon and two mule teams. Hall then proceeded happily down the road to Siboney where an hour and a half later he came upon three Rough Riders left behind at their abandoned camp near Las Guasimas. They loaded up the camp equipage, to include their tents, on their one wagon and proceeded onto Siboney for the mail.

Along the way Hall's escort suddenly jumped to the side of the road with their carbines at the ready. Fifty yards ahead, they saw a party of Spaniards. They soon recognized that it was a party of ten prisoners under the guard of a sergeant and private to be exchanged for Navy Lieutenant Hobson and his crew of the *Merrimac*. Shafter had not received the name of the Spanish officer to be exchanged, so he ordered all three officers brought forward. Both sides met on the road to the right of the cavalry brigade lines. Miley acted as the American commissioner for the exchange. After Miley received the name of the Spanish officer, he signed the papers and returned with the other two officers. Lieutenant Hobson and his crew received a hero's ovation as they paraded through American lines.

After the exchange of prisoners, Miley also issued Shafter's second demand for surrender. Shafter's letter informed Toral that the Spanish fleet had been completely destroyed and demanded that Toral surrender or the siege would restart at noon the next day. Shafter and Sampson had both agreed to a joint army and navy attack on Santiago at noon on the 9th, and Miley informed Toral of such intention. The 8-inch, 10-inch and 13-inch naval guns could easily range the city. Meanwhile, the Fifth Corps brought up and placed eight field mortars in position to the east of the city. The roads, however, were too muddy to bring up the one siege gun that had been disembarked.

About the time Hall arrived at Siboney, the village was crowded with tents and cargo guarded by two Michigan volunteer regiments. Meanwhile, naked soldiers waded into the surf to offload crates from the launches. This was the supply base for Fifth Corps, so army engineers were constructing a pier while transports lay offshore. Hall met up with the postmaster who explained that while he had relocated to Siboney, the mail was still at Daiquiri, and he did not have any transportation. He agreed that if Hall brought the mail forward, he would put his mail clerks to work sorting the Rough Rider mail first. So Hall spent the night in Siboney with his crew.

The next morning, Hall returned to Daiquiri where he presented his written order to the quartermaster in charge of the supplies there. The supply officer was not happy to have to give up a wagon and mules to a line regiment when they had enough problems pushing supplies to the forward depot. Instead, he made Hall wait another day. To pass the time, Hall went out and met an old West Point friend of his, Frank D. Ramsey, in the Commissary Department. He talked him out of a dozen half-rotten potatoes. He then located the sole representative of the post office, who was sick with yellow fever. He agreed to stand by ready with the keys the next day when Hall had the wagons.

That night at the front, Ben Colbert was on duty in the Cossack outpost until 9 p.m. The men continued improving the position when someone accidentally fired a shot. The sound of the Spaniards falling into their rifle pits made Ben laugh.

The next day on the 7th, Hall received two four-mule teams when the muddy roads required six-mule teams to pull a full load. He could only load the wagons to a third of their capacity. Hall loaded the mail and a few hundred pounds of beans and what provisions of lime juice and other delicacies he could purchase with the money Roosevelt had given him. He then proceeded to Siboney where he picked up more rations and proceeded back to the front. All the while, surrender negotiations continued.

After Toral read the latest surrender demand, he responded by asking for permission for employees of the Submarine Cable Company to return to El Caney so he could communicate with his Spanish government. This was done on the 7th. On the 8th, Toral sent his reply. He admitted that bombardment would little affect his army as they were in the trenches outside the city, while the homeowners, whom the Americans had come to protect, would suffer the severest of the damage. He had plenty of provisions and water stored up in cisterns since the Americans had cut off the water supply into Santiago. He stated that his force could outlast the Americans, who would grow weaker from disease the longer they waited, while his soldiers were more acclimated to the climate. Instead of surrender of his army, he offered to evacuate the Province of Santiago. While Shafter waited for a response from Washington, the civil governor brought his family out and surrendered the morning of the 8th. Alger returned Toral's offer.

Rumors about renewing the battle made its way through the ranks. The Rough Riders anticipated an end to their peace and quiet. They continued to improve their positions while a regimental band played that day. David Hughes learned of the impending fight from some Signal Corps men and had recovered enough to rejoin the fighting. He walked over to the pile of equipment and picked out a carbine, pistol, canteen, shelter half, cartridge belt and 100 rounds of ammunition. He hid them under some underbrush and then went to the doctor to bid his farewell. The doctor thanked him for his help with the wounded, checked his wound one last time and then issued him a discharge from the hospital.

Meanwhile, Roosevelt realized that the Santiago Road was lightly defended. He obtained permission to build a redoubt on it and garrison it with Rough Riders. Coincidentally, that night, 30 Spanish soldiers deserted and entered the American lines through that point and surrendered to the Rough Riders. The Americans learned more would follow if the Spaniards knew that they would be treated well. The word circulated through the line that the Spaniards called the Americans, "The Iron Giants," since they would advance once the Spaniards began shooting at them.

On the 9th, the Spanish attack did not materialize. Instead, they offered to surrender their siege guns if they would be allowed to retain their sidearms and march out. Shafter considered the proposal, then sent it to the secretary of war in Washington with the recommendation of his general officers to accept it. He then sent word to the soldiers in the trenches that the truce would remain in effect until an answer returned. The secretary of war was surprised to read the message. Shafter had assured him that if the supply lines into Santiago were cut, he could force the surrender of the Spaniards. Without delay, Adjutant General Henry C. Corbin wired a response from Alger which reminded Shafter that as soon as possible, he should destroy the enemy and take the city. If needed, the invasion force of Puerto Rico could be diverted as reinforcements. Brigadier General George A. Garreston's brigade of 1,800 men had sailed that day from Charleston, South Carolina, aboard the *Yale* and *Columbia* with General Nelson Miles. Shafter passed the word that more reinforcements were on their way.

Washington was a long way from the malaria-infested jungles of Cuba. Alger, as with the delays in Tampa, had little sympathy for Shafter's plight. This response was sent to Toral, and he was given until 3 p.m. on the 10th to respond. If Toral found the terms unacceptable, then the bombardment would begin at 4 p.m.

On the 9th, Colonel Wood also received his appointment to brigadier general. So each troop of Rough Riders went down to congratulate him with three cheers. One determined Rough Rider had also arrived from Tampa. He ran away and hired on as a cook on one of the transports and arrived within ten days. After supper, Ben Colbert and a few other Rough Riders went over to the Ninth Cavalry to hear their quartet sing. The music soothed his weary mind; then he returned and went to sleep without a care.

To pass the time, the men swam in the pond below their position. One day, Sherman Bell slipped and fell, rupturing himself. Four doctors could not help him although the rupture was small. His condition worsened, so they detailed two troopers from K Troop, Bill McGinty and Sherman's friend Benjamin Daniels, also of Colorado Springs, to take him back to the Second Division Hospital at Siboney. They loaded him on his back in a two-wheeled cart with his head toward the rear. When the padded harness was fastened to the mule, it lifted the front of the cart up about a foot. The doctors had shot the sick trooper up with morphine and instructed the two troopers to get him to the hospital before the painkiller wore off.

They started down the hill with Bill riding in the back of the cart with his rifle in hand and Ben walking behind. Since Bill was in a hurry, Ben had trouble keeping up. They argued back and forth above the sound of the squeaky axle. As Bill urged the mule on over the rough road, it bounced the cart around, and Sherman's sedated body absorbed each jolt. Ben thought the ride was going to kill his friend and yelled for Bill to take it easy. They arrived at the Second Division Hospital, and Bill gave the senior surgeon the note from their doctors. The two proceeded back at an easier pace.

Once back at camp, the doctors asked how the trip turned out. Bill told the doctors about Ben's griping. They said that in Sherman's condition it did not matter. They did not have much hope for his recovery anyway. Bill figured that he would never see Sherman alive again.

After the war was over, Bill was admitted to a hospital in New York. Lo and behold, Sherman Bell dropped by to visit him. He introduced Bill to his girlfriend, "Here is the McGinty that saved my life in Cuba." He then told her stories about Bill. Bill had considered Sherman a truthful man but had doubts about his recent claim. Sherman noticed. "You act like you don't know what I'm talking about. Remember when I was in that awful fix in the mountains of Cuba?" Bill acknowledged.[2]

"Well," Sherman continued, "the doctors told me that the trip down the mountainside was what saved my life. My head being lower than my feet, and I being relaxed, the jolts along the rough mountain side worked that rupture slowly back in until when I reached the hospital, the doctors did not need to operate, or do much else, since I was already on the road to recovery."[3]

Sunday, the 10th came, and it rained that afternoon for the first time since the 5th. At 5 p.m., the Spaniards hauled down their white flag. The men remained alert, waiting in their trenches or bombproofs. At 4 that afternoon, the fighting renewed.[4] The American artillery fired most of the rounds. The U.S. Navy threw 8-inch and 10-inch shells into the city. The only Rough Riders to have a chance to fight were those with the Colts and the 20 picked sharpshooters in the fort. At first, they heard one Spanish battery fire but could not locate its position in the outskirts of the city. With the aid of powerful field glasses, they finally located the source of the noise in front of a hospital flying a flag with the red cross. The Gatlings and Colts under the command of Parker put those enemy guns out of action. One of the rounds from the dynamite gun landed in either an enemy trench or building. The fleeing Spanish solders gave the sharpshooters targets to shoot at. The fighting continued until dark, and the Rough Riders lost no men that day.

Some fighting continued just after sunrise on the 11th and continued until a flag of truce was sent over at 1 p.m. The firing continued for another hour. Only two men from

Soldiers relaxing during another truce (Theodore Roosevelt Collection, Harvard University Library).

the Ninth Cavalry were wounded that day. By noon, the Rough Riders were replaced, and one of the Gatling guns was sent over two miles to the right to help guard the road between Santiago and El Caney. There they could relax a little more.

McGinty ran into Frank Weitzel hanging around the headquarters. Bill remembered, "He seemed to not care for anything but a good time, and liked to see everything that was going on."[5] The officers had told them that El Caney was off limits. Curiosity made both want to go and check it out anyway. That night, they borrowed, without permission, Lieutenant Hall and General Wheeler's horses to ride over to the town. Many of the officers had picked up stray Spanish cavalry horses as their mounts, and, because the men often borrowed them, the officers usually had to walk. The sight of emaciated refugees depressed the two. They returned and staked the horses back in the same place where they had found them. The next day they found out that El Caney was off limits because the Spaniards had yellow fever. Both kept quiet about their trip for fear of being quarantined. The two began to fear that they would also get sick, but neither did. Palmer, Haynes and Amrine did unfortunately come down with malaria. Haynes nearly died and remained hospitalized for a considerable time.[6]

By then disease had incapacitated the majority of Shafter's corps. It was the consensus of the officers that the army was too weak to attack. It increasingly appeared as if his army was losing the battle to disease. Consequently, Shafter became more anxious to bring this siege to an end.

General Miles arrived with 1,800 reinforcements on the 12th and so did a telegram from the secretary of war that morning authorizing the safe return of Toral's army to Spain. This gave Shafter two advantages. He sent another demand for surrender, stating that he had reinforcements and that the U.S. government would transport Toral's command to Spain. Toral responded in a message that he would have to wait for permission from his general-in-chief in Madrid. That evening, Linares sent a telegram to Madrid describing the deplorable conditions in Santiago and offering his reputation as a sacrifice for accepting the surrender. His men were not much better off than the Americans.

Over on the road, a low hill covered with trenches dug by the previous regiment separated the Rough Rider camp from the Spaniards. Behind it camped the regiment. Four troops camped on one side of the road and the remaining four on the other. Wilcox ordered Hughes to round up a detail of 18 men and report to Sergeant Tiffany. They reported between 8 and 9 o'clock where to dig pits for his two Colts in front of their new trenches.

The low-hanging black clouds turned the night pitch-black. The men could not see six feet in front of them. Tiffany had previously selected the position for his guns during the afternoon. He led the men, each with their right hand on the shoulder of the next and a pick or shovel in their left. They cautiously walked in lockstep fashion with no smoking or talking other than in a low whisper. A guard was posted between the Rough Riders and the Spanish trenches 200 yards away. They took six- to eight-inch steps and had made about 50 feet when someone stepped on a rock, and it started rolling down the hill. The Spanish outposts opened fire but could not see anything to hit. The detail dropped to one knee and waited until five minutes after everything quieted down. Then they stood up and moved along. Upon reaching their destination, they received another enemy volley. They dropped to a knee as before.

After the firing quieted down, the men began to quietly clear the brush with their pocketknives. This was slow work but not as slow as the digging. One man would scoop up a shovel full of dirt. The other would hold the sandbag with one hand and feel for the shovel of dirt with the other and then guide it to the opening of the sandbag. The sandbags were laid lengthwise with a gap in the middle for the gun to fire left and right. Whenever the picks or shovels accidentally hit a rock, the Spaniards fired in the direction of the noise. They had the two pits pretty well underway by midnight when a thunderstorm poured down on them for about 40 minutes and filled the pits with water up to their waists. At 1 a.m., the detail started back in the same fashion as it had entered.

For the first time since going into action, Roosevelt stripped down to go to sleep in his tent that night. At midnight on the 11th, the worst storm since their arrival hit them and blew his tent over. He ran around in the pouring rain searching for his soaked uniform. Since Woody Kane was on duty that night, Roosevelt had the confidence that the lieutenant would take care of the pickets. The colonel made his way to the kitchen tent where Bert T. Holderman of L Troop wrapped him in a dry blanket. Roosevelt then crawled up on a table and went to sleep.

The rain continued off and on that night, leaving everyone very miserable. Hughes and his bunkie, Jess Toland, returned soaked to the skin and shivered throughout the night. The rain had blown out the mess fires. The poet, Ben Colbert, lamented in his diary, "I wish there was no fighting. I wish there was no war. I wouldn't take a $1,000 for my experience but I don't want 5¢ more."[7] The rain continued until four in the afternoon.

That morning of the 12th at 8 a.m., the British and French consulates passed through the Rough Riders' lines into Santiago, and the rumor circulated after supper that Spain was suing for peace and the Rough Riders would be the first ones home. That news elevated morale.

Toral sent a letter to Shafter explaining that he had sent a request for surrender to his commander in Madrid but insisted that his army be allowed to surrender with honor. Shafter responded that Miles, the Commanding General of the American army, would be at his command that day and requested a personal interview with him at 9 a.m. on the 13th.

The First Illinois Volunteers, which had landed at Siboney on the 9th, came up and took position on the Rough Riders' right. The veterans, wearing the same clothes since they had landed, could easily identify those who had not been in battle, since the new arrivals still had everything the government had issued them. Consequently, the seasoned veterans made sport of their hardships with the untried volunteers.

The First Illinois Volunteer Infantry had left Tampa with 1,350 men on two transports on July 5. This fleet of six transports also brought six batteries of light artillery and 930 recruits as infantry replacements for the Regular Army.[8] There were not enough transports to ship the rest of the Rough Riders this trip. As soon as transports returned from Cuba, the other squadron expected to load up. However, the *Iroquois* and *Cherokee* loaded with sick and wounded left for Key West on July 3 and 5. Once at Key West, the *Iroquois* was ordered to Fort Monroe, Virginia, while the *Cherokee* continued on to Tampa. Unfortunately, once Toral agreed to surrender, there was no need for the rest of the Rough Riders to come to Cuba. They would miss the war. However, several volunteers did manage to slip aboard the transports and arrive in Cuba to enlist in the Rough Riders.

Meanwhile, the storm had swollen the rivers, preventing any more food from reaching the front. Fortunately, Roosevelt had amassed and maintained enough hardtack and salted pork to last his regiment about two days. On two or three occasions, Roosevelt had personally taken his improvised packtrain back to Siboney for provisions. He had not relied entirely on the army transportation system nor did it seem he could count on Hall. When he did not go, Chaplain Brown or another trooper went in his stead. Brown and Charles Knoblauch developed a good penchant for that line of work. Colonel Weston of the Commissary Department never let red tape interfere with getting his job done. He helped the Rough Riders out however he could, and Roosevelt purchased food whenever possible either with his own money or that given him by Woodbury Kane or sent to him by the Red Cross of New York or even Roosevelt's brother-in-law. So the Rough Riders had sufficient provisions of army rations.

The Illinois infantrymen were new and had nothing to eat. They had left the beach with three days' rations. Roosevelt gave them beans and coffee for the senior officers plus a couple of cases of hardtack. He then rode his horse back to the headquarters, half swimming the streams, but succeeded in bringing back half of a packtrain with provisions for them.

Transportation remained a constant problem aggravated by disease. The effects of disease had rendered two entire packtrains without packers. On the 12th, Shafter directed that Wheeler task the Rough Riders for two squads of 12 men each to handle the two packtrains. Roosevelt complied but explained that this further reduced his number of men fit for duty down to 340. He had lost nearly 200 men to disease and wounds.

Whenever soldiers linger in one area for any length of time, the local populace sees the commercial opportunity to benefit from what the army does not issue them. When their situation becomes more austere, the need to trade with soldiers increases even more. All day on the 14th, women and children flocked to the guard line attempting to trade picked fruit, money and jewels for anything edible. They also picked up whatever refuse the soldiers threw away. While their victory depended upon forcing these conditions upon the citizens and military of Santiago, it still saddened the soldiers, nonetheless.

At 9 a.m. on the 13th, Wheeler, Shafter, Miles, Miley and Doctor George E. Goodfellow, who spoke Spanish like a native, met with Toral and two or three of his staff under the shade of a huge ceiba tree along the road between the lines. The trunk measured nearly 50 feet in circumference, and the branches extended broadly across the field, providing good shade. This was the same place as the exchange of prisoners. They talked for an hour and a half. Shafter stated that only Toral's unconditional surrender would be accepted and that he had no hope of escape and had no right to continue to fight. If Toral refused, Shafter stated that he would open fire on Santiago with every gun he had at noon the next day, and the navy's 13-inch guns were ready. This gave Toral something more to consider. They agreed to meet at the same place at 11 a.m. the next day.

Many of the officers thought that Toral was only delaying the negotiations to buy time. They urged that Shafter break off negotiations and attack. Miles made arrangements to land a strong infantry force under Brigadier General Guy V. Henry at Cabanas, which could march against Santiago. Shafter was confident that Toral would surrender in time, but when?

By the 14th, Shafter had 62 guns in place overlooking Santiago. The same delegation rode forward at the appointed time. They passed through the Rough Riders' lines, and a few men standing alongside the road came to attention. Miles optimistically called out, "Well, boys, the rest of the fighting will be done on paper."[9]

Shafter again gave Toral the ultimatum to surrender by noon that day, or he would again begin the siege. The discussion lasted until 12:15. Wheeler remembered that Toral explained that he could not surrender without the approval of the Madrid government. General Blanco had authorized Toral to arrange the terms of capitulation, and the Spanish government usually complied with the recommendations of their general officers. Shafter and Miles, however, understood that Toral had finally agreed to an unconditional surrender. A commission of officers was appointed by both sides to discuss the terms of capitulation later that afternoon. Shafter appointed Wheeler, Lawton and Miley as his representatives. With the siege at an end, Shafter ordered that all soldiers be withdrawn from the trenches except a small guard.

One must understand that John Miley was only a lieutenant colonel in the volunteers on General Shafter's staff. He had graduated from West Point in 1887 and held the Regular Army rank of first lieutenant, and that was how the others referred to him. His views of the negotiations would differ significantly from the two older officers.

They returned, and, with the help of the War Department stenographer, Mr. Leonard Wilson, Wheeler dictated the terms of immediate capitulation. One of his Cuban interpreters, Mr. Aurelius Mestre, mentioned that he did not think Toral had agreed to immediate capitulation. The other officers disagreed, and they completed a document for absolute and immediate surrender.

At 2 p.m.,[10] the commissioners of both parties met under the same tree, which would became known as "El Arbor de la Paz" or "the tree of peace." The American commissioners had arrived with a rough draft of the agreement of capitulation. The Spaniards requested that the Americans repair and immediately reestablish the water system of the city. Second, they wanted all Cuban volunteers who had sympathized with the Spaniards to be allowed to remain in Cuba. The Americans agreed to this as long as they agreed not to bear arms against the United States in the present war.

Finally, the Spaniards requested that their troops be permitted to retain their fire-arms when they returned to Spain. This, at first, was unacceptable to the Americans, who considered the Spaniards as prisoners of war. The Spaniards felt that the return of their arms would allow them to return with honor. Miley believed that they wanted this last issue to take the sting out of the surrender. Lawton agreed to recommend that the arms be returned with them to Spain, and Miley and Wheeler concurred. When asked if they were prepared to sign the amended articles, the Spanish officers said that they would have to return and consult with Toral. Having finished at 4 p.m., they agreed to reconvene at 6 that evening. In the meantime, soldiers erected a tent underneath the tree for the next meeting.

The Americans expected nothing more than for the Spanish commission to sign the document. The Americans opened the meeting by asking that the Spanish troops be withdrawn from their trenches and that they remove the obstacles to the mouth of the harbor so that the Red Cross vessel, *State of Texas*, might begin to enter immediately. They also asked if the Spaniards would assist in getting the railroad operational. The Spanish officers said they would have to consult with Toral on those issues. The Spanish commission also stated that they wanted to discuss two or three other points in

Surrender tree before Santiago (Library of Congress).

connection with the document. This evidently caught the Americans by surprise as they had not anticipated any further negotiations.

The first key point was that any mention of the word "surrender" or "surrendered" should be changed to "capitulated" or "capitulation." The Spanish officers were very sensitive about the wording of the document so as not to discredit their honor. Wheeler agreed to this. Lieutenant Colonel Don Frontan explained that the document required a complete inventory of Spanish property, which would be impossible to complete. Wheeler agreed to modify it to read just arms and military stores. The Spaniards still had concern over disarmament. Wheeler again stated that he and his colleagues would recommend that their government return the arms to the soldiers but that they would have to be disarmed while in Santiago. Lawton reminded them that Washington had to make that decision.

In addition, the Spaniards requested time so they could consult with Linares. Everyone knew that Linares was not in command on account of his wound. Wheeler stated that he had understood that the commissioners were supposed to have the authority to make decisions for their respective commands. It appeared that the Spaniards either misunderstood the surrender agreement between Toral and Shafter, or they were again employing delaying tactics. The Spaniards felt that it was important to postpone the negotiations until the next morning. Wheeler had a serious objection with the idea. He demanded that they resolve the matter with little delay. Wheeler reminded them that Toral had earlier understood and agreed to this.

General Don Federigo Escario offered to go and bring Toral back to clear up any misunderstandings. The young, impetuous Miley stated that this issue could only be settled by them as they had originally agreed. The older Lawton interposed that it was not the American intention to humiliate the Spaniards but to get this distasteful matter over with as pleasant a solution as possible. Wheeler offered that as a courtesy, the Spaniards could store their arms in a Spanish arsenal until the American government replied. Escario appreciated their sentiments and asked to go bring back Toral. The Americans politely offered to accompany the Spanish commissioners to Toral under the excuse that they did not want to burden the general this late by making him return. Escario declined their offer and agreed to bring Toral back at 9:30.

General Toral arrived at 9:40 and objected strongly to the heading of the document, "Terms of the Military Convention for the Capitulation." He preferred "Preliminary Agreement for the Capitulation." He again reminded them that he was willing to surrender but needed the permission from Madrid first, and that response would take time. Miley was the first to speak up by stating that the Spanish attitude was not in accordance with the letter which Toral had sent to Shafter. Wheeler remarked that he had assumed that Toral had received full authority from his commanding general to negotiate. Toral stated that their position was clearly stated in the message Toral had sent to Shafter earlier that morning. Evidently someone had misinterpreted Toral that afternoon.

The Americans had come to respect Toral but feared that he might secretly be waiting for reinforcements. So they consulted with Mr. Robert Mason, the British Consulate, who acted as the interpreter for the Spanish commission. The Americans trusted him, and Mason told them that Toral was honest and sincere in his statements. The commissioners realized that they were merely finalizing a capitulation agreement while waiting for permission from Spain.

During the entire affair, Wheeler observed that Toral had a keen sense of pride and was very sensitive in his feelings. Wheeler suspected that while courteous, if anything during the negotiations encroached upon his honor, Toral would have broken off negotiations immediately. Wheeler also noticed that Toral seemed preoccupied with some other concern. Toral confided in Wheeler, "I would not desire to see my very worst enemy compelled to play the cards I have had to play during the last two weeks. All my generals have been killed or wounded, I have not a single colonel left and I am surrounded by a powerful army. My men counted 67 ships off the coast, all loaded with troops; and besides all this, I have secret troubles there," wearily pointing to the city, "of which I cannot speak."[11]

One of Toral's officers explained to Wheeler that even if Toral received the consent of his government to capitulate, he would still be held accountable for the surrender. He would probably face a court-martial in Madrid when he returned. Toral wished to remove anything from the surrender document that might reflect upon his courage, as it would most likely be used against him in court. By an interesting coincidence, the senior American general officer negotiating the terms of capitulation had himself served on the losing side during the Civil War. They agreed to change the wording.

Wheeler remarked that under the circumstances they should modify the document as the Spaniards requested so they could get them to sign it. He recommended that they review and modify each paragraph so that the Spanish commissioners would agree to sign. Two Cubans translated the draft document; then the Spanish commissioners discussed each point and recommended changes to some clauses. Toral from then on acted as the sole commissioner and made all the changes to the document personally.

Leonard Wilson observed when they reached the issue of disarmament, Toral appealed to Wheeler, not only because he was older and the senior American officer, but because Wheeler had a kind disposition and could sympathize with him in his present situation. Toral said that although his army was outmatched and outnumbered, it had not been conquered or vanquished. They still controlled their trenches and defended the city. If called upon by his country to resist attack, his army would. They were then negotiating an amicable arrangement that would prevent further bloodshed. No one more than Wheeler could identify with that. He and Lawton agreed to let the Spanish troops march under arms out of the city, then stack them somewhere.

Evidently not satisfied with the procedures, Miley recounted the last two days' meetings then summarized that upon their first meeting Toral requested that his army be allowed to march to Holguin. He then said that he would accept surrender if his army returned to Spain. Shafter had left the meeting the other day with the understanding that he had received the surrender of the Spanish Army of Santiago. Wheeler diplomatically concluded that there had evidently been a misunderstanding. Toral apologized for any misunderstanding but had only entered upon a preliminary agreement for capitulation while waiting for confirmation. Miley did not agree, but Toral added that the misunderstanding had arisen out of an imperfect translation of his statements. If his original letter to Shafter had been properly translated, then it would prove he was right. Miley consented that he was probably correct. They read through the articles one more time and agreed to change the phrase "pending arrangements for capitulation" to "pending the confirmation of this preliminary agreement."[12] They finished at half past midnight and agreed to meet at 9 the next morning.

The same officers met again the next day, July 15. Miley stated that Shafter agreed to allow the Spanish Army to march out of the city under arms and even offered to salute their colors. Shafter recommended a few word changes, which the Spaniards accepted with some modification. The one issue that Toral could not comply with was the removal of mines prior to authorization from Madrid. The Americans hoped to allow the Red Cross ship, *State of Texas*, to enter with humanitarian relief for the citizens of Santiago. Toral consented that they could discharge their relief at the mouth of the harbor so long as they agreed not to take any pictures of the harbor defenses. Lawton agreed but stated that they had all the pictures they wanted already. Toral also asked that the salute of the Spanish colors be added to the document. The draft was typed out in Spanish and English with a typewriter on a camp stool. By 3:30, the two documents were completed and signed. All during this negotiation process, Shafter was continually kept informed by field telephone. The anxiety of Shafter and Miles, who was aboard a ship waiting to sail to Puerto Rico, was intense. Miles's army was ready, but he did not want to sail to Puerto Rico until he knew his army was not needed.

On the 15th, the Rough Riders' usual meal of bacon, hardtack and coffee was supplemented with rice, condensed milk and sugar. The cooks even baked doughnuts. Roosevelt walked around and talked with his men. As they asked about their future, he mentioned that he thought that they would next deploy to Puerto Rico as there was a Spanish garrison there that had not been defeated. Nonetheless, the prospects of victory brought singing back to the camp at night.

On the morning of the 16th, Shafter received the long-anticipated letter from Toral announcing that the Spanish government had given Toral permission to surrender. Miley wrote, "Words cannot express the feeling of relief throughout the command that followed."[13] The commissioners met at 9:30 that morning to retype the final version of the document for signatures. Shafter and Toral met at 4 p.m. to sign the document. Over the next two hours they arranged the details of the surrender ceremony.

When the surrender was assured, the Spanish citizens that had evacuated the city before returned on the 16th. For two days a steady stream of wretched-looking refugees gained the sympathy of the Rough Riders. They asked for water and hardtack. They offered whatever jewelry they had just for a hardtack biscuit. Paul Hunter was offered $5 in Spanish gold for two hardtacks. He could not bear to take the money. Besides, the Americans were ordered not to talk to the Spaniards nor give them anything. He, like other troopers, ignored the order and gave away their rations. Some helped carry bundles and children the quarter-mile stretch through their lines. Ben Colbert, who sympathized with them, summarized, "I feel like the hardships that I have undergone have been amply rewarded."[14] Santiago had fallen into American hands.

He went on duty in the Cossack outpost that night from 8 p.m. until 12 a.m. With no threat of enemy attack, the duty was rather monotonous. Only the flutter of some night bird or squall of a cat broke the monotony. A dog wandered close to the trenches, but it ran away when it saw Ben.

Finally, on Sunday, July 17, Shafter and his staff and his generals with their staffs arrived at the agreed-upon field in front of Santiago at 9:30 under the escort of 100 cavalry. There they lined up according to rank from right to left across from Toral and his staff, escorted by 100 foot soldiers. Shafter rode up to Toral and presented him the saber and spurs of Spanish General Vara del Rey, who was killed at El Caney. The Spanish soldiers, along with Shafter and his escort, presented arms while they lowered the Spanish flag. General Garcia and his Cuban army did not receive an invitation to attend the surrender ceremony and felt insulted. The Spaniards then marched to the arsenal where they turned over their arms to Shafter's ordnance officer, Lieutenant Brooke. Afterwards, they would march to a camp on the San Juan Hills.

Shafter and Wheeler then led the procession of general officers, their staffs and their escort of cavalry and the Ninth Infantry in a column of twos into the city. Toral escorted Shafter to the Governor's Palace where civil officials of the province and the archbishop paid their respects to the American general. Toral then retired to his home. At 11 a.m., the Americans were invited to lunch.

The generals then marched out onto the plaza to an awaiting crowd of thousands of Cubans and Spanish. The Rough Riders, along with every other regiment, lined up at attention in front of their rifle pits at 11:45 in full view of Santiago.

The Ninth Infantry, which was designated to occupy the town, came to attention and presented arms in salute. As the cathedral clock opposite the plaza commenced striking the hour of noon, Captain William H. McKittrick, aide-de-camp to Shafter; Lieutenant Joseph Wheeler, Jr., aide-de-camp to his father; and Lieutenant Miley raised the American flag over the palace while the Sixth Cavalry band played "Hail Columbia." That flag had flown over Wheeler's headquarters. All the soldiers cheered in the trenches and congratulated each other. Capron's battery had the honor to fire the 21-gun salute. The Rough Riders swelled with a sense of pride that they had contributed to the raising of Old Glory over the Spanish city.

The U.S. Navy immediately set about clearing the mouth of the harbor of mines. By the 19th, they had cleared it of 18 mines. Some of the transports had entered the harbor on the 18th while the rest entered the 19th bearing provisions.

The regiment also held its raffle for Capron's horse, which must have raised a considerable amount in that D Troop's contribution added up to $35. This money was sent to his widow.

Soldiers in trenches cheering after hearing of the surrender (Library of Congress).

The folks back home shared in the experience of the war in a different way. Right after the announcement of the Battle of Santiago, they anxiously waited for the news of the fate of their loved ones. The Wetmores' fears were finally realized when they read his name on the list of wounded at the battle on July 1. Because of delays, they had no idea of the seriousness of his wound. One confused report even indicated that Holmes and Wetmore had both been killed. Like a good son, Starr had written home regularly up until he was wounded. Then the letters stopped after he was wounded, more likely from the lack of paper. His mother would later learn the truth about the wound, but without any details to his condition, she could only fear the worst. Was his condition critical? Would he lose a limb or die?

Even those who did not see their sons' names among seriously sick, wounded or dead still let their fears overcome them. They would not receive any mail from the front for two weeks. Hearing no news from their son, Paul Hunter's mother wrote Colonel Roosevelt with the fear of all the other mothers that her son's name had not appeared on the list because he was missing in action. She pleaded that an officer should relieve her anxious heart and send a list of those answering roll call to the governor so he could make it public. Evidently, Paul Hunter was one of those who did not think it important to write home after the battle. Roosevelt passed the letter on to Huston to answer, adding by the way the colonel's compliments on Hunter's performance.

Roy Cashion's parents accepted the news of their son's death as best they could. They had also received the letter from fellow Hennessian John Rhoades two weeks later. Then his father quickly wrote Captain Huston on July 18 asking for the details of his son's death. He complimented the company: "He spoke highly of you and all the boys in Troop D. I think your Regt. won lasting honors for bravery."[15] On the 6th of August, Huston received the letter and responded. These are the toughest letters that any officer has to write. The Cashions received the letter two weeks later and posted it in the paper. Huston had explained the details of Roy's death and added, "While I know his death is a great bereavement to you and nothing that anyone can say would lesson your anguish, yet I think you can always feel a just sense of pride in the way he died. No soldier in this army fell so far to the front and so near to the retiring foe…. It is useless to say that he was brave. He died as only a brave soldier can die, and in the noblest cause for which nations ever went to war. You have my deepest sympathy, but I am proud of his record and the manner of his death."[16]

The elder Al Norris received a stained, yellow package also mailed by Captain Huston. His first thought was that his son, Edward, had been killed and that it contained his personal effects. To his relief when he opened it, he found the souvenirs that Ed had sent back from Las Guasimas along with the money to buy the cattle.

The day after the surrender the Rough Riders and the rest of the cavalry division in Cuba were ordered to move their camp about five miles further back up the mountain to a shady area near a spring just west of El Caney. About half of Fifth Corps had come down with malaria and even a few cases of yellow fever, dysentery and typhoid fever. The real fear was an epidemic of yellow fever. At that time doctors believed that sanitation would prevent the spread of the disease. So based upon medical advice, Shafter had ordered the troops to relocate their camps.

The Rough Riders, whose brown cotton uniforms were reduced to almost rags, broke camp at 9 in the morning and marched during the hottest time of the day. Nearly half of the dismounted cavalrymen dropped out of the march from heat exhaustion or

Roosevelt and his Rough Riders on San Juan Hill (NARA).

bouts of sickness brought on by the exertion. Captain Llewellyn had recovered enough to join the march. He carried a pick and shovel for one soldier; then after reaching the camp, he went back with a mule to pick up another trooper who had fallen out. Even this limited physical exertion caused the captain to collapse and bring about the symptoms of malaria, which would usually last for about a week. Guy Endsley, of F Troop, died of fever that day. Fearing that Llewellyn would also die, Roosevelt sent him back to the United States.

A blockhouse topped the hill. The green grass, shaded by a scattering of mango trees and palms, made it an idyllic tropical scene. Once at the new location, the sick rested where they fell, and the rest did the best they could to erect dog tents for themselves and their bunkies. For those who had recovered from the effects of malaria, this work brought it back, and most were unable to walk the next day. Because of the shortage of wagons, the officers' tents would follow a few days later, so the officers had to sleep out in the rain.

A poor military diet combined with exposure to the heat and humidity continued to weaken men. Even the slightest exertion brought about sickness. They laid listlessly under their shelter halves. A few began to show signs of yellow fever, and the new camp near a stream did little to improve the situation. It caused them to vomit blood that resembled a black ink, so they referred to the disease as the "Black Vomit." The longer men waited the more fell victim to the disease. The fever and dysentery caused most to lose up to 30 pounds of weight. Roosevelt's orderly, Bardshar, lost 80 pounds. Not surprisingly, the robust Roosevelt was one of the few in his command not to get sick. However, he lost 20 pounds that he felt he did not need anyway.

Camp behind San Juan Hill after the surrender (Theodore Roosevelt Collection, Harvard University Library).

The military routine still had to continue. Even though sick himself, First Sergeant Palmer had to call muster roll every morning, and even though fewer and fewer reported, he still had to assign out work details. One hundred fifteen men out of 340 Rough Riders were on sick report on the 19th. F Troop only had 38 men stand for roll call that day. Even those who could stand were weak. They would complain, as was every soldier's right, but they did their duties. Rich man, poor man, they were all equal in the eyes of the army and a good first sergeant. At the end of the day, he lined the men up for a retreat ceremony.

To break up the monotony and lift the spirits of his men, Roosevelt allowed a few to go to Santiago for supplies each day. They could purchase necessities such as tobacco, which brought the inflationary prices back down. Most, however, were incapable of making the long walk. There was not much of interest to see except the central plaza, Governor's Palace or Café Venus.

The day after the surrender, Rynning had ridden to the Café Venus with a group of officers. The café did not have anything to eat, so the Rough Riders rode around town scrounging up enough bacon and eggs to make a worthwhile meal. They returned to the café and asked the staff to cook the meal for them. While the American officers had their fill, two Spanish officers walked in and sat down to a skimpy meal of a small piece of fish. The Rough Riders invited them over. The two officers, one with his arm in a sling, slid their table over adjacent to the Americans. It turned out to be none other than General Linares and another officer named Pando. Most of the Rough Rider officers from the Southwest spoke some form of border Spanish, but Captain Luna spoke it fluently. Linares spoke English fairly well but with an accent.

"What are the Rof Riders?" he asked. "In Madrid they tol' us you were all convicts and that you showed no quarter in battle. That is why we fought so hard. We feared to surrender." The Rough Riders broke out in laughter joined by the two Spaniards. Wine helped these former adversaries warm up to each other. Finally, Linares rose to his feet and proposed a toast: "I meet you combate. I meet you socially. I prefer socially." That called for more rounds of wine, and they gained even greater respect for each other as warriors and gentlemen.[17]

Most of the Spanish officers remained in their quarters in Santiago, while their men waited in camps outside the city. As described in the encounter by Rynning, the relations between the former adversaries were very cordial. They showed respect for each other as noble soldiers. After several years of fighting against Cuban guerrillas who used hit-and-run tactics, the Spaniards welcomed the chance to fight in a civilized fashion. Pedro Lopez de Castillo, a Spanish soldier, wrote a tribute to the American army:

> You have complied exactly with all the laws and usages of war as recognized by armies of the most civilized nations of the world; have given honorable burial to the dead of the van-quished; have cured their wounded with great humanity; have respected and cared for your prisoners and their comfort; and lastly, to us, whose condition was terrible, you have given freely of food and of your stock of medicines, and have honored us with distinction and cour-tesy, for after the fighting the two armies mingled with the utmost harmony.[18]

By the 21st, Paul Hunter finally wrote home to the *Daily Leader*. He claimed that they did not know whether they would pack their tents and ship out for Puerto Rico or America. Miles sailed that day with his corps to Puerto Rico. Roosevelt hoped to see more action, but his men had had enough of war. Besides, the heat and disease had taken its effect on the ranks. David Goodrich finally came down with malaria about the time that Huston had recovered. Huston had a new shelter that could keep him dry. The fever had rendered him ineffective as a squadron commander. First Sergeant Palmer also came down with malaria. He wrote that the men did not have enough ambition to even charge an anthill.

The supply situation had improved with Santiago Harbor as its new base, although it still took a team of six mules to pull a 1,500-pound wagon load across the muddy roads. The weight pack mules could carry had been reduced from 200 to just 50 pounds. Nonetheless, the division commissary became well stocked with canned fruit and the most craved of all supplies—tobacco. Each man received a ration of two slices of bacon, two spoonfuls of roasted coffee and one and a half spoonfuls of sugar per day. Mail began arriving daily, but the shortage of paper still made it difficult for Rough Riders to write back. News from home was an important morale factor as it was their only contact with the world they left behind.

The Rough Riders also received an issue of blue flannel shirts and their new cotton khaki uniforms. They were happy to receive the first change of clothes since arriving in Cuba a month ago. They would receive a new issue of shoes and socks on the 29th. Meanwhile, the Regulars had received their conical Sibley squad tents. Roosevelt set out to acquire some for his men. Hunter felt confident that Roosevelt would succeed since he had never failed hem yet.

Roosevelt assumed command of the Second Brigade that day, after Brigadier General Wood was appointed the military governor of Cuba. Wood had picked Luna and a few other Spanish-speaking officers from his old regiment to serve on his staff. Wood likewise relocated his staff to the palace in Santiago and issued instructions for the citizens and soldiers to clean up the city in an effort to eliminate disease.

On the 22nd, Roosevelt sent Rynning into Santiago with a message, but, while there, he rode a couple of miles toward Morro Castle. He happened to look down and saw a Norwegian transport loaded with cattle from South America. Rynning reported this back to Roosevelt, who asked, "Do you think they would sell them?" The lieutenant said, "*Quien savvy* [who knows], but I'll find out." With that Roosevelt wrote out a personal check for several thousand dollars, and Rynning rounded up some old Tonto cowboys from his outfit to herd the cattle back. When they returned, Roosevelt issued the cattle out to the cavalry.[19]

Ben Colbert was assigned as the regimental butcher. From then on, he would cut up one beef a day. That was the only fresh meat they had eaten since June 6. The Rough Riders ate so much that many could not even rise to walk to their tents. They would just sit for about 20 minutes, letting the food digest.

Soldiers of a free and democratic society choose to serve of their own free will. For those democratic values they cherish, they willingly risk life and limb in their defense. From the Spanish–American War forward, all American wars would be fought overseas for the rights of others. In a democratic army, soldiers expect their officers to motivate and inspire, not lead through fear and coercion. This is done in tyrannical societies. They expect their leaders to show courage in battle and look out for their needs and concerns in between. Those leaders who embody this can expect great feats from their men. Since Washington at Valley Forge, there was probably no greater example of this than the relationship between Roosevelt and his regiment.

The Rough Riders loved their commander. They had followed him up Kettle Hill and on to the next. They had performed for him, and he felt an incredible obligation to them. If it was within his means to secure for them what they deserved, he did. No regiment could ask more from a commander. David Hughes later wrote of that incident, "That was the kind of colonel Roosevelt was! That was the kind of a colonel we had! Other regiments did not fare so well."[20] That kind of effort could only come from genuine love for his men.

That day another Rough Rider, James B. Sinnett, arrived, having escaped from Tampa. Charles C. Bull, a Harvard man from A Troop, had been wounded after Las Guasimas but found his way back to his troop. Quite a few eager, young college men arrived at Tampa in June to enlist, but some were not content to wait out the war. As many as nine Harvard, Yale and Princeton men made their way to Cuba to enlist in the Rough Riders. Having a number of vacancies opened by casualties, Roosevelt rewarded them for their determination with enlistment on July 27.

At 7 a.m. on Sunday, the 24th, Chaplain Brown held his first religious services since landing in Cuba, under a tree just outside Roosevelt's tent. Only about 40 men attended. Colbert was one of them. Afterwards, Ben went off to gather mangos and bamboo for him and his bunkie, Edgar S. Adams. The news quickly spread that General Wheeler's daughter, Anna, was riding through camp. Ben and the other men rushed to catch a glimpse of the first American lady they had seen in some time. Under a straw hat, she wore a shirt that buttoned up to her neck and modestly covered her wrists. It tucked in at her trim waist. Her long skirt reached down to cover the ankles of her laced boots. Her lovely image brought back memories of the girls back home. An armed mounted escort of two Regular cavalry men followed behind.

Raised in the refinement of a Southern aristocratic home, Annie shared a sense of devotion to the soldiers who bore the burden of war. Not only did her father serve in the current conflict, but so did her brother. She had applied to work as a nurse for the Red Cross, but they rejected her for her lack of experience. She decided to just show up and help out as best as she could, especially since her father was also sick. The soft voice or caress of a woman to a sick or wounded soldier could lift the spirits better than any medicine that the surgeons could apply. She reminded the soldiers of finer things of home and gave them hope. This angel of mercy did not flinch from any of the hardships or horrors she saw. The surgeons assigned her in charge of the nursing at the Santiago Yacht Club after the First Division Hospital moved into the town. The soldiers dubbed it "Miss Wheeler's Hospital."

That day Roosevelt instructed his men to cut bamboo poles and build floors to raise their beds off the muddy ground. When details searched through the nearby woods for bamboo, they stumbled onto a small clearing covered with corn, lima beans and cucumbers. They picked enough corn and lima beans to supplement their meals. They had not received any vegetables since before the last battle. The steady ration of bacon and hardtack had become pretty monotonous. Lieutenant Woodbury Kane also received a large box of tobacco and several cases of canned peaches from his sister, which he issued out on Sunday. He became immensely popular.

Mail also arrived that day, and nearly everyone received a letter or newspaper from home. That and a good dinner of fresh beef, vegetables and canned peaches for dessert made it what Ben referred to as "a red feather day."[21]

By the 28th, the rumor circulated that Fifth Corps would return to America in ten days to two weeks. The Rough Riders ate a meal of light bread and Porterhouse steaks, thanks to Roosevelt. No one had yet been promoted to replace Lieutenant Carr. So Goodrich still commanded D Troop while Huston remained commander of the squadron.

Over the next couple of weeks after the surrender, Roosevelt sorted out who would fill which vacancies left by casualties and a chain reaction of openings caused by Wood's promotion. Brodie advanced to Roosevelt's position of lieutenant colonel of the regiment, and Jenkins beat out Huston for Brodie's major's vacancy on August 11. Huston's illness during the last battle had cheated him of his anticipated promotion. Major Hersey and his orderly would receive permission to come to Cuba and arrive on the 2nd of August. Huston then returned to command his troop.

Roosevelt recommended Woodbury Kane for promotion to fill Jenkins's captain vacancy in K Troop. Carr would transfer to Kane's place as the first lieutenant, and Willie Tiffany, who had impressed Roosevelt immensely, was recommended for promotion to second lieutenant. Goodrich was promoted to fill Carr's vacancy as first lieutenant. Sergeant Robert H. Ferguson, of New York City, who had shown gallantry in action at San Juan, would be promoted to second lieutenant from the "Knickerbocker Club" and to command Luna's F Troop until he returned. He would then fill Goodrich's second lieutenant vacancy in D Troop when he filled Carr's vacancy. Sergeant William E. Dame, of Santa Fe, would replace Cadet Haskell as the second lieutenant of F Troop.

Since Richard Day had commanded Capron's troop during the charge up San Juan Hill and during the following siege, Roosevelt promoted him to the captaincy while the hospitalized Rob Thomas remained as the first lieutenant. Thomas, although gallantly, only commanded his troop in battle for an hour. Sergeant Frank Hayes was promoted to the second lieutenant vacancy left by Day for his gallantry at San Juan Hill. Frank Frantz assumed command as captain of Buckey O'Neill's A Troop.

After the war, Roosevelt would write Sir George Otto Trevelyan, on January 1, 1908, "Mine was a volunteer regiment; at least half of the officers at the outset were very bad, so that I should have had to make a complete change among them—a change that was already well begun when the regiment was disbanded."[22]

Hall had anticipated the promotions even before the surrender on the 17th. Surprisingly, he had the audacity to approach Roosevelt and ask if he would receive one. There is little doubt about what went through Roosevelt's mind, but he instead thanked Hall for coming to talk with him. The colonel looked furiously at Hall. "I'm glad you have brought the subject up. That makes it easier. After showing the yellow streak in action you have the effrontery to ask for promotion? No, you'll not be promoted—but I'll accept your resignation!"[23]

Hall was shocked with disbelief. He hung his head and said that he did not have enough money to go home. Roosevelt said, "Don't let that bother you. I'll let you have what you need." He reached into his pocket and pulled out a roll of dollar bills. Without counting it, he handed it to Hall and told him to take what he needed and leave. Hall boarded the *Senaca* on July 10 and returned to the United States on July 30. He tendered his resignation on July 29, which was accepted on August 1.[24] While Hall neared the United States, more pressing matters faced the whole Fifth Corps.

The constant rains made the new camp a mess. The tents and all the blankets were damp and moldy. It was hard for the men to stay dry. Dropped food had attracted flies, and maggots covered the ground, making the wet, matted grass all the more slippery. The medical authorities recommended that the regiments relocate their camps every two or three days without understanding the implications of the moves. As he had witnessed with the last move, Shafter knew that each move weakened his men more. There were not enough wagons to move camp equipment, and the men would have to sleep out on the ground until it arrived. The physical exertion of another move would only bring about recurrences of the malaria symptoms.

Finally, the War Department directed that Shafter move the command to a higher elevation, above what Surgeon General George M. Sternberg thought was the yellow fever line. They had even identified the site of the new camp up in the mountains near the end of the San Luis railroad. The health of the soldiers in Cuba was not the real concern of the War Department. There was an incorrect fear in Washington that if the Fifth Corps returned to the United States, they might start an outbreak of yellow fever.

Shafter had urged Secretary Alger time and again to quickly transport the Spanish prisoners home so that they could expedite the shipment of American troops back to a healthier climate. With the telegraph instructing him to move his command, Shafter called for a council of war at the Governor's Palace with his division and brigade commanders and medical officers on the morning of the last day of July. They reviewed the facts. Over half his command was down with some form of sickness, and the situation was only getting worse. The bridges and railroads had not been repaired, and the commanders did not feel that their men had the strength to make the march. Unanimously, they agreed that the move further inland would jeopardize the health of their commands. All feared that a real epidemic of yellow fever would eventually break out in August, killing a significant number of their soldiers. Officers duty bound to follow orders faced a serious dilemma. They had to choose between obeying an order from

Washington or taking care of their men. Unlike the career officers, Roosevelt had nothing to lose by protesting. He quickly penned a letter to Shafter.

Major General Shafter;

Sir—In a meeting of the general and medical officers, called by you at the palace this morning, we were all as you know, unanimous in view of what should be done with the army. To keep us here, in the opinion of every officer commanding a division or a brigade will simply involve the destruction of thousands. There is no possible reason for not shipping practically the entire command north at once. Yellow fever cases are very few in the cavalry division, where I command one of the two brigades and not one true case of yellow fever has occurred in this division, except among the men sent to the hospital at Siboney, where they have, I believe, contracted it, but in this division there have been 1,500 cases of malaria fever. Not a man has died from it, but the whole command is so weakened and shattered as to be ripe for dying like rotten sheep when a real yellow fever epidemic instead of a fake epidemic like the present strikes us, it is bound to if we stay here at the height of the sickness season, August and the beginning of September. Quarantine against malarial fever is much like quinine against the tooth-ache. All of us are certain, as soon as the authorities at Washington fully appreciate the condition of the army, to be sent home. If we are kept here it will, in all human possibility, mean an appalling disaster, for the surgeons here now estimate that half of the cavalry, if kept here during the sick season, will die. This is not only terrible from the standpoint of the individual lives lost, but it means ruin from the standpoint of the military efficiency of the flower of the American army, for the great bulk of the regulars is here with you. The sick list, large though it is, exceeding 4,000 affords but a faint index of the debilitation of the army. Not ten per cent are fit for active work. Six weeks on the north Maine coast, for instance, or elsewhere the yellow fever germ can not possibly propagate, would make us all as fit as fighting cocks, able as we are eager, to take a leading part in the great campaign against Havana in the fall, even if we are not allowed to try Puerto Rico.

We can be moved north, if moved at once, with absolute safety to the country, although, of course, it would have been infinitely better if we had been moved north or to Puerto Rico two weeks ago. If there were any object in keeping us here, we would face yellow fever with as much indifference as we faced bullets, but there is no object in it. The four immune regiments ordered here are sufficient to garrison the city surrendered. It is impossible to move into the interior. Every shifting of camp doubles the sick rate in our present weakened condition, and anyhow, the interior is rather worse than the coast, as I have found by actual reconnaissance. Our present camps are as healthy as any camps at this end of the island can be.

I write only because I cannot see our men who have fought so bravely and who have endured extreme hardships and danger so uncomplainingly, go to destruction without striving so far as lies unnecessary and undeserved.

> Yours respectfully,
> Theodore Roosevelt
> Colonel Commanding First Brigade.[25]

After Roosevelt had taken the initiative, the other general officers similarly united to write a letter of their concerns to General Shafter. They echoed the same sentiments and logic of Roosevelt's letter. To his credit, Shafter telegraphed Roosevelt's letter and a letter of his own accompanied by the written opinions of his general officers and medical officers to Washington on August 3. In addition, Shafter handed a copy of Roosevelt's letter to the correspondent of the Associated Press for publication. It appeared in the newspapers two days later. This press leak would spark the downfall of Alger, which would sour his feelings toward Roosevelt.

Roosevelt was not alone in exerting political influence. General Adelbert Ames sent a telegram to Honorable Charles H. Allen, Assistant Secretary of the Navy: "This army is incapable, because of sickness, from marching anywhere except to the transports. If it is even to return to the United States it must do so at once."[26]

He then turned to a correspondent of the Associated Press and said, "If I had the power, I would put the men on the transports at once and ship them north without further orders. I am further confident such action would ultimately be approved. A full list of the sick would mean a copy of the roster of every company here."[27]

President McKinley held a conference with Secretary of War Russell Alger; Secretary of State William R. Day; Secretary of Navy John D. Long; and Assistant Secretary of the Navy Charles H. Allen at the White House to discuss Shafter's response. The conference occupied a couple of hours, where they presented the needs for prompt action and what means were at hand to move the troops. After a few hours, they finally agreed that there were sufficient vessels off the coast of Cuba for the removal of the Spanish prisoners and American army. They agreed to transport General Shafter's Corps immediately from Cuba to Montauk Point, Long Island, and sent a telegraph with this conclusion on August 4. The news was well received.

Regiments of immunes were on their way to take over the occupation. These regiments had been recruited from the tropical states in the Southeastern United States for service in the tropic islands with the idea that they would be immune to the diseases that plagued the others. Shafter's Fifth Corps was made up primarily of Regular Army regiments, which would have to provide the main fighting force for subsequent actions. It was imperative that they return and regain their strength. So far, only the Spanish garrison of Santiago and Manila had surrendered. There were still Spanish garrisons in Havana and Puerto Rico.

The Rough Riders heard the news and believed that they would go back long enough to recuperate then come back and fight the Spaniards in Havana. All the while, Roosevelt and his officers scrutinized the Spanish cavalry to measure what they were up against. The runty Spanish horses resembled cow ponies. The Rough Riders believed they would eventually be employed as shock cavalry as originally planned. However, the rumors of Spain suing for peace were favorably anticipated by the enlisted men.

Finally on the afternoon of August 6, the Rough Riders heard the news that they had been waiting for. They would move to Santiago at noon the next day and load transports bound for home. The cavalry division would be the first to depart. The order also stated that they would have to put on their new uniforms and leave all their old brown fatigues and tents behind. They could take nothing but blankets and mess outfits. The men then began to silently collect their souvenirs. Ben Colbert wrote, "I hope the retreat of this evening will be the last one in Cuba. I would like to bid farewell to Santiago forever."[28]

They rose early the next day to clean their gear. Most burned their old uniforms as instructed. At 11:30, they received orders to break camp but leave the tents standing. After dinner the Rough Riders boxed up and packed their equipment on the mules. They loaded their blankets and poncho rolls on wagons. Tom Horn supervised the packing. Between 12:30 and 1 p.m., assembly call brought the Rough Riders into formation, standing at attention. What few of them were left stood in two rows. Some stood in blue flannel shirts and others in their new khaki uniforms with carbines and their old blue cartridge belts and khaki canteens. The brims of their campaign hats had lost their shape due to soaking by the constant rains. These were not the same healthy men who had stepped off of the *Yucatan* a little over a month prior. They were emaciated, their health broken down by heat and fever. But now they were going home.

The order was given, and D Troop turned to the right and marched westward toward Santiago, leading the rest of the regiment. Although the rail line was only a couple of miles away, many struggled to walk even that far. Some still suffered bouts of fever. Unable to continue, the extremely sick collapsed alongside the road. Ambulances followed behind to pick up those too sick to finish. Very few of the Cavalry actually came down with yellow fever. Hughes was one though. The black vomit brought him to his knees. His bunkie waited patiently beside him until Hersey came up and offered Hughes his horse. The regiment reached the railroad at 2 p.m. and loaded onto the awaiting rail-cars, then rolled into the station at Santiago. They again fell into line and marched down to the dock. Roosevelt rode at the head of the column.

At 5 p.m., they boarded the transport *Miami* with Major General Wheeler, his daughter and a squadron of the Third Cavalry under Major Henry Jackson. The rest of the cavalry division boarded the *Gate City* and *Matteawan*. The Rough Riders settled in with their meager possessions as the sun sank over the hills. The pay master happened to be waiting for them, and he quickly paid the Rough Riders what the government owed them. As soon as their gear was stowed aboard, the men were permitted to walk about the city. Those who wanted to could buy groceries for the trip and last-minute souvenirs.

Miami leaving Santiago Harbor (Theodore Roosevelt Collection, Harvard University Library).

The healthier ones walked about the narrow, dirty streets bordered by stucco houses looking for a good meal or souvenirs. The windows had iron bars on them with oak shutters. Paul Hunter walked into Café Venus to eat supper. The meal as usual consisted of eggs, after a ten-minute recess a small loaf of bread, followed by a small piece of fish. The waiter then delivered a small cup of black coffee and a small piece of rubber-like jelly for dessert. Upon completion of that, the waiter pulled out the bill from his apron and handed it to the sergeant. While Hunter could not read Spanish, he could read the numbers. The bill to his shock was $1.90, well over three days' wages for a soldier. A sergeant only made $17 a month. The siege had driven up the price of food, and he paid the price. He then adjourned to the wine room where he paid another 75 cents for a bottle of beer and a sandwich.[29]

At 6:30 the morning of August 8, Rough Riders bid Cuba farewell from the deck of the *Miami* while the Third Cavalry band played "Red, White and Blue" followed by "Old Folks at Home," "Dixie" and "Home Sweet Home." Every boat they passed cheered them. It was a beautiful sunny morning that reflected the sentiments of the Rough Riders. Hunter wrote, "The sick smiled, and the well danced and sang, and congratulated each other on their escape from the island, mud, fever and war."[30]

The *Miami* passed the remains of the *Merrimac* protruding from the water. Hobson and his crew had sunk it in a failed effort to block the harbor. The band then played "Yankee Doodle." As the *Miami* slipped out of the bay, the hills rose up like pillars to bid her farewell. The battle-damaged Morro Castle, which had guarded the entrance to the bay, towered on the hill to her left with shore batteries on both sides of the inlet. Blue-clad soldiers cheered and waved from atop the castle as their comrades sailed for home.

At 7:30, the *Miami* cleared the bay and passed into open sea. They left behind several sick comrades suspected of having yellow fever: Lieutenant Willie Tiffany of K Troop, Corporal Edgar A. Schwartz of G Troop, Privates William Hoyle of E Troop, E.F. Whalen of A Troop, Eugene Lutz of G Troop and T.D. Stedman of D Troop. It turned out that they only had malaria. Wheeler assigned Roosevelt the responsibility for the policing and management of the ship. He did the best he could with overcrowding, poor food and water to contain further outbreaks of illness.[31]

Once on board, both the ship's crew and soldiers became intoxicated. Rum had evidently become a favorite souvenir brought from shore. After a complaint from the ship's captain, Roosevelt told his men to turn over their alcohol voluntarily, or he would throw any he found overboard. The men turned over about 70 flasks and Roosevelt found and threw overboard about 20 more as he had promised. Roosevelt wrote that he would give any man a drink who was ill, but for that matter nearly everyone was sick. McGinty wrote that Roosevelt said that he would tend bar during the voyage, and if anyone needed a drink, to see him. He was true to his word. The men had all they wanted to drink, yet no more incidents of drunkenness occurred aboard ship. Who had the nerve to get drunk in front of his beloved commander?[32]

On August 11, Sergeant George Walsh, of A Troop, died of chronic dysentery. He had acquired some rum from the Cubans the first night ashore in Daiquiri and had become intoxicated. Not fully sober, the intoxication had dehydrated him for the long march in the hot sun. He picked up dysentery and never recovered during his stay on the island. At 8:30 the morning of the 12th, he was wrapped with a hammock as his shroud. His comrades placed the American flag over him and readied the port side. The ship's engines were stilled as Chaplain Brown read the funeral service while Walsh's comrades stood nearby with heads bare. The band then played a funeral dirge. The flag was withdrawn and his body given to the sea. The death, although nothing new to the Rough Riders, brought about a somber mood that day.

One day on the open sea was the same as the next. The men gambled with what little money they had and reminisced about adventures long ago and more recent. On the morning of the 14th, they finally sighted land. At 7 that evening, a gunboat pulled up alongside to relay the news of the victory in the Philippines and that Spain had declared a peace. Filled with excitement, the Rough Riders shouted with joy. They had won the war.

Never an idle man, Roosevelt spent the voyage writing the history of his unit. Although he had most of his men around him to provide input, he still made mistakes. Roosevelt was not one to write anything bad about anyone, so he just did not mention Hall. He was drawn to those charismatic personalities like himself.

CHAPTER 9

Following the Drum

After the surrender, nearly everyone's concern shifted to returning home. The first Rough Riders to return from Cuba were the sick and wounded on hospital ships. Hospital ships were merely troop ships improved for comfort and cleanliness to hold the sick and wounded. The army only converted a few such vessels. Since its refitting, the *Relief* was supposed to serve as the hospital ship but was not finished in time for the invasion. The fleet's water carrier, *Olivette,* was hastily outfitted instead as the hospital ship for Cuba. Initially the *Olivette* took on the sick from the other transports after the voyage but later transferred its convalescents to the transport *Iroquois* as the wounded from the Battle of Las Guasimas began to pour in. Major Aaron H. Appel, surgeon of the Second Division, and his assistants, Lieutenants B.C. Howard, L.P. Smith, G.L. Bird and D. Latori, operated on the wounded aboard the *Olivette*. Once the wounded from the Battles of San Juan and El Caney began to crowd the bed capacity, Shafter asked the navy for the help of their hospital ship, *Solace*. The hospital ships were used for the more seriously ill and wounded.

Shafter also sent the milder cases on transports *Iroquois* and *Cherokee* back to Key West on July 3 and 5. On July 8, the *Relief* finally arrived, and the next day the *Olivette* left for New York. Others followed, then returned for more. Since no one army hospital could handle all the wounded returning from the war, the wounded were distributed to different hospitals along the east coast. The individual accounts of the journey revealed more details.

D Troop's Alexander Denham was shot through both hips at Las Guasimas. He waited at Siboney for the next hospital ship. Fellow soldiers took him and another litter patient from the First Cavalry on a rowboat to the hospital ship *Iroquois*. To get them aboard the vessel, the crew hoisted the boat up, but three feet out of the water, one of the lines came loose, and the end of the little boat spilled back into the rough sea. The waves pounded the inclined boat against the hull of the ship until the crew secured the lines. It was a harrowing experience for the two helplessly wounded soldiers. The *Iroquois* set sail on the night of July 3. The two troopers lay on the deck until the *Iroquois* deposited them at the hospital at Key West, Florida, on July 5. That day Adjutant General Henry C. Corbin ordered that the sick and wounded should not be sent to Key West or Tampa but to Fort Monroe, Virginia. Eighty-two of the wounded were then transported by train to a hospital in Cincinnati, Ohio, on July 17, and among them were three Rough Riders. The *Cherokee* continued for Tampa.

The second day of the truce, Frank Knox found a Spanish officer's horse and reported to Roosevelt. Knox wanted to mail a letter to his mother to let her know he had made it through safely. Roosevelt wrote an order for the postmaster to give Knox the regimental mail. Along the way to Siboney, Knox came along a soldier shading his bandaged head with a branch as he walked. "What's the matter, Jack?" He told Knox that he was walking to the hospital. Knox loaned the wounded soldier his hat and told him, "Get on behind here and I'll take you."[1]

Along the way, a sharpshooter fired at them. Knox instinctively swung his leg back to dismount the horse, knocking his passenger to the ground. Their horse fled, and they hid in the brush until the sharpshooter quit firing. He had fired a few more rounds but failed to hit either man nor beast. After waiting a while, Knox raised his hat on a stick to see if the sharpshooter had not completely given up. The sound of the rifle confirmed their suspicions; he was just a bad shot, so the two wormed their way through the brush to safety and caught up with the horse.

Upon arriving at Siboney, Knox learned from Major Brodie, who was in the hospital, that the mail was at Daiquiri. Brodie warned Knox to leave his carbine, as he would not have time to return fire against a sharpshooter, but to keep his revolver instead. Knox reached Daiquiri and found the post office around 4 p.m. The postal clerk warned Knox, "Why, I wouldn't go down to the postal shed for a million dollars. That fellow who came down with yellow fever the other day was working over that mail. The shed is locked. I won't go there, not me!" At that time, the medical authorities still did not know that a particular species of mosquito was the carrier of yellow fever. Knox responded, "Well, I can't go back without the mail and tell my colonel I was afraid and that you were, too."[2]

The clerk answered, "You can tell your colonel anything you please, but I'm not going into that mail shed, and I won't open it for any fool who wants to go in." Knox drew his six-shooter as a mild warning to the clerk that he meant business. The clerk took the hint and opened the shed. At that Knox said, "You're in here now. Why don't you be a good fellow and help me find the mail for my regiment." The clerk did and had a complete change of heart. To prove that he had no hard feelings, he insisted that Knox have dinner with him and remain there overnight. Riding in the hot sun without his hat had weakened Knox, so he consented. His host could not do enough for him. He ate a meal of fried bananas, rice, yams and greasy pork. Early the next morning, Knox rode off, but by the time he reached Siboney, he was too weak to ride further. He rested until the cool of the evening. He was so sick that he had difficulty sitting up in the saddle. His meal had also given him dysentery, and the heat added to his fever.[3]

Upon Knox's return, he reported to Roosevelt's tent, then collapsed from heat exhaustion outside. The colonel came out and found him collapsed flat on his face. The next morning, Knox could not eat anything. Captain Huston sent him back to the Second Division Hospital at Siboney. For a while his condition grew worse, but receiving better treatment from the Red Cross Hospital his condition improved. While still weak and lying in the hospital, he was taken aboard the hospital ship *Breakwater* since the doctors were evacuating the field hospital. The doctor assured Knox that he could spend the night aboard the ship then return to his regiment the next day. That was Knox's first night in Cuba where he slept under clean sheets. That night the sound of the anchor chains being pulled in woke Frank up. The ship was getting ready to sail. Frank pulled off his nightshirt and tied his stable uniform, stiff from dried sweat, around his neck and was about to dive in the harbor when the same doctor stopped him. The doctor said Frank was too sick to be of any use to his regiment. "You've been sick, are still sick, and the fighting is over. You stay on this ship, and if you improve and want some service I'll make you a hospital attendant."[4] The vessel put ashore at Fort Monroe on July 14. There the vessel dropped off her sick and wounded with orders to return to Cuba.

Knox wanted to rejoin his regiment and coaxed Captain Edward L. Munson, the surgeon in charge, to let him remain aboard and sail back to Cuba with the vessel. Munson, at the urging of Knox, wrote a statement verifying that Frank was taken aboard a hospital ship against his will. However, the next day, the ship's orders were changed, and it was put in quarantine at nearby Hampton Roads. While waiting aboard, Frank contracted malaria. The ship then sailed for Governor's Island, New York, where he remained hospitalized for two or three weeks. On August 5, he received a 30-day medical furlough to his home in Grand Rapids, Michigan, with orders to report to Fort Wayne, near Detroit, Michigan, on the 6th of September. From there the government would transport him to his regiment. After Frank read in the paper that his regiment had finally landed in New York, he wrote Captain Huston an explanation of his journey. The War Department directed that the next hospital ships sail directly to New York.

The *Olivette* dropped anchor at the quarantine station with 279 sick and wounded at Staten Island Landing at New York; also at 8 in the evening on the 16th of July Doctor Alvah H. Doty, the health inspector for the Port of New York, boarded a tender, *Charles F. Allen*, to go out and inspect the veterans for contagious diseases. With his usual courtesy, he permitted Governor Roswell P. Flower, newspaper men and a few relatives to join him. Judge John Thomas, from the Indian Territory, numbered among the relatives. Tooting tugs and launches accompanied them at dusk.[5]

If Doctor Doty found any contagious diseases, he would remove the men to quarantine on Swinburne Island. He asked the dreaded question, "Fever on aboard?" "All well," laughed Major Appel, "or rather, there's no illness—only men." After five minutes of inspection, he found none.

With his permission, the awaiting passengers on the tender climbed aboard the *Olivette*. They encountered bandaged soldiers in various stages of dress. Some had no hats, coats or shoes. Some, like Tom Isbell, wore only their cotton long underwear and covered themselves in blankets. He had recovered quickly from his seven wounds. Most had not shaved since going into battle when they had abandoned their haversacks. One-third had wounds to their arms. Some with leg or foot wounds hobbled around with the help of sticks or poles. Those unable to stand lay on mattresses on the deck. A few worse cases, like journalist Edward Marshall, of the *New York Journal*, were berthed in staterooms. His brother, I.D. Marshall, had come to welcome him and take him home that very day.

As the launch pulled up alongside the *Olivette*, a pretty girl sang out, "Three cheers for our brave soldier boys!" The small group on the tender let out an enthusiastic cheer. The soldiers, crowded on the side of the deck facing them, answered with their own cheer.[6]

Of the veterans of Cuba, there were 24 wounded and two sick Rough Riders on board to include Major Brodie, Captain McClintock, Lieutenant Rob Thomas and Lieutenant Horace Devereaux. The wounded from Oklahoma included Fred Beal, Edward Culver, Shelby Ishler, Tom Holmes, Lee McMillan, and Sel Newcomb. Tom Isbell, Joe Kline and George Seaver were the only wounded from the Indian Territory on board.

Judge Thomas recognized his son, Rob, standing next to Major Brodie near the pilot house. He embraced his son and said, "My lad, you were reported killed, but thank God you were not. Tonight I am the happiest old man in America."[7] For those families with a martial tradition there is no greater joy and relief than to know that one's son has served his country and returned alive and in one piece. Meanwhile, the journalist pumped the wounded veterans for their personal accounts of the war. Thomas became something of an instant celebrity in recounting the opening fight at Las Guasimas. They were particularly interested in the truth of the accusation of cowardice of their own Seventy-First New York. The wounded Regulars were smart enough to speak highly of the Volunteers in their own state.

Doty turned the boat and its passengers over to Surgeon General Sternberg. He and Majors Bushnell and Hall spent some time identifying 108 of the walking wounded which would go to the Marine Hospital in Stapleton. Those chosen were lowered onto the Staten Island ferryboat *Westfield*. The wounded had to cross from the deck of the transport over a gangplank to the roof of the cabin of the ferry. Ambulances and a cheering crowd of over a thousand citizens awaited them at Stanton Landing. The police had to push back the crowd as the wounded stepped onto the wharf.

Judge Thomas had received special permission from Secretary of War Alger to take his son ashore immediately. He brought his son up to the battery in a tug. Once ashore, Rob's sister smothered him in kisses while her proud father yelled, "Hurrah! Hurrah!" They then proceeded to the Astor House as Lieutenant Thomas was immediately granted a 60-day medical furlough to go home.

The next morning at 7, the *Olivette* arrived at Dow's stores in Brooklyn where she would transfer the rest of her passengers to the Long Island College Hospital, St. Peter's Hospital or home. The wounded officers would go to Fort Wadsworth on Staten Island. Over 2,000 citizens waited on shore to see the returning heroes. As each wounded soldier in ragged array walked off of the transport, the crowd cheered and men threw their hats in the air. They ran up to the passing ambulances, trying to shake hands with the veterans. One old man whose jacket was adorned with American flags and buttons walked up to grasp the wounded soldier's hand in each passing ambulance and say, "God bless you, my boy!" The first wounded soldiers of this popular little war had received their hero's welcome.

The navy's hospital ship, the *Solace*, arrived in Chesapeake Bay on the 16th of July carrying 44 wounded Americans and 49 wounded Spaniards. They were put in the hospital at Fort Monroe. Among the sick and wounded were Captain A.L. Mills, William M. Greenwood of A Troop, Sergeant Jerry Lee of B Troop, Sergeant William Simms of L Troop, and Lieutenant Tom Hall.

Lieutenant Hall had reported aboard the transport *Seneca* around July 10. He had a letter from Roosevelt authorizing him to return to the United States. He would later write that he returned on account of his sickness, which had caused the portly lieutenant to lose 70 pounds. The *Seneca* carried not only a number of sick and wounded but also journalists and foreign observers. Hall roomed with a Japanese naval attaché.

While Hall waited on board, he heard the artillery bombardment of Santiago on the 10th and witnessed the burning of Siboney on the 11th. The outbreak of yellow fever had become so bad in Siboney that Major Louis LaGarde ordered the buildings vacated and burned, thinking that would prevent the spread of the disease. Yellow fever continued to spread.

The *Seneca* was originally destined for Key West, Florida, but upon sailing, the destination was changed to Newport News, Virginia. This was a disappointment to Major English, whose wife was waiting for him at Key West.

The *Seneca* was a troop transport detailed to return wounded. The ship did not have medical supplies or facilities. While the officers and civilians berthed in staterooms, the enlisted suffered in the cramped quarters below deck. This soon became foul as the toilet rooms filled with filthy water. The wounded were crowded into the cots in the hold. As with the previous trip down to Cuba, the air became foul and the decks became filthy. The quality of the food was good until they set sail. Drinking water for the passengers came from a hot, rusty faucet. The ships officers and crew, as on the trip down, fared much better than their passengers, so Hall purchased distilled drinking water from a ship's steward. There were only two contract doctors aboard, but Hall felt that they were inexperienced. Consequently, the press, which experienced this voyage, dubbed these transports "Horror Ships."

At Newport News, the *Seneca* was not permitted to dock for fear of yellow fever. Instead, it waited out in the harbor until orders redirected it to New York. Supplies were brought alongside in a launch, without touching the transport, and tossed aboard. Another launch brought Mrs. English to within 25 feet from the vessel. When she had previously learned that the *Seneca* was diverted to Virginia, she proceeded there. After her not-so-private conversation with her husband, she left for New York.

The *Seneca* arrived in New York on July 30. Dr. Doty, accompanied by John W. Keller of the Commission of Charities and Corrections, boarded for his usual inspection. From then on the passengers' fare improved. The *Fidelity* pulled alongside her at 4 o'clock to remove those who required surgical attention. A Troop's Charles B. Perry, who was shot in the head on July 2, was the only Rough Rider who was sent to the Bellevue Hospital. The very sick were removed immediately to New York hospitals while the rest remained aboard the *Seneca* as she put in at Hoffman's Island in quarantine. That night Hall came down with the fever again, and the next day he was taken to the hospital at Fort Hamilton where he remained for 28 days.

Corporal McClure, of D Troop, said that the one good thing about getting wounded was that it got him out of Cuba before the fever set in. Most of the wounded were issued 30-day medical furloughs, so they went home.

On the 25th of July, the *Hudson* unloaded the body of Captain Capron at Fort Monroe. Of all the officers to die in the Battle of Las Guasimas, none seemed to capture the attention of the public more than Capron. While in Oklahoma, his charisma and fairness had won the hearts of the citizens. His national popularity probably resulted from the combination of his service in the much-celebrated Rough Riders as having descended from a long line of veterans. His grandfather had been killed in action in Mexico, and young Capron and his father fought in the same war.

The hermetically sealed, iron casket with his body was placed on a steamer and sent upriver to Washington, D.C. His body arrived that night, then went to Birch and Sons in Georgetown for embalming at 7 the next morning. By 11 a.m. the funeral services were ready, and the body was delivered to the St. Paul's Episcopal Church to an awaiting crowd of family, friends and journalists. Capron's wife, Agnes, two sons and mother were in attendance. They stayed with friends at Fort Meyer. His father still served in Cuba. The casket draped in the American flag, for which he had given his life, lost its outline among a large arrangement of flowers. Several bunches of roses sent by the officers and wives at nearby Fort Meyer caught the attention of the journalists because of the yellow ribbons tied on them for Capron's service in the cavalry. Even President McKinley's wife had sent a large wreath. The Reverend Dr. Harding opened the service, and a choir of young women dressed in black caps and gowns sang "Nearer, My God, to Thee" and "Lead, Kindly Light."[8]

Upon conclusion of the service, six soldiers from the Fifteenth Pennsylvania Volunteers carried the casket outside to an awaiting artillery caisson attended by four men from Battery H. A hundred infantry men from four companies of the Fifteenth Pennsylvania Volunteer Infantry from Fort Sheridan, Illinois, came to present arms while the pallbearers loaded the casket on the caisson. Then the infantry returned their rifles to "Order Arms," wheeled to the left by fours and turned onto Pennsylvania Avenue. They waited for family and friends to board, awaiting carriages, then they proceeded at a slow pace to Arlington Cemetery. There Dr. Harding said a final prayer for the fallen warrior. Two soldiers folded the American flag into a triangle and presented it to his widow. A bugler played "Taps," a bugle call written in the last war for putting soldiers to bed. Then a detail from Fort Meyer fired a seven-gun salute, and Capron's body was finally laid to rest.[9]

That day the *Hudson* proceeded up to New York where it landed on the 26th with the body of Ham Fish. The wounded Cadet Haskell was also on board. On Thursday evening, the 28th, the flag-covered casket containing Fish's body was placed in the vestibule of St. Mark's Episcopal Church on Second Avenue in New York City. With funeral services set for 11:30 a.m., a crowd of several hundreds of friends and admirers swelled around the church, greatly exceeding its capacity by ten times. Only a few hundred were allowed in. The police formed a cordon around the church to hold the onlookers back and prevent the obstruction of approaches.[10]

Although a man of wealth and social standing, Fish's body was buried with military honors. By regulation, the military escort for a cavalry sergeant consisted of eight pallbearers and 14 troopers under the command of a sergeant. New York's Squadron A performed this role. The platoon of cavalry lined up, waiting outside across the street while the pallbearers walked in.[11]

At 11:15 a.m., about 75 members of Fish's Delta Psi fraternity marched into the church and took their reserved seats on the right of the main isle. Pews on the left were reserved for members of the family, with the center pews reserved for a dozen wounded Rough Riders and members of the Seventy-First New York. Dressed in blue or khaki, many limped into the church. Fish's family arrived at 11:30, and the organ played "Asa's Death." The mourners passed by the flag-draped coffin in the entrance hall. Then eight pallbearers lifted the casket to their shoulders. Three clergymen waited at the portal to escort the funeral detail to the altar where a beautiful display of wreaths of white lilies and roses honored their fallen hero. The parents of Ham Fish and close friends followed the casket while the organ played the funeral march from "Siegfried." The parents then took their seats as the casket was placed in front of the altar.[12]

While the choir sang "Rock of Ages," the fraternity brothers walked down the main isle with each man laying a sprig of evergreen on the casket until the entire lid was completely covered by a thin layer of green. Afterwards, the military pallbearers lifted the casket to their shoulders and carried it out to the hearse where the military escort came to attention and presented arms. The horse-drawn hearse and mourner's carriages, under the escort of the dismounted cavalry, proceeded to Grand Central Station. There the casket was loaded onto a reserved railcar and the funeral party on another for transport to the family plot at Garrison-on-the-Hudson. At the grave, the Rev. Dr. W. Thompson held the services. After the benediction, the military escort fired three volleys and a bugler sounded "Taps," thus laying their comrade to his final rest.[13]

Meanwhile, back at Tampa, an unpleasant situation arose. While Major Dunn served as court-martial officer, Captain George Curry acted as the squadron commander. Acting Adjutant, Lieutenant Hal Sayre, Jr., reported to Curry that their quartermaster was selling food and grain to Tampa merchants. Curry's First Sergeant, Green Settle, also reported that the troop was not receiving its entitlement of supplies, grain and hay. Curry made friends with Tampa officials, and with the help of the Secret Service and Sayre, they uncovered absolute proof of the quartermaster Lieutenant Schweizer's guilt. He had taken advantage of their ignorance of the supply system to sell large amounts of supplies to local merchants.

Curry removed Schweizer from duty and placed him under arrest, then appointed Lieutenant John W. Green from G Troop as the quartermaster officer. Roosevelt considered a court-martial for Schweizer but allowed him to resign his commission without an honorable discharge, which he did on August 4. While Curry felt Regimental Quartermaster Sergeant Madsen was just as guilty, he was allowed to remain on active duty. That incident might have accounted for why he was not given a commission, as Wood had promised.[14]

Only one other incident occurred in Tampa. The evening of August 4, a huge rainstorm also flooded out the Rough Rider camp. Water stood five to six inches in the tents and extinguished all the campfires. It also blew down the cook tents, so the troopers had nothing to eat for supper. Major Dunn then gave those with financial means permission to find shelter in Tampa for the night. Their friends accompanied them. The rest slept in a string of boxcars along the railroad. They soon had blazing campfires to dry out.

On August 8, the day after their regiment had departed Cuba, the squadron in Tampa escorted the horses to the railroad depot to load their mounts. The train departed for Camp Wikoff. Believing yellow fever was contagious, they planned to isolate the returning troops from Cuba and Puerto Rico at a secluded camp in New York where the climate was cooler. The War Department had leased 5,000 acres of Montauk Point on Long Island from the Long Island Railroad Company on August 2. They named it after Brigadier General Charles A. Wikoff, who was killed in the assault on San Juan Hill.

Along the trip north, troopers took their turn sitting guard on top of the stock cars. Unfortunately for Will Tauer and his bunkie, it rained miserably the night of their turn. The train stopped as usual to unload the horses, then water and feed them each day. Their squadron finally arrived on August 13, several days ahead of their regiment, and billeted in the Fourth Regiment Armory in Jersey City since their tents at Camp Wikoff were not ready yet.

The first evening they arrived, Will Tauer and his bunkie went to town. Will had the time of his life with his celebrity. Dressed in their new khaki uniforms trimmed with yellow, they did not walk anywhere without the escort of a lovely young lady on their arms. For the Easterners, this regiment of cowboys was a novelty. People would stare and point, then run to tell others. Soon a crowd of about 50 followed them. The first time they stopped at a corner to determine which direction to walk, the crowd began to swarm on them with questions. Finally, a police officer dispersed the crowd, and from then on around 15 people followed them. Although their meager army pay of $13 had not lasted long enough to reach New York, their female companions, nonetheless, treated them to a supper in a fine restaurant.

The next morning a couple of wealthy swells Will had befriended sent him a fine breakfast. When he returned to town that morning, a barber called him in and gave them a free shave while another gentleman pumped him for stories about his experiences in the Rough Riders. Another plump Dutchman, who also listened intently to the stories, departed only to return with a big package of sandwiches. The wealthy gentleman then invited Will into his home for dinner to meet his family. After dinner, they convened to the parlor where the gentleman's 12-year-old daughter played the piano and sang for Will.

Afterwards, Will returned to the armory, and upon his arrival, he found another invitation to have supper with a wealthy family. He went into the fine house, and upon completion of introductions to the man's wife, two sons and a daughter, they paraded to an elegantly set table. After a fine meal, servants brought in iced lemon tea and cake. After that, they brought in still more different flavors of cake and ice cream. Upon the signal from his host, the men rose and retired to the smoking room to indulge in fine cigars and further conversation. After 15 minutes, the ladies returned dressed in evening gowns. Will Tauer had never seen such elegance growing up on a homestead in Oklahoma.

Roosevelt, a local celebrity, had become even more popular, and his regiment shared in his celebrity, becoming the toasts of the town. These early arrivals capitalized greatly on the fame of their regiment; however, not all had developed the refined tastes of Will and his bunkie.

Local citizens and the press flocked to the newly arrived celebrities. A reporter from the *Daily Advertiser* found the tall, handsome Captain McGinnis chatting with a Jersey City belle. Mac wrote his name, address and unit on a piece of hardtack for her. A score of other visitors also handed him hardtack to write on.

Captain McGinnis told the reporter the afternoon of the second day, "I had to keep about a score of the boys under guard last night, for the people of this town treated them too well. Late at night we found that the men under guard were getting very jolly. It was discovered that citizens had given them flasks and other things through the barred windows."[15]

While conversing with the journalist, Michael Saville, a trooper from Mac's troop walked up. "Captain, I want to go out for a short time."

"You've been drinking, Saville," said the captain, "and ought to go to sleep."

"Only a little with the jolly men of this town," responded the trooper. "Hain't I always done what I said?"

"Yes, and do it now," instructed Mac. "Go, but don't drink any more." The trooper walked across the street; then, half a dozen citizens ushered him into a saloon. When he came out, the captain was watching.

"All right, Cap," shouted Saville in apology. "Couldn't help it. Had to take one. Won't do it again. When the bugle toots I'll report."

"You see how it is," the captain joked with the reporter. "These generous people are spoiling my men. But I can't blame the men, for they had a rough time at Tampa and are glad to get up North. If we had stayed there another month nearly all the men would have been down with fever. We brought a dozen sick men with us. They are in a hospital down town. We are being treated like lords here."

One slightly intoxicated trooper walked up and insisted upon telling the crowd what a fine fellow the captain was. Mac was patient with him. After he left, the captain commented that the trooper was one of the bravest men he had ever met. McGinnis shrugged off the praise of himself by turning the attention to his men.

"Twelve men from my troop were in the Santiago fight," said Captain McGinnis. "Sergeant Hamilton Fish, who was shot at Santiago, was in my command. So was Hallett Alsop Borrowe, who used to be in Newark. I made him a sergeant. Now he is a captain on some general's staff. He is a brave man. Ham Fish was a man of true grit. He obeyed orders. He would do anything he was told to do willingly and well. My men all liked him. He feared nothing on earth or beyond. I never met a braver man in the Western mining camps than he was. None of the troopers who went to Santiago are with me now."

"Sergeant Fish was a splendid soldier," said a big cowboy trooper. "Some folks think the papers puffed him because he was rich and an eastern man. But he had sand. He was one of the men who die in their boots. There was no airs in him."

"When we started out 700 of our 1,200 horses never knowed a bridle or a saddle, not even a halter, for they were wild horses from the plains. Fish was out with the rest of the boys when these horses made a break. He helped us every time. Every cowboy liked him. Borrowe and Tiffany and the other chaps called dudes, were gritty, too."

Other troopers continued to flock to their commander during the course of the interview to seek permission to leave. One brawny trooper with a long black beard but pale face walked up and asked McGinnis to visit some friends. The captain asked if he had money, and the trooper responded that he had a little. Mac then handed him several pieces of silver and said, "Take good care of yourself. Stop at a restaurant and get some chicken soup."

"That's the kind of a man our captain is," the trooper bragged to the reporter. "He gives all of his pay to the men."

"Oh, he's lovely," the Jersey City belle exclaimed. "I could hug him for being so kind."

Captain McGinnis again shrugged off the compliment and mentioned that his first lieutenant, Frederick W. Wintge, gave up a jewelry business in Santa Fe to join the Rough Riders. "I would like his Newark friends to know that he is a brave fellow and a good soldier. He has gone downtown and may run out to Newark." In this atmosphere the squadron waited for a reunion with their comrades.

At 3 a.m. on the 14th of July, the men aboard the *Miami* began to see a number of steamboats. After seven days at sea, they saw the first signs of civilization. At 4 in the morning, they could make out the light of houses and a lighthouse off in the distance. They steamed for the sound, and the torpedo boat *Comet* came alongside at 2:30 in the afternoon, saluted and cheered the Rough Riders. The Rough Riders returned the cheer. The Regulars felt left out. Colbert wrote, "They don't like the Volunteer but very little."[16] The gunboat *Hornet* came out to announce that Spain had sued for peace through France. There would be no more fighting.

Upon arrival at Montauk Point, Long Island, the *Miami* dropped anchor a mile offshore. Surgeon McGruder, of the U.S. Marine Hospital Service, arrived on the *Pulver* for a quick inspection. The crew of the *Pulver* also brought the passengers of the *Miami* several newspapers. The cavalrymen spent the night aboard the ship, and the band entertained them with several selections of music as the sun set.

Meanwhile, that night on land the citizens of the Ninth Ward of New Jersey honored Dunn's squadron of Rough Riders with a banquet at Phillips Hall on Montgomery Street and Bergen Avenue. The day before, the guests of the armory had received orders to move to Camp Wikoff the next day. As soon as the citizens of the Ninth Ward learned of it, they telegraphed General Young, asking permission for the troopers to stay over Monday night and leave the next morning. Young agreed.

At 9 o'clock the squadron of Rough Riders marched up the street preceded by a band playing music. The crowd around the Hall cheered and lit off Roman candles. Major La Motte, who had been sent back early, Captain McGinnis and Lieutenant Hal Sayre, Jr., led their men up the stairs and were greeted by the Committee on Arrangements and other prominent citizens. The committee ushered them into rear rooms 50 at a time where they sat down to tables, for there were not enough tables and chairs for everyone. Since the committee had no time to coordinate for a guest speaker, the toastmaster, ex-mayor Peter F. Wanser, called on Mr. Benson to make a speech after coffee. He eulogized about the quality of men that the territories had produced such as Washington, Andrew Jackson, Lincoln and McKinley. He added that battles were not won by the commanders but by the men who did the fighting and planted the flag on enemy soil.

McGinnis rose to give the response. He was met by cheers but apologized for not being an orator. He went on to state several times that they regretted that they had not the privilege to go to Cuba and participate in the charge up San Juan Hill. "Our own record was not the brightest. But the record of my regiment, I regard as the brightest of the war. I did not get the opportunity to show what my troop could do in the charge up that hill. If we had been there, there would have been an evaluation."[17]

McGinnis went on to speak praises of his former commander, General Wood. He added a conversation he had with a Second Cavalry man who felt it took two years to make a cavalry man.

The captain explained, "Roosevelt selected for his regiment, men who knew how to handle their horses, use their Winchesters and weapons as skilled as the Regulars if they were not quite as pretty. They could put a bullet from a carbine where it ought to be every time. It was said that they only needed the necessary discipline, that they could not click their heels together; but this regiment was not going to the war for that purpose, but to act in unison, to concentrate their action and act as one man. That we did in 60 days, and we showed those fellows that we could do as well as any one of them. In conclusion, I would say that you are all admirers of our Colonel Roosevelt. Apparently, I'm not talking politics, but I don't want him to leave our regiment."[18]

Someone spoke up, "What's the matter with making him governor?"

McGinnis responded, "He is good at everything, because he is so just. He is unpleasant for those who don't do their duty and very good for those that do. He is the kindest man that is my pleasure to know personally. He is a good fighting American."[19]

The room cheered as McGinnis sat down. Then they shouted cheers for "Teddy" Roosevelt and the Rough Riders. McGinnis did not know it at that time, but he was about to campaign for his commander.

The Rough Riders aboard the *Miami* awoke early the next morning to roll up their blankets, clean their mess kits and sweep the deck for the inspectors. Around 7 or 8 o'clock, Dr. McGruder and his team came aboard the ship. For fear of being quarantined, the men did their best to act healthy. They stood shoulder to shoulder, bracing their buddies up so each could answer "Okay" when the inspecting officer asked about their health. After a quick check to the eyes and teeth and a feel of the pulse, the officer moved on to the next man. Fortunately, they were pronounced healthy and cleared to land.

A tug then came alongside at about 10:30 and towed the transport for 30 minutes to its dock. As the *Miami* came into view and Roosevelt, standing among his men along

Wheeler greeting the commander of Camp Wikoff (Theodore Roosevelt Collection, Harvard University Library).

the bridge, was recognized, the crowd began to cheer and the band played. The reception for other regiments had been quieter. The crowd had reserved their joy for the return of the Rough Riders and New York Seventy-First. It took about 15 minutes to tie the *Miami* to its pier. The First Cavalry, which guarded the deadline at the entrance to the pier, had trouble holding back the surge of the crowd. They pushed them back about 100 yards from the dock.

General Wheeler, in his blue wool undress tunic, breeches, leggings and a white cork sun helmet, was the first to walk down the gang plank. His memento of the war, a machete in its leather scabbard, swung by his side. The old rebel's eyes lit up at the cheering of the crowd, and he raced forward to the end of the pier with the agility of a boy and raised his sun helmet in acknowledgment of their welcome. Roosevelt followed in his brown cotton duck uniform, leggings, broad-brimmed hat and pistol belt with holster fastened behind him. Barely had he stepped on the pier when General Young, commander of Camp Wikoff, wrapped his left arm around him and grasped Roosevelt's right hand with the other. They shook hands for what seemed like five minutes. The rest of the Rough Riders paraded off of the vessel.

The wife of the late John A. Logan, Civil War general and Illinois congressman, made her way through the lines to shake hands with Wheeler. She then greeted each trooper with kind, motherly words as they passed by. Roosevelt greeted friends at the deadline and found himself surrounded by the crowd and the press. They asked how he felt, and he answered that he was "disgracefully healthy" as compared to the suffering condition of his men. Roosevelt went on singing praises about his regiment when

Rough Riders arriving at Montauk Point (Theodore Roosevelt Collection, Harvard University Library).

someone asked about his wound. He went on lauding his regiment like a proud father but admitted that he had not been wounded but merely grazed on the wrist and showed the place on the arm. Before leaving to join his men, he said, "I want you all to bear witness that I have not said a word except about the regiment, and that is worth while talking about."

Dunn's squadron was also there to greet their comrades. How different they looked from the last time they saw them. Lieutenant Curry remembered many years later, "It was a pitiful sight and one I shall never forget as they reached the piers and disembarked. All but a few had been weakened by fever. Many had to be brought ashore on stretchers. They returned victorious, but a regiment of human wrecks. Many never fully recovered."[20] Once ashore, they walked to an assembly point where the weakest crawled into awaiting wagons to carry them to the hospitals. The rest, in not much better condition, formed into a line and struggled about a mile to their new home, Camp Wikoff, where they would go into quarantine for five days.

They looked out over a long, rolling plain of green grass. Dotted across the plain were rectangular rows of white tents with plank floors, which would sleep four men each. Their camp was on the side of a low hill facing the ocean with a nice sea breeze to cool them. This was heaven compared to Cuba.

For men whose physical senses have become used to privation and hardship, returning to the comforts of home comes as a culture shock, which almost seems unreal. Their spirits rise as they near their destination, but not until they step on home soil does the return become something real, something they can touch, smell, see and hear. They have become so accustomed to suffering that they think if they blink, it might disappear. Ben Colbert wrote in his diary that day, "Nice breeze and soft dry grass to lie upon. Such a contrast to what we have recently been compelled to be contented with."[21] Paul Hunter wrote home, "We were afraid that it was all a dream and that we would awake and find ourselves once more in the old tent, with the patter of rain overhead."[22] The Rough Riders were back on home soil. Their health could only get better. Colbert and his friends savored the moment for as long as they could. They sat around the campfire until late that night eating broiled beef that they had stolen.

The Rough Riders residing in the armory joined the rest of the regiment the next day. During their earlier wait, a local barber, Frank Testrial, had recognized a trooper loitering around the armory. Testrial went immediately to the police headquarters and told Police Inspector William H. Lange, of Jersey City, that one of the Rough Riders was wanted for murder in Kansas City. James Redmond had killed a woman named Mrs. Shumaker during a robbery on December 8, 1897, and enlisted under the alias of Michael Saville of I Troop.

Inspector Lange telegraphed Chief John Hayes in Kansas City for confirmation of the murder and a description of Redmond. Hayes wired back that Redmond was in fact wanted for murder and that he could be identified by a wart on his nose and the two tattoos on his arms, both described in detail.

Armed with the description, Lange and Testrial went to the armory where Testrial pointed out Redmond. The alleged murderer turned out to be Michael Saville, of McGinnis's troop. The 29-year-old Saville had enlisted from Santa Fe, New Mexico. They told Mac of their information, and the captain informed them that he legally could not turn Saville over without a proper warrant or order from the War Department. Lange did not go up and check out the tattoos for fear that Saville would escape before they could arrest him. Mac informed them that he would have Saville closely watched.

The same day that the Florida squadron moved to Camp Wikoff, Police Chief Hayes telegraphed that he was sending a police officer to Jersey City with a warrant for the arrest of Redmond. Lange quickly sent Detective McNally to Montauk Point with the news. He reported to Roosevelt, but the colonel would not release Saville without the proper paperwork. McNally returned empty-handed. Over the next three days, Saville became aware of the law's interest in him. There must have been some truth to the allegations. On the 20th, McGinnis telegraphed Lange that Saville had fled the night before. That day, McGinnis listed Saville as a deserter.

Huston, like the others, had lost weight and was sick with malaria. As soon as the five-day quarantine ended, he took a medical furlough to visit the home of Code and Marion, in Worchester, New York, where his wife, Vite, and son had waited since July. Once again command of D Troop fell to Dade Goodrich. First Sergeant Palmer would not take sick leave until September.

With the whole regiment in camp, the men kept themselves occupied with camp maintenance. Notwithstanding, they had a lot of time on their hands. Two Regular Army cavalry regiments also shared the camp and had several unbroken horses. This provided the cowboys a chance to demonstrate their superb horsemanship skill. Roosevelt rounded up four of his best bronco riders to meet this challenge. McGinty and three others provided a regular rodeo as they broke horse after horse without a man getting thrown. The Regulars witnessed the talent for which the volunteer regiment had

Rough Rider officers at Montauk Point. Seated in the second row, left to right: Chap Brown, Col. Roosevelt, Maj. Brodie, Maj. Hersey and Maj. Jenkins (in khaki). Standing behind them, left to right: Surg. Church (in khaki), Capt. Kane (in khaki), unidentified, 1st Lt. Day, unidentified, and Capt. Huston. Capt. Bruce and 2nd Lt. Greenwald (in khaki) are seated on the right in the front row. 1st Lt. Griffin is wearing the white cowboy hat (Library of Congress).

been recruited. The Army had missed a tremendous opportunity in not utilizing these expert horsemen in their intended cavalry role.

With Bardshar near death, Roosevelt picked Private Gordon Johnston, of M Troop, to become his new orderly. Johnston had come down from North Carolina and enlisted in the Indian Territory's M Troop on June 8, after the regiment had left for Cuba. He was the son of Confederate General Robert D. Johnston and nephew of the governor of Alabama. An 1896 graduate of Princeton University, he had played on their football team. Little doubt that Roosevelt took a liking to him and considered him one of the best men in the regiment. He would in later wars measure up to Roosevelt's estimation. Meanwhile, he and Roosevelt would take evening rides on their horses across the rolling plains. On other occasions, Roosevelt would summon some of his favorite officers, Ballard, Church, Ferguson, Greenway, Kane, Goodrich, Frantz and John M. McIlhenny, for rides to the beach, where they would swim. This reminded him of his frolicking days out West.

The Rough Riders were given pretty liberal passes, similar to their days in Texas. Many hustled to get one to go to watch the parade of U.S. Navy battleships in New York City on Saturday, August 20. Ben Colbert and his bunkie, Ed Adams, went into town for the first time since landing and experienced the same reception as had their comrades. They did not pay for a thing except their room in the hotel. Ben woke up Saturday

Seated, left to right: 2nd Lt. Ferguson, 1st Lt. Goodrich, unidentified, 1st Lt. Greenway, Col. Roosevelt, Lt. Col. Brodie, 2nd Lt. Greenwald. Standing, left to right: Adj. Keyes, 2nd Lt. Hayes, Cpt. Kane, 1st Lt. Day, Surg. Church (Library of Congress).

morning, went downstairs for breakfast and a shave, then went for a walk. He visited Grant's Tomb, then walked over to watch the parade of battleships. There he was taken by a chill, the first symptoms of malaria. Ben became unable to enjoy the spectacle and had to return to his hotel room around 2 in the afternoon to sleep. He ended his five-day pass one day early by reporting to a local hospital. He was released on the 25th. The next day he went to visit a friend in the Belleview Hospital, and, to his surprise, he found his sick bunkie, Ed, in there. Ed returned from the hospital on the 30th. With the war at an end, the majority of the soldiers preoccupied themselves with recovery.

On August 24, Paul Hunter reported sick with ten other Rough Riders during morning formation. They were sent to Hospital Number 2, the one nearest Montauk. Colonel William C. Forwood, assistant surgeon general of the U.S. Army, had orders on July 29 to erect a 500-bed temporary tent hospital. The demand would exceed that capacity. By the time that the troops arrived, he had established four wards of the general hospital. Each white canvas tent was erected over frames on wooden floors. The fear of the spread of yellow fever caused Forwood to establish a second hospital as a detention facility. However, this was complicated by a shortage of supplies and medical personnel. Local hospitals and even the New York Stock Exchange donated food and medical supplies. Concerned civilians flooded Camp Wikoff with offers and donations. President McKinley told General Wheeler, the camp commander, to spare no expense in the care of the soldiers. The problems did not grow from want of resources. Some concluded that Forwood was not the man capable of handling the task. By the time Paul and his fellow Rough Riders reported in, the hospital capacity had peaked.

They arrived at 2 in the afternoon and were assisted by stewards to their tents. Paul and another trooper were escorted to a tent in the center row already occupied by four others, three of whom came from the Seventy-First New York. Dinner was being served at that time. It consisted of a small saucer of oatmeal and a cup of black coffee for the very sick and a bowl of beef soup, hardtack and coffee for those with stronger stomachs. This diet was not much better than what had weakened their systems in Cuba.

About 4 a young army doctor wearing shoulder straps and high-top boots walked into their tent with an orderly following close behind. Paul observed that there were about seven doctors in the ward for 300 patients. The doctor walked around the other four and passed out pills. He then walked up to Paul's comrade. "What is the matter with you?"[23]

"I am suffering terribly from pains in my chest and neck and am spitting blood," he replied. The doctor then gave him two white pills and one dark one and said, "Take one now and the others before supper."

The doctor then walked up to Paul and asked, "Well, what can I do for you?" Paul answered, "Doctor, for over three weeks I have had pains in my side from my left shoulder to my hips and can't relish lying down for the pain, and I want something to stop it, and want to know what is the matter." With that the doctor started searching through his pill bag. Paul stopped him and asked for an explanation. The doctor thumped around the trooper's ribs and looking wise, asked what Paul thought was the matter. Paul answered, pleurisy.

The doctor told his orderly, "Put it down as pleurisy." Then he asked what Paul wanted for it. Paul answered that he thought a mustard pack would give him some relief. The doctor applied a mustard pack. Paul did not develop much confidence in the medical help there.

Supper arrived that evening, and it was the same as dinner. Breakfast was no different. Each meal was the same, which the sick men could not eat to maintain their health. Paul then told his tentmates that he would go to the cookhouse to try and get some milk. The others were so sick that they could hardly walk ten feet. Paul watched the medical officers and men finish a supper of bread, milk, butter, roast beef, potatoes, coffee and sugar. He asked one of the cooks for some bread and milk. The sympathetic cook told him to wait until the mess steward walked out, or he would get in trouble giving him the leftovers. Paul returned some milk toast for his half-starved comrades. Their eyes lit up at the sight.

At 4 p.m. the doctor came back around and administered the same regimen of pills. When he reached Paul, he asked how the plaster worked. Paul told him sarcastically that it had succeeded in removing a few feet of skin from his side. The doctor laughed and walked away. Paul asked the others why they did not get out of there. One answered, "Just as well die here as anywhere."

Supper came with the same menu. So Paul again walked over to the cookhouse and reported to the chief steward and asked for milk and bread. He added that the men were starving for common food.

The mess steward unsympathetically answered, "I am not responsible for it, and it is none of my business whether they starve or not." He then demanded, "You go back to your tent and take what is brought to you, and don't come back here again." Paul pleaded for sympathy but found none. He ended his conversation describing the man as a brute who ought to be shot. Paul returned to his tent, resolved to see the senior doctor.

After the usual breakfast at 9 a.m., Paul put on his uniform and walked to the tent of the chief surgeon. He stood before a mean-looking major sporting a beard. Paul saluted then began telling his woes. The old major stopped him and said, "You Rough Riders want the earth. Go back to your tent and stay there."

It was partially true. The Rough Riders did not expect special treatment; they had just come to expect what was properly due to them as common soldiers. Neither did they accept excuses for incompetence for they had a colonel who stood up for them and delivered on what they were due. Paul said, "Sir, I will go to my camp."

The doctor responded with authority, "You can't leave here until I tell you to go."

Confident that he was justified in such action, Paul said, "I am going just the same." While he had been visited by only two doctors during his two-day stay, he would often observe four or five doctors standing on a hill watching the ships come in. He believed that the absence of women nurses in the hospital allowed for that deplorable neglect by the army doctors. He praised the Red Cross though. Paul reported back to his camp at 10 the next morning. By then, two of his sick tentmates had died.

Of the 1,850 patients that had passed through the hospital, 62 died. Contrary to what Paul thought, here were as many as 329 female nurses. On September 8, Surgeon General Sternberg replaced Forwood with Colonel Charles R. Greenleaf to expedite the transfers. Because of the congestion, Sternberg permitted patients to transfer to civilian hospitals in the cities or go home on furloughs in early September.

William Tiffany had finally returned from Cuba aboard the *Olivette* to Boston on August 23. Cleared of yellow fever and put on the convalescent list, he was permitted to select his own lodgings while the more seriously ill were interned in hospitals. He chose to stay at the Parker House until he regained enough strength to go home. His brother, Belmont, had come to the hotel to care for him, but Willy died two days later. His friend, Woodbury Kane, rode up to Montauk Point on Saturday to select pallbearers to escort Tiffany's body to the family plot in the Island Cemetery. There his body was laid to rest next to his great-uncle, Commodore Oliver Hazard Perry. Roosevelt felt that had Tiffany been allowed to return with them on the *Miami*, his health would have recovered.

Adjutant General Henry C. Corbin had issued the order on August 22 governing the mustering out of the volunteers. The order gave instructions on how each regiment would be mustered out. Nothing was simple. It was harder to get out of the Army than into it. Only a Regular Army officer could muster out a regiment. Each troop commander must account for all the men listed on the

Studio portrait photograph of Sgt. Ira Hill in his new khaki uniform (author's collection).

muster-in roll on the muster-out roll. They must turn in all organizational equipment, such as cartridge belts, canteens, haversacks, and tents. Such equipment as needed could be kept until the final date of discharge. Officers responsible for public property had to obtain certificates of non-indebtedness from the government before they could receive their final payment. Mustering officers were empowered to prefer charges against officers who neglected in any manner to take proper measures to prevent loss of property or keep their command together and under proper discipline. That is why the army paid officers so much more money than enlisted men. They had more to lose.

The mustering officer would prepare discharge certificates for every enlisted man and officer except for those held by proper authority or deserters. The discharges would be delivered first to the regiment then troop for issue on the muster-out date of the regiment. The troop officers would forward the discharge certificates with proper addresses and list of account of pay and clothing of those enlisted men absent and on account of sickness could not rejoin their regiment. The muster-out officer would then notify the soldier to apply by letter to the paymaster general for final payment.

On August 25, Lieutenant Colonel Brodie sent a telegram to Captain Huston in Worchester that there was strong talk of mustering out the regiment within ten days. He advised Huston to return to his troop. As his superior and friend, Brodie took a special interest in Huston's military success. The next day, Goodrich also sent a telegram to Huston informing him that they had received orders to muster out immediately. Roosevelt directed that he return at once. Huston had traveled to Dobbs Ferry, so he did not receive the telegram until early September. He sent a telegram back that he was still sick but would leave for Washington that night and should arrive in two days. Rob had received letters from his brother, Had, earlier that month that the Republican Party wanted to nominate him for the congressional bid. The Democratic candidate, Dennis T. Flynn, however, was the clear favorite in the territory. Huston, fortunately, had no ambition for politics but desired to stay in the Army and hoped he could find a vacancy during his visit to the War Department. He, in the meantime, sent his family back to Oklahoma.

A week after Corbin's message, Roosevelt told his men that they would be discharged within 30 days. The next rumor claimed that they would be mustered out on September 5 with a parade through New York the next day. From the beginning of September, the Rough Riders focused their energy on meeting the requirements to muster out. By then the veterans were used to the rumor mill and did not pin their hopes much on any

Studio portrait photograph of William Pollock (courtesy Western History Collections, University of Oklahoma Libraries, Wenner 110).

particular date. They relaxed, visited new friends they had made in the city or went down to the beach to bathe in the surf.

A bunch of the officers were heading to the beach for a swim and dropped by Roosevelt's tent to see if he wanted to go with them. The colonel said he was too busy but for the others to go have a "bully swim." Just as they started off, Roosevelt called Rynning back for a minute and asked him if he thought Doctor La Motte was a coward. Someone had preferred charges of cowardice against him for returning to Siboney during the Battle of Las Guasimas. The lieutenant answered, "I'm a witness for the defense and shouldn't discuss the case with anybody."[24]

His colonel demanded angrily, "Well, you can discuss it with me, can't you?" Rynning refused. He was caught in the quandary where regulations protected him from revealing his testimony, but his silence would incur the wrath of this commander. Roosevelt grew hotter and glared Rynning in the eye. The lieutenant just stared back. Roosevelt finally exploded, "Consider yourself under arrest!"

"Yes, sir," answered Rynning, then he returned to his tent and hung up his towel. Evidently, he was not going to go swimming that day. Half an hour later, Johnston came by and said that the colonel had released him from arrest of quarters and wanted to see him. Rynning hiked over to his colonel's tent and reported in.

A much calmer Roosevelt apologized. "I was absolutely wrong. I had no right to ask you that question and I admire you for your attitude." Roosevelt was not too proud to admit to his subordinate that he was wrong, and Rynning never lost his respect of him for that.

During the trial, La Motte was accused of cowardice for leaving the battlefield and establishing a dressing station further back, out of the line of fire. All the while, Church had cared for men under fire. While heroic, Rynning felt that it was reckless.

William Pollock on horseback at Montauk Point (Theodore Roosevelt Collection, Harvard University Library).

The regiment only had two surgeons and could not afford to lose either. La Motte did the appropriate thing and established a dressing station in a safer location. Doctors were not supposed to take the same risks as infantry or cavalry men. The court agreed, and La Motte was acquitted. Years later, President Roosevelt ran into Rynning at the Grand Canyon and reflected on the affair. "Hello, Tom. You were right and I was wrong. You knew more about military matters than I did."

While Roosevelt tried to be fair, his own personality shaped his judgment of people and their actions. He judged La Motte on how he would have acted under the same

Regimental Quartermaster Sergeant Chris Madsen (courtesy Oklahoma Historical Society).

Little Billy McGinty (far left) with fellow broncobusters (Theodore Roosevelt Collection, Harvard University Library).

circumstances rather than how a surgeon should act. This bias may have also affected the way he judged Huston. Roosevelt liked Huston as much as any other officer and even had a little Rough Rider uniform made for his son.

The muster-out process repeated the muster in. The medical surgeons had to determine if they were in the same condition that they had entered the service. This was where many soldiers commonly claimed injuries or sickness incurred during the service of their country for future disability claims. Roosevelt would later brag that his men belittled their injuries and sickness even though they were gaunt and pale. Instead of being skeptical of claims, the medical officials had to look out for the future interests of the Rough Riders.

Chris Madsen, however, did not hesitate to state his case. Having entered the army weighing in at 200 pounds, he then weighed out at 120. After the surgeon signed his certificate of disability, Madsen did not follow normal procedure and take it to his headquarters. He knew the slowness of army bureaucracy too well, so he carried it straight to General Wheeler and was discharged early on August 26.[25]

Bill McGinty's friends put him up to a trick. During the mustering-out process, they prevailed upon him to walk up and ask the mustering-out officer, a major, when they would go home. In the Regular Army enlisted men did not address officers without being addressed first, and then protocol required that they speak in the third person. They figured that a direct question to a superior officer would get him reprimanded. Bill had no qualms about the challenge. He did as asked, and to everyone's surprise the officer met the little broncobuster with a smile, sat down on a log and had a friendly chat. Not all army officers followed formalities. Bill's buddies had assumed that all Regular Army officers were the same. After that they just continued to pass the time waiting to leave.

Secretary of War Alger visited the camp on August 24 and actually slept under canvas one night. Alger was not deliberately malicious in his demands upon the army; he just had very little understanding of military matters. The civilian qualifications that appointed him for the job in peace did not qualify him to serve in that capacity during war. He left after two days, and on August 26, President McKinley also proposed to visit. As the commander-in-chief, the president held the authority to send men into battle. McKinley, an old Civil War veteran, felt the need to see the men who had faced the dangers and were suffering the consequences of his decision to go to war.

Portrait photograph of Billy McGinty (Theodore Roosevelt Collection, Harvard University Library).

President McKinley, Vice President Garret Hobart, Secretary of War Alger and his wife; Secretaries John Addison Porter and George B. Cortelyou, Attorney General John W. Griggs, Senator Redfield Proctor of Vermont, Commissary General Charles P. Eagan, Quartermaster General Marshall I. Luddington, Colonel Henry Heckler and his wife arrived by train at Camp Wikoff on September 3. Wheeler, his staff and nearly every officer of prominence waited at the station to greet them. The president stepped out in his black frock coat, waistcoat and top hat. After the greetings on the platform, McKinley took Wheeler's arm and walked to an awaiting carriage.

Roosevelt and a group of his Rough Riders were mounted nearby. When McKinley recognized his former Assistant Secretary of the Navy, he stepped out of the carriage and walked over to speak with him. Roosevelt hastily dismounted, pulled off his leather gauntlet to shake hands, and they spoke briefly.

McKinley then climbed back in, and the column of carriages wound their way up the hill escorted by the Third Cavalry and the Sixth Cavalry bands. They came upon an open plain covered by enough white canvas tents to house 18,000 men. The carriage pulled up next to General Shafter's tent, and McKinley stepped out. Shafter, still suffering from the full effects of malaria, was sitting in front of his tent. He attempted to rise, but McKinley said, "Just stay where you are, general. You are entitled to rest." He then congratulated the general on his victory.[26]

McKinley then mounted back into his open carriage to visit the sick in the general hospital. Soldiers lining each side of the road cheered as he passed. He tipped his hat to them in acknowledgment and did not put it back on until he had passed them. He met General Wheeler's daughter, who was the nurse in the first ward. She escorted him through each ward, and the general announced the president when they entered each tent. Some slept, unconscious of what went on around them, while others tried to raise themselves to their elbows. McKinley gently shook hands with many and bowed in acknowledgment to the rest. He seemed to be in no hurry.

As he walked from one end of the long tents to the next, he had to jump from the flooring to the ground as the tents were on an incline. He did this until he came to a slope that was six feet below the floor. At that moment he hesitated, saying, "I balk here. Can't go over this hurdle." Neither would Secretary Alger; then the wiry Wheeler lightly sprang to the ground. The whole experience made him feel young.[27]

After having passed through all the hospital tents, General Briggs stopped the president as he was about to get back in his carriage and told him that Miss Annie Wheeler had promised Lieutenant Prado, who was dying in a tent by himself, that the president would meet him. McKinley said, "Certainly, let us go to him." The other officers waited outside while the president and a nurse went inside. After a couple of minutes, the old Civil War veteran reemerged with his eyes moist and head downcast.[28]

They proceeded to the infantry plain where 5,000 infantrymen of the Ninth Massachusetts Volunteer Infantry, the First Illinois Volunteer Infantry, the Eighth Ohio Volunteer Infantry, the Thirteenth, Twenty-First, Twenty-Second and Tenth Regular Infantry were lined up in close order without weapons. Wheeler addressed the group:

> The President of our great country has come here to greet the soldiers that marched so gallantly up San Juan Hill on July first. He comes here to express the nation's thanks to these brave men. I wish to tell you that when the president sent me here two weeks ago, to command this camp he enjoined me in the most emphatic language that I should, without regard to expense, exercise any and every authority necessary to make comfortable this body of

brave men, who by their courage, have raised this republic to the highest position among the great nations of the earth. I have the honor and pleasure of introducing to you the President of the United States, President McKinley.[29]

McKinley then addressed the troops:

General Wheeler, soldiers of Camp Wikoff, soldiers of the Fifth Army Corps, I trust that you will put your hats on—I am glad to meet you. I am honored to stand before you today. I bring you the gratitude of the nation to whose history you have added by your valor a new and glorious page. You have come home after two months of severe campaigning, which has embraced assault, siege and battle, so brilliant on achievement, so far-reaching on results as to command the unstinted praise of all your countrymen. You had the brunt of the battle on land. You bore yourselves with supreme courage, and your personal bravery, never before excelled anywhere, has won the admiration of your fellow citizens and the genuine respect of all mankind, while your endurance under peculiar trial and suffering has given added meaning to your heroism. Your exertions made easy conquest of Puerto Rico, under the irresistible army commanded by Major General Miles, and behind you, to proceed at a moments summons were more than 200,000 of your comrades, ready to support you, disappointed that the opportunity which you had did not come to them yet filled with pride at your well earned fame and rejoicing upon your signal victories.

You were on the line of battle, they no less than you, were in the line of duty. All have served their country in its need, all will serve it so long as they may be required, and all will forever have the thanks and regard of a grateful people.

We cannot bid you welcome here today without our hearts going out to the heroes of Manila, on sea and land, whose services and sacrifices, whose courage and constancy in that far distant field of operations have never been surpassed by any soldiers or sailors the world over. To the Army and the Navy, and to the providence which has watched over them all, the nation today is full of thanksgiving and praise. The brave officers and men who fell in battle and those who have died from exposure and sickness will live in immortal story, and their hearts and history of a generous people, and those who are dependent on them will not be neglected by the government for which they so freely sacrificed their lives.[30]

The men cheered many times. The president and his party then visited the detention hospital with the same respect that he had gotten through the general hospital. He came out to a graveyard marked by 60 or 70 new wooden crosses. He solemnly raised his hat to them. He then proceeded to visit the last ward, even though he was warned that it was a dangerous ward. He walked in while the rest of his party remained outside.

Upon completion, they mounted their carriages and drove through the lines of cavalry drawn up along both sides of the road. The lines included the First, Second, Sixth, Tenth and Rough Riders. The Third continued to provide the escort. The presidential party then returned to Shafter's tent and sat under the shade of the tent fly for a while. The president then got up to walk over and shake hands with another prominent volunteer officer, Colonel John Jacob Astor, standing among a group of officers nearby. Astor was probably the richest man in America to don the army blue and serve in Cuba. McKinley then had lunch with General Wheeler and his staff, where they were also photographed. McKinley then issued an order directing the Regulars stationed at posts east of the Mississippi to return to their posts with the least possible delay.

That day, Corbin announced the intention of the War Department to muster out of service a number of volunteer regiments to include the First U.S. Volunteer Cavalry— the Rough Riders. By then work had begun in earnest to get the pay- and muster-out rolls in order. Ben Colbert worked five straight days on them and would have worked

Capt. Huston standing by his tent (Theodore Roosevelt Collection, Harvard University Library).

a sixth but came down with another bout of malaria. Huston had returned to Camp Wikoff, and by September 9 had his muster-out reports completed. The delay in mustering out resulted from the work to account for those absent on sick leave. The War Department in Washington had to approve them before Huston and his men could get paid. He estimated that his troop would be discharged on the 13th or 14th while the rest of the regiment would be discharged on the 15th or 16th. Huston had also learned about a major's vacancy for a paymaster of the volunteers. He sent a telegram to his brother, Had, asking for three letters of recommendation.

In September, Tom Isbell came back from his medical furlough in the Indian Territory. While home, he discovered that another Cherokee had run away with his woman, so he killed the man. Tom's tribe tried him according to Cherokee law and sentenced him to death. They released him on his own recognizance until the time of his execution. Rynning asked him if he was going back. The half-blood Cherokee said, "Sure. I'm Indian. I've got to keep my word to go back."[31]

Rynning then went and told Roosevelt about it. The colonel then burned up the wires with telegrams until the chiefs of the Five Nations promised that they would not take his life. No one could expect more from a commander.

At the regimental mess on September 9, the men of the First U.S. Volunteer Cavalry formed the social organization known as "The Order of the Roosevelt Rough Riders" to preserve the memory of their service and pass on the honor to their eldest sons.

They elected Brodie as their first president, Wood and Roosevelt the vice-presidents and Goodrich the secretary. David had quickly become one of the more popular officers in the regiment. Most of the other officers spoke very highly of him. Journalists Marshall and Davis were elected as honorary members along with Lieutenant Parker of the Gatlings.

Brodie stood up and addressed Roosevelt:

The officers and men of the First United States Volunteer Cavalry wishing to perpetuate the name under which they were popularly known, and to transmit to their sons the heritage of renown they won so distinctively before Santiago, propose to organize a military order that they sincerely believe will become an honored and inheritance as any title to nobility. We are proud to be known as members of Roosevelt's Rough Riders and we have therefore given our association that precious name, the name under which our beloved comrades died gloriously on the battlefield. All of the preliminaries have been concluded without your consent but we are confident of your approval.[32]

Roosevelt responded:

Comrades, no happiness can ever equal that which this evidence of your love and respect brings to my heart. They have been spent with you, associated on camp, on social life, or on the activities of actual warfare. That I have retained your esteem is gratification enough for any man.

I can say that to have been a Rough Rider is the pride of my life. I feel that I certainly was born to command this regiment, and you tell me by this graceful method of perpetuating the

Roosevelt saying farewell to the regiment (Theodore Roosevelt Collection, Harvard University Library).

love each of us feels for it, that I have commanded it to your satisfaction and approval. I thank you and am greatly honored as well as made gloriously happy.[33]

They held an informal reception with the idea that every man in the regiment should stand on the same equality. They also planned to design a distinctive badge before the regiment was mustered out.

Their last Sunday together, Roosevelt spoke after Chaplain Brown's sermon. He told them how proud he was of them but warned them not to rest on their laurels. For probably ten days the world would treat them as heroes, but then they would forget, and the men would have to work hard for anything else they wanted. Roosevelt felt a strong bond with the men of his regiment and hoped that they would heed his advice.

On a sunny Tuesday, September 13, Brodie asked Roosevelt to step out of his tent. The regiment assembled in a hollow square with the officers and color sergeant in the center. Brodie invited his colonel into the center. There, William Murphy, on behalf of the regiment, presented their beloved colonel with Frederick Remington's bronze statue "The Bronco Buster," on a pine table in the center of the square formation.

It is fitting that I, one of the troopers from the ranks of your regiment, should try to tell you as well as I can, to what is due the honor given me on making this presentation. It is well known that while you hold your officers on the highest esteem, because of their bravery, gallantry, and ability, your heart of hearts was ever with your men, whether on the tented field or on the trenches before the enemy's lines, or better still, on the trenches which your regiment captured from the enemy.

I want to tell you, sir, that one and all of us, from the highest of us to the humblest of us, will always carry with us in our hearts a pleasant and a loving memory of your every act, for there has not been one among them which has not been of the kindest. As lieutenant colonel of our regiment, you first made us respect you; as our colonel you have taught us to love you deeply, as men love men. It is our sincere hope, now that we are about to separate, that this bronze 'Bronco Buster' will sometimes make you think of us, as we shall ever think of you.[34]

The role of the officer is to accomplish the mission and take care of the men. Efforts to enforce discipline and maintain impartiality may confuse the soldiers as to the commander's concern for their well-being. Every good commander hopes that his men understand this and appreciate the motivation of his efforts. The giving of gifts to a beloved commander is an old tradition but not a requirement. There could have been no better gift that captured the character of the regiment. It removed any doubt that Roosevelt might have had about what his men thought of him.

Deeply touched by the sentiment, Roosevelt then made another farewell speech:

Officers and Men; I really do not know how to answer you. Nothing could touch and please me as this has touched and pleased me. Trooper Murphy spoke quite truly when he said that my men were nearest to my heart, for while I need not tell to my officers on what deep regard I hold them, they will not mind my saying, that just a little closer come my men.

I have never tried to coddle you, and I have never made a baby of any one of you. I have never hesitated to call upon you to spend your best blood like water and to work your muscles to their breaking point. Of course, I have tried to do for you, as you have ever done all that you could ever do for me. You are the best judges as to whether or not I have succeeded.

I am proud of this regiment beyond measure; I am proud of it, because it is a typical American regiment, made up of typical American men. The foundation of the regiment was the 'Bronco Buster,' and we have him here on bronze. The men of the West and the men of the Southwest, horsemen, riflemen, and herders of cattle, have been the backbone of their sections of the country. This demonstrates that Uncle Sam has nobler reserve of fighting men to call upon, if the necessity arises, than any other country on the world.

The West stands ready now to furnish tens of thousands of men like you, who are only samples of what our country can produce. Besides the cow-puncher, this regiment contains men from every section of the country and from every state within the Union. This shows us that the West is not alone in ability to furnish men like you. This gives us double reason to feel proud on this day when we disband.

I have profound respect for you, men of the Rough Riders, not only because you also have those qualities which made men recognize you as fighters, and enabled you to be among the first who found the opportunity of getting into the fight. Outside of my own immediate family, I shall always feel that stronger ties exist between me and you than exist between me and anyone else on earth. If your feeling toward me is like mine toward you, I am more than pleased to have you tell me of it.

I realized when I took charge of you, that I was taking upon myself a grave responsibility. I cared for you as individuals, but I did not forget at any moment that it might be necessary to sacrifice the comfort or even the lives of individuals, in order to insure the safety of the whole. You would have scorned a commander, who hesitated for a second to expose you to any risk. I was bound that no other regiment should get any nearer to the Spanish lines than you got and I do not think that any other regiments did.

We parted with many on the fights who could ill be spared, and I think that the most vivid memories we will take away with us will be not of our own achievements, not of our own dangers, not of our own suffering, but will be of those whom we left under Cuban sod and those who died on the hospitals on the United States—the men who died from wounds and the men who, with the same devotion to their country, died from fevers—I cannot mention all the names now, but three of them, Capron, O'Neill and Fish will suffice. They died on the pride of their youthful strength and they died for their country, like men who were proud to die.

I should have been most deeply touched if the officers of this regiment had given me this testimonial, but I appreciate it ten-fold, as coming from you, my men. You shared the hardships of the campaign with me; when I had none, you gave me of your hardtack, and if I lay coverless, I never lacked a blanket from my men to lie upon.

To have such a gift come from this peculiarly American regiment touches me more than I can say. It is something that I shall hand down to my children, and value more highly than I do the weapons which I carried through the campaign with me.

Now, boys, I wish to take each of you by the hand, as a special privilege, and say good-by to you individually; this is to be our farewell in camp; I hope that it will not be our farewell in civil life.[35]

At several times his voice faltered and tears came to his eyes. If it had not occurred to the men before, it did then. This was the last time they would assemble as a regiment. They would part ways with their commander and with each other. David Hughes looked around and saw not a dry eye among the hardened, weathered veterans.

As each man approached, Roosevelt removed his hat in respect, then reached out his right hand. As he grasped their hands, Roosevelt said something to each one. He knew every man in his regiment by his name or nickname. While they greatly anticipated going home, they realized that this would probably be the last time that many of them would see each other. Colbert lamented, "We will all be scattered all over the U.S. and a thousand miles from each other."[36]

The next day Color Sergeant Albert P. Wright took down the national colors that had been a gift from the ladies of Arizona and served them in battle, and Civil War veteran Sergeant Nevin Guitilias rolled up the yellow regimental standard that the army had finally issued them at Camp Wikoff. Each troop lined up in turn to be paid off and mustered out. Eight troops then mustered out that day, the rest the next.

Color Sergeant A.P. Wright (Theodore Roosevelt Collection, Harvard University Library).

At 3:40 p.m. on the 14th, F Troop assembled for the last time. As each trooper's name was called out, he stepped forward and received his pay and discharge. Each man was paid two months' extra pay plus travel expenses. Once again, they were civilians. It was a solemn moment. The officers and men were equals once more. They walked around shaking hands, saying their good-byes. They then walked back to their tents to pack up their belongings. Once finished, they had no reason to delay around the camp any longer, so they made their way to the railway station. The Board of Trade had prepared a place for them to stay overnight. After supper, Colbert and his two buddies visited New York City one last time before they caught the train the next day and parted company. They were not in a hurry to return. Ben wrote, "I dare say the Fifteenth day of September was born before we returned."[37] Each veteran returned home to pick up where he had left off. They ceased to exist as a collective body of men and would once again pursue their individual goals, forever changed by their experience.

D Troop's turn to be paid off and mustered out came later that evening. The War Department withheld Huston's last month's pay of $250 until he and the other commanders settled their ordnance accounts in Washington, D.C. Huston, however, received $495 travel pay back to Guthrie based upon a day's pay for every day of travel. The government used 20 miles a day for calculating travel days. That amounted to 88 days of travel time back to Guthrie. That added up to more than the two months' leave that most others were paid. D Troop finished at 8 p.m. Consequently, Huston did not leave camp until noon next day.[38]

Huston went over and checked into the new Hoffman House since it offered rooms to Rough Riders at half the normal rate. Not surprisingly, almost all of the Rough Riders stayed there. Brodie planned an excursion to his alma mater, West Point, that day, but Huston felt too sick to attend. He planned to go to Washington to settle his accounts and apply for appointment as a major and paymaster of volunteers. He wanted to stay on active duty. He had received the three letters of recommendation from Had on the 16th and planned to leave the next day with Brodie. The major felt a special loyalty to help Huston.

Roosevelt left for his home in Oyster Bay. He invited five of his favorite officers to accompany him. They included John Greenway, Hal Sayre, Charles Ballard, Robert Ferguson and David Goodrich. Roosevelt and his friends entertained them royally with dinners, parties, dances and fishing.

Roosevelt also asked Bill McGinty to escort Little Texas, the horse he rode up Kettle Hill, to his home in Oyster Bay. Bill did as his colonel asked, but, along the way, souvenir hunters picked hairs out of Texas's tail. By the time Bill and Texas arrived, the legendary warhorse had no tail hair left. Upon seeing his horse, Roosevelt said with his usual flair, "Bully! But he surely doesn't look natural."[39]

Roosevelt was quick to capitalize on his military success. He was a hero in the eyes of his men and the citizens of New York. The Republican Party was quick to nominate him for the candidacy for governor of that state. Roosevelt had earned the respect of his men, who were all too eager to help him in any way. At first, he was willing to surround himself with his Rough Riders, but that was seen as overdoing it a little. He narrowed his veteran entourage to only four troopers. Surprisingly, two of them were from Oklahoma.

McGinnis did not return home immediately. He had impressed Roosevelt enough for the colonel to invite him to help on his Republican campaign for the governorship of New York. Mac initially sent his prized horse back home under the entrusted escort of a black man, Mr. Smith from North Carolina. Smith also delivered a dagger as a gift to Mac's barber, Will Fogg, who proudly hung it up for every customer to see. Mac returned home on October 8, only for a short visit, then rejoined the side of his colonel. He talked about witnessing Wheeler's decision to defend San Juan Hill after Shafter ordered it evacuated.[40] If the Rough Riders had not been Republicans before the war, most, like the former Populist McGinnis, became so after.

The wounded Starr Wetmore also joined the election campaign for his beloved commander. Ambling around on crutches, he presented a visible reminder of the sacrifices of the military campaign.

In celebration, many Rough Riders hung around New York City until their pay ran out, and that would have been a long time. People still paid for their food and drinks. Some hotels refused to accept their money for the rooms. Over time some managed to become penniless, without funds to get home. Albert Wright hunted down Rynning to ask where he could find Roosevelt. Rynning told his former color sergeant, and off they went to the Fifth Avenue Hotel while Wright explained to Rynning the problem. Roosevelt was busy with members of his Republican Party and campaign advisors planning his run for election as governor of New York. Rynning asked one of the guards if he could see Roosevelt. The man said he was busy, and no one could see him. Rynning felt otherwise and waited in the lobby. Finally, Roosevelt came out talking to another, hammering one fist in the other. Rynning spoke up, "Can we speak to you a minute, Colonel?" Roosevelt barked, "Certainly!"[41]

Roosevelt on Little Texas at Montauk Point (Library of Congress).

Rynning explained that about 35 of his former Rough Riders were flat broke in New York City with no way home. Roosevelt asked Wright if he had a list of their names. Wright acknowledged that he had and handed him the list, which showed where they lived and how much money it would cost to buy their tickets. Roosevelt sat down and wrote out a check. He handed it to Rynning with instructions to purchase the tickets and give each man $5 once he was on the train. Roosevelt would for the rest of his life take care of and come to the rescue of his men. He would always be their colonel. He wrote in his book that most of his men were too proud to accept help or money, even when they desperately needed it. Rynning mentioned that when he explained to them that Roosevelt had bought their tickets and given them each a $5 gold piece for travel money, they asked for it then and there. Judging by the wild looks in their eyes, Rynning felt it better to wait until they were loaded on the train bound for home.

Still lingering in New York, Tom Rynning was sitting at the bar of Hoffman House drinking with Alex Brodie when Tom Hall walked in and called Rynning to one side. "I want you to second me in a duel." Rynning began to laugh, "Hell, you don't want to fight any duels. Who are you going to shoot with?" Hall told him that Richard Harding Davis had slandered him in a story he had written, and Hall meant business. Rynning realized that Hall had that determined, hostile look, so he answered, "Hell, yes; I'll be your second. Where'll I find Davis?" Hall did not know, so Rynning assured the former adjutant that he would find him.[42]

Rynning returned to the bar and told Brodie about it. Alex laughed in his own quiet way and said it was a good idea. Hall might actually do all right in a "two-man battle." Rynning left the bar and called on the studio of the artist Chandler Christy, who was a close friend of "Dicky" Davis.

Pretty soon, Rynning found Davis, who had already learned of the challenge. Dicky was a tough war correspondent and ready for any kind of a duel from fists to six-shooters. He accepted and would have Ferguson as his second. They set the time of the duel for early the next morning at Montauk Point. The participants would go out there that night. They even arranged for a few New York surgeons to attend.

Back at the bar, Brodie and Rynning then discussed the subject of dueling between drinks. Evidently Brodie had served as a second on one or two duels while he was in the army. Although dueling had been outlawed in the United States back in 1859, it was still practiced in the territories of the West and Southwest. Brodie explained the rules on how to protect his principal from fouls or bad decisions. He also warned that the most important part of the second's job was to stand well out of the way of fire in the event the opponent began to fire wildly by pulling heavily on the trigger.

As they drank and discussed it more, Brodie suggested they ought to be sober for the duel, but, as the evening progressed, he concluded that it was not necessary. Brodie, however, warned Rynning not to discount Hall. He had heard that men who had shown the white feather in battle showed greater courage on the field of honor when facing only one man. While they speculated on how Hall might do, Rynning received a message from the police commissioner.

Tom reported to the commissioner, who explained that he had heard about the Davis-Hall duel, and there would be no duel at Montauk Point or anywhere else in his state. Rynning tried to explain that it was a matter of honor and everything was in order with seconds and surgeons, even though dueling was against the law. The police commissioner would not relent. Tom had to give in to the commissioner's superior numbers. He had the entire police force at his disposal. Rynning could not help but wonder, with all the participants sworn to secrecy, whether possibly Hall had tipped off the police after he changed his mind.

Roosevelt won the election in November, and the remaining Rough Riders celebrated their last great victory together. Afterwards the last of them trickled back home. The men had used up their ten-plus days of hero worship and then had to go back to rebuild their lives.

Col. Roosevelt portrait photograph showing the final version of his campaign hat (Library of Congress).

Chapter 10

After the War

War becomes a significant emotional event in the lives of those who personally experience it. It steals away men's youth (and now women's) and profoundly changes them. All who take part in battle must confront their fear and discover their true mettle. Each, however, possesses different tolerances for fear. Those with low tolerances may carry the emotional scars of the experience that haunt them in their sleep, while those on the other extreme with higher tolerances find the adrenaline rush of combat exhilarating and addictive. The thrill of danger motives some to even continue to follow the drum of war. Likewise, a number of Rough Riders changed their life trajectory to become professional soldiers. Even among those who do not make the military a profession, the sound of the drum announcing the next war stirs in some a sense of longing to return to that experience that defined them during their youth. For many of them will never again participate, in however so small a way, in an event of history so great.

But veterans also realize that skill, intelligence or toughness often has little to do with who lives or dies. There are just too many indiscriminate factors involved, namely bullets and shrapnel flying around. Those fortunate enough to survive live with a guilt over why they lived and better men did not. The experience humbles men. It strips away all social or racial distinction and makes them realize who they really are and what is truly important in life, family and close friends. The kind who will risk their lives to save yours.

War also brings out the greatest of human virtues: discipline, selfless sacrifice and brotherly love. While nearly all veterans experience this, the Rough Riders experienced something special. They had an élan unlike any other unit. They belonged to the most celebrated regiment in the war. This gave each man who bore the name Rough Rider an advantage in starting his new life and picking up where he had left off. What happened to the Rough Riders who served in the three troops from the Twin Territories provides a sampling of what happened to those from the other territories.

The war would continue to claim casualties long after it had ended. Joseph Carr finally died of his wounds on November 29, 1901, and was laid to rest with full military honors in Arlington Cemetery. Disease often proved more fatal than bullets as most veterans suffered the long-term effects of malaria throughout the rest of their lives.

Hall was a writer before the war and had participated in the great adventure, although not so favorably. Nonetheless, he had been an eyewitness to a story that had captured the interest of the nation. It was only logical that he would write his own version of service in the First U.S. Volunteer Cavalry. The next year, Frederick A. Stokes Company published Hall's *The Fun and Fighting of the Rough Riders*. However, Thomas Hall died of sunstroke in Hannibal, Missouri, on August 2, 1900. His body was transferred to Chicago for burial. Other Rough Riders would die of sickness within a few years of their discharge.

On William Pollock's return from New York, he stopped by the Haskell Institute where he was treated to a large reception. The Pawnee Nation similarly honored him as a warrior returning from the battle. The Native American culture was a warrior culture. A friend presented him with a pony. It was tradition for fellow warriors to give a warrior a new name upon his initiation into battle. As no Pawnee had witnessed his feats and since he had adopted white ways, William decided to keep the same Pawnee name. Not long after his return, William "Buffalo Bill" Cody signed him up in January 1899 for his Wild West show, but Pollock died of pneumonia on March 2, 1899. He was buried with full military honors instead of the Pawnee tradition of slaying his favorite horse over his grave. While disease would claim more lives, most would recover.

Those first wounded Rough Riders to arrive at New York, not suspected of having yellow fever, were granted up to 60 days' furlough to visit home. The returning sick aboard the *Miami* were also given liberal medical furloughs in September. These were the first to return home.

Tom Holmes's wound had healed quickly, so he returned to Newkirk on Sunday night, August 14. As he was the first Rough Rider to return, no one expected his arrival. As the lone Rough Rider, he had to feed the folks' appetite for tales of the heroism of his friends, Roosevelt and the colored cavalrymen. Like many of the veterans, he was reluctant to speak of his own experiences. Family and friends also flocked to hear any word they could about their loved ones.

Most of all, the Wetmores sought anyone with knowledge about the condition of their wounded son, Starr. His mother was nearly sick with worry. Tom knew nothing. Even though both had been hospitalized together, he had lost contact with Starr after he left Cuba. Starr, the most seriously wounded, was the biggest concern of Oklahoma citizens. The Wetmores had written every Rough Rider they knew, but none knew anything about their son after he was evacuated back to Siboney.

From then on, the press and the local citizens waited at the depot every time a train came through, looking for returning Rough Riders. The Rough Riders, however, did not return to Oklahoma with the same fanfare that had sent them off. Because of the medical furloughs, they essentially trickled back home in ones and twos. A train would pull in and off stepped a man in a khaki uniform. Most who had served in Cuba looked emaciated, pale of skin and showed signs of ill health. From D Troop, First Sergeant Palmer, Sergeants Webb and Reay, Privates Albert Thomas, Ed Wright, Clare Stewart, Francis Byrne, William A. Faulk, Walter Cook, Dick Shanafelt, Dick Amrine, and Clerk Johnson returned early. Only about a third of the remainder of the Rough Riders were fit for duty. A deathly ill Milt Haynes remained in the hospital in New York.

When Corporal David McClure returned to Oklahoma City, he told everyone that he was glad he was wounded in battle. His wound just above the left knee did not disable him but fortunately got him out of Cuba before the outbreak of malaria. When granted a medical furlough, he headed for home. Like the others, he was hounded for stories of his experiences in Cuba and battle.

On Monday night, August 15, William Bailey passed through Guthrie on his way south to Norman. Having been wounded in the foot at San Juan Hill, he had received several letters from Starr Wetmore's mother inquiring about her son. He told everyone that Starr was recovering very well in a New York hospital.

The long, dreadful suspense was more than the parents and friends of Starr Wetmore could stand. The Knights of Pythias Lodge in Newkirk wrote to President McKinley, Colonel Roosevelt and anyone else that they thought could provide them an answer. On September 13, they received the good news. Their son had left Cuba for New York on the third of September on the transport *Missouri* and arrived on the 10th. Unfortunately, the seriousness of his wound did not permit the hospital to release him for several more weeks.

Meanwhile, a very thin and gaunt Charley Hunter returned to Enid Tuesday night, August 23. He still had enthusiasm about the adventure that he had nearly missed on account of his height and had the souvenirs to prove it. A similarly emaciated Clare Stewart arrived in Pawnee on August 31. Alexander Denham hobbled off of the train in his hometown of Oklahoma City with the help of crutches in early September.

A thinner O.G. Palmer returned first to Jewell, Kansas, to see his newborn son. However, he had no job to support his increased family. The war had ended quickly. His old job belonged to another. By July, the Ponca City School Board had appointed Professor L.E. Eddy to fill Palmer's vacant superintendent position. With the beginning of the new school year, all education positions had been filled. Fortunately, the Republican Party sought him as their nominee for Kay County Superintendent. He filed his candidacy as soon as he arrived at Camp Wikoff. Palmer returned to Ponca City on Monday, September 5, to campaign for office. He easily won the Republican nomination on the first ballot, 76 to 54, on September 10 but would have to wait until November for the results of the Kay County election.

Governor Barnes was proud of his Oklahoma veterans. On September 15, he invited Palmer and Holmes to join him on a visit to the Trans-Mississippi Exposition in Omaha, Missouri. The khaki-clad veterans of this famed regiment made a smart-looking escort. After their return, Palmer went back to Kansas for a couple of weeks.

The Oklahoma volunteers received their discharges on September 14. They had enlisted, fought a war and returned home in less than five months. Those on furloughs did not get their discharges right away. Ira Hill and Frank Weitzel returned to Newkirk on Saturday, September 17, with their discharges in hand. Ira Hill had dropped in on Starr the night before he left to see how his comrade from Newkirk was doing. Starr informed him that he was healing but feared that he would be slightly lame in that left leg for the rest of his life. If Kay County represented a sampling of what the boys from Oklahoma did, few hung around for prolonged festivities in New York. They wanted to get back to their families and businesses.

It probably did not take them as long to use up their ten days of hero worship among their old companions. The older veterans picked up where they had left off, but most would move on. Much of the attention had been drawn from their service by those Oklahomans still on active duty.

Since the Rough Riders had enlisted in the National Guard before joining the Rough Riders, the governor freed them from their obligations to the territory. None returned to the National Guard. There was no point. For many, service in the militia or National Guard during a time of peace was a substitute for going to war. Others joined just in time to go to war. Once having become veterans they had no more reason to continue their service in the state militia. These men had been the first men bearing the name of Oklahoma in battle. They won honor for their territory, which unfortunately became lost by the militia organization they hoped to honor.

The Oklahoma Territory had felt slighted when it was only called upon only to produce a single troop during the first call for volunteers for the war with Spain. Right after the Rough Riders were mustered in May, Governor Barnes personally visited Secretary of War Alger with an updated census to request a fairer consideration for the next call-up. He received his wish. In June, he learned that Oklahoma Territory would provide a full battalion of four companies for the First Regiment of Territorial Volunteer Infantry. Similarly recruited from Arizona, New Mexico, Oklahoma and the Indian Territory, this regiment became known as the "Big Four."

Governor Barnes again reserved the right to appoint officers instead of allowing elections. After the first call-up, ambitious citizens flooded Barnes's desk with requests to fill the three officer vacancies. Ten asked to replace Huston as the colonel with the promise to raise a regiment. Barnes appointed Assistant Attorney General John F. Stone, of Guthrie, as the major in command of the "Oklahoma Battalion." Forty-five applied for the captain vacancies, each promising to recruit a company in ten days. Armed with many more vacancies than before, Barnes had a greater quality of applicants to select from other than just those dedicated Oklahoma National Guard officers who had built the organization. He gave command of three of the companies to politically influential men.

The governor appointed his son Harry C. Barnes captain of Company I. Fortunately, his other son attended the Naval Academy. Roy V. Hoffman, founder of the *Guthrie Daily Leader* and lawyer, was appointed captain of Company K. Robert Lowry, attorney and member of the board of regents of the A and M College at Stillwater, assumed command of Company L. Captain Fred Boynton, of Kingfisher, was the only National Guard officer to receive a command in that call-up. With one exception, Guard officers filled all the lieutenant positions in the four companies. Captain Charles Barrett, of Shawnee, became the First Sergeant of Hoffman's Company K. The Indian Territory only provided one company this time, and Governor Barnes received permission to appoint Earl Edmundson as its captain. The war brought out a sense of patriotism in leading citizens of the territory, which more importantly would have a lasting effect on the future of the Oklahoma National Guard.

Recruiting began on June 27, 1898, with headquarters at four different locations: Barnes's company recruited from Guthrie, Hoffman's from Chandler, Lowry's from Stillwater and Boynton's from Kingfisher. The lieutenants then recruited men from their own militia companies and surrounding towns. Afterwards they took their recruits to their headquarters for physical examinations and mustering. Each infantry company was limited to 106 enlisted men, yet the officers found plenty more than that ready for service. Former Adjutant General Jamison came out of retirement one more time to assist Hoffman in this endeavor since he had no previous military service.

The recruiting and mustering took weeks, and the battalion was completed by July 15. When mustered into federal service, the companies rendezvoused at Fort Reno, where they began training. They cheered when they heard the accomplishments of the Oklahoma Rough Riders' victory in the battle in Cuba. Yet they secretly feared that the war would end before they could see action, and their fears increased when, on July 17, Toral surrendered Santiago.

They then transferred to Camp Hamilton near Lexington, Kentucky, on September 23, 1898, to rendezvous with the rest of the regiment and continue their training. They thought they might still see action in Puerto Rico. General Nelson Miles, however, took the island with minimal fighting. The news of the armistice, however, took much of the enthusiasm out of these infantry men. The Oklahoma Battalion then transferred to Camp Churchman, near Albany, Georgia, in late autumn, where they heard rumors that they might go instead to the Philippines. That did not happen either. The training period seemed uneventful, and it became clear that they were going nowhere.

The Oklahoma infantry finally received word that they would be mustered out on February 13, 1899. As mentioned, the Oklahomans in the volunteer cavalry had been released by the governor from their military obligations from the territory. The recruiting of the Oklahoma Battalion had unfortunately stripped the Oklahoma National Guard. While they were discharged from federal service, Governor Barnes chose not to release all of them from their obligation to the territory. Lowry was one to muster out and started a law practice in Stillwater with his First Sergeant, Jerome Workman.

While the men in this second mobilization may not have earned battle honors, upon their shoulders fell the responsibility to rebuild the Oklahoma National Guard. Unlike the cavalry volunteers, these infantry men had undergone seven continuous months of military training and discipline. This experience would prove more valuable than anything previous Guard officers had before. From the Oklahoma Battalion of the Big Four came a cadre of officers who rebuilt the Oklahoma National Guard. Again, Barnes had chosen well.

Major John F. Stone became the colonel of the reorganized First Oklahoma Infantry Regiment. He served as its colonel until his untimely death in 1900. Captain Roy Hoffman initially became the lieutenant colonel and followed Stone as the colonel of the regiment. These returning officers created a new efficiency and morale with the new regiment. A renewed awareness of the importance of the Guard in national policy and territorial prestige increased legislative appropriations and modernization with federal equipment.

Hoffman secured $4,000 to fund the first encampment of the new regiment. He skillfully resolved the Crazy Snake Rebellion without the use of arms. He commanded the regiment when it was activated into federal service for the Mexican Border War in 1916. On August 5, 1917, Hoffman became the first National Guard colonel promoted to brigadier general during World War I and commanded the Ninety-Third Division in France. After the war, he commanded the Ninety-Fifth Reserve Division until he assumed command of the Forty-Fifth Infantry Division (Oklahoma National Guard) in 1931. He commanded this division until his retirement June 13, 1933.

Hoffman's First Sergeant, Charles Barrett, and Lieutenant Jake Switzer returned to command the two battalions. Barrett served on through World War I and was instrumental in the reorganization of the Second and Third Regiments, which later became the 179th and 180th infantries after the war. He rose to colonel of the 179th Infantry Regiment, and on two occasions served as the Oklahoma adjutant general on the outset of the Second World War. Barrett had the longest and most distinguished military career of any officer in the Oklahoma National Guard.

Probably the most instrumental man in the creation of a professional Oklahoma National Guard organization and getting it ready for war was James Jamison. After having served his new territory one last time in getting it ready for the Spanish–American War, he finally retired to the life of a country gentleman on his farm. Aside from his contributions to Missouri and Oklahoma, his great adventure was in Nicaragua. He wrote and published a book on his experience in *With Walker in Nicaragua* in 1909. In

1911, the last three survivors of Walker's first expedition held their annual reunion in California. Jamison died in Guthrie on November 19, 1916, the last surviving member of Walker's American Phalanx.

Upon the foundation lain by men like Huston, Jamison and Stiles, the latecomers built a new and professional National Guard that would serve its nation well during other wars. Unfortunately, in their effort to rebuild the Oklahoma National Guard, they overlooked the service of the one company of men to see action in the war with Spain. The new Guard started over, only drawing their lineage from the company recruited in 1890. Since D Troop had been recruited from the National Guard, they could have claimed its battle honors, but for some reason they did not. While Governor Barnes had stacked the deck in favor of that company of men and reminded them of their place in Oklahoma history, the Oklahoma National Guard quickly forgot. Those who had lost loved ones did not.

Almost immediately after the war, citizens of Hennessey began to raise money for a monument for the first Oklahoma soldier killed in combat. Civic organizations raised donations, and many sold buttons with Roy Cashion's picture on them for 25 cents. They raised a total of $800. The 1899 Oklahoma Legislation subsequently passed the Roy Cashion Bill appropriating another $1,200 for the monument, bringing the total to $2,000. Governor Barnes signed the bill in March. In April 1902, S.H. Miller of Oklahoma City won the contract with a bid of $1,950 to erect a monument of Bedford stone. They delivered the monument to Hennessey in September, where it was formally presented and dedicated in the Memorial Park on May 30, 1903. Oklahoma also honored its two fallen heroes, Roy Cashion and Allyn Capron, by naming new towns after them. Cashion was incorporated in 1900.

Frank S. Cashion made several trips to Cuba to find his son's grave but with little luck since Roy's comrades had failed to properly mark it. In 1902, Henry Love, who was fighting in the Philippines, wrote Frank detailing the exact location where the body was buried. This time, Frank successfully located the remains and brought his son's corpse back. Cashion's body lay in state from January 27–30, 1903, when it was buried in the family plot.

Pawnee also erected a stone obelisk to honor its eight volunteers to the Rough Riders. Since Palmer had enlisted with their quota, they inscribed his name on the stone, which was placed in their cemetery. Muskogee constructed a historical marker to remind the local citizens where the Indian Territory volunteers had mustered in. The city later relocated it to their local military museum.

Roosevelt was right; most of the citizens quickly forgot about the war, and the Rough Riders had to work hard from then on for anything they wanted. Their old colonel would always come to their aid. For those who hoped to benefit from their service in politics, none did any better than Theodore Roosevelt. In November 1898, he won the election for New York's governorship. Two years later, the New York Republican Party encouraged him to run for vice president on the William McKinley ticket. They won the 1900 election.

An assassin's bullet ended McKinley's life on September 6, 1901, and propelled Roosevelt into the presidency. Roosevelt continued the American tradition, since General George Washington, that the nation would reward its military hero with the presidency. Roosevelt ran for office in 1904 and again won. In his last two years in office, he began handing out political appointments to many of his old Rough Riders. Nearly anyone with political ambition benefited. At the 1905 Rough Rider reunion, President Roosevelt asked Dick Shanafelt, "Well now Shanafelt, is there anything I can do for you." To the president's surprise, Dick answered, "No, unless you want to make me vice president or something." Roosevelt chose not to run a second time, feeling that he had achieved his political goals in two terms. He later ran again in 1912 but failed to win the Republican nomination. So, he formed his own "Bull Moose Party" and ran as an independent. Roosevelt lost the election, but his party won more votes than the Republican Party candidate. The rest of his life has been well chronicled by other historians. There is little need to recount his achievements other than how his life was forever intertwined with those of his men.

Some of the Rough Riders in Arizona and New Mexico did very well in political life. Most of those Oklahomans who had political ambitions were sorely disappointed, however. While nearly everyone of the previous generation had either served or been affected by the Civil War, the Spanish–American War was a much smaller affair. Those patriots who participated were few in comparison with those who had not. Their personal sacrifice when the nation called was easily forgotten even by the early history books of the state. Their biggest problem was that they were Republicans in a territory that favored Democrats in local elections. Few Rough Riders in Oklahoma rose to great heights in office without help.

Palmer was not so lucky at the polls in November 1898 as Kay County had failed to reward his patriotic sacrifice. He lost in a close election, 1421 to 1576. With no job prospects until the next school year, he called for help, and Governor Barnes came to Palmer's rescue again. Although on his own way out of office, Barnes appointed Orlando as the chief clerk of the territorial legislation in January 1899. Orlando also became a professor of history and physics at the Oklahoma University. This would keep him occupied for a while.

Among Roosevelt's political favors to former Rough Riders, he appointed Major Alex Brodie as territorial governor of Arizona in 1902, who served until 1905. Roosevelt clearly favored Frank Frantz though.

After the war, Frank had gone west but finally returned to Enid in 1900. On April 9, 1901, he married Matilda Evans, and they would have five children. President Roosevelt first appointed him to the position of postmaster in Enid. In 1904, Roosevelt then appointed him the Osage agent to clean up rampant corruption. After this success, Roosevelt appointed Frantz the last territorial governor of Oklahoma Territory in January 1906. Oklahoma gained statehood in November 1907, ahead of Arizona and New Mexico.

Frank was unfortunately defeated in the 1907 election to be first state governor, the result of political infighting. Oklahoma would for many decades never reelect a governor for a second term. Disillusioned, Frank left the state for Colorado and entered into the oil business. In 1915, he moved to Tulsa, Oklahoma, to head the land department of the Cosden Oil Company. Frank returned to politics but was defeated in his 1932 run for Congress. That same year the Oklahoma Memorial Association voted him into the Oklahoma Hall of Fame. His citation for gallantry by Roosevelt was converted to the Silver Star Medal when the medal was first authorized in 1935. Frank became the director of the Investors Royalty Company in 1940; then he died on March 8, 1941. The few surviving Oklahoma Rough Riders—Chris Madsen, Bill McGinty and Tom Meagher—attended the funeral.

Republican Ira Hill did not win his election either. He made an unsuccessful bid for the Kay County attorney. Yet, with a little help, his political career did better than most of his other Oklahoma comrades in arms. He married Laura Coleman Hill the year after he returned from the war and had two sons and three daughters. On April 14, 1906, Governor Frank Frantz appointed Ira as the county clerk of the Sixth District Federal Court under Judge Pancoast. Ira served as the county clerk of Alva until Oklahoma became a state in 1907. That year he moved to Cherokee to become the first president of the Alfalfa County National Bank, yet he still continued to practice law. He suffered a singular defeat in his bid for city attorney of Alfalfa County in 1925. Ira resigned his position from the bank during the Depression since he did not want to foreclose loans. In 1930, the Republicans nominated him for governor of Oklahoma. Ira was seen as a leader sympathetic to the plight of his fellow man. He won the most votes of any Republican up to that time but unfortunately lost to William "Alfalfa Bill" Murray, who coincidentally had the largest Democrat turnout in history. Ira then continued to serve his fellow man in other offices. He served as the mayor for 12 years and the state senator for eight years. His family had two girls, but both sons died while young. He also remained lifelong friends with fellow Rough Rider Frank Knox of New York. Ira died in 1941, proving that at least one veteran did very well with local elections.

Milt Haynes did not return from New York until November. He worked in real estate in Pittsburg, Pennsylvania, for four years, then tried his hand at prospecting in Venezuela. In 1904, he returned to Lawton, Oklahoma, where he entered politics. In 1906, he was elected county treasurer. He then served as the county clerk and as commissioner of finance, then moved back to Newkirk where he served as city and state auditor until he retired. He died at the age of 75 on November 13, 1946.

Schuyler McGinnis returned to practice law in Newkirk and had two more children. He became promoter of a fabulous timber proposition in Mexico where he proposed to sell the timber from a newly discovered island in the Pacific to the government for construction of the Panama Canal. He even made a trip or two to Washington in the interest of the proposition. The isle was never exploited, and the timber was never unloaded on the government for the Panama Canal.

When Roosevelt was handing out appointments, McGinnis received an appointment to the Dawes Commission in February 1906. For 18 months he helped transfer tribal lands in the Five Civilized Tribes to individual allotments. He continued to practice law in the state and became the attorney for Oklahoma City. His brother, Walter F. McGinnis, however, was speculating for oil around Greenwood County, Kansas, buying up oil leases, and in the fall of 1915, oil was finally discovered on one of them, then on others. In the summer of 1916, Schuyler moved to Eureka, Kansas, to join in his brother's fortune. He and his brother invested with the Hastings Brothers, of New York City, in a large block of Greenwood County land to prospect for oil. A few months later the 49-year-old Schuyler married Mrs. Dot Wiershing, of Eureka, and they had one daughter. On a Thursday afternoon in June 1917, Captain McGinnis was stricken with uremic poisoning at his home and died Friday morning at 2 a.m. on June 15.

In 1899, "Buffalo Bill" Cody's publicist, John Burke, recruited 16 Rough Riders for a Roosevelt Rough Riders act in his Wild West show. For some reason, he recruited primarily from the Oklahoma Territory. Former Color Sergeant George Webb served as the sergeant of the troop with broncobuster Bill McGinty as the color bearer. Buffalo

Bill also recruited Tom Holmes, Marcellus Newcomb, Fred Beal, Walter Cook, Volney Miller, Ed Loughmiller, Peter Byrne, R. Ben Miller, Henry Meagher and Lorrin Muxlow from Oklahoma. Tom Isbell, famous for firing the first shot at Las Guasimas, joined them from the Indian Territory, while Jess Langdon joined from North Dakota and John Tait joined from New Mexico. The "Battle of San Juan Hill" replaced "Custer's Last Stand" as the grand heroic spectacle in 1899 and 1900 only to be replaced by the Chinese Boxer Rebellion the next year. This troop continued to perform for several more years.

Rough Rider at Buffalo Bill's Wild West Show (Library of Congress).

Bill McGinty left the show in 1901 and returned to Oklahoma where he married Mollie in the fall of 1902. They moved to Day County, Indian Territory, to homestead a ranch they called "The Crossed Sabers Ranch." The ranch was not profitable on account of cattle diseases and droughts, so the McGintys returned to Ingalls in 1905. In 1912, he went back East to help his old regimental commander form his "Bull Moose Party" for an independent run for the presidency. The McGintys then settled in Ripley a few years later. In Payne County they raised three boys. He formed the Billy McGinty Cowboy Band and played on radio stations. In 1954, four years after David Goodrich had died, Bill was elected President for Life of the Rough Rider Association.

Tom Hornet and Bill McGinty (Theodore Roosevelt Collection, Harvard University Library).

Some Rough Riders sought to continue that adrenaline rush in law enforcement. Lorrin Muxlow joined the Guthrie Police Force but was killed in the line of duty by Lou Green, a local bootlegger, on September 8, 1913. Scott Reay became a deputy sheriff in Newkirk in 1900 then moved to Ceiling, Oklahoma, and finally Napa, Idaho. After Roosevelt appointed Brodie the Governor of the Territory of Arizona, Brodie appointed Tom Rynning to captain of the Arizona Rangers. He helped clean up the territory of outlaws and served as the warden of the Arizona State Prison. He followed an illustrious career in law enforcement at the end of the Old West, as many had known it. But the birth of professional lawmen of the West can be attributed to the "Three Guardsmen" of the Indian Territory.

The 46-year-old Chris Madsen returned to El Reno in broken health. Upon his recovery, he returned to law enforcement. In 1903, he helped round up a gambling ring in Chickasaw. On one occasion, he and another constable broke up the furnishings of a gambling establishment, piled the debris in the middle of the road and set fire to it. In August that year, he shot and killed Elbert Gray after he resisted arrest.

When President Roosevelt handed out appointments in Oklahoma in 1906, he appointed a friend of his, John Abernathy, as Marshal of the Western District of Oklahoma. John picked Madsen as his chief deputy. However, Chris seemed more qualified for the job than John,

Elderly Chris Madsen in his uniform with veteran medals and marksmanship badges (courtesy Western History Collections, University of Oklahoma Libraries, Ferguson 358).

as it appeared that Chris did most of the work. In December 1910, the Justice Department called Abernathy back to Washington to answer charges, but he resigned before he learned what they were.

Chris took over as the marshal for three months until another appointee took over the post. The justice, however, held Chris accountable for all the unpaid debts and missing equipment and withheld his salary until he balanced the accounts. A 64-year-old Madsen finally retired from law enforcement in 1916. Prior to the "Three Guardsmen," there were few career lawmen in the territories. Sheriffs were elected and marshals were appointed. In a time of lawlessness, many who lived by the gun often switched sides of the law. Men like Madsen were rare.

Prior to the Social Security Act, there were few options for retirement. Those with good-paying jobs could put money aside for their "Golden Years." The vast majority would have to move in with their children. Those who had served their nation in war could draw a meager veteran's pension when they physically could no longer work.

The Director of Pensions, like its successor, the Department of Veterans Affairs, had a limited budget to take care of old veterans. On occasions the rules for disability would change, and the veterans would have to justify their claims all over. Chris Madsen, a veteran of both the Indian Wars and Spanish–American War, qualified for either pension. However, in 1933, the Director of Pensions decided to pay him the lesser of the two. Chris appealed the decision with his usual wit and humor.

> Sir, I respectfully request information as to the method of making appeal from your decision, fixing the rate of my pension for participation in the Spanish American War at $20.00 per month, in place of $60.00 per month heretofore received.
>
> I understand that boards will be appointed to review the appealed ones, and that the evidence submitted by me, which did not reach your office in time to be considered before you made your decision, will be available for this board.
>
> However, I beg to call your attention to the fact that I am entitled to the Indian War Pension of $50.00 per month, as per certificate No. 8363, and that instead of giving me credit for such former service in rendering your decision, you penalized me $30.00 per month for participating in the Spanish American War, regardless of whether I was disabled or not.
>
> Thank God, I am too old and feeble to go to any more wars, or I might get into another one and lose the balance of the pension. Respectfully, Christian Madsen.[1]

In 1940, the state in which he had helped clean out of outlaws honored him by inducting him into the Oklahoma Memorial Association Hall of Fame. He died in January 1944 and was laid to rest next to the grave of his wife. The majority of the Rough Riders from Oklahoma followed the paths they had started before the war.

Starr Wetmore returned to Newkirk on December 29, 1898, and married Leota Lorena Balcom from Arkansas City, Kansas, in 1899. He moved to Arkansas City where he opened the Mammoth Racket Department Store. Evidently, he recovered better than he had expected as his children said he did not even walk with a limp; he just needed an extra half an inch added to the heel of his shoe. He eventually became a construction contractor and built a few of the houses in the Sleeth Addition and later opened the Starr Theater. Like many veterans, Starr shunned talking about his experiences in the war. Leota died February 17, 1941, and Starr died at the ripe old age of 93, on November 5, 1965, in the Veterans Hospital in Houston, Texas, near where his children lived.

After Will Tauer returned to Ponca City on September 26, 1898, oil was discovered on his family's property, and they climbed up the social ladder. Will later moved to Mountain Park, Oklahoma, and finally to Houston, Texas. Elisha Freeman moved to Peggs, Indian Territory, after the war to farm and marry. He had four children and retired a farmer. After his wife died, he moved back to Kaw, near Newkirk, to live with his daughter, where at the age of 73 he died of a heart attack on September 26, 1953.

Dick Amrine recovered from malaria and started his business over again. He was quick to capitalize on his fame, and, in January 1899, Dick Amrine reopened his restaurant under a new name, "The Rough Rider Restaurant and Bakery." A decade later he sold his business to Fred Hebieson and moved to Los Angeles, California. That state attracted a number of Rough Riders like Tom Isbell, who retired in San Diego.

In 1904, Paul Hunter moved to Korbel, California, where he married Verna H. Ring that same year. They then settled in Fortuna in 1912, where Paul became politically active, becoming a campaign manager for Clarence F. Lea in his run for Congress in 1918. In 1934, Paul was appointed the postmaster and served in that post until 1948. He also served as commander of the local Veterans of Foreign War post and was one of the original sponsors of Save the Redwoods League in his area. He died at the Redwood Memorial Hospital on the morning of August 28, 1959.

While the veterans of Kettle Hill may not have returned to the National Guard, many continued to wear the army blue. The experience of war had changed the lives of some in an unusual way. Many signed up for the Regular Army. Cadet Earnest Haskell's wound prevented him from graduating with his West Point class of 1900. It, however, did not prevent him from serving as an officer. Roosevelt kept the promise he had made that hot day at the base of Kettle Hill. Immediately upon his discharge from the Military Academy in April 1899, Haskell received a commission as a second lieutenant in the Twenty-First Infantry with which he saw action during the Philippine Insurrection. He later became the distinguished graduate of the School of the Line at Fort Leavenworth, Kansas, and also graduated from the Army Staff College in 1912. He was twice selected to teach at the School of the Line from 1913 to 1915. During World War I, he served as a major in the Twenty-Seventh Infantry, which deployed to Siberia and earned the nickname the "Wolfhounds." He retired after 30 years of service with the rank of colonel. Despite his successful military career, his little adventure that summer in 1898 ruined the chances of future cadets going off to war during their summer vacations.

William S. Simpson, from Dallas, Texas, was the first veteran from D Troop to pick up a commission in the Regular Army. He became a lieutenant on September 3, 1889, before his Rough Rider Regiment was disbanded. They would have to wait until they graduated to get wounded in battle.

Rob Huston enjoyed the army and wanted to become a professional soldier. He received the commission as paymaster officer of Volunteers with the rank of major and remained in that position until June 1899. Volunteer ranks, like the volunteer organizations, were temporary. Regular Army commissions were permanent yet hard to get until Congress authorized its expansion of the army in 1899. Huston applied for and received a commission as captain in the Regular Army. In the fall, he joined the Forty-Seventh Infantry Regiment and shipped out to the Philippine Islands in November that year, again leaving his wife and son behind. He fought in all the actions with his regiment but fell ill with typhoid fever. He died on July 6, 1900, having served less than a year in the Philippines, and his body was sent back to Ohio for burial. His wife, who always appeared helpless, turned out to be very tough when it came to fighting with the Veterans Affairs for her widow's pension from the government. Following in his father's footsteps, Rob's son would seek a military profession and join the U.S. Marine Corps where he retired as a colonel. Rob Huston was not the only Rough Rider from Oklahoma to take advantage of the expansion of the Regular Army in 1899 under the Army Reorganization Bill.

Rob Huston's mentor, Alex Brodie, also sought a Regular Army commission after the expiration of his term as the Arizona territorial governor. This time the old warhorse would not join to fight. Brodie joined the Adjutant General Office as a major on February 15, 1905. He made lieutenant colonel in June of that year and served in the Philippines as the military secretary. He returned to the United States in 1907 to serve as the adjutant general of the Department of the Dakotas. In 1911, he became the adjutant general of California and was promoted to colonel on August 24, 1912. He finally retired on his 64th birthday on November 13, 1913, where he settled in "Greensfield Hall" in Haddonfield, New Jersey, and he died on May 10, 1918.

The inspiration and training of Capron was not lost on his lieutenants, John R. Thomas and Richard Day. Rob Thomas was released on medical furlough and returned to Chicago with his family where they stayed in the home of his aunt. He applied for and received an appointment as first lieutenant in the Seventeenth Infantry on March 13, 1899. He served with that regiment during the Philippine Insurrection, and, by the outbreak of World War I in April 1917, he was a captain in the same regiment. He was then promoted to major in the expanding army with an assignment to the Fifty-Fifth Infantry but transferred to the National Army with the wartime rank of lieutenant colonel. The divisions of the National Army were made up of conscripts, which replaced the volunteer units of

Colonel Brodie greeting President Roosevelt (Library of Congress).

the previous wars. He rose to colonel and earned the Distinguished Service Medal during the war and later the Silver Star Medal for his previous citation for bravery at Las Guasimas. In 1920, he made the eligible list for the General Staff Corps with the promotion to the permanent rank of lieutenant colonel but transferred to the field artillery in 1923. He was finally selected for the General Staff Corps with an assignment as the assistant military attaché in Paris from 1923 to 1924. Rob then attended the Army War College in 1925. Actually, this was not the normal career path of a line officer. They preferred assignments with troop units and shunned schools as unnecessary distractions. They considered experience the best school. Rob retired as a colonel with over 30 years' service.

With the death of Capron and the wounding of Thomas at the Battle of Las Guasimas, Richard Day assumed command of L Troop. After the war, he also received a commission in the Regular Army and served in the Philippines where he became a captain in one of the California Volunteer Regiments. In 1900, Day commanded Headquarters Company of Funston's Scouts. Richard Stanton, from Phoenix, walked into the constabulary in Manila after his discharge from the Fourth Cavalry. He reported to Captain Day, who was in charge of the constabulary, and asked to be released from arrest. Day asked for the trooper's name, then checked the list. Unable to find Stanton's name, he asked where and when he had been placed under arrest. Stanton informed him, "Three and a half years ago while on the firing line at Las Guasimas, Cuba, you ordered me in arrest, and since I am going back to the United States, I'd like to return with a clean slate." Stanton had served in B Troop of the Rough Riders. They sat down for a long chat to reminisce about the old times.

Day also served as treasurer of a province near Manila, and during that time, $1,600 disappeared from his safe, which he had to reimburse. His friends raised $800, and former Rough Rider G.A. Price, who ran a gambling house in the Philippines, donated

LT.COL.ODE C.NICHOLS & 31ST INF. AT VLADIVOSTOK   4884-4

Lt. Col. Ode Nichols with the 31st Infantry at Vladivostok (Library of Congress).

another $800. This may have paid his debt but did not restore his honor. However, it was later revealed that a Filipino who had learned the safe combination stole the money. This cleared Day of any suspicion to his honor, but he died in the hospital in Manila in 1903 before friends could tell him of it.

From the Indian Territory's M Troop, Lieutenant Ode Nichols enlisted in the Thirty-Fourth Infantry, which did not see action in the Philippines either. He rose all the way to regimental sergeant major, then was commissioned to a second lieutenant in February 1900 and then accepted a Regular Army commission in the infantry in June 1901. Finally, during the Great War, it looked like he would see action. He rose to the rank of lieutenant colonel in the Thirty-First Infantry, which did not go to France but served in Siberia. Nichols retired a few years after the war.

Having missed the opportunity to prove his bravery in Cuba, Gordon Johnston, Roosevelt's last orderly, enlisted for service in the Philippines and received a commission in the Forty-Third Infantry on August 17, 1899. Although he had only served a short period with the Indian Territory troop, he would become the most decorated Rough Rider, if not soldier, in the Regular Army. On March 31, 1900, he received his first citation for gallantry in action against the Filipino insurgents at Dagami, Leyte. A month later he earned his second citation in an attack near La Paz. His earlier action in that campaign would 30 years later earn him the Distinguished Service Cross, the second highest award for bravery. In September 1903, he was reluctantly detailed as a first lieutenant to the Signal Corps but volunteered to fight with combat arms units wherever he could. While fighting with the cavalry, he received his third citation for bravery against the Moros in 1905. Two of these citations would later be converted to Silver Star Medals.

1st Lt. Gordon Johnston with the 7th Cavalry (Library of Congress).

In March 1906, he joined up with the Sixth Infantry for General Leonard Wood's attack on the Moro stronghold in the volcano crater, Bud Dajo. They advanced to the first trench line below the cotta, and, while waiting for the infantry to line up for the assault, Johnston asked Major Omar Bundy for permission to advance to the base of the cotta. He did this under fire from a Moro rifle pit to his left and was the first to reach the cotta. When the order was given to charge, he rose up and was severely wounded in the shoulder. For his actions, Bundy recommended him for and he received the nation's highest award, the Medal of Honor, on November 7, 1910.

While a captain in the Regular cavalry, he was made colonel of the Twelfth New York Volunteer Infantry during the Mexican Border Service in 1916. He made news when he resigned his commission in protest to Major General John O'Ryan's insult of making his regiment pass in review a second time. His officers attempted to follow his example, but the affair was smoothed over, and his commission was reinstated. When the Great War broke out in 1917, he rose to lieutenant colonel and chief of staff of the Eighty-Third Division, then he was promoted to colonel and chief of staff of the Seventh Army Corps. He later became chief of staff of the Seventh Division, then held the same duties in the Second Army in France. He served in the last months of the war in France.

He had earned all the Army's medals for valor, equaled only by men like Audie Murphy. In 1934, while serving at San Antonio, he was playing polo for the San Antonio Freebooters against the Air Corps team for the consolation cup. His horse tripped and fell, rolling over the colonel, crushing his head and chest. He died the next day. He was not the only Rough Rider to later receive the Medal of Honor. Assistant Surgeon James R. Church was belatedly nominated for and awarded the Medal of Honor for his actions at Las Guasimas in 1906, while Roosevelt was the president.

George McMurtry returned to Harvard and graduated in 1899, becoming a stockbroker and a member of the New York social elite, joining the Knickerbockers, Brook and the racquet and tennis clubs. When the Great War broke out, he served as a captain in the Seventy-Seventh Division, while his Rough Rider peers became field grade officers. He and Captain Charles Whittlesey commanded elements of the 307th and 308th Infantry Regiments and the 306th Machine Gun Battalion, which became cut off on the rain-soaked slopes at Charlevaux in the Argonne Forest. They held out while surrounded by a superior German force and under constant artillery barrage for five days in October 1918. McMurtry, although wounded by shrapnel in the knee on the first day, continued to move around, encouraging his officers and men to hold out. He was again wounded by a hand grenade two days later but continued to organize and direct the defense against German attacks. Of the 650 men in the "Lost Battalion" only 194 returned. He and Whittlesey received the Medals of Honor for their heroism and leadership.

Col. Gordon Johnston during World War I (Library of Congress).

After the war, McMurtry formed the Benjamin and McMurtry stockbrokers' firm and became the Director for the American Can Company. He died in New York in 1958.

Other D Troop veterans also continued to wear the army blue after the Spanish–American War. Dick Schanafelt enlisted in the Nineteenth Infantry where he served for two years in the Philippine Islands and one year at the Presidio of San Francisco. He returned to Perry after his enlistment in the Army and moved around Oklahoma, then settled in Lawrence, Kansas.

Clyde Stewart, however, enlisted in the Regular Army for the long haul. He served in the Philippines Insurrection, the Boxer Rebellion in China, the Mexican Border

Expedition and finally World War I. During the Great War, he was commissioned as a first lieutenant but returned to rank of first sergeant after the war. He retired after more than 30 years of service. He returned to Pawnee and started his own business. He and his wife finally retired from business to enjoy their golden years. On Sunday, June 22, 1941, Clyde died of a heart attack in his car while visiting his son, Leroy, in Tahlequah, Oklahoma.

His brother, Clare, returned to Pawnee after the war to live but gained a reputation for being a bully and hanging out in saloons. On Saturday afternoon, May 20, 1905, 27-year-old Clare got into a fight with 60-year-old James Stevens in the Diamond Saloon. The fight occurred because Clare either accused James of cheating at cards or told James he had to treat him to a drink. Nonetheless, Clare hit the older man several times, breaking his nose. James went to the doctor,

Capt. McMurty during World War I (NARA).

then returned and stabbed Clare in the stomach. Two friends escorted Clare to the doctor's office where he died at 1 a.m. that night.

Ben Colbert returned to the Cherokee Nation in the Indian Territory after the war and tried his hand as a cattleman near Tishomingo. Evidently that life was too tame for him. When Roosevelt became the president in 1901, he appointed Colbert Chief U.S. Marshal for the southern territory. When World War I was declared, he tried to enlist but was told he was too old. He persisted, and with the help of Democratic Congressmen Bill Murray and Richmond Hobson, he succeeded in enlisting. A prewar trip to a machine-gun factory in Ohio had qualified him as a machine gunner. His unit did not go overseas, so he did not see any action during this war. Afterwards, he tried his hand again at raising cattle and selling stock for an oil company. In 1943, at the age of 70, he tried to enlist when his country was again at war. This time no congressional influence would help.

Upon completion of his term of office, O.G. Palmer applied for and received a commission as a second lieutenant in the Seventh Cavalry on February 2, 1901. He, like many of his fellow Rough Riders, had a taste of adventure and found it intoxicating. Adrenaline is a natural drug produced by the body and, like any drug, can become addictive.

Lieutenant Palmer served with the Seventh Cavalry first in Cuba, then later transferred to the Philippines with the Sixth Cavalry in April 1914. In July 1916, he was promoted to captain with command of F Troop. As a commander, he participated in

Pershing's Punitive Expedition into Mexico against Pancho Villa. By World War I, the Army had expanded. Major Palmer organized and commanded the 320th Machine Gun Battalion of the Eighty-Second Division in August 1917. He commanded that battalion during the Meuse-Argonne Campaign. On July 30, 1918, Palmer was promoted to lieutenant colonel of the cavalry.

After the war on March 31, 1919, Palmer was honorably discharged from the National Army. Since he did not have the required 30 years of service at the age of 60 to draw retirement pay, he instead drew his veteran's pension on January 6, 1925, because of disabilities incurred in the line of duty. He moved to York, Nebraska, in the fall of 1944 where he married Anna B. Cutler. He enjoyed recounting tales of his time with the Rough Riders and the opening of the Strip. At the age of 86, he became ill and entered the York Veteran Hospital, dying several months later on May 31, 1951. However, there was one Rough Rider to leave a lasting impression on the Army.

After the Spanish–American War, the Rev. Henry Brown was invited to preach at several churches where he spoke on the qualifications that made a good Christian soldier. "I have noticed in our Army that the good soldier depends on good preparation made before the campaign. The effectiveness of this fleet of ours was the result of the magnificent preparation of our officers who were in command." He then linked that preparation of the weapons and body to that of the soul. Speaking from firsthand experience, he concluded that the effectiveness of religion was often diminished by chaplains whose only qualifications were that they had the opinion that they had been called upon to preach. Brown realized that the role of the military chaplain included far more than just ministry. He was an integral part of the military unit and the one man free to focus on the morale as well as the morality of the unit.

Brown consequently applied for a commission as a chaplain in the Regular Army, which was enthusiastically endorsed by Roosevelt. Brown received his commission on November 4, 1898. He retired as a lieutenant colonel in September 1915, but when World War I broke out, he returned to active duty. In November 1918, he was assigned as the Commandant of the Training School for Chaplains at Camp Taylor, Kentucky. Chaplain Brown established the training for all army chaplains. His performance in Cuba became the standard for the Chaplain Corps. After the war, he retired a second time in January 1919 and died at the age of 65 in June that same year.

Although the Oklahomans and the social elite enlisted in the Rough Riders for a sense of adventure, it had changed their sense of patriotism forever. While they may not have seen a need to participate in the National Guard after the war, many did not hesitate to answer the call when the bugle of war sounded again. Even social standing did not keep them away.

David Goodrich returned to the family business after Cuba and in 1913 was elected to the board of directors of the B.F. Goodrich Rubber and Tire Company. He, like other Rough Riders, joined

David Goodrich (Theodore Roosevelt Collection, Harvard University Library).

Roosevelt's Bull Moose Party in his second run for the presidency in 1912. It was no surprise that when Roosevelt tried to raise a division in 1917 for the war with Germany, David Goodrich offered to help him recruit.

At that time, Democratic political leadership under President Woodrow Wilson had adopted an isolationist policy and hoped to avoid participation in the war in Europe. Roosevelt and Wood had the loudest voices for preparing for war. This was in stark opposition to the popular sentiment and set them both at odds with Wilson.

When Congress declared war and passed the Selective Service Act of May 1917, Roosevelt had his congressional friends insert a provision for recruiting four volunteer divisions. The old Rough Rider colonel proposed recruiting a division along the same pattern as he had recruited his cowboy cavalry regiment and commanding it. He wanted a hardy stock of volunteers from lumberjacks and cowboys to lawyers and wealthy Wall Street men. The recruits would be ready to enlist on a moment's notice, and he had already selected officers from his former Rough Riders and active duty officers. Former Secretary of War Henry L. Stimson volunteered to serve as his chief quartermaster officer. Rear Admiral Cameron McRae Winslow would be one of his brigade commanders. Roosevelt believed that he could have his "T.R. Division" ready for the field service in 30 days. The Secretary of War, Newton D. Baker, turned Roosevelt's offer down.

The French army and government still recognized Roosevelt as a hero and wanted him. The American soldiers wanted him. Wilson and Baker turned him down without explanation. Quite obviously, a Democratic president did not need a former Republican president leading a division in battle. While Theodore followed the war from his home, his four sons served on the front. Archibald Roosevelt told author Henry Berry, "We all knew how badly Dad wanted to go, so we went for him. He always told us to lead meant to serve." Quentin Roosevelt was killed in action. With Theodore Roosevelt unable to serve himself, many of Roosevelt's former Rough Riders served in his absence.

Goodrich gave up the life of luxury to answer the call of the bugle one more time. He entered as a lieutenant colonel and served in France and finished the war as a colonel, and his Rough Rider friends forever referred to him as "Colonel Dave." In 1927, the Goodrich board of directors elected David as the chairman while his brother, Tew, became the president. During the Depression of the 1930s, David would emerge as one of the most influential directors in the history of the company. No matter how important he became, he always had time to chat with an old comrade. At an annual meeting of the Rough Rider Association in the 1940s, his comrades elected him President for Life. He served as the chairman of the board until his death in 1950. Whatever leadership potential that Wood and Roosevelt had seen in him back in 1898 proved right. He became a great leader both in and out of uniform.

Frank Knox had returned home from Cuba to a hero's welcome, and William Alden Smith asked Frank to speak as his curtain raiser in his run for U.S. Congress. Many politicians saw the advantage of being seen with a Rough Rider. Frank soon married his college sweetheart, Annie Reid, in December 1898, and he needed a job to support his family. During the war, Frank had written home about the cheerful events to alleviate his mother's worries, and the *Herald* had an exclusive run on publishing Frank's letters. His writing style impressed the publisher, E.D. Conger, who offered the young veteran a job as a reporter at $10 a week. This began his long career in the newspaper industry. Frank then rose up through the ranks of different newspapers to city editor and circulation manager.

Frank Knox maintained his friendship with his old colonel and became actively involved in the Michigan Republican Party. He even served as the chairman of the state central committee. After Wilson turned down Roosevelt's offer to recruit his division, Knox met one last time with his old commander. "They won't let you go, but I must go. I have been criticizing slackers and I could not stay behind even if I wanted to."

At 43 years old, Frank Knox's application for the first officers' training camp was turned down. Instead, he enlisted as a private in the First New Hampshire Infantry. Soon he was selected to attend the newly formed Officer Candidate School and received a commission as a cavalry captain on August 14, 1917. His regiment moved to Camp Dix, New Jersey, and formed part of the Seventy-Eighth Division. The new table of organization dropped the cavalry regiments from the division. Knox was assigned to division personnel to assign 50,000 draftees to jobs according to their talents and civilian training. During the construction of the camp, the union electrical workers walked off their jobs because others would not join. Knox identified all the soldiers with electrical experience and asked them if they would finish the job. When the union men heard this, they returned to work. This incident caught the attention of his superiors, and Knox was offered a job as a lieutenant colonel in Washington, D.C. Knox did not want to fight the war with his spurs hooked to a desk.

In December, Colonel Wait C. Johnson, division chief of staff, offered Knox command of the 303rd Ammunition Supply Train in the 153rd Artillery Brigade with the rank of major. It had horses, mules and trucks. He jumped into the job with zeal and energy. Since this was his first command, he inquired of an old West Point officer, "In your years of handling troops you must have sifted some fundamental principles. What are they?"[2]

"There are three things to remember," replied the officer. "First, no social contacts. Avoid social contacts with your men, not because of any feeling of superiority, but because you cannot have social contacts with all of them and, therefore, will be laid open to the charges of favoritism. Hold aloof for that reason only. Second, strict impartiality. An officer is in a sense a judge. He is bound to be called upon to decide petty cases and punish minor infractions of the regulations. Officers should try to develop strict impartiality and firmness. [Third] Keep a sharp eye out continually for the welfare of your men. In the field the soldiers are utterly dependent on their officers for food, camp sites, and protection against mistakes. An officer should be exceedingly industrious in looking after the physical welfare of his men, even before his own welfare or the welfare of his officers." Knox had learned more about the third principle during his Rough Rider days.[3]

The division deployed to France in the summer of 1918 and participated in the St. Mihiel, Meuse-Argonne and Lorraine campaigns. During the upcoming Argonne Campaign, fodder for the animals was scarce, resulting in many deaths. The division officers held a conference to determine the fate of the 2,000 animals in the three regiments. They decided to allot fodder just to the animals in the regiments. Someone in Knox's absence asked, "What about the supplies for the ammunition train?"[4]

"To hell with them," snapped the brigadier general. "That red-headed major will get his himself some way or other. We won't worry about him." He was right. A soldier later described Knox: "Well, he never got very chummy with any of the men. He was summary court officer for the regiment, and he was hard but fair and impartial. But, gosh, what a son of a gun he was for looking after his men in his outfit, rustling food and good camp sites and trying to see that nobody got away with anything we should have."[5]

Lieutenant John Kennedy recalled, "Major Knox often found his ingenuity taxed to the utmost to keep a plentiful supply of shells where the 'red legs' could reach them handily. It was one of the toughest jobs in the A.E.F., but Major Knox was at his best on tough jobs. In turn his unit served the 90th Division, the 78th, the 35th, the 6th, the 42nd, and back again to the 78th."[6]

His commanding officer, Colonel John N. Straat, said, "Knox commanded his section throughout the entire period. Proved himself to be a man of resourcefulness, untiring energy and a good disciplinarian. On the job all the time. When things were pretty hot and many of his animals had been killed by enemy fire, he rigged up packs in which he packed shells and delivered them at the front on pack animals." Knox finished the war as a colonel of the 365th Field Artillery.[7]

After the war, Frank returned to the newspaper business. By 1927, he had become general manager of all 27 of William Randolph Hearst's newspapers and had accumulated enough savings to retire in 1931. In 1920, he entered politics, running unsuccessfully for various New Hampshire offices. In 1934, he began raising money for the Republican Party. He was so successful that many considered him a likely candidate for president. At the 1936 Republican National Convention, it became clear that Kansas Governor Alfred Landon was the overwhelming favorite for the candidacy. Knox withdrew his name from the nomination and became Landon's running mate. Franklin D. Roosevelt won the election, and, in a bipartisan move, appointed Frank Knox as his Secretary of the Navy, a job he had held once. Frank Knox held that critical position through World War II and died in office at the age of 70 on April 28, 1944. If the story of the Rough Riders' lives tells anything, they remained loyal to each other as a group.

The brotherhood formed by the close relationship of men in combat has led to reunions and veteran fraternities. While some keep in touch with a few close comrades in arms after the war, most return to restart their normal lives but in their 50s tend to gain a nostalgia for the past and seek the company of their former brothers in arms. The Rough Riders were unique in respect to the number of celebrities in their unit. Several became governors, and their commander eventually became the president of the United States. The Rough Rider Association remained strong and held well-attended reunions almost immediately after their return. It helped encourage attendance that their former commander was the vice president, then president, of the United States. Teddy Roosevelt visited Oklahoma City on July 2, 1900, for the annual Rough Rider reunion. As he stepped off the train, he was met by a delegation of dignitaries: Mayor Lee Van Winkle, E.W. Johnson, Judge Benjamin F. Burnell, Sydney Clark, D.R. Boyd and Senator Dennis Flynn and the following Rough Riders: Alex O. Brodie, Frank Frantz, Charles Hunter and Anton H. Classen, then president of the Rough Rider Association. The next day the city held a parade in their honor. Roosevelt, not wanting to draw too much attention away from the veterans, did not dress in uniform but only wore his old campaign hat. Nearly 100 veterans from his regiment followed. From then on Arizona and New Mexico would host the reunions.

Roosevelt attended all that he could. This command was probably the pivotal experience in his life. In a letter to a friend Roosevelt wrote:

> The regiment was a wholly exceptional volunteer organization, and its career cannot be taken as in any way a justification for the belief that the average volunteer regiment approaches the average regular regiment in point of efficiency until it has had many months of active service…. They [Rough Riders] were hardy, self reliant, accustomed to shift for themselves in the

open under very adverse circumstances. The two all-important qualifications for a cavalry-man are riding and shooting-the modern cavalryman being so often used dismounted, as an infantryman. The average recruit requires a couple of years before he becomes proficient in horsemanship and marksmanship; but my men were already good shots and first-class riders when they came into the regiment.[8]

Studying the war through the eyes of those who participated in it provides a different perspective than that viewed by most historians. As a small war, the Spanish–American War did not require a draft, but, in fact, the states and territories petitioned for the opportunity of their citizens to serve in combat. It was a time when war brought honor to the participants and their homes. The experience of the Rough Riders in war did not lessen their sense of patriotism but enhanced it. Many readily donned the uniform again when the trumpets of war sounded 19 years later.

Following the same unit through the war also reveals that the casualties of war do not always end with the fighting but continue long after the war has ended. Many of those Rough Riders who would die of disease did so within two years.

The First U.S. Volunteer Cavalry was a unique organization. It not only recruited men with the same special skills of riding and shooting, but it broke down social barriers. The wealthiest sons of America served alongside the poorest and became fast friends. The war took place during a time when the privilege of wealth and culture did not free one from the burden of military service but gave them an increased sense of patriotic duty. With privilege comes the responsibility and obligation for leadership. This leadership first began with selfless service. Many of the elite descended from families with a tradition of military service. Neither would the elite shirk their duties when the next war broke out.

The performance of the Rough Riders steals no credit away from the Regular Army soldier who enlisted for five years. There was nothing that the Rough Riders did at Las Guasimas or San Juan that the Regulars did not do themselves. It just did not take the Rough Riders two years to achieve that same standard of performance. This resulted from the method by which the Rough Riders were recruited and trained. The Rough Riders also reflect that maturity and resource of professional trade skills brought by the militia organization.

When one follows the participants up San Juan Hill and climbs into the trenches with them during the siege, one can see the beginning of a form of warfare that would reach fruition during the next war. The first attempts at the use of barbed wire represented nothing more than fences that could be easily kicked down. During the next war, barbed wire entanglements would be interlaced and anchored down like entangled spiderwebs. Wheeler stumbled onto some of those types of entanglements along the road leading into town after the surrender. These, combined with the firepower of the machine gun, would make the gap between enemy trenches a death trap. The Spanish–American War was the last war when officers would stand exposed to enemy fire to inspire their men. After that, such acts would become suicidal.

The Santiago Campaign represents a transition between the doctrine of the American Civil War and World War I. Besides battlefield tactics, medicine had also advanced. No longer did surgeons have to amputate every wound. They had learned what caused infection and could fuse shattered bones together. None of the Rough Riders returned as amputees even though several like Brodie and Wetmore had shattered bones. However, canning factories had not yet perfected the method of preserving food in a tin can. This would happen by World War I, but the soldiers in Cuba had to sustain themselves on the same army rations as had their fathers in the Civil War.

Following a single unit through the war, one can see the growth of its leaders. Huston seemed to have remained the same professional throughout the campaign, but sickness cheated him of any greater recognition at Kettle Hill. McGuiness never had the chance to measure up to others' expectations. Goodrich, however, surprised many. Among the lieutenants, examples like and Rob Thomas seem to have grown the most during combat.

Of all the heroes of the Santiago Campaign, General Joseph Wheeler stands out. Historians have criticized him for being too aggressive in attacking the Spaniards at Las Guasimas when the Spanish had planned to abandon the position anyway. They criticized the fight as avoidable, wasteful, and headstrong. However, contrary to the critics, the battle did serve a purpose. It provided these regiments a chance to test their combat mettle prior to the eventual battles around Santiago. It also reinforced a psychological advantage over the enemy. It sent the Spaniards a message that the Americans came to fight a winnable battle. Wheeler believed that this would play into his hand when he defended the ridge around Santiago with a thin line.

To many historians, the Santiago Campaign represents a study of military blunders and incompetence. Shafter may be unfairly blamed for this, but he did the best he could with the resources that he had. His decisions at El Pozo, however, did result in serious blunders as he had the divisions line up in full view and range of the enemy, like during the Civil War. Evidently, he did not understand the full effects of modern weapons. Keep in mind the War Department had been deliberately turning down the latest weapon technology for fear of losing control of the battlefield and the men rapidly expending all their ammunition. They did not want to leave their comfort zone, and besides, the army only had to fight inadequately armed Indians. This deliberate avoidance of advancing technology had dire consequences when Lawton was unable to join the battle as planned. Shafter had placed his command post centrally located between the fights at El Caney and Santiago, as doctrine called for. But being sick, he was unable to leave his command post to inspect the front. Fortunately, this did not stop Wheeler.

A puzzling thing about the study of the Santiago Campaign: If it was such an example of military incompetence, then why did the Americans win? While Shafter may have taken a lot of the blame for the things that went wrong during the campaign, clearly many of the successes resulted directly from the actions taken by Wheeler.

By everyone's description, Wheeler was still sick when he went forward to the battle. Although he was still subordinate to Shafter, fortunately, he was not reluctant to assert his authority and make decisions based on his rank. Like Roosevelt, he did not think that he would ever get the chance to command in battle again. While the infantry assault began spontaneously, Wheeler ordered his cavalry division to attack the hill. When officers felt that they could not hold the hill that they had paid a high price in lives to take, he reassured them that they could. He even countermanded Shafter's order to withdraw that night. Otherwise, they would have lost everything they had achieved that day and would have had to charge the hill again. The history of the campaign might have turned out entirely different. Wheeler understood the mind of the retreating foe since he had spent his Civil War career fighting the rearguard action of a retreating Confederate Army.

Finally, Wheeler negotiated the surrender. If Wheeler had not negotiated an honorable way for Toral to capitulate, the Americans might have had to attack the city. This would have cost more American lives and done damage to the very citizens and their property that the Americans had come to help. While Wheeler was much older and wiser than Lieutenant Miley and General Lawton, his real advantage was the fact that he had been in Toral's shoes before. Who better to negotiate an honorable surrender?

It is amazing that after 33 years of civilian life, this old Confederate general had not lost his feel of the battle. This work has examined how to achieve victory against overwhelming obstacles. If this campaign has been set up as a case of military incompetence, then Wheeler should take a lion's share of the credit for its success.

After the war, Wheeler tried to pick up where he had left off but lost his seat in Congress in the 1898 election. Fortunately, he managed to receive another appointment as a brigadier general of volunteers in June 1899 and returned to his first love, the army. After a brief service in the Philippines, he returned to the United States in January 1900 where McKinley appointed him a brigadier general in the Regular Army. Wheeler commanded the Department of the Lakes until his retirement that September. He died on January 25, 1906, while living with his sister in Brooklyn.

Rob Huston guessed right that Colonel Wood would go on to become an important officer in the Army. When the Spanish–American War had started, he was just an army surgeon with the rank of captain. Although he had received the Medal of Honor in the Apache Wars, his career had stagnated. By a great turn of fortune, he happened to be friends with Roosevelt when the war broke out. When commands of volunteer regiments were given out to men of influence, Roosevelt had the wits about him to offer command of the First U.S. Volunteer Cavalry to his friend Leonard Wood. Wood's previous experience campaigning against Apaches had given him valuable field experience leading soldiers. He had also lived among many of the citizens with whom his regiment would be recruited.

Wood finished the war as a brigadier general of volunteers, a temporary rank, and military governor of Santiago, a city of a population of 50,000. Wood set out to first clean up the city and feed the people. Dead animal carcasses as well as dead people littered the streets and houses. Whether willingly or unwillingly, Wood put every able-bodied citizen to work. While this may have constituted forced labor, he paid them for their services. They gathered the dead into piles of 90 to 100, soaked them in petroleum, then set them afire and kept adding cadavers to the flames. Those not collecting bodies delivered food. Wood also pressed every abandoned vehicle into service with his authority as the military governor. When this work was done, he put the Cubans to work building roads with the money gathered from fines. His quick response to a smallpox outbreak in one of the districts in November brought it under control in a few weeks.

Wood appointed government officials, judges, and the police. Although a Protestant, he knew the importance of the Catholic Church in Latin culture and escorted the newly elevated Bishop Bernada to his coronation ceremony. He brought inflation of food prices down by setting fixed rates based upon their cost. At first he did not please many of the citizens with his heavy-handed policies, but results resulted. By the time he left for a visit to the United States the next spring, he had won the citizens over, and they presented him with a scroll in recognition of his service and defense of the people. In December 1899, McKinley appointed him governor general of Cuba with the rank of major general of volunteers "to prepare Cuba, as rapidly as possible, for the establishment of an independent government, republican in form, and a good school system."

In his first six months, he corrected the ills of the prison and judicial system. He

Brigadier General Wood (Theodore Roosevelt Collection, Harvard University Library).

next instituted a government elected by the people and established a public school system that had not existed before. As usual, he set about to clean the city of Havana of its filth and rid it of disease. The medical authorities, unfortunately, still did not know the cause of yellow fever, which broke out during the summer of 1900. During that time, medical doctors in Cuba would identify the stegomyia mosquito as the transmitter of the disease.

Wood served as governor general until an assassin's bullet in September 1901 elevated his friend to the presidency. Roosevelt then promoted Wood to brigadier general in the Regular Army and brought him home in May 1902. Wood jumped from captain to brigadier general in the Regular Army, a thing that other officers would not ignore. Wood left Cuba a functioning democracy, having gained the respect of the people he governed. Not having risen through the traditionally slow promotion process, he would have to prove himself worthy of the rank. He could not rest on the laurels of his Medal of Honor nor his achievements in Cuba.

To avoid criticism of his friendship with the president, Wood sought the post of military governor of the Moro Province in the Philippines in 1903 under Philippine Governor William Howard Taft. There the heaviest insurgent fighting by Muslims continued. Wood shared the burden of living in the field with his men to overcome their criticism of his meteoric rise due to his political connection. As a reflection on Roosevelt's judgment, he also advanced another officer ahead of his peers, John J. Pershing. Wood instituted the same policies as he had implemented in Cuba but dealt forcefully with those who still resisted. His military campaign culminated with the storming of the rebel stronghold at Bud Dajo, where Johnston earned his Medal of Honor. Wood earned his men's confidence. Upon pacification of the province, Roosevelt then promoted Wood to major general in 1906 with command of the American division in the Philippines.

In 1908, he finally returned to the United States to command the Department of the East with his headquarters in New York. On his return, Wood traveled through Europe to observe their military systems. This tour inspired a number of his ideas for the future of the U.S. Army.

After Roosevelt had stepped down from office, he pressured his successor, President Taft, to appoint Wood as the Chief of Staff of the Army in 1910. In that position, Wood set out to implement his ideas. The U.S. Army had adopted a general staff in 1903 modeled after the Prussian system, but it did not function as it should. Wood streamlined it and set out to make the organization work. He also advocated for a universal military service based upon the Prussian system instead of the volunteer system. In spite of the success of the Rough Riders, he knew that the volunteer system had failed to adequately and rapidly mobilize citizen soldiers for war. In his new concept, all citizens would receive mandatory military training and be available for call-up in time of war. This idea was never adopted. Upon completion of his term in office by 1914, Wood had made progress but failed to reform the Army and the general staff as much as he had hoped.

Wood returned to the post of commanding general of the Department of the East. With the outbreak of war in Europe, Wood advocated in earnest, along with Roosevelt, the importance of national preparedness. Unable to sway national policy, he took steps on his own. He immediately initiated a military training program for business and professional men at Plattsburg, New York, paid for by private contributions. Up until this time, only the military academies provided a training and commissioning source for officers. The military instruction at the Land Grant Colleges did not provide a source of commission, nor did the Army keep track of the graduates.

This initiative and his outspokenness for preparation put him at odds with President Woodrow Wilson, who felt that any preparations would lead the nation to war. Wood was quite outspoken on this subject. Fortunately, he had too much political support for Wilson to take disciplinary action against him. Consequently, when Congress finally declared war in 1917, Wilson appointed a more junior general officer to lead the American Expeditionary Force in France, John J. Pershing. Wood instead received command of the Eighty-Ninth Division at Camp Funston, Kansas.

By the end of the year, however, Wood visited France. While he was observing French training with a number of American officers, a round inside a mortar exploded, killing the crew and four officers on both sides of Wood. He escaped with only a wound to the left arm. Upon his recovery, he continued to visit training, but on February 26, 1918, Pershing ordered him back to the United States. There the Mayo examining board found the 57-year-old General Wood unsuitable for the physical demands of leading an army. Wood sat out the remainder of the war, training the Tenth and Eighty-Ninth Divisions at Camp Funston. Both Wood and Roosevelt had been among the loudest critics of Wilson's isolationist policy. Neither would see action in the war for which they had advocated preparation.

In 1920, Wood made an unsuccessful bid for the office of president then threw his support behind Warren G. Harding. Wood hoped Harding would reward him with the appointment as the secretary of war, but Harding offered him instead the civilian post as governor of the Philippines. Reluctantly, Wood retired from the Army in October 1921 and accepted it. He died in office on August 7, 1927, during an operation on an old wound to the head that had grown into a tumor.

Roosevelt's little push to Wood's stagnated career elevated him to the highest rank and post in the Army in a little over a decade. An ambitious man, Wood unfortunately failed to achieve all his high expectations, but he had left his mark. He established democracy in Cuba and the Moro Province. His officer training camps provided Pershing with well-trained officers and established a model for future officer training. He also trained and mentored Roosevelt to become one of the great American military heroes.

It was said during the Civil War that any damned fool could command a regiment. That was partially true. Command of a regiment during that time required no tactical expertise since no regiment fought alone. A commander had to master getting his regiment in line of battle and command and instill discipline to stand up against withering fire. It required tremendous leadership skill to motivate a regiment to greatness though. Theodore Roosevelt provides an example of that kind of leadership.

While this examination of the Rough Riders was not intended as another study of Roosevelt, it was unavoidable. One could not tell the story of the men without telling his. He grew before them as one of the greatest military commanders of American military history but was not destined to go down in American history as one of the great tacticians of his time. In fact, Roosevelt was still learning as the war ended. He provides an example of what kind of traits the men expect from a leader. He was not afraid to make mistakes; therefore, he learned constantly. There was no limit to the efforts he would take to care for welfare of his regiment; neither would he condone poor performance. If a student of military leadership wanted a good role model to emulate, he could find no better example than that of Roosevelt.

Shortly after the war in December 1898, Roosevelt was recommended by Generals Wheeler, Sumner and Wood for the Medal of Honor for leading the charge and conspicuously exposing himself to danger while in the command of men on the battlefield. He not only led the charge up Kettle Hill but led the charge up the next, then organized its defense. The Regular Army Officers Stevens, Mills and Howze, along with Jenkins and Bardshar, wrote statements as eyewitnesses to these facts. By the standards then and today, these actions ranked among the highest of valor.

Unfortunately, Secretary of War Alger was bitter over the letter that Roosevelt wrote to get the men off of Cuba and his testimony at the investigation later. This led to Alger's resignation. In his last act, he disapproved the Medal of Honor for Roosevelt. The War Department, however, did honor Roosevelt with brevet promotions to colonel for his actions at Las Guasimas and brigadier general for his actions at San Juan Hill. The debate over the Medal of Honor would resurface after Roosevelt's death.

Congress passed the Fiscal Year 1996 National Defense Authorization Act on February 10, 1996, which repealed the statute of limitations on military decorations. It was felt that many African Americans had their awards downgraded because of prejudice. This, however, opened the door for another review of Roosevelt's performance. Congressman Paul McHale, Democrat from Pennsylvania and former Marine officer, introduced a bill that year to award the Medal of Honor to Roosevelt. He then introduced a second bill on July 25, 1997, and it gained over 160 co-sponsors. The House Military Personnel Subcommittee then held hearings on the issue on September 28, 1998, and the House of Representatives passed the bill by unanimous voice vote on October 8. Senator Kent Conrad, Democrat from North Carolina, introduced the bill to the Senate, and it passed by a similar unanimous voice vote on October 21. President Bill Clinton held the bill in review for two years. The main opposition to upgrading awards came from the Army. Finally, Clinton rectified the injustice and awarded the Medal of Honor to Tweed Roosevelt, Theodore's great-grandson, on January 16, 2001.

A little more than a month before leading the Rough Riders into battle in Cuba, Roosevelt had been a civilian with political ambitions. On the slope of that hill, he commanded nearly 500 men under fire. He did not hesitate nor did he seek cover but willingly exposed himself to danger. He moved wherever he saw the need to inspire. He alone rode horseback to the summit of the hill. While it was the duty, at that time, for every officer to expose himself to fire, few did it so willingly. They were called heroes. In the following debate over whether he deserved the Medal of Honor, in later years, anyone who would have acted in that same manner would have earned it. This medal had greater significance.

Roosevelt joined Wood, Church, Johnston and McMurtry as Rough Riders who had earned their nation's highest military honor. Roosevelt then became the only president to have earned the Medal of Honor. Although Roosevelt was not alive to appreciate it, the medal did elevate his place in history. He and his son, Theodore Roosevelt, Jr., ranked with Arthur and Douglas McArthur as the only father and sons to earn the medal. This award also made Roosevelt the only recipient of the Medal of Honor to have also earned the Nobel Prize for Peace.

Roosevelt summed up his experience best by his statement at Sorbonne, Paris, on April 23, 1910,

> It is not the critic who counts; not the man who points out how the strong man stumbles, or where the doer of deeds could have done them better. The credit belongs to the man who is actually in the arena, whose face is marred by dust and sweat and comes short again and again, because there is no effort without error and shortcoming; but who does actually strive to do the deeds; devotions; who spends himself in a worthy cause; who at the best knows in the end the triumph of high achievement, and who at the worst, if he fails, at least fails while daring greatly, so that his place shall never be with those cold and timid souls who know neither victory nor defeat.

Chapter Notes

Chapter 1

1. *Portrait and Biographical Records of Oklahoma*, Chicago: Chapman Publishing Company, 1901, p. 29.

2. Robert Huston's obituary, provided by the Heart of Oklahoma Council.

3. The *Guthrie Daily Leader* detailed the incident and investigation from December 23 to 28, 1897.

4. The *Guthrie Daily Leader* covered the accusations, investigation and outcome from March 9 to 31, 1897.

Chapter 2

1. Jo Elaine Cashion Matousek loaned the original copy of Roy Cashion's "Cuba Libre" speech to the Hennessey Public Library for transcription and posting on "Who Was Roy Cashion?"

2. "Governor Is Firm," *Guthrie Daily Leader*, Tuesday, April 26, 1898, Vol. 11, No. 125.

3. *Ibid.*

4. The two local newspapers, the *Ponca City Democrat* and the *Ponca City Daily Courier*, each covered this story in detail. "Insulted the Flag," *Ponca City Democrat*, Monday, May 2, 1898, Extra; "Negroes Narrow Escape," *Ponca City Democrat*, Thursday, May 5, 1898, Vol. 5, No. 33; and "An Unfortunate Occurrance [sic]," *Ponca City Daily Courier*, Monday, May 2, 1898, Vol. I, No. 181.

5. "Want to Fight with Teddy Roosevelt," *Hennessey Clipper*, April 28, 1898, printed in "Who Was Roy Cashion?"

6. "Unwritten History," *Ponca City Daily Courier*, May 7, 1898, Vol. I, No. 186.

7. Paul Hunter described the monthly pay for enlisted in "On the High Seas: Interesting Letters from the Soldier Boys Who Left Tampa," *Guthrie Daily Leader*, Wednesday, June 22, 1898, Vol. 12, No. 22.

8. "Thomas Is a Hero," *Chicago Times-Herald*, Tuesday, July 19, 1898.

9. "Thomas a Fighter," *Chicago Inter-Ocean*, June 25, 1898.

Chapter 3

1. By this time, a company organization in the cavalry was referred to as a troop.

2. *Newkirk and Kay County Republican*, Vol. 5, No. 26, Friday, May 20, 1898.

3. Roosevelt recorded that the regiment expanded from 780 to 1,000 men, Roosevelt, *Rough Riders*, p. 41. Charles Hunter wrote to the *Guthrie Daily Leader* that the troops had been reduced to 65 men. "How Cavalry Boys Enjoy Camp Life," *Guthrie Daily Leader*, Tuesday, May 17, 1898, Vol. 11, No. 144. Tom Rynning wrote that the original two Arizona troops were turned into three skeleton troops. Rynning, *Gun Notches*, p. 142.

4. Robert B. Huston, Papers, Oklahoma Historical Society.

5. *Newkirk and Kay County Republican*, Vol. 5, No. 26, Friday, May 20, 1898.

6. Edward Marshall, *The Story of the Rough Riders*, New York: G.W. Dillingham, 1899, p. ix. Hall wrote that Colonel Wood wanted "to break the men into discipline by degrees, and gradually tighten the bonds." Hall, *Fun and Fighting*, p. 19.

7. David L. Hughes, "A Story of the 'Rough Riders,'" Arizona Historical Society.

8. Marshall, *Rough Riders*, p. 33.

9. *Ibid.*, p. 41.

10. Ogden Wells kept a detailed diary of his time in the Rough Riders, *Diary of a Rough Rider*, St. Joseph, MI: A.B. Moore, n.d., pp. 3–5.

11. George Burgess described the high and weight requirement, "Burgess' Letter," *Guthrie Daily Leader*, Thursday, May 26, 1898, Vol. 11, No. 152. Schuyler McGinnis described the prices, "War Notes," *Newkirk and Kay County Republican*, Vol. 5, No. 26, Friday, May 20, 1898.

12. "Colonel Roosevelt's Pets," *Guthrie Daily Leader*, Monday, May 16, 1898, Vol. 11, No. 143.

13. "Teddy Is Popular," *Guthrie Daily Leader*, Friday, May 20, 1898, Vol. 11, No. 147.

14. "Fitness Rules. Money Is No Object in Wood's Rough Riders, Writes Lieutenant Schweizer," *Guthrie Daily Leader*, Tuesday, May 31, 1898, Vol. 12, No. 3.

15. Robert Huston letter to Vite, 15 May 1898, Huston Collection.

16. "'VIVA OKLAHOMA!' San Antonio Lady Speaks in glowing Terms of Our Cavalry Troop," *Guthrie Daily Leader*, Thursday, May 19, 1898, Vol. 11, No. 146.

17. Robert Huston wrote home that his troop

had a reputation of being the best trained in the regiment. Robert Huston letter to Vite, 15 May 1898. Ira Hill wrote this in a letter to the editor, "From the Front," *Newkirk and Kay County Republican*, Vol. 5, No. 28, Friday, June 3, 1898. Paul Hunter wrote this to the editor, "Breezy Gossip of The Rough Riders," *Guthrie Daily Leader*, Monday, May 16, 1898, Vol. 11, No. 143. Schuyler McGinnis likewise wrote to the editor that D Troop was designated the base troop. "McGinnis Tells of the Troop," *Guthrie Daily Leader,* May 16, 1898, Vol. 11, No. 143.

18. List of color of the mounts in Tom Hall, *The Fun and Fighting of the Rough Riders*, New York: Fredericks A. Stokes, 1899, p. 49.

19. Roosevelt, *Rough Riders*, p. 32.

20. Robert Huston letter to Vite, 15 May 1898, Huston Collection.

21. Hall, *Fun and Fighting*, pp. 41–42.

22. Hughes, "A Story of the 'Rough Riders.'"

23. Roosevelt, *Rough Riders*, pp. 39–40.

24. Robert Huston letter to Vite, 15 May 1898, Huston Collection.

25. Paul Hunter, "How Cavalry Boys Enjoy Camp Life," *Guthrie Daily Leader*, Tuesday, May 17, 1898, Vol. 11, No. 144.

26. Hall, *Fun and Fighting*.

27. "Teddy Is Popular," *Guthrie Daily Leader*, Friday, May 20, 1898, Vol. 11, No. 147.

28. "Thomas Is a Hero," *Chicago Times-Herald*, Tuesday, July 19, 1898.

29. Robert Huston letter to Vite, 15 May 1898, Huston Collection.

30. David L. Hughes, "A Story of the 'Rough Riders," Arizona Historical Society.

31. Thomas H. Rynning as told to Al Cohn and Joe Chisholm, *Gun Notches*, New York: Frederick A. Stokes, 1931, p. 144.

32. Hall, *Fun and Fighting*, p. 41.

33. H.B. Hening, *George Curry, 1861–1947, An Autobiography*, Albuquerque: University of New Mexico Press, 1958, p. 122.

34. Rynning, *Gun Notches*, p. 145.

35. *Ibid.*

36. Hening, *Curry*, p. 123.

37. Hall, *Fun and Fighting*, p. 52.

38. Hughes, "A Story of the 'Rough Riders.'"

39. Roosevelt, *Rough Riders*, pp. 21–22.

40. Hughes, "A Story of the 'Rough Riders.'"

41. Nancy B. Samuelson, "Chris Madsen: Soldier, Oklahoma 89'er, and Deputy U.S. Marshal," *OklahombreS Journal*, Vol. IV, Summer 1993.

42. Harold L. Mueller in collaboration with Chris Madsen, "With the Rough Riders," *Daily Oklahoman*, February 23, 1936.

43. The *San Antonio Express* wrote that Madsen arrived on 27 May, but by his own account, Madsen arrived while Hall was the quartermaster officer. Mueller and Madsen, "With the Rough Riders."

44. Mueller and Madsen, "With the Rough Riders."

45. Hall, *Fun and Fighting*, pp. 32–33.

46. Huston correspondence to the Leader, "HOT" and "M'Ginnis Shows 'Em," *Guthrie Daily Leader*, Saturday, May 21, 1898, Vol. 11, No. 148.

47. John C. Rayburn, "The Rough Riders in San Antonio, 1898," *Arizona and the West*, Vol. 3, No. 2, Summer 1961, p. 122.

48. Robert Huston letter to Vite, 20 May 1898, Huston Collection.

49. Mueller and Madsen, "With the Rough Riders."

50. "OH, DEAH! Horwid Fifth Avenue Willies as Officers. WITH WOUGH WIDERS," *Guthrie Daily Leader*, Wednesday, May 25, 1898, Vol. 11, No. 151.

51. *Ibid.*

52. *Ibid.*

53. Mueller and Madsen, "With the Rough Riders."

54. "Rough Riders Gentlemen," *New York Times*, August 22, 1898, p. 5.

55. "Jaunt of Riders. Sergeant Hunter Tells of the Routine of Daily Camp Life at San Antonio," *Guthrie Daily Leader*, Saturday, May 28, 1898, Vol. 12, No. 2.

56. Ben Colbert's account is detailed in his diary in the archives of the Oklahoma Historical Society.

57. The 25 May 1898 issue of the *San Antonio Express* provided a detailed and lively account of this incident.

58. C.H. Thompson's name is not listed on any of the rolls of the regiment. This account was taken from the *San Antonio Express* the next day. It is quite possible that he was dropped from the rolls since it would have taken him about seven months in the Army to pay that fine. He probably remained in jail after his regiment deployed.

59. "From the Front," pt. 2, *Newkirk and Kay County Republican*, Vol. 5, No. 28, Friday, June 3, 1898.

60. "Complimentary Concert at Riverside Park to the Rough Riders Tomorrow Night," *San Antonio Daily Light*, May 23, 1898.

61. "Jaunt of Riders. Sergeant Hunter Tells of the Routine of Daily Camp Life at San Antonio," *Guthrie Daily Leader*, Saturday, May 28, 1898, Vol. 12, No. 2.

Chapter 4

1. Theodore Miller's experience was detailed in his diary, *Theodore W. Miller, Rough Rider*, 1899.

2. "Jaunt of Riders. Sergeant Hunter Tells of the Routine of Daily Camp Life at San Antonio," *Guthrie Daily Leader*, Saturday, May 28, 1898, Vol. 12, No. 2.

3. Hall, *Fun and Fighting*, p. 69.

4. Hughes, "A Story of the 'Rough Riders."

5. Miley, *In Cuba with Shafter*, p. 29.

6. Joseph Hamblen Sears, *The Career of Leonard Wood*, New York: D. Appleton, 1919, p. 89.

7. MG Joseph Wheeler, *The Santiago Campaign 1898*, New York: Lamson, Wolffe and Company, 1898, p. 4.

8. Mueller and Madsen, "With the Rough Riders."

9. *Hennessey Clipper*, February 24 to July 28, 1898.

10. Norman Beasley, *Frank Knox American; A Short Biography*, Garden City, NY: Doubleday, Doran & Company, 1936, p. 15.

11. Compiled by Frank Oppel, *Frederic Remington Selected Writings*, Secaucus: Castle, 1981, p. 331.

12. Hughes, "A Story of the 'Rough Riders.'"

13. Roosevelt wrote that they had to leave four troops behind, Roosevelt, *Rough Riders*, p. 57. Hall recorded which troops were chosen to go. Hall, *Fun and Fighting*, p. 87.

14. Rynning, *Gun Notches*, p. 154.

15. George Curry wrote in his memoirs in 1947 that Wood had initially chosen Muller and Llewellyn's troops and that either Luna or his troop would have to remain. They tossed a quarter to see who would go and Luna won. Roosevelt claimed that Luna protested on the grounds that he was the only officer of Spanish descent. David Hughes also mentioned seeing Luna arguing the issue of his Spanish ancestry with Wood and the squadron commanders under a pine tree. Ben Colbert, who was in Luna's troop, confirmed in his diary that day, "Our Capt. matched Capt. Curry out of going."

16. Roosevelt, *Rough Riders*, p. 57.

17. Theodore Miller recorded in his diary that the D Troop could only take 70 men, *Rough Rider*, p. 90. Ogden Wells also wrote in his diary that they could only take 70 men from each troop, *Diary of a Rough Rider*, p. 23. Roy Cashion wrote to his parents, June 4, 1898, that the company was only allowed to take 50 men, printed in *Hennessey Clipper*, June 16, 1898, "Who Was Roy Cashion?"

18. Miller, *Rough Rider*, p. 90.

19. Wells, *Diary of a Rough Rider*, p. 23.

20. Hall, *Fun and Fighting*, p. 91.

21. Miley, *In Cuba with Shafter*, pp. 31–32.

22. Center of Military History, *Correspondence Relating to the War with Spain*, Vol. I, Washington, D.C: U.S. Government Printing Office, 1993, p. 30.

23. Some remembered midnight as the reporting time.

24. Hall, *Fun and Fighting*, p. 93.

25. *Ibid.*, p. 97.

26. Marshall, *Rough Riders*, p. 53.

27. "On the High Seas: Interesting Letters from the Soldier Boys Who Left Tampa," *Guthrie Daily Leader*, Wednesday, June 22, 1898, Vol. 12, No. 22.

28. Cashion wrote that the convoy consisted of 31 vessels. Roy Cashion letter to parents, June 15, 1898, on board *Yucatan*, Kingfisher County Historical Society, *Pioneers of Kingfisher County*, Kingfisher, 1976.

29. Marshall, *Rough Riders*, p. 57.

30. Miley, *In Cuba with Shafter*, p. 33.

31. Hall, *Fun and Fighting*, p. 99.

32. Allyn Capron letter to John R. Thomas, John R. Thomas Collection, Research Division, OHS.

33. *Ibid.*

34. Hall, *Fun and Fighting*, p. 98.

35. Allyn Capron letter to John R. Thomas, John R. Thomas Collection, Research Division, OHS.

36. *Ibid.*

37. Hall, *Fun and Fighting*, p. 101.

38. Roy Cashion letter to parents, June 16, 1898, on board *Yucatan*, Kingfisher County Historical Society, *Pioneers of Kingfisher County*, Kingfisher, 1976.

39. Hall described the price of whiskey in *Fun and Fighting*, p. 99–100, while Paul Hunter described the cost of beer in his letter to the *Guthrie Dailey Leader*, "On the High Seas," June 22, 1898.

40. Roy Cashion letter to parents, June 17, 1898, printed in *Hennessey Clipper*, July 7, 1898, "Who Was Roy Cashion?"

41. Roy Cashion letter to parents, June 19, 1898, printed in *Hennessey Clipper*, July 7, 1898, "Who Was Roy Cashion?"

42. Miley, *In Cuba with Shafter*, p. 56.

43. *Ibid.*

44. Hall, *Fun and Fighting*, pp. 99–100.

Chapter 5

1. Hall, *Fun and Fighting*, p. 111.

2. Marshall, *Rough Riders*, p. 96.

3. *Ibid.*, p. 207.

4. Davis, *Notes of a War Correspondent*, p. 50.

5. Edward Marshall remembered that it was Tyree Rivers who went over to Young. Theodore Roosevelt remembered that Wood had sent Smedburg over. Both Tom Hall and Roosevelt remembered seeing Rivers and his horse later near Wood during the battle.

6. Marshall, *Rough Riders*, p. 96.

7. Billy McGinty, *Oklahoma Rough Rider: Billy McGinty's Own Story*, Norman: Oklahoma University Press, 2008, p. 22.

8. Marshall, *Rough Riders*, p. 102.

9. *Ibid.* Robert Thomas recited this story after his return. "Las Guasimas Fight," *The Evening Star*, Wednesday, July 20, 1898, and "The Olivette Arrives," *New York Times*, July 17, 1898, p. 2.

10. Hon. James Rankin Young, *Reminiscences and Thrilling Stories of The War of Returned Heroes Containing Vivid Accounts of Personal Experiences by Officers and Men*, Chicago: C.W. Stanton, 1899, p. 203.

11. "The Olivette Arrives," *New York Times*, July 17, 1898, p. 2.

12. "Las Guasimu's Fight," *The Evening Star*, Wednesday, July 20, 1898.

13. "The Olivette Here," *New York Tribune*, Sunday, July 17, 1898.

14. *Ibid.*

15. Marshall, *Rough Riders*, p. 99.

16. *Ibid.*, p. 104.

17. Roosevelt in *The Rough Riders* and Richard Harding Davis in *The Notes of a War Correspondent* claimed that they deployed across the wire before the shooting started.

18. Marshall, *Rough Riders*, p. 104.

19. *Ibid.*

20. Frank Friedel, *The Splendid Little War*, Boston: Little, Brown, 1958, p. 103.

21. Because the Rough Riders were such a celebrated regiment, many critics sought to discredit the unit. This incident led some to claim that the Rough Riders had inadvertently fired on each other.

22. Davis, *Notes of a War Correspondent*, p. 71.

23. Roosevelt, *Rough Riders*, p. 90.

24. Edmond Norris was listed as a member of K Troop on the muster-out roster but his letters in the *Guthrie Daily Leader* claimed that he was a hospital steward.

25. "Isbell A. Corker," *Guthrie Daily Leader*, Tuesday, July 26, 1898, Vol. 12, No. 51.

26. Davis, *Notes of a War Correspondent*, p. 61.

27. *Ibid.*, pp. 61–62.

28. *Ibid.*, p. 62.

29. "Wounded All Made Snug," *The Sun*, Monday, July 18, 1898.

30. Davis, *Notes of a War Correspondent*, pp. 63–64.

31. *Ibid.*, p. 64.

32. Friedel, *Splendid Little War*, p.106.

33. Captain Robert Huston wrote in his letter dated June 27 that the fire came from his right rear. This did not make sense since L Troop was there. Others described firing coming from the left front during the advance to that position.

34. Rynning, *Gun Notches*, p. 160.

35. *Ibid.*, p. 161.

36. Marshall, *Rough Riders*, p. 109.

37. Robert Thomas recited this story after his return. "Las Guasimu's Fight," *The Evening Star*, Wednesday, July 20, 1898.

38. Marshall, *Rough Riders*, p. 115.

39. "La Quasina Fight," *Guthrie Daily Leader*, Wednesday, July 27, 1898, Vol. 12, No. 52.

40. "Compliment to Captain Huston," *Guthrie Daily Leader*, Tuesday, August 2, 1898, Vol. 12, No. 57.

41. Rynning, *Gun Notches*, pp. 190–191.

42. Marshall, *Rough Riders*, p. 117.

43. Friedel, *Splendid Little War*, p. 106.

44. Hall, *Fun and Fighting*, p. 147.

45. Marshall, *Rough Riders*, p. 115.

46. "What Sergeant P. W. Hunter Has to Say," *Guthrie Daily Leader*, Thursday, July 7, 1898, Vol. 12, No. 35.

47. Roosevelt, *Rough Riders*, p. 97. Beasley, *Frank Knox*, p. 18, mistook Brodie as Roosevelt.

48. Davis, *Notes of a War Correspondent*, p. 70.

49. Hughes, "A Story of the 'Rough Riders.'"

50. Miller, *Rough Rider*, p. 122.

51. David McClure, of Oklahoma City, wrote that "a cook from Ponca City shot a Cuban." As there were only three men from Ponca City, Will Tauer was still in Tampa and O.G. Palmer was the First Sergeant, that only left Freeman as the cook. "Rough Rider Talks," *Guthrie Daily Leader*, Monday, August 15, 1898, Vol. 12, No. 68.

52. Roosevelt did not mention Tom Hall by name but as "one of our men who had dropped out."

53. Davis, *Notes*, p. 74.

54. Marshall, *Rough Riders*, p. 139.

55. *Ibid.*, p. 144.

56. Roosevelt claimed that no one moaned or complained. Robert Huston wrote in a letter home that he heard no "groaning or crying out by any of our wounded" during the battle. Rob Thomas also told reporters upon his return that no one moaned. Marshall, who remained at the hospital all day, mentioned that no one could sleep because of the moaning and pain.

57. Marshall, *Rough Riders*, pp. 185–186.

58. Tom Hall claimed that the prisoner was identified by the Cubans as one of their own and released. Edward Marshall wrote that the Cubans failed to identify him and later killed him. Tom Rynning remembered that Wood ordered him turned over to the Cubans to be hung on the last day of June just before they marched to El Pozo. Nearly every Rough Rider wrote home about the Spanish prisoner's compliment to their fighting abilities.

59. Davis, *Notes*, p. 75.

60. Edward Marshall wrote that officers call was sounded at 11:00 and Roosevelt announced that the funeral would be 30 minutes after that. Ben Colbert wrote in his diary that funeral call was at 10:00.

61. Edward Marshall wrote that only half of the regiment turned out.

62. Edward Marshall also wrote that they sang "Nearer, my God, to Thee." Roosevelt wrote that they sang "Rock of Ages."

63. Young, *Reminiscences and Thrilling Stories*, p. 196.

Chapter 6

1. Hall, *Fun and Fighting*, p. 178.

2. *Ibid.*

3. Marshall, *Rough Riders*, p. 171.

4. Hall, *Fun and Fighting*, p. 179.

5. Shafter's official report claimed Capron's battery began firing at 6:15. George Kennan wrote that it fired at 6:35.

6. Colonel John Miley and George Kennan recorded that Grimes battery commenced firing at 8:00. Miley, *In Cuba with Shafter*, p. 107, and Kennan, *Campaigning in Cuba*, p. 124.

7. Hughes, "A Story of the 'Rough Riders.'"

8. Hall, *Fun and Fighting*, pp. 180–181.

9. *Ibid.*, p. 182.

10. Colonel John Miley recorded that Grimes battery ceased firing at 8:45. Miley, *In Cuba with Shafter*, p. 107. Kennan concurred that Grimes battery ceased firing after 45 minutes. *Campaigning in Cuba*, p. 124.

11. Hall, *Fun and Fighting*, p. 188.

12. *Ibid.*

13. Marshall, *Rough Riders*, p. 180.

14. David Goodrich letter to Mrs. Miller, August 5, 1898.

15. Rynning, *Gun Notches*, pp. 196–197.

16. *Ibid.*

17. Roosevelt, *Rough Riders*, pp. 121–122.

18. Charles Herner in *Arizona Rough Riders* placed this event after they were lined up for the attack in the open. From the description of events by David Hughes, of B Troop, he placed the event while waiting to cross the San Juan to line up. Tom Hall did not describe O'Neill's death but placed it where they lined up waiting to attack. Roosevelt wrote that it occurred just before the charge, after they had crossed the river and lined up in the sunken road.

19. Roosevelt, *Rough Riders*, p. 122.

20. *Ibid.*

21. Wheeler, *Santiago Campaign*, p. 43.

22. *Ibid.*, p. 44.

23. Roosevelt, *Rough Riders*, p. 124.

24. *Ibid.*, p. 302.

25. Hall, *Fun and Fighting*, p. 194.

26. Roosevelt, *Rough Riders*, p. 126.

27. Tom Holmes related this account to Bill McGinty years later. Newcomb was wounded at Las Guasimas and not listed as one of those who returned to duty during the battle. McGinty, *Oklahoma Rough Rider*, pp. 30–31.

28. Charles Herner, *The Arizona Rough Riders*, Tucson: University of Arizona Press, 1970, p. 147.

29. Roosevelt, *Rough Riders*, p. 126; and Marshall, *Rough Riders*, p. 198.

30. Roosevelt, *Rough Riders*, p. 335.

31. " Riders Write Home, Telling About Experiences in and Around Santiago," *Guthrie Daily Leader*, Wednesday, August 3, 1898, Vol. 12, No. 58.

32. Ed Loughmiller wrote this quote. "Commissioned Officers," *Guthrie Daily Leader*, Tuesday, August 16, 1898, Vol. 12, No. 69.

33. Richard E. Killblane, "Assault on San Juan Hill," *Military History*, June 1998.

34. " Riders Write Home, Telling About Experiences in and Around Santiago," *Guthrie Daily Leader*, Wednesday, August 3, 1898, Vol. 12, No. 58.

35. Hughes, "A Story of the 'Rough Riders.'"

36. *Ibid.*

37. Roosevelt, *Rough Riders*, p. 133.

38. Killblane, "Assault on San Juan Hill."

39. Marshall, *Rough Riders*, p. 199.

40. Miller, *Rough Rider*, p. 132.

41. Marshall, *Rough Riders*, pp. 199–200.

42. *Ibid.*, p. 135. Hall wrote that they said, "We didn't hear you, we didn't see you go, Colonel; lead on now, we'll sure follow you. We're waiting for your command." Roosevelt then commanded, "Forward, march!" But there is no evidence that Hall accompanied the men up the hill. Hall, *Fun and Fighting*, p. 194.

43. Edward Marshall claimed that around 300 men followed Roosevelt to the next hill.

44. Roosevelt, *Rough Riders*, p. 143.

45. *Ibid.*

46. Bill McGinty's account written long after the war, claimed as many as 60 men were trapped between the trenches and they did not escape until the third day. Micah Jenkins wrote to John Greenway in 1909 that he had around 20 men and they returned on their own that day after David Goodrich told them Roosevelt ordered them back. Roger S. Fitch in his diary wrote that he went over with about 30 men. Roosevelt wrote that Jenkins had pushed ahead but did not state when they returned or anything about rescue attempts.

47. Sergeant McIlhaney or McKinnery, of D Company, Ninth U.S. Infantry, also claimed to have shot General Linares off of his white horse at the incredible range of 1,100 yards. Lieutenant Hugh D. Wise, of the Ninth Infantry, witnessed this. Young, *Reminiscences and Thrilling Stories*, p. 210.

48. Wheeler, *Santiago Campaign*, p. 46.

49. Young, *Reminiscences and Thrilling Stories*, p. 177.

Chapter 7

1. Rynning, *Gun Notches*, p. 171.

2. Rynning, *Gun Notches*, p. 172.

3. Beasley, *Frank Knox*, p. 22.

4. Rynning, *Gun Notches*, p. 174.

5. Roosevelt wrote that McGinty "simply took a case of hardtack in his arms and darted toward the trenches." McGinty wrote his account late in his life and remembered it as a box of canned tomatoes, but he remembered that he was taking it to those trapped in the forward trench. McGinty, *Oklahoma Rough Rider*, p. 34.

6. Rynning, *Gun Notches*, p. 180.

7. *Ibid.*, p. 181.

8. *Ibid.*, and Hughes, "A Story of the 'Rough Riders.'"

9. Young, *Reminiscences and Thrilling Stories*, p. 227.

10. Clyde and Clare Stewart wrote that Baily accidently shot himself in the foot in a letter home dated July 8, *Guthrie Daily Leader*, Wednesday August 3, 1898, Vol. 12, No. 58.

11. Wells, *Diary of a Rough Rider*, pp. 54–55.

12. Joseph Carr described his wound in a letter to Capt. Rob Huston dated July 16, 1898.

13. Roosevelt claimed he went into battle with 490 men and lost 89 killed and wounded. Roosevelt, *Rough Riders*, p. 153.

14. Roosevelt provided that total number of casualties. Roosevelt, *Rough Riders*, p. 153.

15. Kennan, *Campaigning in Cuba*, p. 138.

16. Hughes, "A Story of the Rough Riders."

17. Roosevelt wrote that they killed eleven guerrillas. Roosevelt, *Rough Riders*, p. 153.

18. Hall, *Fun and Fighting*, p. 214.

19. *Ibid.*

20. Annette Blackburn-Haskett wrote in "A

Souvenir of Hennessey, Oklahoma" that Randolph, Love and Amrine went out to recover Roy's body. Theodore Miller wrote in his diary that Amrine had been left behind in Tampa. All the other details of her paper were correct.

21. Roosevelt, *Rough Riders*, p. 164. At that time, the U.S. Army only had ten regiments of cavalry.

Chapter 8

1. Hall, *Fun and Fighting*, p. 223.
2. McGinty, *Oklahoma Rough Rider*, p. 50.
3. *Ibid.*, p. 51.
4. John Miley wrote in *In Cuba with Shafter* in 1899 that the shooting began at 4:00. Albert Ferris wrote home on July 15, that the flag was hauled down at 5:00 and the shooting began at once. Ben Colbert wrote in his diary that the shooting began at 5:30. Shafter wrote to the Adjutant General on July 11 that the enemy opened fire a few minutes past 4:00. CMH, *Correspondence*, p. 125.
5. McGinty, *Oklahoma Rough Rider*, p. 52.
6. McGinty wrote in his memoirs many years later that this took place after they had relocated their camp after the surrender. John D. Miley wrote that yellow fever broke out in El Caney and became known throughout the Army by the eleventh. The refugees also returned before the surrender so this account more likely occurred after the Rough Riders relocated on the eleventh.
7. Colbert Diary.
8. "First Illinois Reaches Cuba," *Ann Arbor Argus*, July 15, 1898.
9. Hughes, "A Story of the Rough Riders."
10. Wheeler remembered that the meeting commenced at 2:00 while Miley remembered 2:30.
11. Wheeler, *Santiago Campaign*, pp. 131–132.
12. *Ibid.*, p. 164.
13. Miley, *In Cuba with Shafter*, p. 180.
14. Colbert Diary.
15. F. S. Cashion letter to Capt. R. Houston [sic], July 18, 1898, Huston Collection.
16. "Huston Tells of It. Give an Interesting Account of how Roy Cashion Died," *Guthrie Leader*, August 30, 1898, Vol. 12, No. 81.
17. Rynning, *Gun Notches*, pp. 185–186.
18. Miley, *In Cuba with Shafter*, p. 226.
19. Rynning, *Gun Notches*, p. 184.
20. Hughes, "A Story of the 'Rough Riders.'"
21. Colbert Diary.
22. Letter from Theodore Roosevelt to George Otto Trevelyan, Theodore Roosevelt Papers, Library of Congress Manuscript Division. https://www.theodorerooseveltcenter.org/Research/Digital-Library/Record?libID=o201169, Theodore Roosevelt Digital Library, Dickenson State University.
23. Rynning, *Gun Notches*, p. 197.
24. This account came from Thomas Rynning. Hall claimed to have returned because he was sick but did admit that he needed a letter from

Roosevelt authorizing him to board the hospital ship. There is no doubt that Hall was sick but probably not more than the other officers. Paul Hunter wrote in a letter dated July 28 that Hall had been relieved and was already in the South somewhere. The muster-out roll gives the date of his resignation. Tom Rynning was witness to the conversation between Roosevelt and Hall. "Tells All About It. Sergeant Hunter Describes the Last Days of Spanish Santiago," *Guthrie Daily Leader*, Thursday, August 18, 1898, Vol. 12, No. 71.

25. "Roosevelt Writes Sharp-Pointed Letter to General Shafter and Tells of the Necessity for Removal of Troops," *Guthrie Daily Leader*, Friday, August 5, 1898, Vol. 12, No. 60. Marshall, *Rough Riders*, Pp. 219–220.
26. *Guthrie Daily Leader*, Friday, August 5, 1898, Vol. 12, No. 60.
27. *Ibid.*
28. Colbert Diary.
29. "From the Rough Riders," *Guthrie Daily Leader*, Tuesday, August 23, 1898, Vol. 12, No. 75.
30. *Ibid.*
31. *Ibid.*
32. McGinty, *Oklahoma Rough Rider*, pp. 62–63.

Chapter 9

1. Beasley, *Frank Knox*, p. 23.
2. *Ibid.*, p. 24.
3. *Ibid.*
4. Beasley, *Frank Knox*, p. 26.
5. "The Olivette Here," *New York Daily Tribune*, Sunday, July 17, 1898, Thomas Collection.
6. *Ibid.*
7. *Ibid.*
8. This description comes from a collection of newspaper articles in John R. Thomas Collection, Research Division, Oklahoma Historical Society, Oklahoma City.
9. *Ibid.*
10. "Hamilton Fish's Funeral," *New York Times*, July 30, 1898, p. 12.
11. *Ibid.*
12. *Ibid.*
13. *Ibid.*
14. Curry remembered that Chris Madsen was just as guilty, but this was written in his memoirs just before his death in 1947. There were a number of errors in his memory of other events during his time in the Rough Riders. In an interview published in 1936, Madsen made no mention of the accusations but remained on active duty until after the squadron moved to Montauk Point, New York. Because of his illness, he then applied for a discharge for reasons of disability. If he had been guilty, no doubt he would also have been arrested and discharged with Schweizer. However, Schweizer could not have sold the squadron's supplies without Madsen's knowledge. Madsen was obviously more knowledgeable in the supply procedures. The fact that he remained on active duty

and remained on friendly terms with Roosevelt after the war meant that there must have been mitigating circumstances to his compliance with the crime.

15. The following account taken from "McGinnis at Jersey City," *Guthrie Daily Leader*, Friday, September 2, 1898, Vol. 12, No. 81.

16. Colbert Diary, Oklahoma Historical Society.

17. "Capt. McGinnis Makes a Speech," *New York Times*, Tuesday, August 16, 1898.

18. *Ibid.*

19. *Ibid.*

20. Hening, *Curry*, p. 125.

21. Colbert Diary, Oklahoma Historical Society.

22. "From the Rough Riders," *Guthrie Daily Leader*, Tuesday, August 23, 1898, Vol. 12, No. 75.

23. Paul Hunter's account taken from "Sergeant Paul Hunter Tells of Suffering at Camp Wikoff," *Guthrie Daily Leader*, Wednesday, August 31, 1898, Vol. 12, No. 82.

24. The following account taken from Rynning, *Gun Notches*, pp. 190–191.

25. Mueller and Madsen, "With the Rough Riders."

26. "McKinley's Visit," *Guthrie Daily Leader*, Monday, September 5, 1898, Vol. 12, No. 86.

27. *Ibid.*

28. *Ibid.*

29. *Ibid.*

30. *Ibid.*

31. Rynning, *Gun Notches*, p. 188.

32. "Rough Riders Organize," *Guthrie Daily Leader*, Saturday, September 10, 1898, Vol. 12, No. 91.

33. *Ibid.*

34. Marshall, *Rough Riders*, pp. 251–252.

35. *Ibid.*

36. Colbert Diary, Oklahoma Historical Society.

37. Colbert Diary.

38. Huston to Vite, Sept. 16, 1898.

39. McGinty, *Oklahoma Rough Rider*, p. 76.

40. McGinnis would claim to have stood next to Wheeler when Roosevelt challenged him to countermand Shafter's order to evacuate the high ground. Roosevelt would treat every member of his regiment as if they had participated in Cuba and would not list the names of the troops that were left behind. It is quite possible that when he had to narrow the list of Rough Riders who would accompany him on the election campaign, he may have selected Mac as consolation for his promotion causing him to be left behind.

41. Rynning, *Gun Notches*, pp. 188–189.

42. *Ibid.*, 197–198.

Chapter 10

1. Mueller and Madsen, "With the Rough Riders."

2. Beasley, *Frank Knox*, p. 103.

3. *Ibid.*

4. *Ibid.*, p. 104.

5. *Ibid.*

6. *Ibid.*, p. 106.

7. *Ibid.*

8. Roosevelt, *Rough Riders*, pp. 222–223.

Bibliography

Newspapers and Internet Sources

"Buffalo Bill's Wild West at Olympia." *The Navy and Army Illustrated,* January 31, 1903.

The Chicago Chronicle, Tuesday, August 2, 1898.

Chicago Inter-Ocean, June 25, 1898, to August 7, 1898.

Chicago Times-Herald, Monday, July 18, 1898, to August 2, 1898.

Daily Oklahoman, February 21, 1906.

Democrat-Herald, Vol. 13, No. 29, March 23, 1906, to No. 44, July 6, 1906.

Eureka Herald Newspaper, June 21, 1917.

The Evening Star, Wednesday, July 20, 1898

The Evening Telegram (New York), July 17, 1898.

Grand Rapids Press, July 18, 1898.

The Guthrie Daily Leader, Thursday, December 23, 1897, Vol. 11, No. 20, to Saturday, September 10, 1898, Vol. 12, No. 91.

Hennessey Clipper, February 24 to July 28, 1898. "Who Was Roy Cashion?" http://www.hennessey.lib.ok.us/

The Humbolt Beacon and Fortuna Advance, August 19 and 20, 1959.

Letter from Theodore Roosevelt to George Otto Trevelyan, Theodore Roosevelt Papers, Library of Congress Manuscript Division. https://www.theodorerooseveltcenter.org/Research/Digital-Library/Record?libID=o201169. Theodore Roosevelt Digital Library, Dickenson State University.

Mueller, Harold L., in collaboration with Chris Madsen. "With the Rough Riders." *Daily Oklahoman,* February 23, 1936.

New York Daily Tribune, Sunday, July 17, 1898.

New York Journal, Sunday, July 17, 1898.

New York Times, May 7 to September 19, 1898; August 25, 1900; November 30, 1901; July 10, 1916; August 9, 1927; April 29, 1944; June 26, 1948; and November 24, 1958.

Newkirk And Kay County Republican, Vol. 5, No. 16, Friday, March 11, 1898, to Friday December 9, 1898, Vol. 6, No. 3.

Newkirk Democrat, Vol. V, No. 36, Wednesday, March 16, 1898, to January 4, 1899, Vol. VI, No. 26.

The Ponca City Daily Courier, April 26, 1898, Vol I, No. 176, to Saturday, March 4, 1899, Vol. 2, No. 130.

Ponca City Democrat, Monday, May 2, 1898, Extra, to Thursday, February 16, 1899, Vol. VI, No. 22.

San Antonio Daily Express, May 5 to May 28, 1898.

San Antonio Daily Light, May 2 to May 28, 1898.

The Sun, Monday, July 18, 1898.

The Times Record (Blackwell), Thursday, April 7, 1898, Vol. 5, No. 29, to Thursday, October 6, 1898, Vol. 6, No. 3.

Washington Post, Thursday, Sunday, July 17, to Thursday, July 28, 1898.

Published and Unpublished Works

Arnett, Nancy. "David Leahy of the 1st U. S. Volunteer Cavalry ('Rough Riders') Writes Home." http://www.spanamwar.com/1stuscavletters.htm.

Ballard, Charles L., paraphrased by Janet Barum. "Family History Stories Paraphrased, Charles L. Ballard Part I & II." http://www.newmexicogeneology.org/wpac23.htm.

Beasley, Norman. *Frank Knox, American: A Short Biography.* Garden City, NY: Doubleday, Doran & Company, 1936.

Bell, William Gardner. *Commanding Generals and Chiefs of Staff, 1775–1995.* Washington, D.C.: Center of Military History, 1999.

Berry, Henry. *Make the Kaiser Dance: Living Memories of the Doughboy.* New York: Arbor House, 1978.

Blackburn, Brenda. Paper for 1980 Senior Writing Class, April 2, 1980. Hennessey Public Library.

Blackburn-Haskett, Annette. "A Souvenir of Hennessey, Oklahoma." n.p., n.d.

Blackford, Mansel G., and Austin Kerr. *B. F. Goodrich: Tradition and Transformation, 1870–1995.* Columbus: Ohio State University Press, 1996.

Butts, Joseph Tyler. *Two Rough Riders: Letters from F. Allen McCurdy and J. Kirk McCurdy of Philadelphia, Pennsylvania Who Volunteered and Fought with the Rough Riders during the Spanish American War of 1898 to Their Father J. M. McCurdy.* New York: F. Tennyson Neely, 1902.

Center for Military History. *Correspondence Relating to the War with Spain.* Washington, D.C: U.S. Government Printing Office, 1993.

Clark, J. Stanley. "Career of John R. Thomas." *The Chronicles of Oklahoma* 52, Summer 1974.

Colbert, Ben H. Diary. Oklahoma Historical Society.

Connelley, William E. *Kansas and Kansans.* Chicago: Lewis, 1918.

Croy, Homer. *Trigger Marshal: The Story of Chris Madsen.* New York: Duell, Sloan and Pearce, 1958.

Cutler, William G. *History of the State of Kansas.* Chicago: A. T. Andreas, 1883.

"Distinguished Member of the Regiment Biography for COL (Ret.) Gordon Johnston." Regimental Division, Office of the Chief of Signal, http://www.gordon.army.mil/ocos/museum/SCMOH/Johnston.asp.

Feuer, A.B. "Spanish Fleet Sacrificed at Santiago." *Military History,* June 1998.

Friedel, Frank. *The Splendid Little War.* Boston: Little, Brown, 1958.

Fuller, J.F.C. *Decisive Battles of the U. S. A.* New York: The Beechhurst Press, 1953.

Gardner, Mark Lee. *Rough Riders: Theodore Roosevelt, His Cowboy Regiment, and the Immortal Charge Up San Juan Hill.* New York: HarperCollins, 2016.

Gibson, Dana, and E. Kay Gibson *Over Seas: U.S. Army Maritime Operations, 1898 Through the Fall of the Philippines.* Camden, ME: Ensign Press, 2002.

Gillett, Mary C. *The Army Medical Department, 1865–1917.* Washington, D.C.: Center for Military History, 1995.

Gooch, George H. *Route-Book: Buffalo Bill's Wild West,* Buffalo, New York: The Matthews-Northrup Co., 1899.

Goodrich, David M,. to Mrs. Lewis Miller. Letter, August 5, 1898. Houghton Library, Harvard University.

Greenway, Lieut. John. Letter to Mr. Greenway, October 14, 1909. Hennessey Public Library.

Greenwood Historical Society. *The History of Greenwood County, Kansas,* Vol. I. Wichita: Kelly Wright, Josten's Publications, 1986.

Hall, Tom. *The Fun and Fighting of the Rough Riders.* New York: Frederick A. Stokes, 1899.

Hart, Albert Bushnell, and Herbert Ronald Ferleger, ed. *Theodore Roosevelt Cyclopedia.* New York: Roosevelt Memorial Association, 1941.

Hening, H.B. *George Curry, 1861–1947: An Autobiography.* Albuquerque: University of New Mexico Press, 1958.

Herner, Charles. *The Arizona Rough Riders.* Tucson: University of Arizona Press, 1970.

A History of the Oklahoma-State and People. New York: Lewis History Co., 1929.

Hughes, David L. "A Story of the 'Rough Riders." Archives, Arizona Historical Society.

Huston, Robert B. Collection. Research Division, Oklahoma Historical Society.

Hutton, Paul Andrew, "Col. Cody, The Rough Riders and the Spanish American War." http://www.bbhc.org/pointsWest/PWARticle.cfm?ArticleID=26.

Infantry Drill Regulations, United States Army. Washington, D.C.: Government Printing Office, 1891.

Jamison, James C. *With Walker in Nicaragua: Reminiscences of an Officer of the American Phalanx.* Columbia: E.W. Stephens, 1909.

Jenkins, Micah. Letter to Lieutenant John Greenway, October 14, 1909. Arizona Historical Society.

John R. Thomas Collection. Research Division, Oklahoma Historical Society, Oklahoma City.

Kennan, George. *Campaigning in Cuba.* New York: The Century Co., 1899.

Killblane, Richard E. "Assault on San Juan Hill." *Military History,* June 1998.

Kingfisher County Historical Society. *Pioneers of Kingfisher County.* Kingfisher, 1976.

Marshall, Edward. *The Story of The Rough Riders, 1st U.S. Volunteer Cavalry: The Regiment in Camp and On the Battlefield.* New York: G.W. Dillingham Co., 1899.

McCurdy, F. Allen, and J. Kirk McCurdy. *Two Rough Riders: Letters from F. Allen McCurdy and J Kirk McCurdy.* New York: F. Tennyson Neely, 1902.

McGinty, Billy, author, Jim Fullbright and Albert Stehno, editors. *Oklahoma Rough Rider: Billy McGinty's Own Story.* Norman: Oklahoma University Press, 2008.

McRill, Leslie A. "The Story of an Oklahoma Cowboy." *The Chronicles of Oklahoma.* Oklahoma City: The Oklahoma Historical Society, 1956.

McSherry, Patrick. "Camp Wikoff." http://www.spnanwar.com/campwikoff.html.

"Medal of Honor Awarded to Theodore Roosevelt." http://www.theodoreroosevelt.org/life/MedalofHonor%20Quest.htm.

Miley, John D., *In Cuba with Shafter,* New York: Charles Scribner's Sons, 1899.

"Military Record of Colonel Gordon Johnston."

Miller, Theodore Westwood. *Theodore W. Miller, Rough Rider.* n.p., 1899.

Millis, Walter. *The Martial Spirit.* Cambridge: The Riverside Press, 1931.

Peery, Dan W. "The First Two Years." *Chronicles of Oklahoma* VII, December 1929.

Portrait and Biographical Records of Oklahoma. Chicago: Chapman, 1901.

Post, Charles Johnson. *The Little War of Private Post.* Boston: Little, Brown, 1960.

Rayburn, John C. "The Rough Riders in San Antonio, 1898." *Arizona and the West: A Quarterly Journal of History,* Vol. 3, No. 2, Summer 1961.

Roosevelt, Theodore. *The Rough Riders,* Executive Edition. New York: P.F. Collier & Sons, Scribner's Sons, 1899.

Roth, Russell. *Muddy Glory: America's Indian Wars' in the Philippines, 1899–1935.* West Hanover, MA: The Christopher Publishing House, 1981.

Rynning, Captain Thomas H., as told to Al Cohn and Joe Chisolm. *Gun Notches: The Life Story of a Cowboy-Soldier.* New York: Frederick A. Stokes, 1931.

Samuelson, Nancy B. "Chris Madsen: Soldier, Oklahoma 89'er, And Deputy U.S. Marshal." *OklahombreS Journal,* Vol. IV, Summer 1993.

Sawicki, James A. *Infantry Regiments of the US Army.* Dumfries, VA: Wyvern Publications, 1981.

Sears, Joseph Hamblen. *The Career of Leonard Wood,* New York: D. Appleton, 1919.

Simmonds, Frank H. *History of the World War,* Vol. 4. Garden City, NY: Doubleday Page & Company, 1919.

Spiller, Roger J., ed. *Dictionary of American Military Biography.* Westport, CT: Greenwood Press, 1984.

Stallings, Laurence. *The Doughboys: The Story of the AEF, 1917–1918.* New York: Harper & Row, 1963.

Trask, David F. *The War with Spain in 1898.* New York: Macmillan, 1981.

War Department. *Register of the Army of the United States.* Washington, D.C.: Adjutant General's Office, 1888–1935.

Weigley, Russell F. *History of the United States Army.* New York: Macmillan, 1967.

Wells, Ogden J. *Diary of a Rough Rider.* St. Joseph, MI: A.B. Moore, n.d.

Wheeler, MG Joseph. *The Santiago Campaign 1898.* New York: Lamson, Wolffe, 1898.

"Who Was Frank Knox?" The Frank Knox Memorial Fellowships. http://www.frankknox.harvard.edu/who.html.

"Who Was Roy Cashion?" February 12, 2004. http://www.hennessey.lib.ok.us/War.htm.

Wright, Kelly. *The History of Greenwood County, Kansas,* Vol. I. Wichita: Josten's Publications, 1986.

Young, Hon. James Rankin. *Reminiscences and Thrilling Stories of The War of Returned Heroes Containing Vivid Accounts of Personal Experiences by Officers and Men.* Chicago: C.W. Stanton, 1899.

Index